Gl🌐bal
BANKING

By Peter K. Oppenheim

AMERICAN
BANKERS
ASSOCIATION ®

This publication is designed to provide accurate and authoritative information in regard to the subject matter covered. It is sold with the understanding that the publisher is not engaged in rendering legal, accounting, or other professional service. If legal advice or other expert assistance is required, the services of a competent professional person should be sought.

From a Declaration of Principles jointly adopted by a Committee of the American Bar Association and a Committee of Publishers and Associations.

The American Bankers Association is committed to providing innovative, high-quality products and services that are responsive to its members' critical needs.

To comment about this product, or to learn more about the American Bankers Association and the many products and services it offers, please call **1-800-338-0626**.

CONTENTS

LIST OF EXHIBITS

ABOUT THE AUTHOR

Peter K. Oppenheim began his banking career in 1957 in foreign exchange trading in Los Angeles with Bank of America N.T. & S.A. In the following years he had a variety of international operational, credit, and training assignments, including five years in New York. He retired in 1987 as a Vice President in that bank's World Banking Division in San Francisco.

He began authoring the American Bankers Association's *International Banking* series in 1968 with the second edition and has continued with each subsequent edition. He is also the author of *The Language of International Finance in English: Money and Banking,* published in 1976. His articles have been published by the Committee for Economic Development, *American Peoples Encyclopedia Yearbook*, *Verbatim*, and *Scott's Monthly*.

Mr. Oppenheim holds a credential as an instructor in the California Community Colleges in banking, finance, and government. He has taught at the Stonier Graduate School of Banking, School for International Banking, San Francisco City College, University of California Extension, and the American Institute of Banking. He has testified as an expert witness on international banking in U.S. federal court.

He graduated from the University of California at Berkeley with a Bachelor of Arts degree in English. Following service in the U.S. Air Force in Europe, he earned a Master of Arts degree at Berkeley in international relations.

In recent years he has been presenting seminars to U.S. bankers on the business of banking and to foreign bankers on the various phases of global banking. The latter have been presented in Moscow, Bulgaria, Istanbul (for Eastern European, Central Asian, and Middle Eastern bankers), London, Hong Kong, Trinidad, and The Bahamas.

PREFACE

This book continues the series that appeared under the title *International Banking* from 1966 through the sixth edition in 1991, with its "Supplement" in 1993. The new name, *Global Banking*, recognizes that international banking is no longer the business of only commercial banks. The activities of investment banks, corporations, and individuals have been assuming greater influence as the governmental barriers erected as a result of two world wars, the Great Depression, and postwar reconstruction have effectively vanished. The financial world in general, and the role of the United States in particular, at the end of the twentieth century has returned to freedom that has not been known for nearly a century. The description of global banking in the 1860s could, with just a slight change of names and dates, accurately describe the situation today in the United States.

> Indeed in retrospect the 1860s marked a unique decade: capital, goods and labour flowed almost unhindered round much of the known world in unprecedented quantities, the nearest we would ever come to a fully liberal, free-trading system. And at the heart of that system lay the City of London, providing not only unrivalled entrepôt facilities in terms of physical trade but also credit accommodation on a worldwide basis. In the words of a parliamentary committee in 1858. "The trade of the world could hardly be carried on without the intervention of English credit. A man in Boston cannot buy a cargo of tea in Canton without getting a credit from [London merchant bankers]." Moreover, as a concomitant of this, the London money market found itself becoming increasingly sophisticated, increasingly international, with domestic bills of exchange gradually starting to give way in importance to foreign or external bills as London's great contribution to the provision of short-term commercial credit—bills guaranteed by the City's growing array of accepting houses. The pattern was similar in long-term finance. . . . London during the third quarter of the century consolidated and immeasurably strengthened its position as the world's leading international capital market, providing a string of foreign loans to capital-hungry states seeking to enjoy the fruits of scientific progress and industrialization. British investments . . . increased about fivefold over the next twenty years and, in conjunction with the permanent effects of the railway boom, a fully fledged . . . class [of people living on investment income] was born.[1]

The rise in the participation in global banking by investors becomes apparent when the search for solutions to the Mexican debt crisis of 1982 is compared with that of 1995. In 1982, the crisis was caused by debt owed to a few hundred foreign commercial banks, which sought to solve it themselves. In 1995, the crisis was caused by debt owed to thousands of investors and owners of shares of Mexican stocks, who owned their shares both directly and through mutual funds. Mexico's rescue came from foreign governments; the commercial bankers were on the sidelines.

The primary objective of this first edition of *Global Banking* remains as it was for the six editions of *International Banking:* to provide the current practices, procedures, and facts so that all participants can meet their customers' needs in global business. Some of these practices and procedures relate solely to commercial banks; others are shared with investment banks and their customers.

The book is organized into five sections, each a cluster of chapters: Global Structure, Global Payments, Global Trade, Global Financing, and Global Risk Management. The reader interested in a particular topic can go directly to it and its related subjects. For example, global financing is not just about the process of making the credit decision, but also about the options of sources of funding. Each section opens with an overview and historical background. This serves a dual purpose: to add to the reader's understanding of the topic by showing how it developed to its present structure; and to emphasize, paraphrasing the often quoted adage of George Santayana, that bankers and investors who do not know what led to problems in the past will have them again. One need only look at the history of Latin American investments and loans. The causes of the losses in the last part of the twentieth century bear remarkable resemblances to the causes of the losses in the nineteenth century.

Each edition in this series has reflected the recent changes in this area of banking. This edition explains the uses of certain derivatives as well as the roles of new institutions, such as the World Trade Organization. Information about the role of the Bank for International Settlements is expanded; changes in the format and classification of reporting balance of payments has been incorporated; and the movement toward a single European currency is updated, as are each of the major products. The appendices have been updated with the new International Chamber of Commerce publications concerning international collections (No. 522) and letters of credit (No. 500).

One major underlying theme runs throughout the book: banking is a business of managing risks, and global banking means managing risks around the world. These risks may be inherent in the products themselves or in the fact that the global bank does business through personnel at a great distance from the senior management of the bank. In recent years, the cost of the failure to recognize such risks has been vividly evident, with widely publicized losses in distant units that have destroyed or severely damaged entire banks. While the loss initially appeared to have been triggered by a single person, subsequent analysis has put most of the blame on senior management itself in what one government post-mortem bluntly summarized as "institutional incompetence."[2] The final chapter looks at several major failures in discerning lessons that can be learned so that the future global banker does not repeat them.

A number of people, to whom I acknowledge my great appreciation, assisted in the completion of this book. First, the members of the American Bankers Association's advisory committee were very generous with their time in reviewing the manuscript both for its factual accuracy and its clarity. Their expertise in the field as well as their experience in having taught the sixth edition at American Institute of Banking chapters provided an essential contribution. Thanks to:

John Ahearn
Vice President
Bank of New York
West Paterson, NJ

George Gruber
Vice President
Meridian Bank
International Department
Philadelphia, PA

Kiel Hoffman
Assistant Vice President
First Security Bank of New Mexico
Albuquerque, NM

David Hornbach
Assistant Vice President
Chemical Bank-Delaware
Wilmington, DE

Fred Mussler
Vice President
International Department
National City Bank
Columbus, OH

Ann Parr
Assistant Vice President & International
    Documentary Consultant
U.S. Bank
Portland, OR

Janet Parr
Houston Community College System
Central College
Houston, TX

Peter Senica
Vice President
First Fidelity Bank, N.A.
Baltimore, MD

Second, as with previous editions, the ABA has provided strong support in shaping this new edition, particularly the guidance, ideas, and reviews of Associate Directors George T. Martin and Howard Robinson.

Third, I thank a number of individuals who were kind enough to respond to requests for information about specific activities: Edwin M. Truman, Staff Director, Division of International Finance, Board of Governors of the Federal Reserve System, for details about the Fed's role with the Bank for International Settlements and certain applications of the Risk-Based Capital Guidelines; Linda Kamel, Public Affairs Officer, International Monetary Fund, for assistance in obtaining material in time for us to meet our printing deadlines; Tom Huse, Vice President, Bank of America, for reviewing the section on interest rate swaps.

Notwithstanding the assistance of all these people, I remind the reader that the opinions expressed are my own, as has been the choice of supporting materials. Any errors that remain should be attributed solely to the carelessness or stubbornness of the author.

Peter K. Oppenheim
January 1996

Notes

1. David Kynaston, *The City of London, Volume 1: A World of Its Own 1815-1890* (London: Chatto & Windus, 1994), p. 167

I

GLOBAL STRUCTURE

Global banking is a business with many different participants, not all of which are banks. Even within the broad term "bank" there is a considerable variety of what those are and what they do. The term "global" likewise has many different characteristics and types of transactions, some of which cross national boundaries; others stay completely within one country. Therefore, the consideration of the structure of global banking begins with an understanding of each of these two words as they are used in the actual business of banking.

Much banking as it is done today in the United States developed from British banking practices. In the nineteenth century and up to the outbreak of World War I in 1914, London was the financial center of the world. "The name 'London Banker'," wrote the editor and economist Walter Bagehot in 1873, "had especially a charmed value. He was supposed to represent, and often did represent, a certain union of pecuniary sagacity and educated refinement which was scarcely to be found in any other part of society. . . . [He] possessed a variety of knowledge. . . . Banking is a watchful but not a laborious trade." [1] That banker could view a foreign borrower as little different from a domestic one. In the nineteenth century, the London banker financed American railroads and sovereign foreign governments as easily and as readily as a local textile mill.

The English banking system was far more specialized than the systems prevalent in continental Europe. The banks proper were the clearing banks, which collected deposits, and which were in principle limited to providing short-term loans. The merchant banks specialized in accepting bills of exchange and issuing foreign loans, while the bill brokers specialized in discounting bills. . . . A little on the fringes of the English banking system proper, some English banks acted as clearing banks abroad or in the colonies. The different specialties were complementary: the clearing banks supplied cash to the bill brokers, who discounted the bills of exchange accepted by the merchant banks.[2]

Banks were identified by ownership or activities. There were *private banks* ("the bank's capital was in the hands of the partners with unlimited liability"[3]), *joint stock banks* (the ownership was held by individual investors who had limited liability), *colonial banks* (headquartered in London but located to do business in specified British colonies), *foreign banks* (similar to colonial banks, but located in foreign countries that were not British colonies), *discount houses* (short-term financing for foreign trade), and *merchant banks*. "All the merchant banks started out in trade and progressively moved away from it to specialize in purely financial functions." The difficulty in identifying these latter banks is that they continued to call themselves only "merchants," a term that could be applied to any of a wide variety of commercial activities.[4]

Many of these specialized banks coalesced into fewer, but broader, institutions. The City of London began to lose its dominance in global financing with World War I. Its dominance was further diminished by the Great Depression of the 1930s. By the end of World War II, the hub of global financing had shifted to the United States.

The structure of banking for global activities in the United States is basically in two parts. First are the **commercial banks**, which are defined by the Bank Holding Company Act as those that both accept demand deposits that may be withdrawn by check and make commercial loans. Second are the **investment banks**. These do not accept deposits but are in the business of underwriting equity and debt issues, which will then be sold to such institutional investors as pension funds, insurance companies, mutual funds, and so forth. The boundaries between these two are becoming less clear as the twentieth century ends, leading to the use of the term *universal bank.*

Modern commercial banks have consolidated the varied activities of nineteenth-century London banking. They make short-term loans for financing international trade, extend multiyear loans to foreign governments and businesses, accept bills of exchange to provide short-term trade financing, and are the system through which payments flow both domestically and globally. The investment banks continue to raise long-term funds, for either equity or debt, for foreign governments and multinational corporations. Both commercial and investment banks now trade foreign exchange, create risk management programs for their customers, and trade deposits around the world. They have many of the same customers. Thus the global bankers of today are both commercial bankers and investment bankers. Additionally, corporations doing business in several countries have taken on some of the aspects of a bank. They finance a subsidiary in one country with the surplus funds of a subsidiary in another country; they transfer payments between these companies; and they borrow funds in one country to use in another. Independent companies borrow and lend directly with each other, often across national borders.

The concept of "global" likewise has undergone significant evolution, ultimately returning to the point where it started. The London banker of the last century made little or no distinction between a domestic and a foreign borrower. There were few problems about the currency used for repayment: gold was the world money and, through one means or another, it was relatively free to move.

All this changed in the mid-twentieth century. Two world wars and a depression locked the economies of countries within their own borders. The money of one country could not always be exchanged for that of another. Thus bankers were forced by the decisions of their own governments to distinguish between financing for a domestic customer, which could be repaid in local currency, and financing a customer in a foreign country, which might have plenty of its own country's currency, but not much of the lending country's currency. Governments made these barriers high and rigid.

As this century ends, those barriers have mostly crumbled. Money is again free to move to be deposited or borrowed, in the form of either a bank loan or an investment bank marketed bond. At the same time, business has become truly global. Companies manufacture in many countries, assemble at some convenient location, and sell everywhere on the globe. A local banker may be financing a factory across the street, whose product enters into that global marketplace. The boundary between banking a domestic customer and financing in another country is rapidly becoming indistinguishable.

This, therefore, is the global banking discussed in the next 14 chapters. *Global* now refers to the almost borderless business environment (chapter 1, The World of Global Banking). *Banking* refers both to commercial and to investment bankers, some of whom continue the name and history of the merchant business in which their company originated (chapter 2, Organization of U.S. Banks).

Notes

1. Walter Bagehot, *The Collected Works of Walter Bagehot*, ed. Norman St. John-Stevas, vol. IX, (London: The Economist, 1978), pp. 183-184
2. Youssef Cassis, *City Bankers: 1890-1914* (Cambridge: Cambridge University Press, 1994), pp. 5-6
3. Ibid., p. 14
4. Ibid., p. 29

1

THE WORLD OF GLOBAL BANKING

Learning Objectives

After studying this chapter, you will be able to

- outline the history of business transactions between nations
- describe the basic global activities in which customers are engaged
- understand the uses of the balance of payments report

Overview

No modern nation can prosper relying solely on its own resources—mineral, human, manufacturing, or capital. Transactions with other countries, therefore, are a national business necessity. Adam Smith, writing in the *Wealth of Nations* in 1776, commented: "When the produce of any particular branch of industry exceeds what the demand of the country requires, the surplus must be sent abroad and exchanged for something for which there is a demand at home. Without such exportation a part of the productive labour of the country must cease, and the value of its annual produce diminish."[1] Professor Michael Porter's description of the modern world in 1990 is remarkably similar: "No nation can be competitive in (and be a net exporter of) everything. A nation's pool of human and other resources is necessarily limited. . . . A nation can thereby specialize in those industries and segments in which its firms are relatively more productive and import those products and services where its firms are less productive than foreign rivals, in this way raising the average productivity level in the economy. Imports, then, as well as exports, are integral to productive growth."[2]

A nation's international economic activities are broadly grouped into three categories: the movement of goods (raw materials, manufactured goods), the movement of services (engineering, scientific, personal, processing), and the movement of capital (long-term plant investments, short-term financing). Because the bank's customers are engaged in such activities, the banker is asked to provide the skills and products that those customers need to do their business. This is the basis for the myriad global banking products. Banks (both commercial and investment) and businesses benefit when the banker provides the products the customer needs. The determination of which products a bank should offer begins with examining what that bank's customers do and what they need, then what products and services the banker has to meet those needs, and lastly how to deliver the products to the customers.

This chapter examines the world in which business is conducted and from which the needs arise for global banking skills and products. It introduces the separate activities and how these are reported as movements of finance in the structure of balance of payments reports. Although many of these are shown as separate topics, they are, in fact, interconnected and interdependent. Even though the text explains what "nations" do, remember that "Firms, not nations, compete in global markets."[3]

Background

The history of trade parallels the history of human development. "Archeologists have . . . concluded that the people of [9,000 years ago] traded goods across long distances. It has been possible . . . to trace the obsidian trade more or less all over the Near East . . . [and] through the analysis of trace elements in pottery to identify the pottery's origin and conclude that it was made and traded out of a particular central site."[4] Within the span of written knowledge there is vast evidence that the spread of trade has been a catalyst for development, change, and a rising standard of living. It was one of the forces behind the explorations of Columbus, Magellan, and Vasco da Gama. Between Rome and China the trading link was the Silk Road, along which Marco Polo's family made its living.

In the sixteenth and seventeenth centuries, the Portuguese, Dutch, and British went to Asia, initially to trade for spices, later building what were to become colonial bases to monopolize and develop sources of supply. Along the way they traded textiles from India for pepper in Sumatra and then for other spices, coral, elephants, and silk that they brought back to Europe. This trade interlocked with trade for other goods from the

Baltic and from America as Venice, Amsterdam, and London became great trading centers and subsequently financing centers.[5] Trade was big business. "In the minuscle Banda Islands of Run, Ai, Lonthar, and Neira, ten pounds of nutmeg cost less than half a penny and ten pounds of mace less than five pence. Yet in Europe the same quantities could be sold for respectively £1.60 and £16, a tidy appreciation of approximately 32,000 percent."[6]

International trade was a big business, often involving dangers. "Until about 1670 the Dutch East India Company was the richest corporation in the world. . . . [It] mustered 150 trading ships and 40 ships of war, with 20,000 sailors, 10,000 soldiers and nearly 50,000 civilians on its payroll."[7] With trade automatically went finance and credit.

In the seventeenth, eighteenth, and nineteenth centuries, one of the great trade commodities was tea. A look at some of the details of this commerce, which eventually was to have such an effect on the American colonies, shows how trade in one commodity affected the growth of other industries and how these changed the ways people lived.

Tea replaced wine as the everyday temperate drink when a cheap supply of a sweetener became available. Before sugar was plentiful, the tea drinker relied on a very limited supply of honey. Sugar cane at that time could be grown on a large scale only in the tropics, but for Europeans to be able to live and work there, a control for malaria, which was widespread, was needed. The discovery in 1638 by the court physician to the Spanish Viceroy in Lima, Peru, of the native Andean bark, *quinquina* (quinine), made control of this disease possible.

Once tea trade began on a large scale, other trade developed. Porcelain, for example, came to Europe in quantity because ships bringing tea and silk from China needed ballast, which was provided by the porcelain. Along with the 4,000 tons of tea being imported each year in the eighteenth century into England, 240 tons of porcelain were simultaneously being imported.[8]

Trade with Asia traditionally demanded gold and silver for payment. "China and India [became] bottomless pits for the precious metals in circulation."[9] Thus the silver and gold mines of the Americas became crucial for Europe's ability to buy from Asia. Europe acquired the money to pay for these metals, and for tobacco, by selling the colonists processed goods, such as furniture, and foods, among which was tea.

This trend has continued. By the mid-1990s, world trade was nearing $4 trillion annually. The United States accounted for about 12 percent of that; Germany, 11.5 percent; and Japan, 9 percent. In the United States and most industrialized countries, this trade is generally conducted by individuals and companies. In some other countries, it is done by government entities, such as government-owned development banks, utilities, steel companies, and so forth.

Visible Trade

Trade between nations takes place today for a number of reasons. This movement of goods, whether raw materials or manufactured goods, is referred to as **visible trade.** It consists of **imports** (what a nation buys from abroad) and **exports** (what a nation sells abroad). A nation pays money for its imports; it earns money from its exports. Obviously one nation's imports are another nation's exports; one nation's income is another nation's expense. The principal reasons for trade are as follows:

A nation does not have a particular item. For example, the United States does not grow tea or cocoa. For people in the United States to have these commodities, the country must buy them from countries where they are grown. The same is true for every country and for a whole range of foods and minerals that are unevenly distributed in the world. Some countries manufacture specialized goods and can sell them to those that do not manufacture them. Agriculture, mining, and manufacturing require many different resources, and therefore trade to acquire what one needs but does not have is an absolute necessity for all countries. No modern nation can completely eliminate foreign trade. In fact, nations that actively import and export generally have higher standards of living than those who, for political or cultural reasons, limit foreign trade to a bare minimum. Complete self-sufficiency, even if it were possible, has few benefits.

A nation does not have enough of a particular item. The United States grows some coffee beans and sugar beets, but not enough to meet its internal demands. Some countries have large iron ore reserves but only small coal deposits. In this case, they must trade in order to have the capability to produce steel. The change in political boundaries in recent years, primarily in Europe, has created new foreign trade from what had been domestic self-sufficiency. For example, in the former Soviet Union, cotton was principally grown in Uzbekistan and processed into fiber in Russia. When these two became separate nations, new foreign trade became necessary for both countries. Also, Uzbekistan can consider other buyers; Russia, other sources of supply. Competitive global prices may have an important effect on this trade as well as the means of payment.

A nation can produce an item at a lower cost than can other nations. Economic theory suggests that foreign trade should take place because one nation has a comparative advantage in producing an item. Such an advantage, which could result in lower costs, can arise because of the concentration in one area of a high level of producer skills leading to greater efficiency and the spread of innovation in particular industries (see below), greater ease of access to raw materials, or higher education levels leading to more skilled and productive labor. Corporations routinely establish production plants in countries where the cost of manufacturing will be lower and then transport the parts for centralized assembly in another country. About one-third of U.S. foreign trade may be for this purpose, and this is true for other countries, such as Japan. Thus each nation should produce what it most efficiently can and trade the surplus for another nation's products. Internal political pressures have often made this difficult to do. Part of the problem has been assessing whether one country's lower cost is the result of more efficient production or because of favorable tax or subsidy treatment by a government.

A nation produces items with a desirable style or innovation. In the United States, many consumers prefer foreign-made automobiles or electronic products. Both are produced in the United States, but the consumer's selection is based on a style preference, quality, or innovative feature. Sometimes an item labeled "finest imported" is bought solely on snob appeal.

A nation's ability to have innovative export products is directly linked to its domestic market.

> National passions translate into internationally competitive industries with striking regularity. . . . Germans cherish their cars and polish them on Sunday between bouts of high-speed driving on the autobahns. . . . Success in durable, high-performance cars is no surprise. Americans have an unusual interest in popular entertainment (sports, movies, television, records), contributing to American world leadership in these industries. The British are known for gardening, and British firms are world class in garden tools. Italians are known for their sophistication about clothes, food, and fast cars, all areas of Italian international success.[10]

This domestic concentration leads to many local companies competing, which in turn develops specialized labor skills and pushes managers constantly to innovate to maintain their position in that market. Thus national specializations will be concentrated in those domestic industries that consequently create innovative products for exports. "In Italy, for example, over 40 percent of total exports are due to clusters of industries all connected to food, fashion or the home. . . . Active feuds between domestic rivals are common, and often associated with an internationally successful national industry. . . . Vigorous local competition not only sharpens advantages at home but pressures domestic firms to sell abroad in order to grow." [11]

Features of Trade

The difference between what a nation imports and exports is its **balance of trade**. When a nation buys more than it sells, it is said to have an unfavorable or deficit balance of trade; when it sells more than it buys, it has a favorable or surplus balance of trade. A favorable balance of trade brings with it net international income.

A nation often has a choice about where to obtain its imports. This *direction of trade* can be determined by availability, comparative cost from each source of supply, or political factors such as alliances or former colonial ties. The former colonies of England and France continue to do much of their trade with their previous colonial rulers because of long-standing relationships, established customer preferences, or reduced tariffs granted by the former parent country. Other factors, such as regional animosity or availability of transportation, affect the pattern of trade. "Even though a number of East African nations have a preferential trade agreement, jealousies are pervasive. Thus neighboring Tanzania prefers to buy its sports equipment in Europe rather than 'make Kenya rich' [a Kenyan trader] said. 'They pay 45 percent more for Adidas in Europe, and then the freight back, even though the products are made next door'. . . . Also the idea of doing business across the continent—from Kenya in the east to the Ivory Cost in the west [is almost impossible]. 'If I want to export to the Ivory Coast, it's often easier out of Paris'. . . . There is no direct flight to the Ivory Coast from Kenya." [12]

Trade Protectionism

When a country decides to reduce imports, it may do so by imposing a **tariff** or a **quota**. A tariff is a tax levied by a government on imported goods. The amount of the tariff, referred to as duty, can be calculated either as a specific charge per item or weight (such as 10 cents per pound) or *ad valorem*, a percentage of the import value (such as 8 percent). Thus a buyer of an import will have to pay the seller's price plus a charge to the government. The intent is to raise the overall cost so high that the buyer will not purchase the foreign-made goods. If the buyer still makes the purchase, then the government has produced income for itself. A quota is a limit on the amount of a particular product that may be imported. The intent is to limit the local buyer's access to foreign-made goods. In some cases, the effect of a quota or tariff can be accomplished indirectly. "If a powerful government is worried about the harm imports are doing to its producers . . . it requires another government, on pain of retaliation, to restrict its country's exports of the good in question." [13] Both the tariff and the quota will protect the domestic industry and encourage the purchase of its goods rather than those made in other countries.

Governments have many other means to discourage imports. The inventiveness of the bureaucratic mind is virtually limitless when the political goal is to hamper the flow of imports. The government can, for example, indirectly increase the buyer's costs by requiring the importer to deposit the merchandise payment in advance, mandating specialized inspections, or requiring special packaging or labeling. It can require that imports from a country be balanced with an equal amount of purchases of its own goods by that country.

Trade protectionism is as much a complex political decision as an economic one. One historic argument in support of trade barriers is to shelter nascent industries. This means giving a new industry a chance to develop within the country before it has to compete against similar goods imported from another country, where the industry may be well established and able to sell at a lower cost. Deciding how long an industry is nascent rather than inefficient becomes problematic.

Even when an industry is mature, the government may seek to protect it because it represents an important domestic political base. Japan has sought to prevent the importation of foreign-grown rice to protect the livelihood of a powerful segment of the electorate, despite the consequence of Japanese consumers paying higher prices.

Similarly, foreign trade protectionism may be sought to counteract sales by foreign producers who are perceived to be receiving government subsidies or other unfair economic support that might lead to the destruction of a domestic industry. The term *dumping* is used to describe such sales. It can become very difficult to differentiate between dumping and the results of comparative efficiency. Strong political forces can be marshalled to support protectionism. When protection is maintained for a long period, it can encourage high costs and inefficient local businesses that thrive behind such trade walls. Thus, on one hand, any protection—whether through tariffs, quotas, or administrative means—has a cost to consumers and consequently to a country's economy. On the other hand, protection can lead to the development of new industries or reestablishment of waning industries in a country, which in time can compete locally and

internationally, thereby benefitting a country's economy.

Nations apply different tariff rates to similar goods from two different countries. When nation A says it is granting country B *most favored nation* status, it means it is applying the tariff rate that it grants to its most favored trading partners, in other words, the lowest tariff it gives to any nation. This is usually reciprocal. "That does not mean that B's tariffs will be identical to A's, merely that neither will give an advantage to any third country in the tariffs they impose on each other's products." [14] The residue of political empires remains in preferential trade, aid, and investment provisions for now-independent former colonies and dependencies of European countries. The largest of these is the Lomé Convention, which grants special privileges to 70 poor countries in Africa, the Caribbean, and the Pacific in their trade with the European Union. This convention has been declining and is scheduled to expire in 2000.

Reducing imports can also be a goal when a country needs to reduce its foreign expenditures. Some goods are imported, however, to be processed into other goods, which are then exported. The United States facilitates this by giving a rebate, called *drawback,* of almost all of the tariff paid.

A nation may use the techniques described above to try to get the benefits of exports (particularly the creation of jobs) while at the same time trying to keep imports out to protect local jobs from foreign competition. When carried to an extreme, usually during times of severe economic depression as in the 1930s, this policy is referred to as beggar-thy-neighbor (trying to get rich at the other nation's expense). It backfires because it leads to retaliation in which the other country will move to ban imports from the first country. Since the 1950s, lengthy international conferences under the General Agreement on Tariffs and Trade (GATT) have been successful in reducing national barriers to trade on a reciprocal basis that, overall, has been to every nation's benefit. This has led to the development of free trade areas (the European Union and the North American Free Trade Area [NAFTA], for example) to reduce and eliminate tariffs, quotas, and other barriers to global trade.

Effect of Trade

Exports and imports are part of the economy of both the selling country and the buying country. In the United States, exports are about 8 percent of the domestic production. For some countries, such exports account for a higher percentage of the economy than in the United States. In Japan, exports are 15 percent of production; in Germany, Canada, and the United Kingdom, they are between 20 and 30 percent.

Imports and exports have both benefits and costs. A nation that generates exports creates jobs, revenue, profits, and taxes in its own economy. If a particular industry, such as steel, can export part of its output, then its cost per ton of steel may be lower because it can spread fixed costs over a larger production. This can benefit that industry's domestic sales. The global market for a product can be very competitive, since some countries will subsidize an industry's costs to maintain a market share. Such a country may have no other item to sell internationally to earn foreign currency, or it may want to keep local employment high, calculating that it is cheaper to do this than to pay the economic and political costs of domestic unemployment. Such subsidies end up being paid by the taxpayer or consumer.

Imports can benefit a country by supplying goods or commodities that it may not have or may not have in sufficient amounts. When imports are cheaper than similar locally produced goods, the buyers benefit from the lower price, but the local competing industry suffers through unemployment or low wages. This can be offset if new industries provide employment for those displaced. The United States has had to wrestle with these competing effects in such basic industries as steel and copper.

Consequently, a nation's international trade policy can become hostage to regional domestic politics as areas that will be hurt by international competition seek to maintain the protection of tariffs and quotas, while areas with industries benefitting from global markets seek freer trade policies to avoid retaliatory trade-restricting acts from other countries.

Invisible Trade

In addition to international trade in commodities and manufactured goods, there is trade in services, often referred to as **invisible trade.**

One type of invisible trade is *transportation.* For example, when a tobacco farmer in Virginia sells a crop to a buyer in the United Kingdom, arrangements must be made to ship the tobacco from the seller to the buyer. The cheapest method for such bulk shipments is by ocean vessel. Other nations, such as Hong Kong and Norway, have large maritime fleets that provide such transport service. Space in an ocean vessel is rented for the cargo, and payment is made to the maritime nation for the service. The nation of the company owning the vessel earns money by providing this service, just as it would if it had exported a commodity.

Insurance is another invisible trade item. While at sea, a cargo is vulnerable to many dangers, the most obvious of which is the ship's sinking. Cargo can also be damaged by leaking pipes or an accident at an intermediate port. To protect against financial loss from such occurrences, the international trader purchases insurance. Some nations, such as the United Kingdom with its Lloyd's of London, are major providers of maritime insurance. Again, the company providing the insurance earns money from the insurance premium, just as if it had sold a commodity.

Some countries do not have commodities to sell abroad, but they do have a healthy and attractive climate, preserved antiquities, unique vistas, or superior sporting locations that bring tourists from other countries. For example, during the winter the warm climate and attractive beaches of The Bahamas, Mexico, and the Caribbean countries attract many visitors from the northern United States. The money that tourists spend for hotel accommodations, restaurants, and personal purchases is another example of invisible trade. *Tourism* is estimated to be a $750 billion-a-year business worldwide, and it includes not only vacationers but also the business traveler. Tourist travel is very sensitive to political instability. Many countries have suffered sudden declines in the number of foreign visitors, and the consequent earnings, when there has been an industrial accident, natural disaster, internal political violence, or war.

Invisible trade also includes transfers of funds to individuals in another country, which can occur for many reasons. For example, the United States has been described as a nation of immigrants, and many Americans regularly send money to help relatives in the "old country." Individuals who go to other countries to work often send money back home to support their family. In recent decades, this has been an important source of income for such countries as Bangladesh, the Philippines, and Egypt. When the work was no longer available, the return of those workers and the loss of that foreign income has resulted in severe economic shock to the home countries. Businesses headquartered in one country regularly pay salaries to employees they have located in other countries. Payments are made to support students attending foreign schools, pension payments are made to retirees living in another country, and royalties are paid to foreign artists and writers.

Payments between businesses include fees for engineering and construction design of projects such as dams (the subsequent shipment of equip-ment and materials are merchandise trade); licensing fees for patents, motion picture rentals, and telecommunications and computer services; legal services; financial advisory services for pension funds, mergers and acquisitions, and financial underwritings (the stock sale itself is an investment); and contributions to charitable and public service organizations for disaster relief, poverty alleviation, and other social service programs.

Investments

An important contribution to the world economy is made by the flow of **investments**—the transfer of savings from one country to another. This flow of investments may be beneficial for many reasons: it can enable the receiving country to have or to accelerate economic development that otherwise might be impossible because of a lack of domestic savings, and it can offer the investors a more attractive rate of return than might be possible in their own economy.

Investments take different forms. The money may be transferred from one country to another for, say, constructing a manufacturing plant, developing a mine, or establishing a branch of a retail store. This is **direct investment**. The investors expect that the new plant, mine, or store will become profitable in the future, and then they will receive a flow of dividends as earnings. Ultimately, the investors might sell their plant, mine, or store to other foreign or local investors and receive more money than they spent because the business is now a profitable and going concern. The original investors took the risk that their investment might not succeed; the subsequent investors are willing to pay the higher price because that risk is now diminished. Everyone benefits from such investments. The investors make a profit, and their country has a stream of income in future years. The receiving country gets the financial means to create a business it otherwise might not have been able to create from its own resources. That, in turn, means more jobs and perhaps increased exports or reduced imports, which represent new wealth for that country.

Another form of investment is **portfolio investment.** This may be for the purchase of shares or bonds that in turn provide funds to a business or government. Individuals and financial institutions may do this to acquire an earning asset. Portfolio investors differ from direct investors because direct investments usually are made by a company that has management responsibility in that investment. Portfolio investors usually have little, if any, meaningful influence on the management of the company whose shares or bonds they hold.

Historically, investments flowed from wealthier countries (the United Kingdom, the United States) to less wealthy countries (in Latin America, in Africa). In past centuries when large colonial empires existed, investments were made by the parent country primarily in its colonies. In recent decades the pattern of investments has broadened. Businesses now invest in specific areas to have access to sources of raw materials, specialized labor skills, or lower production costs or to protect their share of a particular market. Japanese companies, for example, make investments to establish manufacturing facilities in Southeast Asian countries to lower production costs, to establish automobile plants in the United States to maintain an important share of the total car market, and to own shares in U.S. entertainment companies that, because of their innovation and specialized skills, command world markets. Japanese insurance companies also purchase U.S. government bonds because they have a higher yield than bonds available in their own country. Investors in many countries purchase shares in foreign companies, either directly or through mutual funds that specialize in shares of companies in particular countries. These investors do this to increase their overall portfolio yield and

for the potential for added earnings attributable to appreciation of the currency in which those shares have been issued.

Many of the objectives associated with direct investments can also be achieved with transfers in the form of loans. There are significant differences, however, in the characteristics of loans and direct investments. A *loan* has a fixed schedule for repayments of principal and interest; a *direct investment* will not pay dividends until the investment becomes profitable, and there is no schedule for payment of the principal amount. Investments are made for a longer term. Direct investment creates ownership for the life of the company, but once a loan is repaid, the lender has no further control in the company. For this reason, loans have been preferred by some countries that severely limit incoming investments.

Another reason for investing may be for *humanitarian* or *national security purposes*. These do not necessarily carry an expectation of a monetary profit and are usually made by governments instead of corporations or individuals.

The sum of these separate decisions constitutes the global financial activities of a nation.

Classifying Countries

Economic terms are commonly used to group countries for descriptive purposes. Such terms are *developed countries* and *developing countries*. Expressions that are applied to the latter also include *underdeveloped country*, *emerging market*, *less developed country (LDC)*, or *third-world country*. It is not always clear precisely which countries a particular speaker or analyst is referring to when any of these terms is used. Classifying the former Soviet bloc countries as they evolve from state-run economies toward market economies has also been problematic.

As a guide the International Monetary Fund (IMF) divides countries into three groupings (A few countries are not included, for various reasons such as lack of data. They are not significant in size.):[15]

- Industrial countries: 23 countries consisting of Western Europe, the United States, Canada, Japan, Australia, and New Zealand. These countries have 55 percent of the total world gross domestic product and account for 70 percent of the world's total exports of goods and services.

- Countries in transition: 28 countries consisting of the successor states of the former Soviet Union, central and eastern European countries of the former Soviet bloc, and Mongolia. These countries have 5 percent of the world's gross domestic product and 4 percent of the world's total exports of goods and services.

- Developing countries: 132 countries, those not classified in either of the above two groups. These countries have 40 percent of the world's gross domestic product and 26 percent of the world's total exports of goods and services.

Sometimes the distinction between industrial countries and developing countries is made with the broad terms *North* (industrial countries primarily in the Northern Hemisphere) and *South* (developing countries primarily in the Southern Hemisphere). Whatever terms are used, they have differing elements of imprecision and reflect arbitrary decisions. The IMF groupings, for example, classify Iceland as an industrial country but China, Mexico, and Hong Kong as developing countries.

Historically the pattern of trade had been that the industrial countries imported food, ores, and other raw materials from developing countries and, in turn, sold them processed and manufactured goods. This was one of the rationales for colonial empires and a particular target of Marxist writers. This colonial pattern was shattered

politically after World War II and subsequently was altered economically.

There is no disagreement about the changes in the pattern of North-South trade over the past few decades, during which developing countries have ceased to be merely exporters of primary products. The South's exports of manufactures to the North, which were negligible in the 1950s, had risen to about $250 billion by 1990, involving growth of about 15% per year in real terms. These extra earnings have financed a big increase in the North's manufactured exports to the South. However, the labour-intensive parts of Northern manufactured exports have vanished, as developing countries have learned to make these goods for themselves. . . . The old pattern of trade, in which manufactured goods from the North were exchanged for primary products from the South, has thus largely been replaced by a new pattern, in which the North and the South each specialize in different sorts of manufactured goods.[16]

Since World War II the assumption has been that moving from developing-country status to developed-country status was a desirable goal. Such change has generally involved movement of people from the countryside, where they practiced agriculture and mined ores, to cities, where factories are located. The benefits of such movement have not been without social costs, usually evidenced by the slums that surround most large cities in the developing countries, pollution, and the disruption of political and social structures. Moving an economy from developing to developed status has turned out to be more complex than many had realized. "Carried away by the power of money to finance great capital undertakings, many people seem to think of such investments as being development itself. Build the dam and you have development! But in real life, build the dam and unless you also have solvent city markets and transplanted industries, you have nothing." [17]

Balance of Payments

The **balance of payments** is the basic and most easily available source of information about a country's economic transactions with the rest of the world. It organizes and summarizes all the activities discussed above over a specific period, usually a calendar year or quarter. In essence, it is everything a country does economically with the rest of the world. These activities, shown in exhibit 1.1, take place continuously and represent flows of funds into and out of each country.

It is important for the banker to be aware of what the balance of payments is—and what it is not. The latter is perhaps less well understood, and some analysts may expect the balance of payments report to provide information that it was never intended to give.

Each nation assembles its own data of the international activities of its residents and then arranges that data in accordance with the procedures established by the IMF.* The data are reported in the equivalent of U.S. dollars so that each nation's information is compatible with that of every other country. The balance of payments is published by the IMF and readily available to the public. It should not be assumed, however, merely because the information is published by a respected international financial institution and looks like a balance sheet, that all the numbers are precise in the same sense that a bank's own balance sheet is considered to be exact and accurate. Data for a year will often be revised in subsequent years, as more refined information becomes available.

There are certain conventions unique to the balance of payments report. Notwithstanding its

---

* Readers of *International Banking* should take particular note that the procedures presented in the 1993 (fifth) edition of the IMF Manual were substantially and significantly modified from those in the 1977 (fourth) edition. The change is especially evident in the classification of investments.

Exhibit 1.1   Activities Represented in a Balance of Payments

Income	Payments
Received for:	**Made for:**
Exports	Imports
Services we do for others	Services others do for us
Foreign tourists visiting us	Our tourists in other countries
Money sent by people in other countries	Money sent to people in other countries
Others' investments in our country	Our investments in other countries
Interest and dividends on our investments in other countries	Interest and dividends on others' investments in our country

name, it is not a report of payments but rather of transactions, and the data will not balance.

An import-export transaction is recorded at the time merchandise moves from the seller to the buyer, regardless of when the payment actually occurs. Barter (merchandise is paid for with other merchandise rather than money) shows as though it had been paid in money. Similarly, other items appear at times other than when the funds actually move. For example, interest on investments is reported on an accrual basis, and loan repayments are reported when they are due to be paid. Since the balance of payments is a double-entry accounting system, in such cases an offset is reflected as a financial claim or liability that is later eliminated when the payment is actually made.

The difficulty in having a nation's income and expenditures exactly offset each other to a zero balance results from the different sources of data which in some cases can be only an approximation or offset by other discrepancies. Thus the category **net errors and omissions** (sometimes referred to as a *balancing item* or *statistical discrepancy*) is included. "Some of the errors and omissions that occur . . . usually offset each other. The size of the residual item does not necessarily provide any indication of the overall accuracy of the statement. Nonetheless, interpretation of the statement is hampered by a large net residual." [18]

A country's balance of payments does not exist in isolation and is affected by domestic activities that do not show in its balance of payments. For example, a country with a high rate of internal savings can fund the building of new factories to increase exports without having to attract foreign investments.

from sources that are, however, only as good as each nation's ability to assemble data, and it is modified when necessary by the most competent people available to make such judgments. Some categories can be precise measures. For example, foreign trade can be inventoried as it passes through a nation's customs control. Small values, however, are usually exempted, which means that even this category cannot be completely accurate.

Balance of payments practice is to make the entry into the accounts when the merchandise crosses the border. Recording the merchandise at the free on board (FOB) value (see chapter 6 and appendix A) permits the freight and insurance revenues to be recorded as separate entries.

Data in the service and investment categories can be more difficult to assemble. Tourist expenditures are often determined by asking departing visitors how much they spent during the stay and by making estimates based on hotel revenue. Investment figures likewise depend on a number of sources, and investment categories may be understated because of difficulties in assembling data. "Recorded flows fail to include direct investment financed through capital markets in the host country". [19] There may also be a problem in identifying the amount of foreign ownership in a company or the sales of a foreign-owned affiliate in the country of location. For a country with rigorous exchange controls, all foreign investment requires government approval; where there are few exchange controls, authorities rely on surveys and reports from investors. Data about a country's reserves are usually precise. The government itself controls many of the reserve categories or can depend on accurate reports from the country's banks.

Sources of Data

The balance of payments is usually the best information readily available. It is developed

Balance of Payments Categories

A nation's balance of payments is presented in several broad categories:

- current account—visible and invisible trade
- capital and financial account—investments
- net errors and omissions (see above)
- changes in reserves

The IMF's *Balance of Payments Statistical Yearbook* presents a series of tables that provide these categories of information about individual countries. Exhibit 1.2, the report on Australia taken from the 1995 edition of the IMF yearbook, shows these categories.

Current account categories include the sale and purchase of merchandise goods (visible trade) valued as of the time of sale. An import is a debit; an export is a credit. Many of the transactions related to services (invisible trade) are detailed specifically in the supporting tables. *Transportation* covers both passengers and merchandise goods; the goods and services, other than transportation, purchased by a tourist or business traveler (hotel, meals, local tours, and so forth) are classified under *travel*. Fees and interest arising from banking or brokerage services, legal and accounting fees, and foreign exchange trading are also categories of services. The category *income* reflects dividends and interest on investments (see below) as well as compensation of employees. *Transfers* from either government or private sources describe items that are given away (charity, disaster relief) or for which there is no offsetting transaction such as gifts, dowries, inheritances, support remittances to a student, lotteries, and so forth. Each of these service categories can be either a credit or a debit to a balance of payments, depending on whether the country is paying for the service provided by another country (a debit) or performing the service (a credit).

Income received by a country in any category can be used to pay for any category of expense. The debits and credits in any category tend to be independent of each other. A country's earnings from tourists coming into the country will, for example, be shown as a credit, while those of that country's tourists going abroad will be a debit. These represent separate activities unrelated to each other.

Capital and financial accounts refer to investments, that is, payments made from one country to another for a long-term use. This is in contrast to the various current accounts where the payment is for a transaction that could be completed in a short period, usually less than a year.

Capital accounts consist of government or private sector transfers for acquiring fixed assets such as land, transfers of transportation equipment or machinery itself, debt forgiveness, and the net worth of long-term migrants.

Financial accounts include foreign direct investment (acquiring ownership in a company), portfolio investment (purchase of shares of stock), and other investments (loans and deposits).

Obtaining accurate investment data may be difficult. If a country requires government approval for such investments, it may have fairly accurate information. Otherwise it will rely on surveys, reports, and estimates from businesses.

Reserve assets is an important component of balance of payments statistics and an essential element in the analysis of an economy's external position . . . [It] consists of those external assets that are readily available to and controlled by monetary authorities for direct financing of payments imbalances, for directly regulating the magnitude of such imbalances through intervention in exchange markets to affect the currency exchange rate, and/or for other purposes."[20]

The balance of payments report reflects changes during the period in the reserves. It does not reflect what the country's total reserves are nor the composition of those reserves, such as percentages held in gold, foreign currency holdings (and in which currencies), and so on. That

Exhibit 1.2   IMF Balance of Payments Transactions Data for Australia

Australia
193

Table 1. ANALYTIC PRESENTATION, 1987–94

(In millions of U.S. dollars)

	Code	1987	1988	1989	1990	1991	1992	1993	1994
A. Current Account[1]	4 993 Y .	**–8,459**	**–11,714**	**–19,227**	**–16,585**	**–11,658**	**–11,776**	**–10,707**	**–15,224**
Goods: exports f.o.b	2 100 ..	27,014	33,182	36,893	39,332	42,005	42,375	42,236	47,073
Goods: imports f.o.b	3 100 ..	–26,739	–33,898	–40,311	–38,964	–38,491	–40,820	–42,363	–50,272
Balance on Goods	4 100 ..	*275*	*–716*	*–3,418*	*368*	*3,514*	*1,555*	*–127*	*–3,199*
Services: credit	2 200 ..	6,510	8,921	9,417	10,737	11,534	11,682	12,331	14,451
Services: debit	3 200 ..	–9,157	–11,379	–13,845	–14,735	–14,391	–14,636	–13,913	–14,782
Balance on Goods and Services	4 991 ..	*–2,372*	*–3,174*	*–7,847*	*–3,630*	*657*	*–1,399*	*–1,709*	*–3,530*
Income: credit	2 300 ..	2,455	2,916	3,484	3,148	3,048	3,443	3,935	4,190
Income: debit	3 300 ..	–8,467	–11,391	–14,894	–16,411	–15,346	–13,672	–12,685	–15,451
Balance on Goods, Services, and Income	4 992 ..	*–8,385*	*–11,650*	*–19,258*	*–16,892*	*–11,641*	*–11,628*	*–10,459*	*–14,791*
Current transfers: credit	2 379 Y .	979	1,204	1,366	1,758	1,414	1,232	1,118	1,186
Current transfers: debit	3 379 ..	–1,053	–1,268	–1,335	–1,450	–1,432	–1,380	–1,366	–1,619
B. Capital Account[1]	4 994 Y .	**1,092**	**1,538**	**1,913**	**1,735**	**1,847**	**1,303**	**531**	**612**
Capital account: credit	2 994 Y .	1,311	1,790	2,213	2,077	2,212	1,657	842	976
Capital account: debit	3 994 ..	–219	–252	–300	–342	–365	–353	–311	–363
Total, Groups A Plus B	4 010 ..	*–7,367*	*–10,176*	*–17,314*	*–14,849*	*–9,811*	*–10,473*	*–10,176*	*–14,611*
C. Financial Account[1]	4 995 X .	**8,313**	**19,323**	**16,598**	**13,822**	**12,602**	**9,675**	**11,600**	**10,992**
Direct investment abroad	4 505 ..	–5,114	–4,984	–3,319	–186	–3,126	–113	–1,087	–5,908
Direct investment in Australia	4 555 Y .	3,921	8,056	7,936	7,077	4,903	4,912	3,381	3,789
Portfolio investment assets	4 602 ..	–950	–1,665	–2,350	1,450	–2,532	591	–2,361	280
Equity securities	4 610 ..	–950	–1,665	–2,350	1,450	–2,532	591	–2,361	280
Debt securities	4 619 ..	...	...	...	...	...	...	...	...
Portfolio investment liabilities	4 652 Y .	5,273	7,497	2,820	1,024	7,030	–1,110	6,395	15,229
Equity securities	4 660 Y .	3,204	1,106	1,401	1,665	2,416	704	7,498	7,716
Debt securities	4 669 Y .	2,069	6,391	1,419	–641	4,614	–1,815	–1,103	7,514
Other investment assets	4 703 ..	–2,702	396	–2,487	–831	–817	–1,811	–2,521	1,282
Monetary authorities	4 703 .A	...	...	...	...	...	...	...	...
General government	4 703 .B	–114	250	–297	319	149	113	–184	141
Banks	4 703 .C	–343	–215	–131	–833	898	–887	–1,038	–968
Other sectors	4 703 .D	–2,245	361	–2,059	–317	–1,864	–1,037	–1,299	2,109
Other investment liabilities	4 753 X .	7,885	10,022	13,997	5,287	7,145	7,206	7,793	–3,681
Monetary authorities	4 753 XA	...	...	...	...	...	...	...	...
General government	4 753 YB	1,433	–1,141	803	–312	1,667	5,253	8,062	76
Banks	4 753 YC	2,282	4,274	9,428	3,333	5,100	1,573	2,418	2,013
Other sectors	4 753 YD	4,169	6,890	3,766	2,265	377	379	–2,687	–5,770
Total, Groups A Through C	4 020 ..	*947*	*9,147*	*–716*	*–1,027*	*2,791*	*–798*	*1,424*	*–3,619*
D. Net Errors And Omissions	4 998 ..	**–576**	**–3,896**	**1,344**	**2,754**	**–3,107**	**–3,940**	**–1,479**	**2,664**
Total, Groups A Through D	4 030 ..	*371*	*5,251*	*628*	*1,727*	*–316*	*–4,737*	*–55*	*–955*
E. Reserves and Related Items	4 040 ..	**–371**	**–5,251**	**–628**	**–1,727**	**316**	**4,737**	**55**	**955**
Reserve assets	4 800 ..	–374	–5,279	–601	–1,740	324	4,726	42	960
Use of Fund credit and loans	4 766 ..	...	...	...	...	...	...	...	...
Liabilities constituting foreign authorities' reserves	4 900 ..	4	28	–28	13	–8	11	13	–4
Exceptional financing	4 920 ..	...	...	...	...	...	...	...	...
Conversion rates: Australian dollars per U.S. dollar	0 101 ..	1.42818	1.27991	1.26460	1.28106	1.28376	1.36165	1.47056	1.36775

[1] Excludes components that have been classified in the categories of Group E.

From the 1995 *Balance of Payments Statistics Yearbook,* copyright 1995 by the International Monetary Fund. Reprinted with permission.

information may be found in other sources, such as the IMF's monthly publication *International Financial Statistics*.

Reserves are actually existing assets that a nation's government has immediately available to make payments when that country's income is less than its expenses. These include monetary gold, reserve positions in the IMF, and foreign bank deposits. It also includes foreign assets that the government may not own but can control. An example of this would occur when a country's monetary authorities allow commercial banks to hold foreign balances under regulations and authorization of the central monetary authorities. It does not reflect lines of credit (see chapter 10), foreign exchange swap agreements (see chapter 5), or foreign holdings of residents that could be seized by the government in a national emergency.

Achieving a Balance

These broad categories (current account, capital and financial account, net errors and conversions, and reserve changes) tend to offset each other to achieve an overall balance. For example, a developing country (other than the few oil producers) tends to be a net importer: its purchases of industrial machinery and manufactured goods cost more than it earns from its exports of raw materials, expenditures by foreign tourists, and remittances from its workers in other countries. It is therefore normal for it to run a deficit in its current account. To pay for this import gap, it needs to be a net borrower of money, attract investment, or receive gifts—all of which are reported as items in the financial account, in which the country will show a net credit. Since it is difficult for the current account and investment categories to exactly match in any given year, the balance is achieved by changes in the country's reserves. When the level of investment inflow is less than is needed to cover the current

account deficit, the reserves will be drawn down; when it is greater, the reserves will go up.

An industrialized country, in contrast, is expected to be a net exporter of goods and services. Its manufactured goods will earn more than it spends on raw materials, or its residents spend as tourists abroad, and so forth. Industrialized countries are the sources of the investment, loans, and gifts that the developing countries need. Therefore, as a general rule, the balance of payments of the industrialized countries will show a net inflow in the current account and a net outflow in the capital and financial account. The balance between these two categories will, as for the developing countries, be reflected in changes in the reserves. Since the 1980s, the United States because of its internal domestic policies, was an exception to this generalization.

Although the current account and the capital and financial accounts are separate categories in a nation's balance of payments, they are not incompatible with each other. This is particularly evident from the perspective of businesses. There

are numerous ways of competing globally involving choices about where to locate and how to coordinate activities. . . . Most global strategies involve an integrated combination of trade and foreign direct investment. Finished products are exported from some nations that import components produced elsewhere, and vice versa. Foreign investment reflects the dispersion of production and marketing activities. Trade and foreign investment are complementary, not necessarily substitutes.[21]

Within the balance of payments statement there can be a number of levels of "balance." The difference between merchandise imports and exports is the **trade balance.**

When international payments (for imports, outgoing capital, services bought from other countries, and so forth) exceed income (from exports, incoming capital, services done for others, and so forth), a nation has a **balance of payments deficit**. Conversely, when the receipts are greater than the payments, the nation has a **balance of payments surplus**. The long-term threat of a deficit is that, if not corrected, eventually the country will have neither the means to pay for future imports of food, raw materials, machinery, or needed services nor the ability to meet its international debt-servicing obligations.

A deficit can be financed by using previously accumulated reserves or by borrowing from the IMF or foreign banks. In this sense, a country acts much like an individual. When the money going out exceeds the amount coming in, a country draws on its reserves, and an individual draws on savings. If the deficit persists, both borrow from a financial institution. If the deficit still continues, then lifestyle changes must be made.

If the country's currency is widely used, as is the case with the U.S. dollar, a balance of payments deficit can be covered by encouraging other countries to hold more of the country's currency. Thus, foreigners who sell goods to the United States are encouraged to invest those dollars in the United States. If a nation has a persistent balance of payments deficit, it must take further measures. These usually involve immediately reducing payments. Since imports are usually the largest category of international payments, the nation can take steps to reduce imports through tariffs, quotas, or foreign exchange controls. Investments in other countries can be held down through capital export restrictions or other administrative measures. The country can restrict payments for invisible trade by forbidding its citizens to travel abroad or by limiting payments for services. Debt repayment can be renegotiated so that the immediate year's interest and principal amounts may be reduced by permitting a longer time to repay. At the same time that it is taking steps to reduce the level of its payments, the nation can also seek to increase its foreign earnings through devaluations, liberalized investment rules, tax reductions, and other measures. A deficit can seldom be met by only one of these methods.

While most focus is on the problems of a country with a balance of payments deficit, a surplus in a country's activities with the rest of the world can also create domestic economic problems.

Connections to the Domestic Economy

The domestic economy of a nation is not isolated from its activities with the rest of the world, which are represented in the balance of payments. For example, an investment from a U.S. corporation to build a factory in Zimbabwe for tomato processing would show as a direct foreign investment credit to Zimbabwe's balance of payments. Jobs would be created there, first for the construction, and then for the operation of the factory. Tax revenues will be generated over time from the earnings of the workers and the earnings of the factory. The plant to process tomatoes into tomato paste and juice needs local farmers to supply it with the tomatoes, which would increase the agricultural output of the country now that there is a buyer for the expanded crop. The factory needs local suppliers of fuel and office materials; it needs janitorial, secretarial, security, and local transportation personnel besides the workers on the processing line. Thus a ripple effect can be expected through the domestic economy from the single investment. In the future, this new product could generate exports to neighboring countries.

Likewise, domestic economic events will be reflected in the balance of payments. A country running a large governmental budget deficit, for example, will often have a high rate of inflation. This will cause the costs in local currency for goods and services to rise. If such a country is trying to maintain a fixed exchange rate, either for domestic political purposes or to lessen the apparent impact of inflation, imports become increasingly cheaper and are thereby encouraged. Meanwhile, exports become more expensive, which makes them less attractive to foreign buyers.

When such a country seeks to hold down food prices for its workers living in cities, it may find that it becomes cheaper to import food that was formerly grown domestically. Not only can this increase payments for imports, it can also discourage farmers from continuing to produce, thereby eliminating a source of export income. Many of these farmers will leave farming and move to the cities, thus accelerating the demand for cheap food in those cities and reducing the future capability of the country to change its policy. Eventually the decline in exports and growth in imports causes a payments crisis for the country.

It is interesting to note the different policies that developing and developed countries have for agriculture. The developing countries may want cheap food at the expense of the farmer for those who live in the city; the developed countries often have policies to protect the farmers, which can mean higher direct food prices or government subsidies paid by the taxpayers.

Fears of possible future economic changes can accelerate outgoing funds transfers as a country's citizens seek safety for themselves or their money. This is sometimes called **capital flight**, which can be disguised through many different balance of payments categories. For example, a government imposing controls on imports to reduce a balance of payments deficit may require a permit to get the foreign exchange to pay for an import. An importer gaining such a permit might arrange for the foreign seller, who could be a subsidiary or agent, to "over invoice"—that is, bill at an artificially high price. Then, when receiving the payment, that seller would put the excess over the real cost into a bank account for the buyer in the foreign country. Human ingenuity demonstrates a record of considerable success when frightened people are desperate to get their money to a safe haven.

Even though capital flight can seriously affect a nation, it is almost impossible to determine the amount of capital flight or to distinguish it "from 'normal' capital outflows—that is, trade credits, working balances, natural portfolio diversification, and the attraction of higher interest rates. The term 'capital flight' implies a further set of factors, such as the fear of inflation, exchange depreciation, political upheaval, tax avoidance, evasion of exchange control laws, etc., but it is statistically impossible to classify capital movements, especially the unrecorded movements, according to motive." [22]

Beginning in 1928, international organizations have expanded an analytical System of National Accounts[23] to report the details of domestic economies. The country's activities with the rest of the world is an integral part of this.

Summary

This chapter has examined the world in which global banking exists. It has classified the activities of the banker's customers, since the products the banker has will meet the needs of those customers dealing in the global economy. Trade between nations is a necessity for every nation; services from another country supplement the needs of each economy; countries with surplus savings invest them wherever in the world they can be effective.

The chapters that follow will discuss the specialized products the banker provides for those customers to conduct their business. When you have finished the last chapter you should be able to answer four basic questions:

- What global activities are my customers engaged in?

- Because they are engaged in those activities, what services do they need from their banker to do their business?

- What products do bankers have to meet those needs?

- How does the banker deliver those products to meet those needs?

The banker's customer may be a business, an individual, another bank, or even a government. Regardless of the size of your bank, your customer needs services, products, and advice from you, and your bank must be able to provide these in an efficient, effective, and profitable form.

Questions

1. Why does trade take place between countries?
2. What is invisible trade?
3. Why are foreign investments important to countries?
4. What are the components of a country's balance of payments?

Problem

Identify 10 items you own that are imported. Are these items also made in the United States? If so, would you ever be willing to purchase them? If not, why not?

Notes

1. Adam Smith, *An Inquiry into the Nature and Causes of the Wealth of Nations* (London: Strahan & Cadell, 1776). Reprint (London: Penguin Books Ltd., 1970), p. 472
2. Michael Porter, *The Competitive Advantage of Nations* (New York: The Free Press, 1990), p. 7
3. Ibid., p. 33
4. "Prehistoric Society: A New Picture Emerges," *The New York Times*, December 16, 1986, p. 17
5. Fernand Braudel, *The Perspective of the World* (New York: Harper and Row, 1984).
6. John Keay, *The Honourable Company* (New York: Macmillan Publishing Company, 1991), p. 4
7. Henry Hobhouse, *Seeds of Change* (London: Sidgwick & Jackson, 1985), p. 100
8. Ibid., p. 108; chapters 1, 2, 3
9. Braudel, *The Perspective of the World*
10. Porter, *The Competitive Advantage of Nations*, pp. 91, 119, 131
11. Ibid.
12. *The New York Times*, August 24, 1990, p. C2
13. "Survey of World Trade", *The Economist,* September 22, 1990, p. 8
14. Rupert Pennant-Rea and Bill Emmott, *The Pocket Economist* (New York: Cambridge University Press, 1983), p. 121
15. International Monetary Fund, *World Economic Outlook*, October 1995, pp. 83-87
16. Adrian Wood, *North-South Trade Employment and Inequality* (Oxford: Clarendon Press, 1994), pp. 1-2
17. Jane Jacobs, *Cities and the Wealth of Nations* (New York: Random House, 1984), p. 105
18. International Monetary Fund, *Balance of Payments Manual*, 5th Ed., paragraph 148
19. *Financial Times*, November 14, 1994
20. International Monetary Fund, *Balance of Payments Manual*, paragraph 424
21. Porter, p. 61
22. International Monetary Fund, *Report on the World Current Account Discrepancy* (Washington, D.C., International Monetary Fund, 1987), p. 163
23. Commission of the European Communities, International Monetary Fund, Organization for Economic Co-operation and Development, United Nations, World Bank, *System of National Accounts 1993* (Brussels: 1993), section XIV

2

ORGANIZATION OF U.S. BANKS

Learning Objectives

After studying this chapter, you will be able to

- describe the various organizational elements available to a bank for global banking
- analyze the advantages of these elements
- describe the placement of international activities in a bank's financial statement

Overview

Before the enactment of the Federal Reserve Act in 1913, U.S. national banks had no authority to establish foreign operations or to accept drafts arising from international trade. Customers needing international banking services went to the few state-chartered banks that had overseas branches, to foreign banks, or to British merchant banks. "During the nineteenth century London's merchant banks, while continuing to remain the foreign traders' chief source of commercial credits, also emerged as the dominant force in international finance." [1] It was not until after World War II that U.S. commercial banks began to expand their international capabilities with an array of organizational structures.

To conduct international activities, banks may organize in a number of ways, including establishing international departments, overseas branches, Edge Act corporations, foreign representative offices, subsidiaries, and joint ventures. The appropriate combination of the many available elements will vary among banks, depending on the needs of a bank's customers and management's decision on how best to serve these needs. Even if a bank now has no international structure of its own, the account officer with a domestic customer can serve that customer's global needs through the bank's domestic correspondent banking relationships that have an international organization.

No matter how large and important an international department may become, it is still part of the parent banking institution; its operations must comply rather than conflict with the objectives of that bank. Presumably, the bank's paramount purpose is to combine service to customers with profit for stockholders. Consequently, the international department should not engage in exotic services for which its customers have no need, nor should it permit the glamour of far-flung overseas relationships to obscure their possibly disproportionate cost.

The international activities of a commercial bank are combined with its domestic business into a single financial statement. Bank regulators apply ratios to the total bank to measure the adequacy of the level of the bank's capital to its assets. With the change to the Risk-Based Capital Guidelines, more international activities have been brought into that calculation. Bank management needs to assess the bank's international business ventures and the borrower's country, not only for the present risk criteria and costs, but also for their differing impact on the level of bank capital each requires.

Similarly, the investment or merchant bank will view international business as supplementary to its domestic business.

This chapter concentrates on how the commercial bank organizes itself for the needs of its global banking business.

International Departments

The move into global banking begins with establishing a section or department in the commercial bank's head office for handling international business transactions. The organization of this department should be tailored to meet particular needs. It may be small, with every individual capable of performing nearly every task, or it may be large and highly specialized. In any case, the international department must have a single responsible head with enough knowledge to coordinate the activities of the department as it expands and with the authority to share in the formulation of bank policy.

Until the volume of business becomes substantial, the international department can use the bank's existing domestic facilities. For example, domestic collection clerks can handle international collections until there are enough such collections to justify the assignment of personnel solely to international transactions. Foreign sections in the bookkeeping and audit-control divisions of the domestic organization are relatively easy to create. By using the protection arrangements of a large bank, a smaller bank should be able to achieve the maximum expansion of its money transfer capacity with minimum investment of time and capital. Such protection arrangements, for example, permit the smaller bank to draw its foreign drafts or make remittances through the existing "Due From" or "Due To" accounts maintained by the larger bank with its own correspondent banks (see chapter 3). Unsuccessful and costly experiences can be avoided by proceeding slowly in the expansion of a specialized international department.

Most banks active in international banking develop international departments in their head offices. Comparatively few of these banks establish overseas branches or Edge Act corporations, and then only after they have developed active international departments at home.

The international department of a bank active in overseas business is a miniature bank. An international department carries on nearly every operation performed by a commercial bank engaged in domestic banking. It accepts deposits and maintains its own deposits in other institutions. It pays checks against the accounts on its books and draws against its own funds abroad. It receives and pays out cash, makes funds transfers using the most advanced electronic systems, has a collection section dealing with both incoming and outgoing items, lends money to its local customers, and maintains credit information and correspondent bank relations.

All these functions have their counterparts, usually on a larger scale, in the bank's domestic activities. An international department, however, also handles numerous transactions not usually found in domestic divisions, such as the opening and negotiating of commercial letters of credit, trading in foreign exchange, purchase and sale of foreign currency banknotes, creation of bankers' acceptances, and lending to borrowers in other countries.

An international department's operations reveal the kinds of services it offers its customers. The international department can have a number of sections that carry on its major activities. The more important and active parts of the international department are examined in greater detail in later chapters; these show what the various sections of the department do and how they serve the customer.

Foreign Branches

U.S. banks were slow to develop foreign branches for several reasons. First, it was not until the passage of the Federal Reserve Act in 1913 that national banks were clearly permitted to establish foreign branches. Before that time, the few overseas branches that did exist had been formed under state banking laws. Second, the United States was a debtor country, with much of its developmental capital coming from foreign banks. Even though the foreign trade of the United States expanded after the Civil War, it was being financed by European banks that had well-established techniques and capabilities for financing trade, including accepting bills drawn on them.

The first overseas office of a U.S. commercial bank was opened in 1887. By 1967, 15 U.S. banks had established a total of 295 branches overseas. Three of these banks accounted for approximately 75 percent of the branches. By the end of 1994, there were 128 U.S. banks with a total of 768 branches in foreign countries and overseas possessions of the United States.[2] (These made up 1.2 percent of the total 10,450 commercial banks in the United States at that time.) This represented a decline from the peak in the early 1980s, when there were 166 banks and a total of 917 branches.[3]

U.S. banks have branches in virtually every major foreign market. Banks with only a few overseas branches have located them in the major money centers, such as London, or in such countries as The Bahamas or the Cayman Islands, where laws permit a branch for special purposes to be established at a low cost. Many branches offer a full range of banking services to individuals and to local and U.S. companies. Some countries, however, prohibit U.S. banks from offering certain services, such as taking deposits. Some countries also require that U.S. banks establish separate subsidiaries instead of a branch. Regardless of the form, to open a branch or subsidiary in another country, the U.S. bank must obtain permission of the host government as well as approval of the Board of Governors of the Federal Reserve System.

U.S. banks expanded their overseas branch systems to serve clients whose foreign activities are increasing and, in many cases, to compete with local banks for local business. The foreign branch must comply with all the banking rules, exchange controls, and regulations of the host country and is subject to examination by both the host country and U.S. banking authorities. U.S. banking regulations permit overseas branches more freedom than their head offices have. For example, overseas branches do not maintain reserves in a Federal Reserve Bank against their deposits, may pay interest on demand deposits, and can issue certain guarantees, such as shipside bonds (see chapter 7), which the bank may not do in the United States. Deposits in overseas branches are not insured by the Federal Deposit Insurance Corporation (FDIC).

In most cases, a branch's capital is segregated from that of its parent bank. The branch thus resembles a small unit bank in its operations and must do its own hiring, complying with all the local labor laws and union regulations. Most overseas staff members are hired locally, and all, including the few officers from the head office, are expected to be fluent in both the local language and English. The branch clears its checks directly with the local clearing house, if one exists, or directly with other banks. Deposits at that branch are subject to local regulations. The branch is responsible for maintenance of premises, construction, and printing of forms and stationery. It deals in the local money market for placement of its short-term cash surplus and maintains reserves at the central bank. It must also comply with all the reporting requirements of the country's regulatory agencies.

These are just a few of the activities for which the local overseas manager is responsible. In the United States, most of these are handled by the head office on behalf of all its branches. In addition to the administrative responsibilities of operating the branch, the overseas manager is also the parent bank's representative in the foreign country, a position that necessitates attendance at official and unofficial functions. The hours the overseas branch manager must devote to the job far exceed those of a domestic branch manager. With all this, the branch's basic objective is still to show a profit.

The overseas branch of a U.S. bank has a dual function. It is a foreign bank competing with the local banks in the local market for local customers. The lobby traffic in an overseas branch can often exceed what a banker is accustomed to in his own head office. In addition, it is the local link in the parent bank's international chain of offices. The overseas branch generates international financial business for its system and serves the bank's customers from other markets.

Overseas branches offering full banking services are expensive, and their attractiveness has been declining over recent decades. The impetus for creating them came in the 1960s and 1970s, primarily as a means of funding foreign business while the U.S. government had a series of restraint programs for balance of payments problems. There was also prestige in having a foreign branch. The debt crisis of the 1980s caused most U.S. banks to reconsider the size and scope of their international business, one factor of which was the profitability of overseas branches. As a result, a number of banks closed or sold many of their branches. Those that remain are primarily concentrated in the larger business centers or are "shell branches" (see below).

Shell Branches

Some overseas branches are established, not for general banking in the local market, but for a special purpose. Most U.S. branches in The Bahamas and the Cayman Islands are domiciling units for Eurodollar deposits and loans originating through the efforts of the bank's head office or other overseas branches (see chapter 11). They often have a tiny staff or, in some cases, only a designated local banker who serves in the nominal role of manager. These are sometimes called **shell branches** and are used for tax or other reasons to "garage" or "warehouse" loans that originated in some other foreign country.

Such branches, being in countries with low tax rates, can offer important tax savings for a bank. "The tax savings relate to foreign, rather than to U.S. taxes. Foreign branch . . . earnings are immediately attributable to the parent U.S. banks for U.S. tax purposes." Banks paying taxes on their earnings in some countries that have rates higher than the U.S. "attempt to lower their overall foreign tax rate by booking [some] loans in tax-free centers." [4]

Edge Act Corporations

In 1919, the Federal Reserve Act was amended by the enactment of Section 25(a) to permit national banks to incorporate subsidiaries for international banking and investment. These subsidiaries are established in the United States and are called **Edge Act corporations*** after the bill's sponsor, Senator Walter Edge of New Jersey. Such corporations are permitted to establish domestic offices outside of their home state to transact only international business;

hence, the Edge Act corporation can deal only with overseas customers and that portion of any local (U.S.) customer's business that is international, such as export-import financing. A number of such corporations were established immediately following the passage of the act. By the end of the 1920s, few remained. After World War II, however, interest in Edge Act corporations revived.

Edge Act corporations may be established for banking or for foreign investment purposes. Some banks therefore have one for each purpose. Edge Act banking corporations constitute the majority by number and over 90 percent of the total by assets. After reaching a high in 1983, the total has been declining. At the end of 1994, there were 76 Edge Act corporations with 32 branches.

Most Edge Act corporations are located in New York City, even though the parent banks are located in other states. Through these corporations, the parent bank can offer international clients and correspondent banks the services of an office in New York City in addition to the services available in the home state, a combination not possible under normal branch banking permits. Edge Act banks are now also located in other cities, such as Chicago and Miami.

The law requires that "an Edge must have minimum equity capital of $2 million. Combined with the legal restriction that prevents any national bank from investing more than 10 percent of its equity in Edges, this requirement effectively limits the ownership of Edges to banks with assets exceeding $300 million." [5] Although Federal Reserve Regulation K generally governs their operations, Edges are not members of the

---

* State-chartered banks are permitted under an earlier amendment to Section 25 to create "agreement corporations," which are very similar to Edge Act corporations. The company "agrees" with the Federal Reserve to limit its activities to those permitted to Edge Act corporations.

Federal Reserve System and their deposits are not insured by the FDIC. They are required to maintain the same level of reserves against deposits as does any national bank.

An Edge Act bank may have a small staff or a large staff of more than 500 employees. In either case, it is organized as a complete bank, providing all the services of a full-sized foreign department. It may also establish branches in other states. The International Banking Act of 1978 permits foreign banks to establish Edge Act corporations.

The basic difference, in summary, between a foreign branch and an Edge Act corporation of a U.S. bank is that the branch is located outside the United States, while the Edge Act corporation is in the United States.

The International Banking Facility

Since 1981, banks in the United States have been permitted to establish a separate set of accounts in their domestic office in order to participate in the Eurodollar market (see chapter 11) without incurring the expense of maintaining an overseas branch. This is an **International Banking Facility** (IBF), which essentially has the attributes of an overseas shell branch while being physically located in the United States. It may take Eurodollar deposits from nonresidents free of Federal Reserve regulations on reserve requirements and make Eurodollar-funded loans. Facilities are also exempt from the insurance coverage and assessments imposed by the FDIC. An IBF may be established by any U.S. bank, Edge Act corporation, or U.S. branch or agency of a foreign bank. Federal Reserve approval is not required, merely notification in advance and agreement to comply with Federal Reserve regulations. Even though an IBF deals in the Eurodollar market, it is located in the United States and thus is a U.S. country risk, since it is

subject to the laws of the United States. Various states have passed laws to exempt IBFs from state taxes.

Although exempt from some Federal Reserve regulations, IBFs were from the beginning bound by others. They may "conduct business only with foreign residents (including banks), other IBFs, or the IBF's own establishing entity. . . . Credit provided to foreign nonbank customers may be used only outside the United States." [6] This regulation insulates IBFs from the U.S. market, where reserve requirements must be followed. Deposits (a minimum of $100,000) placed by corporations in an IBF must remain for a minimum of 48 hours, while banks in foreign countries may place overnight deposits. Also, IBFs may not issue negotiable instruments, such as certificates of deposit.

The advantage of establishing an IBF, or several in different offices, is that it reduces expenses by sharing them with other activities of the bank. The same staff can negotiate and process international transactions for an IBF and perform other domestic money activities for the parent bank. It is a vehicle for attracting Eurocurrency activities to the United States. Many foreign customers, however, have continued to prefer to domicile their businesses in offshore banking areas, such as The Bahamas and the Cayman Islands.

"An entity that establishes an IBF does not obtain any new powers by doing so. . . . In meeting loan limitation requirements, establishing entities must include loans made by the IBF." [7]

Representative Offices

A bank often establishes a **representative office** in a foreign city, usually the capital, when it wants a presence there but does not have sufficient business to justify the expense of a branch, or when the country does not permit branches. The bank's assigned representative, usually an experienced officer from the head office of the U.S. bank, develops new business for the bank and calls on existing customers. His presence in the foreign country can also help domestic customers of the bank doing business in the country. The office staff is usually very small, often consisting of only the representative, an assistant, and a secretary. Representatives cannot do any banking business, such as taking deposits or making loans, but will direct business to the head office of the bank or its branches.

In many instances, establishment of a representative office has preceded establishment of a branch. In some countries, new branches of foreign banks are prohibited; hence, many U.S. banks maintain their presence in such countries through representatives.

In the United States in 1994 there were 239 foreign bank representative offices.

Subsidiaries and Joint Ventures

In addition to overseas branches, banks have **subsidiaries** or **joint ventures**. A foreign subsidiary is a foreign company in which a U.S. banking organization has majority ownership or some other form of control. A joint venture is a foreign company in which the U.S. banking organization does not have a controlling interest. Such definitions differentiate the two types of entities from a bank regulatory perspective; definitions for taxing and accounting purposes may vary.

Banks establish foreign subsidiaries to improve their competitive position, to minimize foreign tax liabilities, and to take advantage of opportunities they would otherwise miss. Although most banks prefer to operate their own branches to develop local consumer business that should have a separate identity, such as with a finance company, a subsidiary may be used where branches are not permitted or to perform functions prohibited to branches, including such investment activities as security underwriting and warehousing.

The joint venture can be a bank established by several different banks that share ownership and, in some cases, management of the bank. The joint venture allows foreign banks with local investors to establish a presence in a country that does not encourage foreign-owned branches and to specialize in certain fields. Each shareholder provides a portion of the capital for the joint venture and has a proportionate representation on the board of directors. Daily management may be provided by the shareholders, who will "lend" officers, by one of the shareholders under a management contract, or by a manager hired from outside the member banks. The joint venture has its own name and functions as an independent bank, usually receiving only policy direction from the shareholders through the board of directors. While most joint venture banks are owned by major international banks, the joint venture also provides a way for smaller banks, which might not feel they have the expertise or capacity to be in a foreign country on their own, to have a presence in a particular foreign market.

The joint venture participants share the profits in proportion to their capital contribution. This can be a major risk exposure, since a participant bank also shares the losses in the same ratio but without having full control over the management.

Export Trading Company

In 1982, U.S. bank holding companies were permitted to establish **export trading companies** (ETC). The purpose of these companies is to improve U.S. export capability in both goods and services, with corresponding benefits for U.S. balance of payments, employment, and economic growth. A wide range of export-related services is permitted to an ETC: consulting, marketing, financing, insurance, freight forwarding, warehousing, and the like. Authority to create ETCs was thought to be necessary because the U.S. export business is fragmented among a large number of small businesses. Many businesses in the United States do not now export. To encourage them to do so, an ETC can bring together many fragmented export services along with financial resources and thereby offer a business a centralized source of all it will need to engage in exporting. However, the assumption that ETCs would be popular was apparently not accurate, as the level of activity in ETCs has been disappointingly low. At the end of 1994, only 48 ETCs existed.

Merchant and Investment Banks

Merchant bank, originally a British term, describes what in the United States is referred to as an investment bank, as distinguished from a commercial bank. A merchant bank specializes in such corporate financing needs as underwriting stocks and bonds, handling mergers and acquisitions, and undertaking a range of other financial advisory services. Its antecedents in Europe, from about the fifteenth century on, were the initial providers of international banking services before commercial banks entered the field. The original merchant banks began as commercial trading companies, which then added banking services.

> Giovanni Medici (1360-1429) . . . headed an international trading and banking company that dealt in woolens, silks, furs, and leather; invested in and supervised a variety of domestic industries; financed a miscellany of overseas commercial ventures; and provided its many clients with most of the foreign

exchange, banking, and credit facilities they required. . . . The growth of commerce, both in scope and volume, made international traders increasingly dependent upon the safe and efficient transfer of funds from one principality and kingdom to another. Europe's great merchant bankers with branches and agents in distant cities, such as the Medici, with a half-dozen offices outside Italy enjoyed the confidence of large entrepreneurs and commanded the machinery to serve them efficiently." [8]

Some U.S. investment banks likewise can trace their origins to financing various types of global commodity trading, such as cotton from the South in the nineteenth century.

In the nineteenth century, particularly, and even into the 1930s, the larger European merchant bankers had influence and power on a scale unknown today, internationally and domestically. The French prime minister in 1818 would say of one of them, "There are six great powers in Europe: England, France, Prussia, Austria, Russia, and Baring Brothers." [9] "By the time of the [American] Civil War, Barings was the agent bank for Russia, Norway, Austria, Chile, Argentina, Canada, Australia, and the United States." [10]

Many of the international services that were unique to the merchant banks are now done by commercial banks, so that today's merchant banks are focused on providing investment banking expertise that supplements the lending and operational capabilities of the commercial banks.

In the United States, an **investment bank** describes an organization with a different focus than a commercial bank, sharing some of the attributes of the British merchant bank. Its primary business is raising equity capital and long-term debt for governments and corporations, and offering financial advisory services to them.

Some are active in foreign exchange and global money markets trading. They provide their services not only to domestic companies, but also to customers in other countries. Chapter 11 discusses their contribution to global funding.

Foreign Banks in the United States

Foreign banks have come to the United States for reasons similar to those motivating U.S. banks to expand overseas: to serve their customers, develop a share in the largest business market in the world, and have a direct means of attracting and investing U.S. dollars. This banking presence takes many forms. As of year-end 1994, 277 foreign banks operated 494 state-licensed branches and agencies, 73 branches and agencies licensed by the Office of the Comptroller of the Currency, 12 Edge Act corporations, and 4 commercial lending companies. In addition, foreign banks held an equity interest of at least 25 percent in 85 U.S. commercial banks. Altogether, these U.S. offices of foreign banks control approximately 21 percent of U.S. banking assets.[11] By comparison, the 82 foreign banks in Japan in 1990 made less than 2 percent of all loans.[12]

The basic difference between a branch and an agency relates to deposits. "U.S. agencies, as opposed to branches, of foreign banking organizations are *not* allowed to accept deposits from U.S. citizens or residents. Agencies may, however, may maintain 'credit balances' for U.S. citizens and residents, in addition to taking deposits from foreign residents."[13] A credit balance is generally one that arises from the specific purpose of a loan, wire transfer, or letter of credit; is not used for routine operating expenses; and is withdrawn after the specific purpose is completed.

"The vast majority of branches and agencies of foreign banks . . . are not insured by the FDIC and do not accept consumer deposits."[14] The Federal Reserve has the overall responsibility for the supervision of these foreign branches and agencies, although much of the examination may be done by other federal and state agencies. "It is important to keep in mind that branches and agencies are not U.S. banks. A branch or agency is an integral part of a foreign bank."[15] Therefore, the U.S. regulators are expected to work closely with the regulators of the foreign parent bank to ensure the sound operation of these United States-based units. The U.S. policy is that such foreign branches have the same rights and privileges as domestic banks. However, the U.S. branch or agency of a foreign bank must comply with U.S. laws and regulations even if these differ from those applicable in the parent bank's country. Failure to do so can result in penalties or even expulsion of not only that branch or agency from the United States but all of a foreign bank's U.S. units.

Setting up a Foreign Bank in the United States

Foreign investment in U.S. banking can be traced to the beginning of this country's history, with the charter of the First Bank of the United States in 1809, which housed large foreign holdings. In the late nineteenth century, Japanese, Canadian, and British banks were established, initially on the West Coast. By 1911, Massachusetts, Oregon, California, and New York permitted foreign banking. The 1920s saw a boom in foreign banking, but that died out with the Great Depression, and it was not until the 1960s that the present rush of foreign bank openings in the United States began.

The steps by which foreign banks become involved in the United States are similar to the sequence that U.S. banks undertake when setting up their international business. For the foreign bank these are:

- trade finance and correspondent banking
- medium-term lending to overseas corporations and governments as a participant in credits of other banks
- development of banking units with a dollar source of funds for disbursing dollar-denominated loans
- aggressive seeking out of banking relationships with prime international corporate and sovereign risk names through a growing overseas network
- development of specialist skills in an effort to establish a strategic competitive advantage

Foreign banks now consider a presence in the United States vital to their global strategy in order to establish "a dollar funding base and . . . some form of international corporate lending and trade financing capability." Thus U.S. banks find that their prime customers are exactly the same companies that foreign banks consider the best targets for their business development effort. "Fortune 500 names are almost universally regarded, at least initially, as the highest priority, although many banks subsequently focus on smaller, even middle-market, firms as they come up against the problem of developing a profitable relationship with these sought-after names." [16]

Most foreign banks in the United States have avoided the retail market—soliciting accounts of the general public with the accompanying demand for personal loans—and have specialized in corporate customers.

Global Management

The decision about establishing which of the above entities, how many, or their location is based on a U.S. bank's overall global strategy.

> Large, multinational banks are managed and operated on a worldwide consolidated basis. . . . Branches of [foreign]

banks will be influenced by factors specific to their home country as well as to the local environment in which these branches are operating. In some cases, a foreign branch operating in a less regulated environment might engage in activities that otherwise would have been undertaken by the bank's home country office had it been less regulated, particularly in cases of limitations on interest rates or quantitative restraints on particular activities. In fact, Eurocurrency banking largely owes its existence to banks' seeking to avoid regulatory restraints in their domestic banking markets. [17]

This trend is evident in several ways. U.S. banks use overseas shell branches to warehouse loans for tax benefits or as sources of funding; merchant banks use the branches to conduct investment banking activities outside the U.S. The expansion of branches in the 1960s and the contraction in the 1980s were both the result of the prevalent global strategy that prevailed during each of their respective decades.

This has also been true for foreign banks. For example, Japanese banks, the largest foreign banks as of the mid-1990s, have substantial branch presences in both London and the United States. They use these branches differently, partly because there are restrictions in Japan on the rate of interest banks may pay on the bulk of their local deposits. "The main difference is that offices of Japanese banks in London serve as an important net funding source for their related offices in other countries [principally Japan, to finance loans to local Japanese companies], while offices in the United States . . . are heavily concentrated in lending to locally based companies. . . . In the United Kingdom, Japanese banks lend largely to nonlocal borrowers in nonlocal currencies." In fact, "Little of the activity of Japanese banks in the United Kingdom is oriented toward the U.K. economy." In the United States, "a large proportion of activity by Japanese banks is with customers identified as U.S. residents".[18]

Bank Accounting for International Banking

The **balance sheet** of a U.S. commercial bank is a statement of the financial position of that bank as of a stated date. International banking transactions are merged with domestic ones and presented in a single balance sheet. The balance sheet has four general categories of accounts: assets, liabilities, capital, and contingent (sometimes referred to as "off-balance sheet" items).

The **income statement** or **statement of operations** measures the flow of revenues and expenses over a period of time, usually one year. It likewise combines the international and domestic business.

Each country has its own set of regulations and capital definitions for their banks, which were often inconsistent with those of other countries, creating inequalities as banks spread globally. Some banking activities were excluded by some countries from capital requirements but included by others.

Risk-Based Capital

To address these problems, several meetings were held during the 1980s at the Bank for International Settlements in Basel, Switzerland, by bank regulators from 12 countries: Belgium, Canada, France, Germany, Italy, Japan, Luxembourg, The Netherlands, Sweden, Switzerland, the United Kingdom, and the United States. Out of this came the **Risk-Based Capital Guidelines,** which each country's bank regulators agreed to apply to banks under their jurisdiction. Each country fully retains all of its sovereign powers to regulate and

supervise its banks, while agreeing to substitute these commonly agreed-upon guidelines for their previous separate rules and thereby achieve greater global consistency than at present. There is no international organization with power to regulate and supervise the banks of any country.

Today most other countries have voluntarily adopted these formulas for their own banks with that result that there is a global uniformity in the capital requirements for most commercial banks. As applied to the U.S.,

the guidelines are designed to achieve certain important goals: Establishment of a uniform capital framework, applicable to all federally supervised banking organizations; encouragement of international banking organizations to strengthen their capital positions; and reduction of a source of competitive inequality arising from differences in supervisory requirements among nations.

The guidelines establish a systematic analytical framework that makes regulatory capital requirements more sensitive to differences in risk profiles among banking organizations, takes off-balance sheet exposures into explicit account in assessing capital adequacy, and minimizes disincentives to holding liquid, low-risk assets.[19]

The Risk-Based Capital Guidelines redefine capital, increase the amount of required bank capital, and assign a risk-weighting to each asset so that a bank will have to allocate more capital for higher-risk assets. Each asset is multiplied by a risk weight percentage (0, 20, 50, or 100 percent), and the resulting total determines the base for calculating required capital. Contingent account categories (sometimes referred to as off-balance sheet, such as letters of credit, foreign exchange contracts, and so forth) are now brought into this calculation.

The impact of these guidelines falls heavily on a bank's international transactions. For example, a bank will have to hold more capital for its loans to some foreign governments than to others; certain international business transactions that did not require capital in the past, now do have such a requirement. Banking organizations are required to have capital equivalent to 8 percent of assets, weighted by risk.

In the chapters that follow, the guidelines' applicability for and impact on the international banking business will be examined in detail for each of the types of assets.

Summary

The U.S. bank seeking to expand its international banking activities has a number of options, each with its advantages and costs. It is therefore prudent to proceed only when there is business capable of supporting it. Organizing an international department in the head office is the logical first step. The establishment of an Edge Act office, overseas branches, or a joint venture can be justified only when there is enough business or potential profit to cover the very substantial expenses. With the authorization of IBFs, many banks may be able to participate in Eurodollar activities without the expense of establishing a branch overseas.

Regardless of its organization, a bank can meet the international banking needs of its customers with just a capability in its head office, or solely through the international organization of a major city correspondent bank.

While U.S. banks have been expanding their presence in foreign markets, the U.S. market has been attracting foreign banks in growing numbers. U.S. banks now find themselves facing new competitors in their own serving area. This will certainly continue in the future.

Questions

1. What is the difference between a foreign branch and an Edge Act corporation?
2. Does a U.S. bank need to have overseas branches in order to provide international banking business to its customers?
3. Why do foreign banks have banking offices in the United States?
4. What is an IBF?

Problem

Looking at the area that your bank serves in the United States, identify the competition from foreign banks through their local banking offices and other efforts.

Notes

1. Vincent P. Carosso, *The Morgans: Private International Bankers, 1854-1913* (Cambridge, Mass.: Harvard University Press, 1987), p. 11
2. Board of Governors of the Federal Reserve System, *Annual Report* (Washington, D.C.: 1994), pp. 267–268.
3. James V. Houpt, *International Trends for U.S. Banks and Banking Markets,* Staff Study 156, Board of Governors of the Federal Reserve System (Washington, D.C.: 1988), p. 7
4. Houpt, ibid., p. 9
5. James V. Houpt, "Edge Corporations," *International Banking: U.S. Laws and Regulations* (Washington, D.C.: American Bankers Association, 1984), pp. 10-14
6. Houpt, *International Trends*, p. 16
7. *Federal Reserve Bulletin*, October 1982, p. 567

8. Carosso, *The Morgans*, pp. 3-4

9. Philip Ziegler, *The Sixth Great Power: Barings, 1762-1929* (London: Collins, 1988), p. 10

10. Ron Chernow, *The House of Morgan* (New York: Atlantic Monthly Press, 1990), p. 25

11. Board of Governors of the Federal Reserve System, *Annual Report*, p. 255

12. *The New York Times*, March 21, 1990, p. C1

13. Board of Governors of the Federal Reserve System, *Examination Manual for U.S. Branches and Agencies of Foreign Banking Organizations* (Washington, D.C.: 1995) Section 3150.1, p. 4

14. William Taylor, Staff Director, Division of Banking Supervision and Regulation, Board of Governors of the Federal Reserve System, October 16, 1990, quoted in *Federal Reserve Bulletin*, December 1990, p. 1,032

15. Ibid., p. 1,033

16. Peter Merrill Associates, *The Future Development of U.S. Banking Organizations Abroad* (Washington, D.C.: American Bankers Association, 1981), pp. 22-23

17. *Federal Reserve Bulletin*, February 1990, pp. 41-44

18. Ibid., pp. 41-44

19. Board of Governors of the Federal Reserve System, Press Release, January 19, 1989

II

GLOBAL PAYMENTS

Central to all economic activity is the ability to send and receive payments. At its primitive level—barter—goods are paid for with other goods. Over the centuries, barter evolved into the money system: goods are exchanged for some mutually acceptable token that, in turn, can be used to acquire some other goods or service from someone else.

The capability to make global payments begins with the development of separate national monies. A bit of background is useful to see how that evolved to national payments systems. Then we can see how today global payments are possible without having a global money.

Barter was cumbersome, geographically limiting, and restrictive because it required the double coincidence of each party wanting what the other had. A simpler system of exchange was needed. "In the time of Homer, money chiefly took the form of axes." [1] Such "tokens" were replaced in ancient Greek societies with coins: "a flattened piece of metal, of regulated weight, with a device stamped on one or both sides making it clear . . . what individual or community had put it out and would receive it again. It [was] . . . used in primitive societies to measure value and store wealth; and it follows that for a long time coins circulated roughly at their bullion value." [2] These coins were made of different metals, principally bronze, silver, and gold, which had intrinsic worth. "By a law of Constantine (A.D. 325) the imperial treasury had to accept both minted and unminted gold at the same rate, and gold coins had to be valued according to their actual weight." [3] (Modern money names still reflect this connection to metal weight [see chapter 4].) Coins, too, had their limiting factors, such as their weight and the fraudulent practice of debasing by surreptitiously replacing some of the gold or silver with alloys of similar weight but less value. Another problem that remained even centuries later was seen in "the needs of the merchants of booming Amsterdam, who had great trouble sorting out debased gold and silver coins (with less than the full bullion content) from the real thing. Standardization there was not. The Dutch parliament in 1606 listed 341 silver and 505 gold coins; and as many as fourteen mints in the Dutch republic were churning out coins." [4] The next step was paper money.

"Paper money . . . [developed] with the goldsmiths of Europe who held the private gold hoards deposited by wealthy citizens for safekeeping. The goldsmith issued a receipt for the gold deposit, and over time, it became clear that the receipt itself could be used in commerce since whoever owned that piece of paper could go to the goldsmith and claim the gold." [5] This concept continued with the development of banks that issued their own paper money backed by a promise that it would be redeemed in gold. "In nineteenth-century America, the money in use consisted mainly of these privately issued bank notes, backed by gold or silver guarantees. The money's value was really dependent, therefore, on the soundness and probity of each bank that issued notes. Scandals were recurrent, particularly on the frontier, where ambitious bankers . . . sometimes printed paper money that had no gold behind it." [6] Bank paper money was geographically limiting, since people's willingness to accept such private bank notes was constrained by their knowledge of the soundness of the bank as well as distance. "A note which cannot be converted without travelling a hundred miles is not in fact convertible: it may be so in law and theory, but it may also be at a discount in practice," [7] as the famous editor Walter Bagehot observed. "Forged, depreciated, and counterfeit notes were so prevalent [in the mid-nineteenth century] that various publications of the time list as many as 5,500 types of worthless paper." [8]

The payments problem became acute as a national economy grew. Within the nineteenth century, governments in Europe and the United States began to replace the paper money issued by individual banks with currency and coin issued by the national government, thereby broadening the geographic area of acceptability while retaining the backing of gold. (In 1879, a person could demand 25.8 grains of gold for the dollar. This was ultimately abandoned in 1933.)[9] The U.S. Supreme Court ruled in 1933 that debts that had been incurred with gold could be repaid by government paper money—it was "legal tender." This also led to all paper money being accepted at par. Today only a few countries (for example, Hong Kong and Scotland) still use bank notes issued by commercial banks, and these are heavily regulated by their respective governments.

"Within a country the action of a government can settle the quantity, and therefore the value, of its currency; but outside its own country, no government can do so. Bullion [in other words, gold] is the 'cash' of international trade; paper currencies are of no use there." [10] That was a nineteenth-century description. In the eighteenth century, trade was accomplished without any movement of gold, coins, or paper money. The Virginia planters of colonial America shipped tobacco to an agent in London, who sent back the furniture, fashions, tea, and other commodities that the colonists wanted.

As economies became more sophisticated, other means of exchange provided greater convenience and were safer and more flexible than paper money and coins. As bank accounts became common, payments were made by means of checks, and in recent years, the use of credit and debit cards that facilitate the actual payment by electronic entries in computer systems has become widespread.

The Roles of a Central Bank

"The single theme of a contemporary central bank's functions is to provide stability—stability in the purchasing power of the currency of the country and stability of the financial system, including the payments system."[13]

The contemporary central bank is the part of each country's national government that runs that nation's monetary system. In the United States, it is the Federal Reserve. For other major countries it is the Bank of England (for the United Kingdom), Bundesbank (Germany), and Bank of Japan (Japan). The Sveriges Riksbank (Bank of Sweden), founded in 1668, is the oldest surviving central bank. The Bank of England began in 1694, the Federal Reserve in 1913, and the Bundesbank (in its present form) in 1957. While some, such as the Federal Reserve, were created in the twentieth century specifically as central banks, this was not the pattern earlier. The Bank of England, for example, was a privately owned bank for over 200 years. "Confidence in the Bank [in the 18th century] . . . rested entirely on its standing and reputation as a sound commercial organization."[14] Its shares were owned by individuals who received an attractive rate of return.

A central bank is traditionally concerned with maintaining the day-to-day operations of its country's financial system.

- It prints and/or distributes the currency and coin to ensure that there is an adequate supply available for the functioning of the economy.

- It supervises the banking system by examining commercial banks to ensure that they are financially sound. When a bank has a liquidity problem, the central bank traditionally acts as "the lender of last resort." That means, for example, that if there is a panic run on a bank by depositors seeking to withdraw their deposits, the central bank will supply the cash to regain the depositors' confidence. It will support a bank with short-term liquidity.

- The central bank is concerned that payments can be made from one part of the country to another, either through a functioning commercial banking system or through branches of the central bank itself. For example, a crucial task in transforming the post-Soviet Union economy in Russia was to modernize the central bank's capability to provide intracountry payments for businesses that were completed in a few days rather than in weeks.

In times of sudden financial panic, such as the one caused by the U.S. stock market crash in 1987, the central bank can immediately add liquidity and confidence to the payments market to enable orderly transactions to continue. In dire circumstances, some central banks have taken over failing commercial banks to protect the means of payments needed for commerce.

- It acts as the government's banker for domestic payments. The central bank is each nation's coordinator with other central banks to maintain a stable international payments system. This involves establishing uniform policies for the commercial banks in such areas as capital requirements and inspections. The central banks provide credit lines and facilities to each other to support orderly foreign exchange markets.

Virtually every country now has its own central bank recognized as fundamental to a modern economy. According to former Federal Reserve Chairman Paul Volcker, "At the most fundamental level, central banks are institutions that, by their nature, provide support for the principles of a market system, of competition, and of openness. Whether fully recognized or not, in acting as lender of last resort, they are part of the essential underpinning of modern financial markets."[15]

After having created a uniform national paper currency, the government's role shifted to support the changes in the business world. The transfer of bank balances, primarily through the use of checks, became almost wholly the business of the commercial banks. These checks had to be "cleared" back to the bank where the account was. The government had to provide that this payment capability would be orderly by establishing the means to clear and settle interbank transfers through the development of a central bank in each country (see "The Roles of a Central Bank" below).

Thus today within most countries there exists a single currency (paper money and coin), accepted at full face value everywhere in the country as payment for goods, services, taxes, and debts. A central bank provides and regulates the supply of money, supervises the commercial banks who provide the system of check payments, and oversees the orderly, rapid interbank clearings and payments. The importance of domestic interbank check clearing varies considerably even in industrialized countries. In the United States, the average number of checks written per person per year is 229; in Japan, 3; and in Switzerland, 3. This difference reflects that in the United States, more than 3,000 banks must be involved to account for 90 percent of the deposits, while in most other industrialized countries it takes no more than 10 banks.[11] Japan remains very much a cash economy. ("On the 10th and 20th of each month, [Tokyo] traffic is said to be particularly heavy as businessmen visit suppliers and clients to pay bills or receive payment in cash."[12]) The Swiss are heavy users of automated payment systems.

Today no international money exists and no world central bank exists. Just as the acceptability of paper money issued by banks in the mid-nineteenth century was confined to the immediate region, so today, at the end of the twentieth century, global payments rest on the acceptability of the money of each country. The absence of a world central bank means that there is no single authority to back a commitment that payments can always be made from one area to another, nor to guarantee the solvency of the individual paying agents, the commercial banks. The joint actions of the various national central banks provide the only stabilizing forces for maintaining the international payments system.

Thus today's global payments are made daily through a structure that is decades behind what businesses and individuals have come to expect as basic in their own country. Nonetheless, global payments are essential for the functioning of global business and investments.

The chapters in section 2, Global Payments, examine how this system works. The discussion begins with the structure and techniques of payment between countries (chapter 3, Money Transfers). Then the problems of establishing value between the currencies of the differing regions are examined (chapter 4, Principles of Foreign Exchange), and then today's practices and problems in moving toward a true global money (chapter 5, The Foreign Exchange Markets) are discussed. Chapter 5 also examines central banks' recent struggles to maintain an orderly global payments system.

Notes

1. N. G. L. Hammond and H. H. Scullard, eds., *The Oxford Classical Dictionary*, 2d ed. (Oxford: Clarendon Press, 1987), p. 698
2. Ibid., p. 258
3. Ibid., p. 698
4. Marjorie Deane and Robert Pringle, *The Central Banks* (London: Hamish Hamilton, 1994), p. 34

5. William Greider, *Secrets of the Temple* (New York: Simon and Schuster, 1987), p. 227

6. Ibid., p. 228

7. Walter Bagehot, *The Collected Works of Walter Bagehot*, ed. Norman St. John-Stevas, vol. X, (London: The Economist, 1978), p. 287

8. Paul A. Carrubba, *Principles of Banking* (Washington, D.C.: American Bankers Association, 1994), p. 4

9. James Grant, *Money of the Mind* (New York: Farrar, Straus and Giroux, 1992), p. 70

10. Bagehot, *Collected Works*, vol. IX: 69

11. David B. Humphrey, *Payments Systems: Principles, Practice, and Improvements* (Washington, D.C.: The World Bank, 1995) pp. 15, 46

12. *The New York Times*, November 23, 1995

13. Deane and Pringler, *The Central Banks*, p. 2, quoting the former President of the New York Federal Reserve Bank, Gerald Corrigan

14. Richard Roberts and David Kynaston, eds., *The Bank of England: Money, Power and Influence, 1694-1994* (Oxford: Clarendon Press, 1995), p. 15

15. Deane and Pringler, *The Central Banks*, p. ix

3

MONEY TRANSFERS

Learning Objectives

After studying this chapter, you will be able to

- explain how correspondent banking relationships are structured
- outline the different instruments used to transfer funds
- describe the different systems for settlements
- examine the effects on float of different types of settlements

Overview

Global business requires that a person or business in one country be able to make a payment to a resident or business in another country. Commercial banks provide this capability. Practically all the activities that constitute a nation's balance of payments (see chapter 1) are reflected in transfers through the network of commercial bank accounts. While central banks have the capacity to do this for occasional large transfers, they depend on the commercial banking systems to make the hundreds of thousands of daily transactions that are the core of the international activity of customers around the world.

The international payments structure differs from that within a country. In each nation, commercial banks play a central part in their nation's payments system. In the United States, for example, a bank's customers routinely make payments by writing checks against their accounts, using credit cards, or requesting their bank to transfer funds for them. The banks clear the checks, credit card transactions, or other payments. The Federal Reserve, the U.S. central bank, provides a structure so that orderly interbank settlements can be done quickly and efficiently. Internationally, however, no such central bank service exists. The link from one national payments system to another rests on the foundation of banks throughout the world being active customers of one another. They readily assist each other in transferring funds as well as other aspects of their business (exchanging funds, financing international trade, and extending credit). This is called **correspondent banking.**

A payment has two parts: a message to pay someone and the actual transfer of funds to settle the payment. The distinction between these two parts can be particularly evident internationally, where the U.S. dollar is widely used to make payments to many other countries in their own currencies. The actual settlement of the dollars will be done through accounts in the United States where the dollar is legal tender. Similarly, for example, a payment in pounds sterling would be settled through accounts in the United Kingdom.

This chapter begins by examining the principles of correspondent banking. Then it considers how the payments are made and settled between countries by U.S. banks.

Correspondent Banking

Global banking works because banks in different countries are willing to cooperate in doing business with each other. Each bank participates in correspondent banking as it serves its own national or local market and at the same time is willing to assist the other bank, thereby accommodating each other's customers. Only about 1 percent of U.S. banks have branches in another country, and even the majority of these do not maintain a large global network of branches or subsidiaries. Thus it is the active foreign correspondent banking relationships that enable a U.S. bank to offer a full range of services in another country. Not even the largest banks can afford to have branches in all the countries where their customers do business and will also need to have an active network of correspondent banks.

Major banks become international correspondents of each other to provide their customers with services in each other's markets. Small banks become correspondents of large international banks to obtain services in a major market and also to obtain specialized assistance, including lines of credit to support their operations. Larger banks become correspondents with smaller banks to have access to regional markets. Small banks in foreign countries particularly need the financial help of major U.S. banks for banking and financing foreign trade and for obtaining working capital to enable their customers to borrow for business needs. In providing services and funds to a correspondent bank, the large international bank is putting surplus funds from a developed country to short-term use for development in another country. Within the United States, correspondent banking relationships enable a regional U.S. bank with only an occasional international transaction to offer its customers the same range of services as a bank with its own active international department. Thus both banks benefit from a correspondent banking relationship.

At the initiation of a relationship, the two banks will exchange information ("terms and conditions") on the services they can perform for each other and the fees for these services. The banks also exchange signature books and confidential telegraphic test keys.

A bank's **signature book** contains facsimiles of the signatures of individuals authorized to commit the bank and states each bank's policy as to whether one or two officers must sign for various transactions. Policies for correspondent banks differ from those for commercial customers. Banks do not require corporate resolutions to open such accounts, and signature cards are not used. A unique characteristic of correspondent banking is that both banks exchange signature books. Even though usually only one account is opened, each bank needs to have the other's authorized signatures on file. It is always the responsibility of the receiving bank to be certain that signatures on any instructions received from another bank are bona fide. The **telegraphic test keys** are code arrangements that enable banks receiving teletransmissions from other banks to verify in the absence of written signatures that these are authentic.

Accounts in an International Department

The foundation upon which global payments rest is the practice of banks in one country maintaining deposit accounts with banks in other countries to serve the needs of the customers of both banks. When funds are debited from or credited to in such an account, money is said to "move" from one country to another. Global payments are made through changes in bank account balances and only rarely by the physical movement of large quantities of currency.

The accounts in a U.S. bank's international department are established by foreign governments, banks, individuals, and businesses in other countries or the United States who, being actively engaged in international business, require the special expertise of the international banker. These are demand accounts that pay no interest. In some instances, however, the depositor may establish a time deposit that will earn interest.

Due To Accounts

A demand account maintained by a foreign bank in a U.S. bank is referred to by the U.S. bank as a **Due To** or vostro account (meaning "your account with us," derived from Italian and reflecting the early Italian influence in the creation of banking practices). Such an account is held in U.S. dollars and originates at the beginning of a correspondent banking relationship. The major U.S. banks solicit Due To accounts from banks around the world. These accounts are useful for the foreign banks because much of world trade and finance is denominated in U.S. dollars. Having such a Due To account enables a foreign bank to make direct payments to other countries, handle foreign collections, and settle drafts under letters of credit. Due To accounts are opened routinely at major banks and can be profitable for those banks because they provide deposits for them.

The bookkeeping or accounting section of the international department prepares and sends out statements on all of the bank's Due To accounts. These statements usually use a simplified, standard descriptive posting supported by explanatory vouchers. The international department also receives statements on its accounts in foreign banks.

These statements must be reconciled with the international department's own entries. Discrepancies often emerge between the statements and the international department's entries. Thus a bank's foreign account (as well as accounts the bank has from other banks) is almost never free from "we debit—you do not credit" or "we credit—you do not debit" items. Regardless of the time needed for such corrections, however, they must be made to prevent losses to the bank.

Due From Accounts

An account maintained by a U.S. bank in a foreign bank is referred to by the U.S. bank as a **Due From** or nostro account (from the Italian "our account with you"). Such an account is generally denominated in the currency of the foreign country, and the account will be under the control of the foreign exchange trader (see chapter 4). The usual procedure in the U.S. bank's international department is to keep the record of the account on its own ledgers in both the foreign currency and its U.S. dollar equivalent. By this means the international department can reflect the activity as it will actually be posted in its account in the foreign currency and at the same time have a U.S. dollar equivalent for its own financial statement; thus the Due From account is also called a **dual currency** account.

A U.S. bank does not establish a Due From account for each Due To account. A large U.S. bank may maintain one or two Due From accounts in a particular country, at the same time receiving several hundred Due To accounts in dollars established by banks in that country.

Many factors influence an international department's decision about the location of its Due From account and the size of its balances. Basically, the accounts will be established in countries where a bank's customers need to make payments and in countries whose currencies will be needed for trading activities by the foreign exchange trader. A bank does not want to have more Due From accounts in foreign currency than are needed to serve its purposes. "The U.S. bank must maintain adequate balances in its nostro accounts to meet unexpected needs and to avoid overdrawing those accounts for which interest must be paid. However, the bank must not lose income by maintaining excessive idle nostro balances which do not earn interest." [1] Also, holding foreign exchange can be risky, as it can change relative to the dollar. Once it determines it needs such an account, a bank will therefore tend to establish a Due From account in its best correspondent bank in that country.

In the operation of Due To and Due From accounts, each bank in a correspondent relationship views the same account differently. When a foreign bank establishes a U.S. dollar account in a U.S. bank, the U.S. bank considers it a Due To account ("due to foreign bank"), while the foreign bank will consider it to be a Due From account ("due from U.S. bank"), but there is only one account. Conversely, a foreign currency account maintained by a U.S. bank in a foreign bank is a Due From account as far as the U.S. bank is concerned but a Due To account from the point of view of the foreign bank. Thus it can often be confusing in bank-to-bank correspondence to use the terms "Due To" and "Due From." Often the accounts are called "your account" or "our account" for clarity.

Using the Accounts

One account is sufficient for the conduct of all the business: a transfer of funds from one country to another between two banks, payments to be made in either country in either currency, or payments to a third country in that country's currency. This account is usually the Due To account established by the foreign bank in the U.S. bank.

Once this network of accounts between correspondent banks has been established, money can move from one country to another. For example, an American tourist makes a purchase at a Greek store and pays for it with a traveler's check. The store takes that traveler's check, and all others it has received from tourists, to its local bank. The bank credits the store's bank account with the Greek drachma equivalent. The bank in turn sends all the U.S. dollar traveler's checks it has received from its clients or cashed at the bank itself to its U.S. correspondent bank with a transmittal letter (a **cash letter**) and requests that these be deposited in its account with the U.S. bank. Once this is done, the money has effectively moved from the United States to Greece. Occasionally even accumulated cash is shipped. When these funds are in its account, the foreign bank can send instructions to make payments to individuals in the United States on behalf of one of its clients to the debit of its account or to draw checks against its account for payments. A commercial bank is willing to buy a check or draft drawn in one currency and pay out another because it knows that another customer will need the first currency in another transaction, and in the process the commercial bank expects to show a profit in the conversion.

Conversely, the U.S. bank uses the account established on its books to credit the foreign bank with the proceeds of collections, letters of credit, and payments that it requests the foreign bank to make. This Due To account can also be used to make payments to third countries. The foreign bank may send instructions for such a payment, and the U.S. bank will debit the Due To account for the equivalent in U.S. dollars of the foreign currency amount, which it will instruct a third bank to make by debiting, in turn, the U.S. bank's account in that currency. Once a foreign bank establishes an account with a U.S. bank that has an active international banking department,

that foreign bank has global access for all its needs and can provide its customers with worldwide coverage.

The large volume of transfers through a bank's account will occasionally result in a mishandling of instructions. When this happens, the bank that made the error will compensate the other bank for the earnings it lost because the funds were not available for its use.

International departments of major banks in the United States also make their facilities available to other banks in this country. Assume that the international business of a small domestic bank is limited to occasional requests from its customers for the remittance of funds to pay for their purchases and so forth. Without facilities for handling such transactions, the small bank would probably resort to the issuance of its own cashier's checks.

This would be inappropriate for the bank and inconvenient for the payee, primarily because the check is not payable in the payee's own country. A local bank will probably negotiate the check only on a collection basis, which means a delay of weeks and the additional cost of a collection fee. Moreover, charges for the accommodation are shifted from the purchaser of the check, by whom they should be paid, to the payee or the recipient of the funds.

A large bank benefits by encouraging such business because it provides an opportunity to generate transaction volume from a regional market to which it might not otherwise have access. Increasing volume through such operations may lower the per-unit costs for all other business.

Basic Instruments

The basic means by which banks transfer funds upon request of a client is through the network of correspondent bank accounts, both foreign and domestic. Instructions to do this are given through **remittance orders** or **foreign drafts**. An essential part of these instructions is **settlement**, the means by which the money is transferred from one bank to the other. The sending bank may credit the account of the receiving bank, the receiving bank may debit the account of the sending bank, or a credit may be made to the receiving bank's account at a third bank. In international payments the selection of settlement will be determined by the currency used and the existence of accounts between the two banks.

The simplest way to transfer funds is by bank-to-bank instructions. A bank in one country sends a message to a bank in another country telling it to pay a third party. This can be sent by either air mail or teletransmission.

Remittance by Air Mail

An air-mail remittance letter specifies the details of payment: the amount, the name and address of the beneficiary, and the name of the sender. The letter contains the proper number and class of authorized signatures and indicates how the settlement between the two banks will take place.

When a U.S. customer wants to remit funds to a beneficiary in a foreign country, the U.S. bank receives the money plus its commission and air-mail expenses along with the payment instructions. The U.S. bank writes a letter to a foreign bank advising additionally that, in reimbursement, the U.S. bank has credited the money to the Due To account of the foreign bank (when the remittance is in U.S. dollars) or has authorized the foreign bank to debit the Due From account when the payment is denominated in that foreign currency. The foreign bank, upon receiving this remittance letter, verifies its authenticity by comparing the signatures on the letter with the facsimiles on file in that bank's signature book. If the signatures compare favorably, then the paying bank knows it is acting on bona fide instructions.

It should be noted that in all remittances or foreign drafts, the foreign bank will usually pay the beneficiary in the local currency; if the transfer is stated in U.S. dollars, the foreign bank will convert this amount into the equivalent local currency. There are many reasons for this practice. The laws or regulations of the paying country may require it, but equally important is the fact that the foreign bank usually will not have U.S. dollars on hand because dollars are not the legal currency of that country. The conversion will be at the rate of exchange as determined by the paying bank.

Remittance by Teletransmission

A remittance by teletransmission is exactly the same as a remittance by air mail, except that the message between banks is sent using a telegraphic or electronic communication system. The expression "cable remittance" is sometimes used; this term originated in the past when the only fast option was through international cable companies. This method of remittance is used when speed is important or the amount is large or when it is simply more convenient for the remitting bank. In today's global banking world, this is the most often used method for sending payment messages. Instructions from bank to bank can even be sent by telephone. Since there is no signature to verify the message's authenticity, a code or **test key** arrangement must be used for verification. These codes are kept under very strict security.

Although test keys vary in format from bank to bank, they generally consist of a group of tables of numbers, perhaps one for the day of the month, another for the month of the year, another for the currency, and another for the amount (omitting decimals) or—if more than one amount is mentioned in the message—the amount of the total. The table for the amount provides numbers for the thousands, hundreds, tens, and digits. This test key may be used by a number of banks.

A large bank may use it with all its correspondents. Therefore, to make it a bilateral test key applicable to only one correspondent, a special fixed number is added. The fixed number will be different for each correspondent bank and known only to the two banks. A variable number, based on the number of messages sent on a given day, may also be included. A prefix may be substituted for the variable number. To arrive at a test number, the indicated numbers are totaled; the total usually precedes the text of the message. The receiving bank uses the same procedure, employing its copy of the code, and if it arrives at the same test number, then it can assume that the message originates from the other bank.

Exhibit 3.1 shows the computation of a test for $15,000 sent on August 31. Additional pages of the test key would cover currency.

Payment orders sent by data transmission may use the services provided by a number of independent companies. A widely used system is the **Society for Worldwide Interbank Financial Telecommunications (S.W.I.F.T.),** which provides an automated international communications and information system between member banks. It is organized as a cooperative to provide member banks with standardized message formats in place of unstructured messages or incompatible message systems. This facilitates processing and transmission. More than 120 message types cover customer and bank funds transfers, foreign exchange, loans, collections, letters of credit, and statements. Payment transactions are settled through designated correspondent accounts, since S.W.I.F.T. is only a communications system. S.W.I.F.T. transmits the message through its own communications network, which is linked directly to the member banks.

S.W.I.F.T. is often used instead of other teletransmission systems for sending teletransmission remittance orders because its standard formats have allowed participating banks to link this system directly to automated processing systems in the bank. While its emphasis has been on international transactions, it is used for intracountry transactions in the United States, Japan, and several European and Asian countries. Because S.W.I.F.T. uses a standardized message format, it also becomes part of an automated funds transfer system when linked directly to a regional payments system such as the Clearing House Interbank Payments system (CHIPS) (described later in this chapter). Such standardized message formats facilitate translation as well as processing. For example, in a transfer of funds, instead of the statement "by order of," S.W.I.F.T. uses "50:" and then the name of the person sending the money. In whatever language they use, both the sending and receiving banks know what this means.

These messages also have various security features that authenticate the sender, the receiver, and verify that the message has not been altered in transmission. While being transmitted through the system, the messages are encrypted separately from the test keys established bilaterally between the two banks.

Foreign Draft

A foreign draft (exhibit 3.2) is a negotiable instrument drawn by a bank on a foreign correspondent bank. It can be issued in any currency and is used when the client wants a negotiable instrument to mail rather than sending payment instructions to a bank—that is, a remittance order. A foreign draft must be received by the beneficiary in order for that person to receive payment, whereas a remittance order makes it the responsibility of the two intermediary banks to make the payment.

A bank's customer may request a foreign draft to attach to an invoice to pay a foreign bill. By doing so, she makes it easier for the recipient to apply the funds to the correct account. When the foreign bank is presented with the foreign draft for payment, it will first verify the authen-

Exhibit 3.1   Telegraphic Test Key

<table>
<tr><td colspan="8" align="center">Table 1—Fixed Number</td></tr>
<tr><td colspan="8" align="center">829</td></tr>
</table>

<table>
<tr><td colspan="8" align="center">Table 2—Month</td></tr>
<tr><td>January</td><td>86</td><td>April</td><td>42</td><td>July</td><td>22</td><td>October</td><td>36</td></tr>
<tr><td>February</td><td>51</td><td>May</td><td>30</td><td>August</td><td>81</td><td>November</td><td>58</td></tr>
<tr><td>March</td><td>38</td><td>June</td><td>51</td><td>September</td><td>18</td><td>December</td><td>67</td></tr>
</table>

<table>
<tr><td colspan="14" align="center">Table 3—Date</td></tr>
<tr><td>1st</td><td>20</td><td>7th</td><td>12</td><td>13th</td><td>53</td><td>19th</td><td>85</td><td>25th</td><td>75</td><td>31st</td><td>191</td></tr>
<tr><td>2nd</td><td>37</td><td>8th</td><td>90</td><td>14th</td><td>62</td><td>20th</td><td>142</td><td>26th</td><td>136</td><td></td><td></td></tr>
<tr><td>3rd</td><td>10</td><td>9th</td><td>74</td><td>15th</td><td>19</td><td>21st</td><td>33</td><td>27th</td><td>91</td><td></td><td></td></tr>
<tr><td>4th</td><td>4</td><td>10th</td><td>77</td><td>16th</td><td>66</td><td>22nd</td><td>120</td><td>28th</td><td>230</td><td></td><td></td></tr>
<tr><td>5th</td><td>61</td><td>11th</td><td>83</td><td>17th</td><td>44</td><td>23rd</td><td>99</td><td>29th</td><td>72</td><td></td><td></td></tr>
<tr><td>6th</td><td>26</td><td>12th</td><td>17</td><td>18th</td><td>138</td><td>24th</td><td>95</td><td>30th</td><td>93</td><td></td><td></td></tr>
</table>

<table>
<tr><td colspan="18" align="center">Table 4—Amount</td></tr>
<tr><td>100,000</td><td>54</td><td>10,000</td><td>27</td><td>1,000</td><td>48</td><td>100</td><td>60</td><td>10</td><td>88</td><td>1</td><td>79</td></tr>
<tr><td>200,000</td><td>29</td><td>20,000</td><td>110</td><td>2,000</td><td>14</td><td>200</td><td>220</td><td>20</td><td>.52</td><td>2</td><td>35</td></tr>
<tr><td>300,000</td><td>3</td><td>30,000</td><td>11</td><td>3,000</td><td>16</td><td>300</td><td>5</td><td>30</td><td>9</td><td>3</td><td>49</td></tr>
<tr><td>400,000</td><td>39</td><td>40,000</td><td>131</td><td>4,000</td><td>167</td><td>400</td><td>137</td><td>40</td><td>81</td><td>4</td><td>32</td></tr>
<tr><td>500,000</td><td>43</td><td>50,000</td><td>1</td><td>5,000</td><td>23</td><td>500</td><td>171</td><td>50</td><td>129</td><td>5</td><td>13</td></tr>
<tr><td>600,000</td><td>87</td><td>60,000</td><td>56</td><td>6,000</td><td>59</td><td>600</td><td>251</td><td>60</td><td>65</td><td>6</td><td>205</td></tr>
<tr><td>700,000</td><td>15</td><td>70,000</td><td>89</td><td>7,000</td><td>68</td><td>700</td><td>47</td><td>70</td><td>112</td><td>7</td><td>96</td></tr>
<tr><td>800,000</td><td>6</td><td>80,000</td><td>161</td><td>8,000</td><td>156</td><td>800</td><td>45</td><td>80</td><td>230</td><td>8</td><td>92</td></tr>
<tr><td>900,000</td><td>2</td><td>90,000</td><td>97</td><td>9,000</td><td>71</td><td>900</td><td>34</td><td>90</td><td>98</td><td>9</td><td>7</td></tr>
</table>

<table>
<tr><td>1,000,000</td><td>78</td><td>10,000,000</td><td>46</td></tr>
<tr><td>2,000,000</td><td>25</td><td>20,000,000</td><td>94</td></tr>
<tr><td>3,000,000</td><td>73</td><td>30,000,000</td><td>40</td></tr>
<tr><td>4,000,000</td><td>64</td><td>40,000,000</td><td>114</td></tr>
<tr><td>5,000,000</td><td>24</td><td>50,000,000</td><td>10</td></tr>
<tr><td>6,000,000</td><td>8</td><td>60,000,000</td><td>84</td></tr>
<tr><td>7,000,000</td><td>82</td><td>70,000,000</td><td>76</td></tr>
<tr><td>8,000,000</td><td>28</td><td>80,000,000</td><td>57</td></tr>
<tr><td>9,000,000</td><td>55</td><td>90,000,000</td><td>70</td></tr>
</table>

Note: The test for this message is 1151.

Exhibit 3.2   Foreign Draft

No. 035531   NEW YORK 1978-04-27

THIS CHECK IS ISSUED WITH THE UNDERSTANDING THAT IT WILL BE
FORWARDED IMMEDIATELY FOR PRESENTATION TO THE DRAWEE.
THE DRAWER WILL NOT BE RESPONSIBLE SHOULD THIS DRAFT BE
DISHONORED AS A RESULT OF DELAY IN PRESENTATION.

ADVISED BY AIR MAIL

SPECIMEN

PAY TO THE ORDER OF   J.R. BUCKINGHAM & CO.- - - - - - - - - - £7,551.90- - - - - - - - - - -

SEVEN THOUSAND FIVE HUNDRED FIFTY ONE POUNDS 90- -

IF DRAWN IN U.S. DOLLARS, PAYABLE AT DRAWEE'S
BUYING RATE FOR EXCHANGE ON NEW YORK.

DRAWER   ENGLISH BANK LTD.   First National Bank

LONDON, ENGLAND   *Joan Smith*
                                              AUTHORIZED SIGNATURE

---

ticity of the draft. This may be done in one of two ways: **signature verification** or **advice**. With the signature verification method, the bank will compare the signature on the draft with those in the other bank's book of authorized signatures and with that bank's instructions as to the number of signatures required on foreign drafts. With the advice method, a bank will pay a foreign draft only after receiving a separate advice, that is, a letter from the issuing bank with an authorized signature or a tested teletransmission message. The advice method may be used by a bank with a large number of domestic branches whose officers do not have their signatures on file at the foreign correspondent. The advice method can present problems for the paying correspondent bank since the draft may be presented for payment before the advice is received. The receiving bank must then exercise its own judgment.

A bank with a large international network may place special drawing arrangements at the disposal of its domestic correspondents. This permits them to draw foreign drafts directly on the first bank's foreign correspondents. In this case, the foreign bank will usually have to wait for an advice to arrive and confirm that the draft has been drawn under the "protection" of its correspondent.

When an original foreign draft is lost, a duplicate may be issued only after a stop payment order has been placed on the original. Some banks insist that the purchaser furnish a bond of indemnity before placing the stop payment. The ability to place the stop payment order will depend on the laws of the country of the paying bank. In some countries, there is a minimum elapsed time required before such a stop payment can be placed, which might present problems for the original purchaser.

Operations

A bank with domestic branches or a number of active domestic correspondent banks will set up a system to enable these offices to issue foreign drafts or take instructions for remittance orders from their customers rather than insisting that the customer go to the foreign department. This system enables the branch or correspondent to serve customers at a convenient location, making the bank's specialized service easier for the customer to use and thereby increasing the volume of this business.

The domestic office needs to have a supply of foreign draft and remittance order forms plus an **arrangements book,** also called a **drawing guide,** or some comparable on-line computer information capability. This is a listing by country of the bank's foreign correspondents in various cities on which the domestic office may draw drafts. It will indicate whether drafts may be drawn on that bank in U.S. dollars or foreign currency. The arrangements book should also provide instructions to the domestic office personnel on how to fill out the draft. Although this may seem obvious to the international banker, it often is a matter of concern and trepidation to the domestic banker who infrequently issues foreign drafts.

For remittance orders, the foreign department may select the foreign correspondent when it receives the instructions from the domestic office. The customer may wish to know what bank will be making the payment, and, consequently, the selection of the foreign bank may already be made when the instructions arrive at the foreign department.

Drafts and remittances from U.S. banking offices can be issued in U.S. dollars or in many foreign currencies. If the customer has no preference, it is usually more advantageous for the bank to issue the payment in the foreign currency than in U.S. dollars. The reason is simple: When the payment is issued in U.S. dollars, the foreign bank sets the exchange rate at which it converts the U.S. dollars into the other currency paid to the payee. When the payment is issued in the foreign currency, the U.S. bank sets the exchange rate, and so makes any profit on the conversion. Drafts drawn on a foreign bank in U.S. dollars usually contain a statement that the draft is "payable at drawee's rate for bankers' drafts on New York," which means that the foreign bank sets the conversion rate.

After the domestic branch or correspondent bank has sold the foreign draft and given it to the customer or taken the instructions for the remittance order, the information and money must be processed promptly. When settlement is being made by a book entry, the items issued in U.S. dollars will be credited to the Due To account of the foreign bank; those drawn in foreign currency will be posted to the Due From account. Depending on the bank's procedures, an advice may be sent for the foreign draft. For remittances, the message will indicate to the foreign bank that in reimbursement "we credit your account" (U.S. dollars) or "charge our account" (foreign currency).

Exhibit 3.3 summarizes the advantages and disadvantages of the three basic ways to transfer funds.

Traveler's Checks

Probably the most widely used negotiable instrument in international banking is the **traveler's check,** which is also used domestically. Banks began regularly issuing traveler's checks in the late nineteenth century. Because of their worldwide acceptability, traveler's checks in U.S. dollars constitute the most common deposits to Due To accounts in U.S. banks. (Traveler's checks are also issued by many major foreign and U.S. banks in yen, deutsche marks, pounds sterling, and other major currencies.) The traveler's check in the United States is issued by a few large banking and travel organizations in pre-

Exhibit 3.3　Summary of Transfer Methods

Method	Advantages	Disadvantages
Foreign draft	a. Can be attached to invoices and bills for ease in paying small amounts.	a. Must be received by beneficiary. Customer is responsible for mailing. b. Stop payment on lost drafts are time-consuming.
Remittance by air mail	a. Bank-to-bank instructions with banks responsible for making payments.	a. Beneficiary must await notification from bank. b. Depends on international air-mail service.
Remittance by teletransmission	a. Fastest way to transfer funds. b. Bank-to-bank instructions with banks responsible for making payments.	a. expensive b. Beneficiary must await notification from bank.

printed denominations: $20, $50, $100, $500, and $1,000. The issuer commits itself to pay the stated sum to any payee and undertakes to repay the sum to the buyer if the check is lost or stolen before it is negotiated. Travelers thus feel that their money is safe.

The bank or agency that issues traveler's checks in the United States arranges for the design and printing of distinctive traveler's checks, distributes them to banks and travel agencies around the world to be available for sale, maintains comprehensive records of the inventory held by each seller, and replenishes that inventory. When the traveler's checks are sold, the money is received by the issuer, who also maintains a record of the purchaser of each traveler's check. When the check is cashed, the issuer pays the amount to the bank where it was deposited. Equally important, the issuer must be prepared to replace lost or stolen checks.

Settlement

Settlement is the process of actually moving the funds from the sender to the recipient to complete the money transfer, accomplished by moving balances in bank accounts. It can be as simple as moving funds from one account to another within the same bank. Larger transactions, such as foreign exchange trading or money market trading related to Eurodollars settlement, may generally involve several banks. In such cases, settlement will be done through Fedwire (see chapter 11) or CHIPS.

Other Money Transfer Instruments

Payment instruments that have been developed for use within a country are sometimes used for payments between countries. These are usually for small-value transactions.

Float Calculations in Global Payments

Besides the obvious expenses incurred by a bank in transferring money (forms, staff, and processing), there is **float**. A bank in one country receives funds from its customer and requests a bank in another country to pay out an equivalent amount. The lapse of time between the transfer of funds (settlement) from the first bank to the second bank can create a cost (float), or, if the second bank receives the funds in settlement before making the payment, can create an earnings potential.

A simple formula for such calculations for dollar items is based on using the amount of $27.75. This is the approximate amount that $1,000,000 invested at 1 percent per annum will earn in one day.* U.S. Federal Reserve regulations require that if a check is presented to the bank on which it is drawn by 8 a.m. local time on a business day, the proceeds must be settled that day in **federal funds**.[2] These are immediately available funds in a bank's account at its regional Federal Reserve Bank that represent the bank's required reserves and are used for overnight lending between U.S. banks.

The following examples illustrate the effect of this for banks in dollar transactions:

Traveler's checks. The foreign bank pays out cash at its office to the person cashing the traveler's check. Before the bank can collect these funds for other uses, it must deposit the traveler's check in its account in the United States, where its correspondent bank will clear the traveler's check back to the issuing bank or company. The sooner that traveler's check is deposited, the sooner the foreign bank will be in good funds to offset the cash it has paid out.

Where the volume of such traveler's checks, money orders, and other dollar checks is sufficient, the foreign bank can coordinate its processing schedule with airline flight schedules so that it can send the check to the United States overnight or as quickly as possible. The bank will use either its own personnel, a courier service (usually consolidating its pickups with those from other local banks), or help from its U.S. correspondent bank.

If, for example, a bank cashes $1,000,000 worth of such checks, with a federal funds overnight lending rate of 5 percent per annum, the difference between getting these cleared through a U.S. bank in 2 days using the methods described above or 5 days using mail services would result in the potential earning of slightly over $400 (less transportation costs, which can be reduced when shared with other local banks) ($27.75 × 5 × 3 days). While float in such transactions cannot be fully eliminated, its cost can thus be reduced.

Foreign drafts and bank-to-bank remittances. For these types of payment instruments in dollars, the remitting bank collects the funds from its customer and then credits those funds to the foreign correspondent bank's Due To account. Thus *before* the foreign bank makes the payment to its customer, it has already received the reimbursement or is receiving it the same day it is making the payment and so has no float cost. In the case of foreign drafts, there will be a certain period while the foreign bank has the funds before the draft is presented to it for cashing. Once the foreign bank knows the funds are in its account, it can invest them, and the float can be an earning rather than a cost.

When the draft or remittance is issued in the foreign currency (usually that of the paying bank), the foreign bank will have no float cost since when it pays out cash, it will immediately reimburse itself by debiting the account of the U.S. bank on its books (the Due From account of the U.S. bank).

Large items. For large item payments, the two banks will want the funds to move on the same date because of the cost-earnings potential. These messages will be sent by teletransmission and will indicate a **value date**, which is the date on which the remitting bank will credit the account of the paying bank (who is expected to make its payment contemporaneously).

---

* By market custom in the United States, interest on some financial instruments is calculated on a 360-day factor. The amount will be slightly less using a 365-day factor.

Personal or business checks present difficulties when sent to foreign countries. A store or some other recipient may be reluctant to give immediate credit since they are unable to verify easily that the check represents good funds. They will often send the check back to the drawee bank on collection and wait until this has been paid by means of a foreign draft or bank-to-bank remittance.

The *Giro* system is widely used within European countries for small recurring payments (for example, monthly rent or pensions) or nonrecurring payments (for example, gifts, utility payments, or department store accounts). It allows small payments to be made without the use of checks or cash. Giro is an automated interbank system in which the payer instructs her bank (or post office in some countries) to debit her account and credit the account of the recipient. The linkage of the national Giro systems among European countries has facilitated the system for international payments. Some banks have also formed direct links with a correspondent in another country for rapid automated transfer of small payments. These are mostly small systems among European banks, although some have expanded to the United States and Asia: Inter-Bank On-Line System (IBOS), Relay, Tipa-Net, and the Clearing Bank Association.

Credit cards have expanded as a means of payments, often replacing the use of traveler's checks by the business traveler and tourist. The card is accepted by the foreign merchant, hotel, or restaurant and is processed through the issuing company's procedures, ending up as a charge to the customer's account with the foreign amount converted into the user's local currency. Travelers also benefit from the increasing availability of linked networks of automated teller machines (ATMs), which permit them to withdraw cash from their accounts while in a foreign country.

Large Value Settlements

Banks usually keep only **working balances** in their accounts, which means sufficient funds to cover the normal day-to-day transactions. Such accounts do not earn interest, represent exposure to foreign exchange fluctuations, and otherwise commit resources that could be more profitably employed elsewhere in the bank's global business.

Payments for large amounts (each bank determines this level for itself) can necessitate specific settlements. To reduce float exposure (see box on page 56), the value date for this will be controlled.

In the United States there are two major systems for large-dollar settlements, discussed below.

Fedwire

Fedwire is a message and payment system of the Federal Reserve System for transfers within the United States. The network consists of computer systems linking the twelve Federal Reserve Banks in an automated message switching station. All banks in the United States, including branches of foreign banks, are required to maintain reserves that are a percentage of the deposits on their books. For larger banks, these reserves (federal funds) are held in that bank's account at one of the Federal Reserve banks. These accounts are available for settling payments. As a credit payments system, Fedwire

> is a real-time, gross settlement service in which the sender of the funds initiates the transfer. . . . In general, depository institutions (including U.S. branches and agencies of foreign banks) that maintain

a reserve or clearing account on the books of a Federal Reserve Bank may use Fedwire directly to send or receive payments. Approximately 11,000 institutions use the Fedwire funds transfer service. . . . Fedwire funds transfers are primarily used for payments related to interbank overnight loans, interbank settlement transactions, payments between corporations, and settlement of securities transactions. . . . Each transfer is settled individually when it is processed and is final (that is, irrevocable and unconditional) at the time of receipt.[3]

Thus a receiving bank considers that it is in good funds at the moment it receives the Fedwire payment. The average size of a transfer is about $3 million. Payments intended for third parties are to be promptly transferred. Although Fedwire is used for settling larger international payments, it focuses on the needs of the domestic U.S. banking system.

Fedwire is also used for transferring all marketable U.S. Treasury securities and many other securities issued by U.S. government agencies that are in book-entry form (securities in which certificates are not issued but are represented by ledger accounts). These also include some international organizations, such as the World Bank. This is "a system that supports the immediate and simultaneous transfer of securities against funds."[4]

CHIPS

The **Clearing House Interbank Payments System (CHIPS)** is a private, on-line, real-time, large-dollar network for U.S. dollar transfers that is owned and operated by the New York Clearing House Association. There are 120 participants, of which 18 participate in the end-of-day settlement (as of October 1993). These latter, referred to as settling banks, are those that "have the size and financial strength to handle huge payment volumes."[5] Participants are in New York City and include banks headquartered there, New York branches of certain other U.S. banks, agencies of foreign banks (about two-thirds of the participants), and Edge Act corporations (see chapter 2).

CHIPS enables payment messages to be sent during the day, with each transaction considered irrevocable but with the actual settlement done at the end of the day based on each participant's net position. As messages are sent and received between the member banks, CHIPS calculates the net position between payments made and payments received by each bank. Thus a bank sending payment orders of $50 million to various banks during the day and receiving orders for $40 million would make one transfer of dollars at the end of the day to settle its net of $10 million (see box on page 59).

> The payments transferred over CHIPS are primarily related to interbank transactions of an international nature, including the dollar payments resulting from foreign [exchange] transactions (including spot and currency swap contracts) . . . Eurodollar placements and returns . . . settling obligations on other payment or clearing systems, adjusting correspondent balances and making payments associated with commercial transactions, bank loans and securities transactions."[6]

Comparable systems have been established in other countries, including CHAPS (Clearing House Automated Payment System) in London, BOJ-NET (Bank of Japan Financial Network System), and SIC (Swiss Interbank Clearing System).

Risk Management

When more money is paid out of an account than is in that account, an **overdraft** is created. This is a form of a loan and, generally, interest will be assessed by a bank when the overdraft exists at the end of a business day. To operate the huge volume of daily payments, however, banks routinely have to overdraw accounts temporarily during the day. They do so with the confident expectation that other covering funds will come in later in the day, so that no end-of-day overdraft will remain.

These overdrafts are referred to as **daylight (intraday) overdrafts**. If, however, the crediting funds were not to appear, it could present a very serious problem for the paying bank, perhaps causing it to exceed its legal lending limit and even impair its capital. Both Fedwire and CHIPS have an element of credit. The Federal Reserve will permit banks a daylight overdraft in their account at the Federal Reserve bank up to an amount determined by the Federal Reserve, for which they charge interest based on the number of minutes the overdraft exists within that day.[7] CHIPS likewise permits member banks to send out messages to make more payments than they receive, and all payments are executed during that working day—even though the net settlement does not take place until the end of the day. To protect intermediaries and ultimately the entire U.S. payments system, banks, CHIPS, and the Federal Reserve System now establish *caps*— predetermined limits on the amount of daylight

---

Settling through CHIPS

Every participant in CHIPS has a terminal computer, linked by leased telephone lines to the central CHIPS computer, through which it can directly send and receive payment messages. The central CHIPS computer immediately processes all such messages. Then, at 4:30 p.m. [Eastern Time], it produces for each participating bank item-by-item detailed reports of payments made to and received by it and by institutions holding accounts with it; the printout also indicates the bank's gross position with CHIPS, the gross and net positions of any banks for whom the bank settles, and finally, if the bank is a settling bank, its net net—the dollars it must send out or will receive due to CHIPS settlement. Also, by netting debits and credits, CHIPS figures each participating bank's net position vis-a-vis every other participating bank and the system as a whole. . .

After CHIPS figures come out at 4:30 participants who are not settling banks settle their accounts at one of the settling banks. Each settling bank that, on a net-net basis, has a debit balance with CHIPS sends over the Fedwire to the [settlement account] that CHIPS maintains at [the Federal Reserve Bank of New York] the sum required for it to settle. After CHIPS has received these monies, it in turn wires out, again over Fedwire, all monies it owes settling banks who have ended the day on a net-net basis with a credit balance at CHIPS. Monies are supposed to flow into CHIPS' account from settling banks with a net-net debit balance by 5:30 p.m. and to go out to settling banks with a net-net credit balance by 6 p.m.; at that time, the balance in CHIPS' account at the Fed should return to zero.

Reprinted, with permission, from *The Money Market*, 3d ed., by Marcia Stigum, (Homewood, Ill.: Business One Irwin, 1990), pp. 894-895.

overdraft they will permit to other banks.[8] For example, a bank receiving instructions from an overseas correspondent bank to make payments totaling $10 million, for which it has established a limit of $5 million, will pay out whatever funds are in the account and then $5 million. The remaining payment orders will be held until sufficient funds come into the account during the day.

Accounting

Due To accounts of foreign banks are listed with other deposits in the financial statement of a bank as liabilities. The Federal Reserve requires reserves to be held against these deposits in U.S. offices, as with all other domestic balances in a U.S. bank. Deposits in overseas branches or IBFs do not require maintaining reserve balances at the Federal Reserve Bank.

Due From accounts are listed as assets. The Risk-Based Capital Guidelines (discussed in chapter 2) risk-weight these accounts, which have a maturity of one year or less, at 20 percent, without differentiation for the country in which they are located.

Summary

The foundation upon which all the features of international business rest is that of the ability of payments to be made from one country to another. The commercial banks provide the network that makes this possible through correspondent banking. Transfers of funds consist of two parts: the message and the settlement. Through the accounts that banks maintain with each other, settlements are made for different types of remittances, foreign drafts, redemption of traveler's check payments, and so forth.

Small-value payments from one country to another will usually be made through bank-to-

bank remittances or foreign drafts, which (like the S.W.I.F.T. system) are the message part of the payment. Each of these provides instructions to the bank that settlement is to be made by debiting or crediting an account on their books and, in turn, crediting or debiting another account either in that bank or another bank. Interbank transfers then use CHIPS or Fedwire to complete the settlement.

Large-value payments require prompt settlement, either on a gross or on a net basis. In a gross payment, settlement is made for each transaction. Fedwire is an example of a gross payment settlement. A net settlement system accumulates payments, and the settlement is calculated and made in a single funds transfer for the difference between credits and debits either at specified times during the business day or at the end of the business day. CHIPS is an example of an end-of-the-day net settlement system.[10]

Questions

1. What is the difference between Due To and Due From accounts?
2. What is a correspondent bank?
3. What is float, and how do the different types of payments affect it?
4. How are funds transferred by a foreign draft?

Notes

1. U.S. Department of the Treasury, *Comptroller's Handbook for National Bank Examiners* (Englewood Cliffs, N.J.: Prentice-Hall, Inc., 1982), Section 202.1, p. 2
2. Federal Reserve Regulation CC, §229.36(f)
3. Bruce J. Summers, ed., *The Payments System* (Washington, D.C.: International Monetary Fund, 1994) p. 203
4. Ibid., p. 205

5. Marcia Stigum, *The Money Market*, 3d ed. (Homewood, Ill.: Dow Jones-Business One Irwin, 1990), p. 895

6. Summers, *The Payments System*, p. 209

7. Although permitting daylight overdrafts as necessary for the flow of payments, the Federal Reserve emphasizes that it is not condoning these in their accounts and expects such use to be reduced. See "Federal Reserve Policy Statement of Payments System Risk," *Payment Systems Handbook* (Washington, D.C.: Board of Governors of the Federal Reserve System, 1995), p. 9.350

8. For full details on the application of Federal Reserve policies to net credit limits and net debit caps, see "Risk-Reduction Policy," *Payment Systems Handbook* §9-1000 ff.

9. For details of the payments systems in the major industrial countries, see Humphrey, *op.cit.*

4

PRINCIPLES OF FOREIGN EXCHANGE

Learning Objectives

After studying this chapter, you will be able to

- show how banks trade in foreign exchange
- explain how the foreign exchange market operates
- demonstrate how the bank's foreign exchange trader participates in this market
- identify participants in the market

Overview

Both the currency of a foreign country and the process of exchanging it for the currency of another country are referred to as **foreign exchange**—a practice with an aura of mystery that has been encouraged by foreign exchange traders and fiction writers.

One attribute of sovereignty is a nation's power to have its own money, named or renamed as it wishes.[1] From at least the time of the Greek and Roman Empires, the names of coins have reflected their value—usually determined by the weight of the gold or silver content. Pound sterling, peso, peseta, drachma, lira, kyat, baht, ouguiya, mark—refer to weights; guilder, birr, zloty, rupee, rupiah—refer to gold or silver. The dollar takes its name from a sixteenth-century German silver mine. Other currency names reflect national heroes: bolivar, sucre, lempira, colón, balboa. Some countries call their currency after the name used by another country; dollar, for example, is used by 18 countries other than the United States, each of which is a distinct currency. A few countries use another country's money or have joint currencies. Regardless of the name, each currency is **legal tender**, which means it can legally be used for payments in that country. Foreign exchange trading, as a consequence, is the acquisition of purchasing power in one country with the money of another.

Trading one currency for another arises from the elements that make up a nation's balance of payments: movement of international trade, short- or long-term capital and financial transfers made and redeemed, dividends on previous investments, the payment for services, and tourist and immigrant movement. Whenever any international transaction takes place, one currency is exchanged eventually for another. The trading of foreign exchange is similar to trading any other commodity—such as cotton or wheat—and also attracts speculators and hedgers. Many of the major challenges in international business begin with first establishing a value for one currency in terms of another (for example, how many deutsche marks will one dollar buy?) and, second, obtaining sufficient quantities of each. Within a commercial bank, these activities are centered in the foreign exchange trading section.

Background

Foreign exchange trading originally was considerably simpler than it is today. Countries used gold or silver coins or had paper money that was payable on demand in gold. To determine the value of one country's currency for another, one assessed the gold weight of the coins. If, for example, a certain quantity of gold could buy more wheat in one country than in another, people brought their gold to that country and exchanged it for wheat to take home. This increase in demand and reduction in supply would cause the price of wheat to go up in the country where it was cheaper as well as increase the amount of money in circulation, thus deflating it in the other country. As the wheat price rose, people no longer came to buy the wheat since it was no longer cheaper. Thus the international monetary system tended to balance itself.

This is a much-simplified explanation of the **gold standard**: "To be on the gold standard a country needed to maintain the convertibility between [bank]notes and gold and to allow gold to flow freely across its borders."[2] This system was essentially destroyed by World War I, although an attempt was made to restore it in the 1920s. By the 1930s, the gold standard was gone, victim of industrial protectionism, economic depression, a shortage of gold, and national politics that required internal control and manipulation of the money supply that was incompatible with the freedom of the gold standard. Even though the gold standard has not been used in more than 70 years, its memory exerts a powerful influence on exchange rate policy today—particularly in the effort to regain stability, as shall be seen in this chapter and chapter 5. Of the total gold produced throughout history (approximately 115,000 tons), 31 percent is still being held by governments and central banks.[3] The United States is the single largest holder of this official gold, accounting for about 25 percent. The holdings of Germany, Switzerland, France, and Italy follow, in that order.[4]

The Foreign Exchange Rate

A **foreign exchange rate** is a numerical expression of the price of the currency of one country in terms of that of another country (see exhibit 4.1). The rate of exchange between any two currencies may be stated in terms of one unit of either currency. For example, a rate between U.S. dollars and yen may be stated as follows:

1 U.S. dollar = 200 yen (European terms)
1 yen = 0.005 U.S. dollar (U.S. terms)

Each rate is merely the reciprocal of the other. The trader must be careful in quoting rates because when the rate changes each number moves in the opposite direction:

1 U.S. dollar = 100 yen
1 yen = 0.01 U.S. dollar

At any given moment, a wide range of rates exists that depends on the underlying transactions. There is a rate for buying the currency and a rate for selling. The difference between the buying and selling price is called the **spread**. A bank will quote one rate of exchange for large cable transfers and a different rate for the purchase of a few dollars' worth of foreign banknotes. A bank will quote one price at which it will sell a foreign draft for £100 to a customer and a different rate at which it will buy a British bank check for the same amount from a customer. The trading of bank balances constitutes what is primarily referred to as foreign exchange trading. At a given moment, traders at different banks may quote differing rates for the same transaction, depending on their immediate supply of, or need for, a particular currency. A bank with a large inventory of pounds in its account and no immediate need would have less incentive to buy more pounds than would a bank with a shortage of pounds.

The International Monetary Fund was created by the principal countries of the world after World War II. Each country was required at that time to establish a **par value** for its currency. "Par values were established for the currencies of IMF member countries in terms of gold or the 'U.S. dollar of specified gold content.'"[5] Once this par value was established, the government was required to support that price within 1 percent as importers, exporters, investors, and others bought and sold that currency for their needs. In the case of the United Kingdom, for example, when the par value of the pound sterling equated to $2.40, the British maintained the price between $2.38 and $2.42. Whenever the price in the market dropped to $2.38, the Bank of England bought pounds with dollars; when the price rose to $2.42, it sold pounds for dollars.

This system descends from the gold standard, even though the convertibility into gold no longer exists. The idea of maintaining the value within a narrow band owes something to the old "gold points": "The currencies of those countries that adhered to the gold standard could fluctuate in price among themselves only by minor variations—the so-called gold points . . . [which was] the cost of shipping gold from one country to another, plus insurance charges and loss of interest for the duration of the shipment."[6]

In the post-World War II period, whenever a country changed its rate of exchange by an amount

Exhibit 4.1 *Financial Times* **Guide to World Currencies**

From *Financial Times*, January 2, 1996; © 1996 Financial Times. Used by permission. ▶▶▶

FT GUIDE TO WORLD CURRENCIES

The table below gives the latest available rates of exchange (rounded) against four key currencies on Friday, December 29, 1995 . In some cases the rate is nominal. Market rates are the average of buying and selling rates except where they are shown to be otherwise. In some cases market rates have been calculated from those of foreign currencies to which they are tied.

		£ STG	US $	D-MARK	YEN (X 100)
Afghanistan	(Afghani)	7374.85	4750.00	3318.66	4604.72
Albania	(Lek)	145.712	93.8500	65.5698	90.9796
Algeria	(Dinar)	81.0069	52.1750	36.4529	50.5792
Andorra	(French Fr)	7.5928	4.8905	3.4168	4.7409
	(Sp Peseta)	188.355	121.320	84.7621	117.609
Angola	(Kwanza)	8837.40	5692.00	3976.80	5517.91
Antigua	(E Carib $)	4.1920	2.7000	1.8864	2.6174
Argentina	(Peso)	1.5523	0.9999	0.6986	0.9693
Armenia	(Dram)	626.117o	403.270	281.751	390.936
Aruba	(Florin)	2.7792	1.7900	1.2506	1.7353
Australia	(Aus $)	2.0872	1.3443	0.9392	1.3032
Austria	(Schilling)	15.6351	10.0706	7.0360	9.7626
Azerbaijan	(Manat)	6893.54o	4440.00	3102.08	4304.20
Azores	(Port Escudo)	231.936	149.390	104.374	144.821
Bahamas	(Bahama $)	1.5526	1	0.6987	0.9694
Bahrain	(Dinar)	0.5853	0.3770	0.2634	0.3655
Balearic Is	(Sp Peseta)	188.355	121.320	84.7621	117.609
Bangladesh	(Taka)	62.5678	40.3000	28.1562	39.0674
Barbados	(Barb $)	3.1228	2.0113	1.4052	1.9498
Belarus	(Rouble)	17854.9o	11500.0	8034.65	11148.3
Belgium	(Belg Fr)	45.6916	29.4300	20.5617	28.5299
Belize	(B $)	3.1052	2.0000	1.3973	1.9388
Benin	(CFA Fr)	759.280	489.050	341.682	474.092
Bermuda	(Bermudian $)	1.5526	1	0.6987	0.9694
Bhutan	(Ngultrum)	54.5954	35.1650	24.5686	34.0895
Bolivia	(Boliviano)	7.6696	4.9400	3.4514	4.7889
Botswana	(Pula)	4.3753	2.8177	1.9686	2.7315
Brazil	(Real)	1.5090	0.9720	0.6791	0.9423
Brunei	(Brunei $)	2.1961	1.4145	0.9883	1.3712
Bulgaria	(Lev)	110.017	70.8600	49.5074	68.6928
Burkino Faso	(CFA Fr)	759.280	489.050	341.682	474.092
Burma	(Kyat)	8.8591	5.7060	3.9866	5.5315
Burundi	(Burundi Fr)	395.096	254.474	177.792	246.691
Cambodia	(Riel)	3570.98	2300.00	1606.93	2229.65
Cameroon	(CFA Fr)	759.280	489.050	341.682	474.092
Canada	(Canadian $)	2.1175	1.3639	0.9529	1.3222
Canary Is	(Sp Peseta)	188.355	121.320	84.7621	117.609
Cp. Verde	(CV Escudo)	128.819	82.9700	57.9683	80.4324
Cayman Is	(CI $)	1.2859	0.8282	0.5786	0.8029
Cent. Afr. Rep	(CFA Fr)	759.280	489.050	341.682	474.092
Chad	(CFA Fr)	759.280	489.050	341.682	474.092
Chile	(Chilean Peso)	631.345	406.650	284.112	394.213
China	(Yuan)	12.9132	8.3174	5.8111	8.0630
Colombia	(Col Peso)	1538.19	990.750	692.203	960.448
Comoros	(Fr)	569.940	367.088	256.472	355.860
Congo	(CFA Fr)	759.280	489.050	341.682	474.092
Costa Rica	(Colon)	297.727	191.760	133.976	185.895
Côte d'Ivoire	(CFA Fr)	759.280	489.050	341.682	474.092
Croatia	(Kuna)	8.2686	5.3257	3.7209	5.1628
Cuba	(Cuban Peso)	1.5526	1	0.6987	0.9694
Cyprus	(Cyprus £)	0.7089	0.4566	0.3190	0.4426
Czech Rep.	(Koruna)	41.4003	26.6660	18.6306	25.8504
Denmark	(Danish Krone)	8.6042	5.5420	3.8720	5.3725
Djibouti Rep	(Djib Fr)	248.416	160.000	111.787	155.106
Dominica	(E Carib $)	4.1920	2.7000	1.8864	2.6174
Dominican Rep	(D Peso)	20.6651	13.3100	9.2992	12.9029
Ecuador	(Sucre)	4532.04o	2919.00	2039.40	2829.72
	(Sucre)	4108.96a	2646.50	1849.02	2565.56
Egypt	(Egyptian £)	5.2843	3.4035	2.3779	3.2994
El Salvador	(Colon)	13.6008	8.7600	6.1203	8.4921
Equat'l Guinea	(CFA Fr)	759.280	489.050	341.682	474.092
Estonia	(Kroon)	17.7897	11.4580	8.0053	11.1076
Ethiopia	(Ethiopian Birr)	9.0051	5.8000	4.0523	5.6226
Falkland Is	(Falk £)	1	0.6441	0.4500	0.6244
Faroe Is	(Danish Krone)	8.6042	5.5420	3.8720	5.3725
Fiji Is	(Fiji $)	2.2180	1.4286	0.9981	1.3849
Finland	(Markka)	6.7414	4.3422	3.0337	4.2094
France	(Fr)	7.5928	4.8905	3.4168	4.7409
Fr. Cty/Africa	(CFA Fr)	759.280	489.050	341.682	474.092
Fr. Guiana	(Local Fr)	7.5928	4.8905	3.4168	4.7409
Fr. Pacific Is	(CFP Fr)	138.167	88.9908	62.1748	86.2690
Gabon	(CFA Fr)	759.280	489.050	341.682	474.092
Gambia	(Dalasi)	15.2970	9.8525	6.8836	9.5512
Germany	(D-Mark)	2.2222	1.4313	1	1.3875
Ghana	(Cedi)	2232.64	1438.00	1004.68	1394.02
Gibraltar	(Gib £)	1	0.6441	0.4500	0.6244

		£ STG	US $	D-MARK	YEN (X 100)
Greece	(Drachma)	367.302	236.580	165.290	229.344
Greenland	(Danish Krone)	8.6042	5.5420	3.8720	5.3725
Grenada	(E Carib $)	4.1920	2.7000	1.8864	2.6174
Guadaloupe	(Local Fr)	7.5928	4.8905	3.4168	4.7409
Guam	(US $)	1.5526	1	0.6987	0.9694
Guatemala	(Quetzal)	9.2338	5.9473	4.1552	5.7654
Guinea	(Fr)	1547.94	997.000	696.570	966.507
Guinea-Bissau	(Peso)	28002.7	18036.0	12601.1	17484.4
Guyana	(Guyanese $)	216.588	139.500	97.4639	135.233
Haiti	(Gourde)	29.4994	19.0000	13.2747	18.4189
Honduras	(Lempira)	15.6657	10.0900	7.0495	9.7814
Hong Kong	(HK $)	12.0046	7.7322	5.4022	7.4957
Hungary	(Forint)	212.125	136.630	95.4587	132.451
Iceland	(Icelandic Krona)	101.276	65.2300	45.5740	63.2349
India	(Indian Rupee)	54.5954	35.1650	24.5686	34.0895
Indonesia	(Rupiah)	3549.91	2286.50	1597.50	2216.57
Iran	(Rial)	4657.80u	3000.00	2096.00	2908.24
Iraq	(Iraqi Dinar)	0.4827o	0.3109	0.2172	0.3014
Iraq	(Iraqi Dinar)	3881.50m	2500.00	1746.66	2423.54
Irish Rep	(Punt)	0.9687	0.6239	0.4359	0.6048
Israel	(Shekel)	4.8690	3.1361	2.1911	3.0402
Italy	(Lira)	2463.04	1586.45	1108.40	1537.93
Jamaica	(Jamaican $)	56.6699	36.5000	25.5013	35.3837
Japan	(Yen)	160.153	103.155	72.0708	100
Jordan	(Jordanian Dinar)	1.1008	0.7090	0.4954	0.6873
Kazakhstan	(Tenge)	98.9938	63.7600	44.5469	61.8099
Kenya	(Kenya Shilling)	86.8680	55.9500	39.0903	54.2388
Kiribati	(Australian $)	2.0872	1.3443	0.9392	1.3032
Korea North	(Won)	3.3381	2.1500	1.5021	2.0843
Korea South	(Won)	1204.39	775.750	541.990	752.024
Kuwait	(Kuwaiti Dinar)	0.4647	0.2993	0.2091	0.2901
Laos	(New Kip)	1428.39	920.000	642.772	891.862
Latvia	(Lats)	0.8339	0.5371	0.3753	0.5207
Lebanon	(Lebanese £)	2477.87	1596.00	1115.07	1547.19
Lesotho	(Maluti)	5.6599	3.6455	2.5470	3.5340
Liberia	(Liberian $)	1.5526	1	0.6987	0.9694
Libya	(Libyan Dinar)	0.5520	0.3555	0.2484	0.3446
Liechtenstein	(Swiss Fr)	1.7865	1.1507	0.8040	1.1155
Lithuania	(Litas)	6.2104	4.0000	2.7947	3.8777
Luxembourg	(Lux Fr)	45.6916	29.4300	20.5617	28.5299
Macao	(Pataca)	12.4053	7.9900	5.5823	7.7456
Macedonia	(Denar)	61.0178	39.3004	27.4578	38.0984
Madagascar	(MG Fr)	6357.90	4095.00	2861.04	3969.75
Madeira	(Port Escudo)	231.936	149.390	104.374	144.821
Malawi	(Kwacha)	24.2000	15.5980	10.8925	15.1145
Malaysia	(Ringgit)	3.9419	2.5390	1.7739	2.4613
Maldive Is	(Rufiya)	18.2741	11.7700	8.2233	11.4100
Mali Rep	(CFA Fr)	759.280	489.050	341.682	474.092
Malta	(Maltese Lira)	0.5471	0.3524	0.2462	0.3416
Martinique	(Local Fr)	7.5928	4.8905	3.4168	4.7409
Mauritania	(Ouguiya)	209.275	134.790	94.1731	130.668
Mauritius	(Maur Rupee)	28.2651	18.2050	12.7192	17.6482
Mexico	(Mexican Peso)	11.9624	7.7050	5.3832	7.4693
Miquelon	(Local Fr)	7.5928	4.8905	3.4168	4.7409
Moldova	(Leu)	6.9790	4.4950	3.1405	4.3575
Monaco	(French Fr)	7.5928	4.8905	3.4168	4.7409
Mongolia	(Tugrik)	714.475	460.180	321.512	446.105
Montserrat	(E Carib $)	4.1920	2.7000	1.8864	2.6174
Morocco	(Dirham)	13.1488	8.4689	5.9169	8.2099
Mozambique	(Metical)	15370.7	9900.00	6916.79	9597.21
Namibia	(S A Rand)	5.6599	3.6455	2.5470	3.5340
Nauru Is	(Australian $)	2.0872	1.3443	0.9392	1.3032
Nepal	(Nepalese Rupee)	84.2286	54.2500	37.9026	52.5908
Netherlands	(Guilder)	2.4888	1.6031	1.1200	1.5541
N'nd Antilles	(A/Guilder)	2.7792	1.7900	1.2506	1.7353
New Zealand	(NZ $)	2.3749	1.5295	1.0686	1.4827
Nicaragua	(Gold Cordoba)	12.3550	7.9576	5.5597	7.7142
Niger Rep	(CFA Fr)	759.280	489.050	341.682	474.092
Nigeria	(Naira)	34.1572o	22.0000	15.3706	21.3271
	(Naira)	133.675m	86.1000	60.1551	83.4666
Norway	(Nor. Krone)	9.8091	6.3181	4.4142	6.1249
Oman	(Rial Omani)	0.5978	0.3851	0.2691	0.3733

		£ STG	US $	D-MARK	YEN (X 100)
Pakistan	(Pak. Rupee)	53.1218	34.2158	23.9054	33.1693
Panama	(Balboa)	1.5526	1	0.6987	0.9694
Papua New Guinea	(Kina)	2.0728	1.3351	0.9328	1.2943
Paraguay	(Guarani)	3046.98	1962.50	1371.13	1902.48
Peru	(New Sol)	3.5763	2.3035	1.6094	2.2330
Philippines	(Peso)	40.7234	26.2300	18.3260	25.4278
Pitcairn Is	(£ Sterling)	1	0.6441	0.4500	0.6244
	(NZ $)	2.3749	1.5295	1.0686	1.4827
Poland	(Zloty)	3.8298	2.4668	1.7235	2.3914
Portugal	(Escudo)	231.936	149.390	104.374	144.821
Puerto Rico	(US $)	1.5526	1	0.6987	0.9694
Qatar	(Riyal)	5.6529	3.6409	2.5438	3.5296
Reunion Is. de la	(F/Fr)	7.5928	4.8905	3.4168	4.7409
Romania	(Leu)	4083.34	2630.00	1837.49	2549.56
Russia	(Rouble)	0.9921o	0.6390	0.4465	0.6195
	(Rouble)	7258.40m	4675.00	3266.26	4532.01
Rwanda	(Fr)	341.572	220.000	153.706	213.271
St Christopher	(E Carib $)	4.1920	2.7000	1.8864	2.6174
St Helena	(£)	1	0.6441	0.4500	0.6244
St Lucia	(E Carib $)	4.1920	2.7000	1.8864	2.6174
St Pierre	(French Fr)	7.5928	4.8905	3.4168	4.7409
St Vincent	(E Carib $)	4.1920	2.7000	1.8864	2.6174
San Marino	(Italian Lira)	2463.04	1586.45	1108.40	1537.93
Sao Tome	(Dobra)	2746.18	1768.76	1235.77	1714.66
Saudi Arabia	(Riyal)	5.8229	3.7505	2.6203	3.6358
Senegal	(CFA Fr)	759.280	489.050	341.682	474.092
Seychelles	(Rupee)	7.5379	4.8550	3.3920	4.7065
Sierra Leone	(Leone)	1412.87	910.000	635.786	882.168
Singapore	($)	2.1961	1.4145	0.9883	1.3712
Slovakia	(Koruna)	46.0004	29.6280	20.7001	28.7218
Slovenia	(Tolar)	201.650	129.879	90.7418	125.906
Solomon Is	($)	5.3447	3.4424	2.4051	3.3372
Somali Rep	(Shilling)	4067.81	2620.00	1830.50	2539.87
South Africa	(Rand)	5.6599	3.6455	2.5470	3.5340
Spain	(Peseta)	188.355	121.320	84.7621	117.609
Spanish Ports In N Africa	(Sp Peseta)	188.355	121.320	84.7621	117.609
Sri Lanka	(Rupee)	83.0615	53.5000	37.3786	51.8637
Sudan Rep	(Dinar)	128.090	82.5000	57.6399	79.9767
Surinam	(Guilder)	652.092	420.000	293.440	407.154
Swaziland	(Lilangeni)	5.6599	3.6455	2.5470	3.5340
Sweden	(Krona)	10.2894	6.6274	4.6303	6.4247
Switzerland	(Fr)	1.7865	1.1507	0.8040	1.1155
Syria	(£)	65.0539	41.9000	29.2741	40.6185
Taiwan	($)	42.3645	27.2870	19.0645	26.4524
Tanzania	(Shilling)	853.930	550.000	384.266	533.178
Thailand	(Baht)	39.1088	25.1900	17.5994	24.4196
Togo Rep	(CFA Fr)	759.280	489.050	341.682	474.092
Tonga Is	(Pa'anga)	2.0872	1.3443	0.9392	1.3032
Trinidad/Tobago	($)	8.8654	5.7100	3.9894	5.5354
Tunisia	(Dinar)	1.4723	0.9483	0.6625	0.9193
Turkey	(Lira)	94550.4	60900.0	42548.7	59037.4
Turks & Caicos	(US $)	1.5526	1	0.6987	0.9694
Tuvalu	(Australian $)	2.0872	1.3443	0.9392	1.3032
Uganda	(New Shilling)	1560.36	1005.00	702.159	974.262
Ukraine	(Karbovanets)	278536.4	179400.0	125340.6	173913.0
U A E	(Dirham)	5.7023	3.6729	2.5661	3.5606
United Kingdom	(£)	1	0.6441	0.4500	0.6244
United States	(US $)	1.5526	1	0.6987	0.9694
Uruguay	(Peso Uruguayo)	10.9769	7.0700	4.9396	6.8538
Vanuatu	(Vatu)	177.224	114.150	79.7527	110.659
Vatican	(Lira)	2463.04	1586.45	1108.40	1537.93
Venezuela	(Bolivar) (1)	449.672o	289.625	202.351	280.767
Venezuela	(Bolivar) (1)	527.154m	339.541	237.225	329.156
Vietnam	(Dong)	17095.7	11011.0	7693.01	10674.2
Virgin Is-British	(US $)	1.5526	1	0.6987	0.9694
Virgin Is-US	(US $)	1.5526	1	0.6987	0.9694
Western Samoa	(Tala)	3.9177	2.5233	1.7629	2.4461
Yemen (Rep of)	(Rial)	77.6300o	50.0000	34.9333	48.4708
Yemen (Rep of)	(Rial)	217.364r	140.000	97.8132	135.718
Yugoslavia	(New Dinar)	7.3508(2)	4.7345	3.3078	4.5897
Zaire Rep	(Zaire)	16494.8	10624.0	7422.62	10299.1
Zambia	(Kwacha)	1499.33	965.690	674.694	936.154
Zimbabwe	($)	14.4683	9.3188	6.5107	9.0337

Special Drawing Rights December 28, 1995 Utd Kingdom £0.956618 Utd States $1.48735 Germany DM2.13137 Japan Y152.974 European Currency Unit Rates December 29, 1995 Utd Kingdom £0.847242 Utd States $1.31424 Germany DM1.88397 Japan Y135.590

Abbreviations: (a) Free rate; (m) Market rate; (o) Official rate; (r) Parallel rate (t) Tourist rate (u) Currency fixed against the US Dollar (v) Floating rate (1) Venezuelan Official rate devalued on 11/12/95. Market rate derived from Brady bond trading. (2) Yugoslavian Dinar devalued on 26/11/95; Some data derived from THE WM/REUTERS CLOSING SPOT RATES & Bank of America, Economics Department, London Trading Centre. Enquiries: 0171 634 4365.

To obtain a copy of this table by Fax from the Cityline service dial 0891 437001. Calls charged at 39p/minute cheap rate, 49p/minute at all other times

Friday, December 29, 1995

greater than this 1 percent band, it was required to restate its par value. Changing the par value downward (in terms of gold) is **devaluation**; changing the par value upward is **revaluation**. Such a drastic step is not taken lightly and would be the result of many factors, such as a higher rate of inflation in one country compared with that of another or loss of confidence in a government.

This was a form of a **fixed rate of exchange** whereby the government of a country declares the price at which its currency may be converted into that of other countries. In the years after the end of World War II, use of a fixed rate of exchange was customary for all the non-U.S. dollar currencies because there was limited availability of national reserves, world trade was curtailed as national economies were rebuilt, and there was a crucial need to use export earnings for essential imports such as food and raw materials for factories. To maintain a fixed rate of exchange requires extensive controls and regulation by the government and is as much a political decision as an economic one. At the extreme, the government can require that export earnings and all other foreign receipts be sold to the government at that rate and that all payments for foreign purchases be approved by the government. Such a system can be very costly, requiring constant inspections and supervision and ever more complex regulations. When a government tries to maintain a fixed exchange rate while permitting direct trading between buyers and sellers, it can also require use of its reserves of foreign currencies and gold to support the rate.

By 1973, the maintenance of a country's official exchange rate within a fixed range of a par value was abandoned. For the industrial countries, the structure had become too rigid and protected speculators when the market rate moved close to the range limits. The speculator knew that the government had to support the rate. Although still officially obligated to return to par values, the governments of industrialized countries have abandoned that system of fixed rates

and at present allow the rate of exchange for their currency to **float.**

A *floating rate of exchange* is one in which the rate is determined by supply and demand. Importers, investors, and others who need the currency will bid for it from those who have it—exporters and others. When the demand is greater than the supply, the price rises; when supply exceeds demand, the price falls.

From time to time, central banks enter the market to support a rate, but this is solely their own decision. When a central bank allows the currency rate to float, that country's reserves suffer no direct impact whenever the rate changes. It is only when the central bank attempts to manage the float that the nation's reserves can be affected, and those reserves can be seriously depleted if the country tries to maintain an exchange rate that the rest of the world deems unrealistic. When a central bank does intervene in the market to attempt to affect the rate of exchange, this is referred to as a "managed" or "dirty" float.

Many smaller trading countries still maintain a fixed par value, but do so by linking their currency to a major currency to determine its value for international transactions. This can be done by actually having the foreign currency, as Hong Kong, for example, has done since 1983 to maintain the rate of about HK$7.8 per US$1.[7] In 1992, 55 percent of the developing countries linked their currency to either the U.S. dollar, pound sterling, French franc, or a basket of currencies.[8]

A market exists between currencies when there is sufficient supply of and demand for each currency. Between the major currencies, for example, enough buyers and sellers exist to enable rates to be quoted in terms of each. For many others, however, demand is insufficient, and trading one for the other necessitates going through a third currency, usually U.S. dollars. For example, between Greece and Brazil there would be a very small demand for each currency. To make such a trade when a need arose, the foreign exchange trader would sell drachmas for dollars and then dollars for cruzeiros. The resulting exchange rate for cruzeiros expressed in drachmas is a **cross rate.**

With floating exchange rates, one of the factors influencing the price of a country's exchange rate is the trend of its balance of payments, which is influenced in turn by many factors and events. Despite the importance of this trend, temporary influences may be the most important consideration in making a pricing decision. For example, supply and demand, seasonal factors, political considerations, international events, or the timing of large payments may be reflected in the quoted price. "Foreign currency decisions are crucially dependent upon expectations . . . and exchange rate expectations are influenced by every conceivable economic, political, social, or psychological factor, not just balance of payments trends." [9] For the major currencies, exchange rates can also be affected by the comparative levels of short-term interest rates in the domestic markets (see chapter 5).

Market Participants

The foreign exchange trading day is continuous, reaching a peak of activity in each market as the business day moves around the globe. It starts when a calendar business day opens in Tokyo, Hong Kong, and Singapore and then moves to the Middle East, to Western Europe, to New York, to the West Coast of the United States, and back to Asia. In many industrialized countries, foreign exchange trading has few restrictions. At the other extreme are countries that severely restrict trading by anyone other than the government. A currency is said to be freely convertible when there are no restrictions on its being traded for a major currency, such as dollars, marks, yen, and so on.

The principal foreign exchange market in the United States is in New York City, where most financial activity takes place. However, there is no central market place and traders rarely see each other. There is no official setting of rates, just as there are no fixed hours or rules of trading except the acceptance of an unwritten code of financial and moral conduct that has evolved over time. Its tangible framework is the system of telephone and other direct rapid communications equipment that links participating institutions: domestic banks, U.S. branches and agencies of foreign banks, investment bankers, brokers, businesses, and even individuals whose commercial pursuits require participation in the market. The U.S. foreign exchange market is basically conducted over the telephone. The physical location of traders is therefore of little consequence.

U.S. banks that make and maintain the market—because of their size, historical position in the international banking community, or management attitude toward exchange trading—engage in foreign exchange business with sufficient regularity and quantity that they can handle it with limited risk. They balance their positions when required to by the volume and direction of business. In fact, as the frequency and volume of their transactions increase, the risks inherent in exchange trading are minimized, and the opportunity for trading profits increases.

Agencies and branches of the many foreign banks that are in constant contact with their head offices add to the breadth and depth of the market, particularly in their respective currencies. Some investment banking firms participate in the market because of their special interests and overseas connections. Other active participants include a number of nonbank foreign exchange dealers.

Foreign Exchange Traders

Each bank's foreign exchange trading is the responsibility of a designated trader or dealer.

The Gold Standard: Descriptions and Definitions

Fixing the value of a country's monetary unit in terms of a specific weight of gold constituted the essence of the gold standard. For example, the United States went back on the gold standard in 1879 by defining a dollar to equal 23.22 fine grains of gold or, equivalently, by setting a price of $20.67 for one troy ounce of gold. Before the First World War, most countries were on a form of the gold coin standard. These countries minted gold coins that circulated, along with notes that were fractionally backed by gold reserves, in the payments system as legal tender. To economize on gold reserves after the war, many countries, including Britain but not the United States, stopped circulating gold coins. Instead, these countries instituted a gold bullion standard, under which notes could be exchanged for gold bars.

Under the international gold standard, currencies that were fixed in terms of gold were, necessarily, tied together by a system of fixed exchange rates. The fixed relative quantity of gold between two currencies in the system was known as the parity. The prewar parity between the dollar and the pound sterling was $4.8665 to 1 pound, but the dollar-pound exchange rate could move in either direction away from the parity benchmark by a small amount to the gold export point, where it became profitable to ship gold to the country with the stronger currency. Before the First World War, many central banks held pounds as a reserve asset, and the pound usually served in lieu of gold in international transactions; this system was known as the sterling exchange standard. At the Genoa Conference of 1922, all European governments declared the reestablishment of the international gold standard to be their ultimate and common financial objective and, to economize further on gold reserves, resolved to adopt a gold exchange standard under which gold-based assets would serve as reserve assets. This goal was achieved by the mid-1920s.

However, the extensive holdings of foreign exchange reserves (primarily dollar-and pound-denominated deposit balances) under the gold exchange standard went beyond what the participants at the conference had envisioned. In the 10 years before World War I, total foreign exchange reserves in European central banks fluctuated between $250 million and $400 million. In contrast, at the end of 1924, foreign exchange holdings totaled $844 million; at the end of 1928, they were $2.513 billion.

Reprinted, with permission, from: "The International Gold Standard and U.S. Monetary Policy from World War I to the New Deal," *Federal Reserve Bulletin*, June 1989, p. 425.

Large banks employ many traders working under a chief trader who is responsible for meeting the needs of the bank's customers. For example, a U.S. business purchasing a machine made in Germany will need deutsche marks to pay for it. A bank's foreign exchange trader in the company's bank will supply the marks in exchange for dollars from the U.S. company. The practice of the trader trading solely for the bank's own profit is called "proprietary trading."

To do this job properly, the trader must keep informed about market activities, since the bank's larger customers will often seek advice about the present market and about expectations for the future. For larger banks, this requires continuous participation in buying and selling currencies. Active traders constantly monitor several video screens that display the rates quoted by major banks, along with immediate news information.

The trader must be a competitive person who enjoys the activity of trading, the tension, and the mental effort. "Most traders, including many experienced ones, are under 35 years old. In a rapidly fluctuating market, experience is compressed and those who don't learn quickly go on to other pursuits." [11]

A trader's activity contributes directly to the improvement of the bank-customer relationship. A variety of factors have a bearing on the pricing decision and must be resolved in a matter of seconds during a conversation with a customer before a quotation is given. This unending process of gathering facts, evaluation, and reappraisal makes the work of a foreign exchange trader challenging and stimulating.

Foreign Exchange Brokers

Foreign exchange brokers provide breadth to the functioning of the market. They do not trade for their own account nor deal directly with the public. They specialize in locating bank and business buyers and sellers and bringing them together. Foreign exchange brokers account for about 40 percent of the market. Having limited capital resources, the broker does not act as a principal in an exchange transaction. For example, a regional bank with only occasional foreign exchange transactions can use a broker to locate a needed buyer or seller. When there are a number of buyers or sellers, the broker can assist the regional bank in finding the best price without the bank's having to make numerous calls to gauge the market. When many such banks communicate their needs, the broker has the opportunity to match these or use the market-making capabilities of the larger banks' foreign exchange traders. When two parties with offsetting needs are located, the broker will work between them, to agree upon a rate. Only then will the identities of the two parties be revealed to each other. If they are willing to trade with each other, the deal is closed between them, and the broker is paid a modest commission. Such willingness to trade will depend on the credit relationship between the parties.

Operations in the Foreign Exchange Market

All activities that make up a nation's balance of payments will influence trading in that country's currency. Regardless of whether the currency used is one's own currency or a foreign currency, almost every international transaction involves one party's being exposed to exchange risk.

Payments for Imports and Exports

If all of its international trade were priced in U.S. dollars, the United States would have no need for a foreign exchange market. There would, of course, be a lively supply of, and demand for, dollars in foreign exchange markets abroad. The demand would be reflected on the ledgers of U.S. banks by transfers of dollars among foreign accounts. Dollars earned by foreign exporters, for example, would flow into the accounts of their banks, and dollars paid by foreign importers of U.S. products would flow out of foreigners' bank accounts here and into the bank accounts of U.S. exporters. The U.S. exporter, quoting a price in U.S. dollars, is merely putting the exchange risk on the importer.

In practice, many U.S. firms and individuals receive foreign exchange in payment for goods and services sold abroad. Others make payments to foreigners in their currency rather than in U.S. dollars. A U.S. firm selling in the United Kingdom, for example, may invoice its sales in pounds sterling. International business is highly competitive, and to make a foreign sale, many U.S. firms prefer to quote prices in the local currency and then undertake the problem of conversion into U.S. currency. If the U.S. business deals only in dollars, it will discover that many other sellers are eager to make a sale and willing to quote prices in the buyer's currency. The years after World War II, when the U.S.

business attitude was "dollars or nothing," are gone—probably for good.

Some large firms with a substantial volume of imports and exports may establish their own foreign currency accounts through which they can make payments and receive the proceeds of their sales. They would consequently be carrying the risks of changes in the value of their foreign currency balances. In practice it is difficult to balance these needs exactly. Similarly, it is extremely difficult for other importers or exporters to find exact counterparts with the proper amount of foreign exchange to complete a trade transaction. As a result, the foreign exchange market, like other financial and commodity markets, has developed as a means through which these needs can be easily met.

A country's balance of payments is reflected in the value of its currency against other currencies. A country with a balance of payments deficit will have an increasing supply of its currency in the market as importers, investors, and individuals pay their foreign counterparts; thus the value of the country's currency will decline as supply exceeds demand. A balance of payments surplus usually brings a rising value for that country's currency as more foreigners seek it to pay in that country, and demand for the currency exceeds supply.

Trading in Foreign Currencies

To satisfy the needs of their customers, commercial banks hold foreign exchange inventories in the form of working balances with foreign banks or have access to such balances through their major correspondent banks. In U.S. banks, such accounts are Due From accounts. These inventories are maintained by the purchase and sale of balances owned by firms, individuals, and other banks—domestic and foreign—and by the purchase of bills of exchange, traveler's checks, dividend warrants, and so forth that are denominated in foreign currencies. Within the operating principles of the bank, its foreign exchange traders must manage these balances and make every important trading decision themselves, usually in a matter of seconds. Once a trade has been completed, operations personnel handle the posting, confirming, and settling of the transaction. The size and number of these Due From accounts reflect to some extent the amount of activity the bank experiences in a given currency.

The transfer of ownership of a given amount of foreign exchange from one person to another is fundamental to any foreign exchange transaction. Chapter 3 described methods of transferring funds: foreign drafts and remittances. These are equally applicable whether transferring foreign exchange or U.S. dollars.

Spot Trading

As a bank's customers require the money of another country for their business needs, they communicate with the bank's foreign exchange trader to learn the price at which the bank is willing to sell the foreign currency for local currency. This is the foreign exchange rate. Conversely, a customer who has received foreign currency from a business transaction will seek the price at which the bank will buy it. In each transaction, between a bank and a commercial customer or between two banks, one party is buying while the other party is selling. Both parties must clearly understand which currency they are buying or selling. In U.S. banks, many traders find it convenient to quote all transactions as buying or selling dollars. This facilitates the operations of a trading room, since the bank will report its daily balance sheet in terms of dollars.

Once a trade has been completed, settlement (delivery of the currencies on the designated value date) occurs. For example, bank A purchased 1 million pounds sterling from bank B as a **spot transaction** on June 1, which means delivery occurs two business days later. Bank A has sold dollars and bought pounds; bank B has bought dollars and sold pounds. The price is $1.51 = £1. As soon as the trade has been agreed, both traders notify their operations units. Bank B sends a tested cable, usually using the S.W.I.F.T. format, to its correspondent bank in London to "charge our account 1 million pounds and pay to X London bank for credit to the account of bank A value June 3." Bank A will send a message to its London correspondent telling it "you will receive" the amount. If the funds do not arrive, the London correspondent bank will notify bank A. While sending the instructions to London, bank A arranges to pay $1,510,000 in the United States to bank B, also on June 3, usually through Fedwire or CHIPS. A spot trade is settled two business days hence to provide time for these messages to be sent and for the London banks to have time to pass their necessary entries, taking into account the difference in time zones.

Events elsewhere in the market have a critical bearing on an exchange rate the trader will quote for a given transaction. To trade more favorably, the trader often attempts to anticipate what the market's position will be in the immediate future. The bank's own position in a given currency has a direct bearing on this decision, as does the cost involved in carrying or **covering** a position, which means protecting against possible loss from a change in the rate by an offsetting transaction.

Forward Trading

A **forward** contract between two parties calls for delivery at a future date of a specified amount of one currency against payment of another, *with the exchange rate fixed at the time the contract is made*. When the delivery falls due, the spot rate for the currency may be above, below, or the same as the rate specified for the transaction; this fact has no effect on the contracted rate. Settlement occurs on the maturity date of the contract. Forward rates can be obtained for many of the major currencies that a substantial number of businesses need to either buy or sell for delivery in the future.

While forward contracts are often for periods of time such as one, three, or six months, they can be arranged for any number of days. Longer forward quotations can often be obtained for some actively traded currencies. Contracts may also allow the customer to take delivery on any day between certain specified dates (*option contracts*). The bank is exposed to more risk when a customer is involved in a forward transaction rather than a spot transaction because of the future date of settlement.

Forward trades are used to reduce price uncertainties in international business when an immediate decision must be made about completion and payment in the future. For example, a U.S. company bidding on a contract to sell equipment to a buyer in the United Kingdom will need 90 days to assemble the order. To meet competition from European suppliers, the company wants to quote its price in pounds sterling. The problem is how to quote a sterling price to be paid on delivery of the equipment in 90 days, then convert the foreign exchange into dollars and show a profit, when the company has no idea what the spot rate will be in 90 days. The company's interest is in the business deal, not in currency speculation. The U.S. bank can arrange a forward contract with the company, setting a U.S. dollar price today at which it will buy the pounds sterling when the company is paid in London in 90 days. Regardless of what happens to the exchange rate, the conversion rate is fixed. Such protection is called **hedging**.

Similarly, an importer may buy forward foreign exchange needed to fix the U.S. dollar cost of imports. For example, a U.S. business may be deliberating between a machine made in the United States and a similar one made in Canada. Based on today's exchange rate, they may be nearly equally priced. However, it will take six months before the machine will be ready, at which time payment will be made. By checking with its bank, the importer may discover that the forward Canadian dollar rate is lower than the spot rate. With a forward contract, the Canadian machine becomes cheaper than the machine made in the United States. The U.S. business would therefore be likely to buy the Canadian-made machine.

In cases in which capital transfers are involved, an investor may wish to buy or sell forward the amounts expected to be paid or received in order to take advantage of prevailing *premiums* or *discounts* in the forward market. A forward is at a discount when the forward rate is lower than the spot rate; it is at a premium when the forward rate is higher than the spot. Thus a U.S. investor due to receive 1 million deutsche marks in three months may wish to sell these forward if the deutsche mark spot rate is $0.40 and the forward rate $0.405. If the investor waits until the deutsche marks are in hand ("uncovered"), then the spot rate might be higher or lower, and the investor benefits or loses accordingly. However, with a forward contract entered into now, the investor will receive $405,000 in three months. If the spot rate in six months is unchanged or lower, the investor has profited by the forward contract; if the spot rate turns out to be higher, he has still benefited by having replaced risk with certainty for the period.

The difference between the spot rate and the forward rate usually reflects the difference in short-term interest rates between the two countries (see chapter 5).

Forward transactions do not usually replace foreign exchange transactions that would otherwise take place in the spot market to cover exports, imports, or capital transfers; they simply shift the timing of such exchanges. Importers, exporters, and capital remitters and recipients often cover their activities in response to changes in expectations concerning the movement of exchange rates. These shifts can have material effects on the exchange market.

The use of the forward market to hedge is widely practiced by investors making short-term investments. For example, a corporate treasurer with surplus funds wants to invest them until they are needed for the company's operations and is seeking the highest return for comparable safety. Because of the relative freedom for money to move from country to country, the treasurer evaluates the rates in different markets for short-term investments. To calculate the true yield on any investment, the treasurer considers not only the rate on the investment itself but also the cost of converting currency to make the money market investment, as well as the cost of converting back into the original currency upon maturity.

Another activity in the foreign exchange market is **speculation**. This is the purchase or sale of foreign exchange, usually on a forward basis, for the sole purpose—or at least with the fervent hope—of subsequently being able to cover the open position at a profit. The defensive operator, or hedger, buys or sells exchange—again, usually on a forward basis—as a means of avoiding an exchange risk or of ensuring against loss from an exchange rate change. The speculator hopes to profit from a rate change; the hedger tries to avoid the consequences of a change.

A form of speculation can occur when market participants anticipate that a country with fixed exchange rates is going to change the par value, or a country with floating exchange rates is going to support the rate in the market. If the expectation is that the rate will go down, anyone with payments to make for commercial transactions in that currency will delay payment as long as possible to benefit from the new lower rate. Conversely, anyone in that country with payments to make in a foreign currency will prepay

to make the conversion at the current, more favorable rate. These practices are known as *lags* and *leads*, respectively. These speculative maneuvers tend to aggravate the situation and, in effect, become a self-fulfilling prophecy forcing government action. The government suffers heavy outflows of reserves as its citizens prepay foreign debt, while facing delayed income to its reserves as foreigners wait before paying their local debts.

The global financial markets of the 1990s have become so complex and interwoven that it is difficult to determine whether the underlying business motive for a company entering into a foreign exchange contract is hedging or speculation, as will be seen in chapter 5.

Maintaining the Position

The foreign exchange trader buys and sells continually. It is not necessary, nor is it often desirable, for traders at major banks to offset each transaction immediately. These banks maintain active foreign exchange trading departments that operate within general guidelines established by bank management. The guidelines set the maximum **position** the trader can have in any one currency at the end of the day, which is the net balance of purchases and sales. While traders may want to keep their bank's position as balanced as possible and thus be protected against major rate changes, they may nevertheless let the position be unbalanced. This decision depends on the trader's opinion of what the future trend of that currency will be.

As trades are made, they are taken into the position and recorded by the clerk who maintains this record and reflects all changes. The position clerk keeps a record of the delivery dates of all forward transactions so that they will be reflected in the spot position at maturity. For example, at the beginning of a day, the bank's pound sterling position may be as shown in exhibit 4.2.

In this example the total of spot and forward purchases minus sales plus the cash in the account leaves an overall position that is short £75,000—more sales than purchases. If the trader's position limit is £100,000, then he is within that limit. The cable transfer sales and purchases would be expected to go through his account on this day; he can estimate how many days it will be before the drafts will be reflected in that account. He therefore has ample cash in the account to meet all these transactions. The immediate question is when the forward contracts will mature, as shown in exhibit 4.3.

An analysis of this position shows that if he does nothing, he will have ample cash in the account to meet the maturing forward sales for 60 days. For today, however, he has more cash in the account than he is going to need. This cash balance is not earning any interest. Since the forward contracts do not mature immediately, the trader may decide to reduce the large cash position by means of a **swap.**

Exhibit 4.2   Example of Opening Balance Position

Opening balance with correspondents		£200,000
Purchases not yet credited to account		
Cable transfers	£350,000	
Drafts	65,000	
Forward contracts	100,000	515,000
Total balance and purchases		£715,000
Sales not yet charged to account		
Cable transfers	£400,000	
Drafts	40,000	
Forward contracts	350,000	
Total Sales		£790,000
Overall position		−£ 75,000

Exhibit 4.3   Example of Forward Contract Maturity Dates

	30 Days	60 Days	90 Days	180 Days
Sales	−£ 50,000	−£100,000	−£100,000	−£100,000
Purchases		+ 50,000		+ 50,000
Cash balances in account today: £175,000*				
Cash position	+£125,000	+£ 75,000	−£ 25,000	−£ 75,000

* From Exhibit 4.2: opening balance plus cable and sight draft purchases less cable and sight draft sales.

A swap transaction is a simultaneous purchase and sale of a certain amount of foreign currency for different value dates. The key aspect is that the bank arranges the swap as a single transaction with a single counterparty, either another bank or a nonbank customer. This means that, unlike outright spot or forward transactions, a trader does not incur any foreign exchange rate risk, since the bank contracts both to pay and to receive the same amount of currency at specified rates.[12]

In this case, the trader could sell spot and buy for forward delivery on a date close to the delivery date of the other forward sales contracts. Although this would not change the overall position, it would reduce the cash position. Swaps can be made between any two dates: one month against three months, two months against six months, or between spot and a future date. Applicable rates are quoted for these various dates. Thus the trader would sell the sterling spot, receiving dollars at the rate for a spot sale, and buy forward at the rate for that future date. In this way, the trader has flexibility in adjusting maturities to coincide with the needs of clients, while at the same time remaining within the limits established by the bank's management.

Controlling Risks

There are a number of external and internal risks involved in foreign exchange trading that could expose a bank to loss.

The first external risk is that the customer on whose behalf the bank is initiating the trade will not be able to pay for the transaction. The bank will therefore establish a limit, based on a credit assessment of the customer, before any transaction will be done. A spot transaction where settlement with the customer will take place in two days may have less risk than a forward contract. If the customer is unable to deliver his part of the transaction at the future date, the bank may suffer a loss, since it has committed itself to another party for the offsetting transaction or has taken the contract into its position for other operations. The bank may have even delivered the funds. Because of time differences, the bank may have instructed the foreign bank to pay out before debiting the customer's account. The basic question is whether the customer has the financial resources to meet his contractual obligations and will indeed do so.

The second external risk is the potential exposure with the **counterparty** to the trade—that is, the bank or company with which the bank has made the trade. Each bank will make its own determination of the maximum amount in outstanding forward contracts it wishes to have at any time with a particular bank or corporate customer, either domestic or foreign. Banks can fail, so there is a risk in entering into foreign exchange trades. If a bank goes bankrupt, other banks will be unable to realize contracts with that bank and will have to replace the amounts, perhaps at a considerable loss. Bank management will also limit the amount of exposure on settlement from a correspondent or customer in any one day, which would guard against a customer being overcommitted to come up with cash at any one time.

Internally, the operation of a foreign exchange trading section requires management direction and subsequent supervision. At the outset, limits are established for each currency. Management will determine the maximum exposure it is willing to have in a currency. The trader may enter into any number of trades, spot and forward, but at the end of each day the difference, if any, between total sales and purchases must be within the limit, either *long* (more purchases than sales) or *short* (more sales than purchases).

Strong internal audit controls are very important. Foreign exchange traders are not infallible, and they may not always judge the direction of the market accurately. In the heat of trading activity, mistakes will be made. Bank management must expect that this will happen. It is important that the trader recognizes such mistakes or misjudgments and cuts losses quickly. The skilled trader will do this and go on to the next transaction. There have been instances, however, in which traders remained convinced that a situation would turn around and, to recover the loss, took greater and greater risks. The results were substantial losses to the banks. In a few cases, the bank failed as a consequence.

Strong, independent in-bank auditing of daily positions is vital for a foreign exchange section. It is important that the back-office operation and the audit function report to separate offices outside the trading activity to ensure a measure of immediate control against manipulation.[13]

Such managing of risks will be discussed in greater detail in chapter 14.

Local Correspondent Services

Banks with extensive Due From accounts frequently make these accounts available to their domestic correspondent banks for drawings. In addition, regular foreign exchange rate sheets or on-line information services can be made available, giving the U.S. dollar price at which the correspondent can issue foreign payments in any of several foreign currencies. Correspondents authorized to use such facilities are thus able to arrange foreign exchange transfers for their own customers without incurring the expense of their own network of foreign currency accounts and, in most cases, without first having to communicate with their principal foreign exchange correspondents. Banks with a large branch system will use the same system so that their branches can easily issue drafts and remittances in foreign currency without having to contact the foreign exchange trader for small amounts.

Currency

A service performed principally for travelers by the foreign exchange trader is that of buying and selling foreign banknotes and coins. The price spread between buying and selling for this type of trading is always wide, because the market is small and moving cash from one market to another inherently poses certain problems. If a bank buys a larger quantity of banknotes from returning travelers than it can expect to sell, it can sell the surplus to specialized brokers or, in some cases, mail the bank notes to a correspondent in the country of origin for deposit in its account. The expense of registered insured mail plus the handling costs of maintaining a current inventory must be taken into account in determining the rates of exchange.

Currency buying and selling—of banknotes—is basically a service a bank provides to individual customers. Tourists and business travelers are often well advised to have a small amount of local currency when they arrive in the foreign country, to facilitate getting to their hotel. Only a few countries prohibit tourists from bringing in such a small amount of local currency.

Nonbank Markets

In addition to the foreign exchange markets established by banks, foreign exchange is bought and sold in some specialized markets as a commodity for future delivery in the same manner as is corn, wheat, copper, pork bellies, and so forth. This involves contracts for a prefixed standard amount for delivery on only specified dates. In foreign exchange, for example, a standard contract may be for DM125,000 maturing on the third Wednesday of March, June, September, or December. There is an important distinction between *forward* transactions and *futures* contracts. "The former are individual agreements between two parties, such as a bank and a customer. The latter is a contract traded on an organized market of a standard size and settlement date, which is resalable at the market price up to the close of trading in the contract." [14] Contracts are available in only certain major currencies.

Summary

Converting the money of one country into that of another country is a service banks provide for their customers through foreign exchange trading. This is a continuation of the concept outlined in the previous chapter in which money is moved from one country to another through accounts maintained by banks with each other.

The need for the foreign exchange service arises from international trade, investments, invisible trade, and other payments between countries. In each transaction, one of the parties needs to convert the money to that of another country. A designated trader who is knowledgeable about the spot market and the forward market provides this service to the bank's customers. The foreign exchange trader is supported by an operational staff and must operate within guidelines established by the bank's management that will limit the bank's exposure in the volatile exchange markets. The foreign exchange trader is experienced in dealing in a very complex market and can provide advice to the bank's customers to guide them through the foreign exchange marketplace.

Questions

1. How is the foreign exchange rate determined?
2. Who are the major participants in the foreign exchange market?
3. What is the difference between a spot trade and a forward trade? Why would a business use one or the other?
4. Why does foreign exchange trading exist?

Notes

1. For a full discussion of the meaning of money names, see Peter K. Oppenheim, "Money of the Realm," *Verbatim, The Language Quarterly*, Spring 1989, pp. 7-9
2. *Federal Reserve Bulletin*, June 1989, p. 426
3. Kenneth Gooding, "U.S. Group Charts All the World's Gold: History's 115,000 Tonnes," *Financial Times*, February 9, 1995, p. 25
4. Samuel Britton, "Free Bankers and Gold Bugs," *Financial Times*, June 16, 1994
5. B. Dianne Pauls, "U.S. Exchange Rate Policy: Bretton Woods to Present," *Federal Reserve Bulletin*, November 1990, p. 891
6. Allan M. Loosigian, *Foreign Exchange Futures* (Homewood, Ill.: Dow Jones-Irwin, 1981), p. 10
7. Simon Holberton, "Hong Kong Wakes Up to Cost of Dollar Link," *Financial Times*, January 16, 1995, p. 3
8. Michael Mussa, Morris Goldstein, Peter B. Clark, Donald J. Mathieson, and Tamim Bayoumi, *Improving the International Monetary System* (Washington, D.C.: International Monetary Fund, 1994), p. 8
9. Roger M. Kubarych, *Foreign Exchange Markets in the United States* (Federal Reserve Bank of New York, 1978), p. 40
10. *The Economist*, April 15, 1995, p. 74
11. Kubarych, *Foreign Exchange Markets*, p. 28
12. Ibid., p. 10
13. For a full description of the operation of such a control system, see *Foreign Exchange Trading Techniques and Controls* (Washington, D.C.: American Bankers Association, 1977)

14. K. Alec Chrystal, "A Guide to Foreign Exchange Markets," *Federal Reserve Bank of St. Louis Review*, March 1984, p. 8

5

THE FOREIGN EXCHANGE MARKETS

Learning Objectives

After studying this chapter, you will be able to

- explain the uses of the foreign exchange markets
- demonstrate the relationship between foreign exchange and interest rates
- understand how governments attempt to influence foreign exchange rates
- illustrate some of the problems and alternatives facing the markets

Overview

As discussed in chapter 4, the ability to receive and make payments in another country's currency is essential for the global trade in goods and services as well as short- and long-term investments. In the past this was readily done because of the existence of the gold standard or the willingness of British bankers to provide financing in sterling by accepting the "bill on London." In the immediate decades after World War II, when governments played a controlling role in maintaining stable rates of exchange, the value of currencies reflected the timing and changes in demand of a particular currency to meet trade needs. In the case of sterling, for example, the exchange rate with the dollar usually came under pressure in the autumn, when the British had to make large purchases of tobacco and other harvested crops in the Northern Hemisphere. The British government imposed limits on the uses of sterling based on the country of the users; capital uses were segregated from those for imports and exports.

Today, however, the major force in determining the rates of exchange between the currencies of the industrialized countries is speculation, sometimes described in gentler terms as "proprietary trading," "trading for one's own account," or "position taking." Perhaps as much as 75 percent of foreign exchange trading is done just to try to make a profit from often very short-term movements in rates by commercial banks, investment banks, corporations, governments, and pools of funds assembled for the sole purpose of profiting from high-risk position taking. During the course of even a quiet trading day, the value of a dollar in terms of yen or deutsche marks can fluctuate 1 percent, giving ample opportunity for short-term trading profits or losses. In contrast to markets trading commodities, equities, or bonds, there is a seemingly unlimited availability of currency, particularly in times of trading turmoil, in foreign exchange trading.

Into that maelstrom must come those who need to buy or sell foreign exchange for imports and exports of goods and services, make long-term investments for the development of factories and mines, or acquire equities or bonds as part of managing a pension portfolio. Every participant in the foreign exchange market affects the other participants. A sudden flow of funds from one country to another for short-term investment opportunities or speculation affects the prices for the importer or exporter seeking another currency. Regardless of what may have been the original purpose, a participant may have to adopt a different strategy to protect himself or herself.

> . . . [T]hose who deal in the market may have different goals and views. A central bank, for example, is not looking to maximize profit, but to support the currency for some economic or political end; a bank dealer has a time horizon of minutes, while a corporate treasurer may think in terms of months. In short, market participants are heterogeneous." [1]

This chapter begins by examining the objectives of the major classes of participants. It then examines some techniques available for these participants seeking stability for their transactions and concludes by reviewing some government-directed efforts toward a more stable market for the beginning of the next century.

Market Characteristics

The global trading of the money of the industrial countries is an unregulated financial market that operates beyond the control or supervision of any government or international organization. No government permits its *national* money market or stock exchange such an absence of supervision, licensing, or control.

Many developing countries—for the purpose of solving balance of payments problems, rationing limited foreign exchange earnings for essential imports, and so forth—do restrict the use of their currencies. Many countries limit access to foreign exchange, and certain developing countries maintain fixed exchange rates under the direct control of government. While acknowledging the existence of these markets and their importance to the residents of those countries, this chapter focuses on the activities of the market for the currencies of the major industrial countries, in which there are relatively few or no restrictions.

Participants

There are four major classes of participants in the global foreign exchange markets: governments, central banks, businesses, and traders. Each has certain objectives, some of which overlap with those of other participants. These objectives reflect not only short-term conditions, but also long-held beliefs.

Governments

The search for stable exchange rates has been a continuing goal of governments and businesses. Stability means that the price for one currency remains basically constant in terms of another major currency or the currency of a nation's major trading partner. It is generally accepted that such stability benefits global trade and investment decisions by enabling them to be based on the competitive advantages of markets and not warped by attempts to outguess short-term swings in price and cost differentials arising solely from exchange rate fluctuations. Into the early decades of the twentieth century, governments and businesses believed that this stability could be accomplished through the gold standard.

For interwar observers, the mystery of the prewar gold standard was how it worked so well. For a third of a century the gold standard had been synonymous with exchange-rate and balance-of-payments stability over much of the world. Exchange-rate stability, in the popular if dominantly British belief, had been responsible in turn for the stability of price levels and the rapid expansion of international trade that served as the basis for the impressive growth of the industrial economies. "There can be no question," concluded . . . a leading academic expert, in 1935, "that the development of an international gold standard in the second half of the nineteenth century and the enormous growth of international trade and investment which then took place are no mere coincidences." [2]

The collapse of the gold standard in the wake of the economic tumult of the 1930s did not diminish the belief in the importance of exchange-rate stability. In the immediate post-World War II world, stability was forced on the major industrial countries of Europe because the shortages of reserves and insufficient payment resources mandated massive controls. The first goals of the IMF after its creation in 1945 were to stabilize the value of each currency by requiring each country to establish a par value (defined in terms of gold) for its currency and then maintain the price of its currency in the then-limited foreign exchange trading market within a narrow band.

As economic prosperity was restored with the rebuilding of Europe, the IMF encouraged countries to dismantle their exchange controls and allow their currencies to be freely convertible, which meant that the exchange rate would be determined primarily by the demand for and supply of each currency freely trading in a market. (A country did this formally when it accepted Article VIII of the IMF Articles of Agreement.) By the mid-1970s, this had been accomplished for the industrial countries.

Exchange rates floated; trading was basically a free market; rate stability remained a major political objective. The conflicts among these became more evident by the 1990s.

Countries have different levels of economic activity, as is reflected in rates of inflation, government deficits, and unemployment: they can be in recession or inflation at different times in the business cycle. At any one given time during that period, different countries had conflicting economic policies as each government endeavored to restore or maintain internal economic prosperity by such acts as raising or lowering internal interest rates, depending on the conditions within the particular country. Political forces were also at play in each country; of course, European governments faced regular elections and had to be in harmony with the moods and goals of their voters.

In Germany, for example, the populace was acutely sensitive to any hint of inflation. German voters were familiar with their parents' and grandparents' experience of the financial devastation triggered by the 1922-1923 hyperinflation when "the wheelbarrow replaced the counting scales as the instrument for measuring the money supply." [3] "On paydays . . . men would ask their wives to wait by the factory gates to pick up their paychecks to rush to the store to buy milk. . . . Shopping had to be done early in the day, . . . and eventually it became customary for shops to close at lunch time and reopen in the afternoon with new price tags." [4] "If inflation stays above 50 percent a month for any length of time, barter rapidly replaces money, which loses all value. During the great German inflation in 1922-1923, the average monthly inflation rate was 322 percent a month or 40 percent a week." [5] Consequently, today's German government has to recognize that the voters will not tolerate inflationary economic programs.

With the signing of the Treaty of Rome in 1957, Western Europe moved toward a common market, which meant harmonizing all phases of economic life including removal of trade barriers between the member countries, and standardization of business practices.

Stability of the exchange rates between these countries became an increasingly important part of this movement toward a common market. In 1979, the European Monetary System (EMS) was created "to manage the way in which eight European currencies float against each other. The EMS [was] the successor of the first international attempt to dampen wilder fluctuations in exchange rates after the dollar had been allowed

---

Hyperinflation: Postage for Mailing Postcards in Germany

October 1, 1922	1 mark
April 1923	29 marks
July 1923	60 marks
October 1, 1923	400,000 marks
November 1, 1923	20,000,000 marks
November 26, 1923	16,000,000,000 marks

Source: *The American Philatelist*, January 1985, p. 66

to float in 1971." [6] These eight Western European countries (later expanded with several neighboring countries unofficially shadowing them with the same policy) created an exchange rate mechanism (ERM). This was a descendant of the older systems of par value with trading bands and, before that, the gold standard. Under the ERM, a central rate value was agreed upon for each of the participating European currencies so that each currency had comparable purchasing power. From time to time there were small, official, multinational realignments of these central rates (11 from 1979 to 1987). Each country was then required to maintain its currency's exchange rate in free market trading with the other ERM countries within a range between a floor and a ceiling price.

In December 1991, the countries of the European Community agreed at a meeting at Maastricht, The Netherlands, to take steps to achieve a common currency for their countries by 1999. The process was to be completed in three stages. By the start of Stage II on January 1, 1994, the governments would endeavor to bring their economies in line with each other preparatory to "convergence"—that is, replacing their individual currencies. Formulas were established for levels of consumer price inflation, interest rates for long-term government securities, keeping the currency within the ERM without unilateral realignment, and a sustained level of general government deficit as a percentage of gross domestic product (GDP). "At the start of Stage III, which could begin as early as 1997 but not later than January 1, 1999, member states that participate in the final stages will irrevocably fix their exchange rates and subsequently introduce a single currency." [7]

Central Banks

Although often seen as one, the objectives of the government and its central bank may differ at times, but usually not in public. The government's focus is on the political consequences of an action; the central bank may be more concerned with the monetary effects.

Much of the operational responsibility for implementing the ERM fell to the central bank of each country. When a country's exchange rate, for example, declined in free market trading (that is, there were more sellers than buyers), that country's central bank was committed to restore balance in the market either by entering the market as a trader to buy up its currency with its foreign currency on hand (or in its reserves), or to raise its internal interest rates to attract short-term foreign investors who would take advantage of the higher return by buying the currency to invest in that country's money market. Other central banks assisted in market support actions. Under the rules of the ERM, the Bundesbank, for example, "was required to intervene to support a weaker currency when it nears the limit of its permitted range of movement. But the other country's central bank must repay the Bundesbank." [8]

"Of European central banks, most of the larger ones—including the Bank of England—are under direct government control. Several smaller central banks, in The Netherlands, Switzerland, and Sweden, for instance, are, like the Bundesbank, independent from their governments." [9] This independence is relative. "In a strict sense, the field in which [the Bundesbank] can unambiguously apply its independence is rather narrow. Its competence is massively concentrated on monetary policy. Its [authority] extends to neither fiscal matters nor to social or wage policies. . . . [It] is not directly involved in either banking supervision or affairs of industrial policy [and] the government . . . has the final say over decisions on the exchange rate." [10] Article 3 of the law creating the Bundesbank specified its responsibility to regulate "the quantity of money in circulation and of credit supplied to the economy, using the monetary powers conferred on it by this Act, with the aim of safeguarding the currency."[11]

The reunification of East and West Germany highlights the balance of power between the government and the central bank. The West German government wanted to present political and monetary reunification to the voters in the most positive way.

The Bundesbank based its misgivings about monetary union, and particularly its opposition to a 1 to 1 conversion rate, on sound economic logic. At the beginning of 1990, the rate used for exchanging East Marks against D-Marks in commercial transactions was 4.5 [East Marks] to 1 [D-Mark]. On the free exchange market (illegal according to the East German authorities), the rate was 7 to 1. Monetary union on a 1 for 1 basis would involve a substantial revaluation of the East Mark which would cripple East Germany industry, by sharply increasing East German companies' costs, making their output uncompetitive.[12]

The government had the final say, unification came about, monetary union was basically set at one to one, and the governing party won the elections. There was an initial burst of economic euphoria as the East Germans spent their new money, and within a year the Bundesbank's predictions came true. For several years, this had serious negative economic consequences on the economy of the unified Germany. In time the government was forced to do the politically unpopular: raise taxes to prevent greater inflation.

By the 1980s, the Bundesbank was the dominant central bank in Europe. "The Bundesbank's direct monetary command spreads across reunified Germany, the world's third most important economy, and the home of one-quarter of the European Community's gross national product.

Its sphere of influence, however, stretches far beyond Germany's enlarged borders. The Bundesbank has taken over from national governments as the driving force behind monetary policy across Europe, a region accounting for roughly one-third of world economic output."[13] The success of the Bundesbank's policies gave it a growing stature above other central banks. "The bank's very name is a watchword for anti-inflationary rectitude. Its counsels find grave and attentive listeners at the tables of the mighty; and its writ runs wide. As the guardian of the Deutsche Mark, the quintessential strong currency which became the symbol of Germany's post-war recovery, the Bundesbank holds sway across a larger area of Europe than any German Reich in history."[14]

The Bundesbank's view of its responsibilities, echoing from the events of 1922-1923, was stated by the head of the bank in 1992: "The D-Mark is currently the leading currency in Europe, and it would not be in the interest [of our neighbors] if the Mark became a currency of inflation."[15]

Businesses

As businesses become increasingly more international, manufacturing plants are built in different countries to take advantage of the availability of raw materials, skilled labor, and transportation infrastructures as well as the location of markets, tax structures, political stability, and so on. Businesses have a strong motive to support governments' goal of maintaining stable exchange rates. "In a world of increasingly international industries, companies do not know where to build new plants if no confident predictions can be made about exchange rates three to five years out. So investment decisions are often delayed."[16]

The desire for stable exchange rates is equally strong among investors in long-term bonds and equities issued in one country but financed from pools of money (pension funds and mutual funds, for instance) in other countries.

The establishment of the Exchange Rate Mechanism provided investors and businesses with a degree of freedom from concern about exchange rate volatility.

> Although the [Maastricht] treaty did not provide for fixed exchange rates within the system for several more years, market participants came to assume that few of these governments would countenance devaluation in the interim. As a result, investors felt increasingly secure holding securities denominated in ERM currencies other than the mark. Investors purchasing assets that carried even higher yields than DM-denominated assets appeared to give little weight to exchange rate risk in . . . calculations of risk-adjusted returns. During the long interval since the last general ERM realignment in 1987, the total amount of assets allocated on the basis of this view reached substantial sums." [17]

> Institutions "invested hundreds of billions of dollars in Britain, Italy and Spain, where interest rates are high, on the assumption that the European Monetary System was providing them inexpensive protection against adverse currency fluctuations." [18]

Cross-border sales, foreign market share, corporate profitability, and costs of raw materials are also affected by changes in exchange rates. A business will be faced with difficult decisions when exchange rates are volatile and require it to balance its ability to be competitive in a foreign market against its need to maintain a level of profitability necessary for its survival.[19]

Traders

In a world in which a country's currency is freely convertible into that of other currencies, the rate of exchange since the early 1970s has been primarily determined by free market trading between buyers and sellers.

> The foreign-exchange market is one of the world's slickest. It is screen-based, genuinely international and open for business 24 hours a day. There are many buyers and sellers; prices adjust rapidly and for the most part smoothly. And it is huge.

> [In 1992] traders put daily net turnover in foreign exchange (including derivative products like futures, options, and swaps) at about $900 billion, only $50 billion or so less than the total foreign-currency reserves of all IMF members. If they are right, foreign-exchange trading has grown by more than a third since April 1989, when a central-bank survey estimated turnover at $650 billion, or double the previous survey's figure for 1986. Perhaps a quarter of the business is done in London; New York probably handles $150 billion and Tokyo $100 billion, with most of the rest spread among Frankfurt, Singapore, Hong Kong, Zurich, Sydney and Paris.

> Only a fraction of the turnover seems to reflect customers' foreign-exchange needs. Less than 5% relates to underlying trade flows, the demands of companies that buy and sell abroad or those of globe-trotting individuals. Another 10-15% may represent capital movements, such as pension-fund investment abroad. Though distinctions are hard to draw, most of the rest is the

dealing that banks and investment banks, mainly, do among themselves.[20]

The survey by the major central banks estimated that total *daily global* trading in April 1995 had reached $1.2 trillion, of which 30 percent was done in London, 16 percent in the United States, 10 percent in Japan, and 5-7 percent each in Singapore, Hong Kong, and Switzerland.

The emphasis for foreign exchange traders has shifted over the decades from meeting the needs of importers and exporters to trading for profit. "According to the Comptroller of the Currency, foreign-exchange dealing [in 1991] accounted for half of all the profits made by New York money-centre banks in the past four years."[22] But the psychology of the trader hasn't changed since Benjamin Strong, head of the New York Federal Reserve Bank, described it in 1925: "The speculator is more influenced by apprehension of things to happen then he is by the happenings."[23]

The Objectives Collide

The incompatibility among objectives for foreign exchange became obvious in 1992. Traders wanted profit; governments and central banks wanted stable exchange rates and to be able to manage their own internal money markets to maintain national economic growth and prosperity; businesses wanted stability for long-term investment decisions. And overall there was the longer-term political goal among members of the European Community to meet the Maastricht convergence targets.

Tensions had been growing in the summer [1992], following the Danish referendum rejecting the Maastricht treaty in early June and the subsequent strengthening of the deutsche mark within the ERM. The lira and sterling experienced particularly strong downward pressures. For the lira, market concern over the country's high level of public debt and its excessive budget deficit contributed to these pressures. . . . In the United Kingdom, the continued recession and a weak current account position influenced market perceptions that the pound sterling might be devalued within the ERM, given the apparent constraints on interest rate policy in the country. The rise in the Bundesbank discount rate on July 16 and further declines in short-term interest rates in the United States added to the tensions by putting upward pressure on the deutsche mark relative to other EMS currencies.[24]

The Bundesbank fought to dampen the inflation resulting from West Germany's merger with economically weak East Germany by maintaining high internal, official interest rates (8.75 percent to 9.75 percent). Most of the other major European countries (and also the United States) struggled to overcome internal recessions by lowering interest rates as a spur to economic activity. Many of these countries saw a movement, which quickly became a flood, of traders selling Swedish krone, Italian lire, and Finnish markkas and buying deutsche marks. When they did not have enough of those currencies, traders borrowed more. The traders calculated that after the currency was devalued, those borrowings could be repaid by selling the marks for krone, for example, paying off the local loan, and still having a substantial profit.

Against this tidal wave of trading, each European country, whether officially part of the ERM or merely shadowing it, sought to maintain a stable rate of exchange between its currency and that of Germany. These central banks intervened in the market—buying their own currency and paying for it with their holdings of foreign currencies. In spite of needing *lower* interest rates for internal recoveries from their recessions, they tried to support the stability of their exchange rates by *raising* internal interest rates, hopefully for just a short time, with two objectives: to reverse the flow of money by offering higher interest rates than Germany, and to make it too expensive for traders to borrow local currency to sell in the market.

These conflicts came to a crisis in September 1992.

Selected Chronology for Three Weeks in September 1992[25]

September 3 [Thursday]: The Bank of England borrowed $14.5 billion worth of deutsche marks to augment its reserves. The rate goes up to DM2.8 = £1.

September 4: The U.S. dollar drops to historic low against the deutsche mark.

September 8: Finland allows the markka to float; it drops 13 percent against the deutsche mark. Sweden raises internal official lending rate to 25 percent and then to 75 percent.

September 10 and 11: The Italian lira remains below its ERM floor despite massive intervention in the market by the Bank of Italy and the Bundesbank.

September 13: The Italian lira is devalued 7 percent.

September 14: The Bundesbank reduces internal interest rates by 0.25 percent and 0.50 percent. Sweden reduces its internal rate to 20 percent.

September 15: The Italian lira drops; sterling falls to a new low against the deutsche mark; the Spanish peseta drops.

September 16: At 8:30 a.m., Sweden raises its internal interest rate from 20 percent to 75 percent, "but this was insufficient to stem the outflow and it was forced to boost the rate again at 3:30 p.m. to 500 percent."[26] Massive intervention fails to keep the Italian lira above the ERM floor.

Sterling, a much more widely used currency, was assaulted by a tidal wave of selling. A member of the ERM, the Bank of England had a central rate of DM2.95 = £1, and a floor of DM2.778. By the end of the day, the Bank of England had spent £15 billion of foreign exchange reserves (about a quarter of its total reserves) buying pounds in an attempt to support the rate and had raised its minimum lending rate from 10 percent to 12 percent, only to raise it to 15 percent a few hours later. (Because so many other loan rates are tied to this minimum lending rate, this sudden increase would have raised other rates for business borrowing for inventory and even for home mortgages.) By evening, the Bank of England had succumbed to the pressure, withdrawn from the ERM, stopped buying pounds in the market, dropped its internal rate back to 12 percent, and allowed the pound to float freely. (By the following February, the pound was down to DM2.38 = £1, and the minimum lending rate was down to 6 percent.)

September 17: Italy withdraws from the ERM. The Bank of England cuts its rate to 10 percent. The French franc, Danish krone, and Irish pound fall to ERM floors. Spain devalues the peseta by 5 percent.

September 18: Heavy market selling continues. Ireland raises its interest rates to 300 percent. (In January 1993, Ireland gave in to heavy market selling, angrily devaluing the Irish pound by 10 percent.)

September 21: Sweden lowers its rates from 500 percent to 50 percent. (By mid-November, Sweden gave up trying to maintain a fixed rate and devalued its currency, which fell 9 percent against the deutsche mark.)

Consequences

Not all of the sellers of pounds sterling in September 1992 were simply speculators, although many were drawn by the "'scent of blood' buoyed by the handsome profits won on the devaluation of the lira [the week before]."[27] Long-term investors were forced to protect the value of those investments. For example, a year before, a German company might have built a factory in the United Kingdom, investing £10 million that had been acquired when the exchange rate was DM2.8 = £1. The company would show that investment in its financial statement as assets at DM28 million. Since this was close to the ERM floor rate of DM2.778, the company would have perceived little risk. When the pound was under attack in mid-September, however, the German company would have seen peril to the value of its investment. Realistically, it could not sell the factory overnight. But it could have borrowed £10 million, sold those for deutsche marks, and, when the devaluation actually occurred, sold the marks back to pounds in December 1992, when the rate was DM2.45.

September: £10 million at DM2.8 to £1
= DM28 million

December: DM28 million at DM2.45 to £1
= £11,428,000

Profit: £1,428,000

This profit on the company's foreign exchange trading (less interest on the loan plus interest earned on the deutsche marks in that same period) would have offset the translation loss it would have shown in its financial statement on the factory investment.

A **translation loss** (or **gain**) is an accounting procedure used by many companies in which, for example, long-term investments in foreign assets are shown in the company's financial statement based on the current, rather than the original, rate of exchange. The same would be done for its foreign currency debts and other liabilities. Thus the company's financial statement will reflect the current valuation of all its assets and liabilities.

Within five months, 5 of the 10 ERM currencies had devalued, as had several other European currencies. "From early September to mid-December, sterling depreciated by about 15 percent and the Italian lira by about 16 percent."[28] Both had dropped out of the ERM. Although the rate for sterling dropped as a consequence of the massive speculation against it in September 1992, there was a benefit in the next years. British goods became cheaper for European buyers and thus British exports increased.

In January 1993 the Bundesbank reported that it had spent the "equivalent of $68.7 billion intervening in support of other European currencies, . . . [of which] $22.4 billion was in one day [in September]. . . . [It] is expected to register a profit of more than $6 billion for 1992."[29] This heavy intervention in the market during this crisis resulted in Germany's foreign reserves (excluding gold) jumping from $63 billion at the end of 1991 to $91 billion at the end of 1992.[30]

The conflicts that ignited the foreign exchange crisis in Europe involved the U.S. dollar, too. Traders always had the option of selling a European currency for the safe haven of the U.S. dollar or selling dollars to speculate or hedge with a European currency, just as they were selling one European currency for another. Thus the rate for the dollar rose or fell in response to the actions of the European currencies with the same implications for imports, exports, and investments. The trading rooms of U.S. banks and multinational corporations were as heavily involved in the immediate trading turmoil as were those in Europe. The uncertainty was seized as an opportunity for sizable profits from trading. Such profits from foreign exchange trading were reflected in the 1992 annual reports of many commercial banks. One private, non-bank trader reported a profit of $1 billion. While such profits tend to get the most publicity, trading also has high risks. That same sophisticated trader reportedly lost over half of that profit later on a position in Japanese interest rates. This situation also attracts less knowledgeable participants. One former communist country "bought a screen-based trading system and experimented with currency trading." That country lost an amount equivalent to 25 percent of the country's annual gross domestic product.[31] Another such country lost the equivalent of their entire foreign currency reserves.[32] What was frightening to those in the United States who needed these major currencies to pay for imports, exports, and investments was the speed with which everything happened. However, the profits lured more speculation in the next years.

By the summer of 1993, the speculators were on the prowl again, this time against the French franc, Spanish peseta, Portuguese escudo, and Danish krone. They sought to profit by that same commitment of the ERM to keep their rates within a narrow band. As the rates fell to the floor of that band, they sensed another opportunity for what appeared to be certain profits. The governments responded, as they had in 1992 by changing the interest rates, with the Bundesbank lowering its rates to help. Finally, over the last weekend in July, the countries met. To give the central banks greater flexibility while maintaining the spirit of their commitment toward the goals of the Maastricht treaty, and to diminish the power of speculators, the ERM bands were widened to permit some of the currencies to fluctuate 15 percent above or below the central rate (rather than the previous 2½ to 6 percent) before central banks had to intervene. In spite of this, some currencies had to devalue because of internal inflation and loss of competitiveness for their exports—but such a 30 percent range of fluctuation (±15 percent) reduced speculation.

According to the IMF summation: "The recent episodes have illustrated the extent to which the private sector is willing to take positions when a currency is felt to be overvalued. Indeed, both the size of the market and the number of private operators able to inject very large sums into currency markets are clearly much greater now than in the past, and both have probably been underestimated."[33] The head of the Bundesbank had a terser summation: "an unfriendly domino game in which speculators knock down one currency after another."[34]

The example of the German company protecting the value of its investment in its factory in the United Kingdom during the crisis in the fall of 1992 illustrated a way of hedging a capital exposure.

Using the Markets

The foreign exchange markets reflect the vast number of individual transactions that the participants conduct each day. The participants have a number of ways to conduct their day-to-day business in such markets. The spot and forward markets are used for settling import and export transactions as well as short-term investments.

One of the characteristics of international finance today is the relative freedom of money to move from one industrialized country to another for short- or long-term investment. Each currency remains a domestic currency whose market interest rates are basically determined by conditions within that country: rate of inflation, monetary policy, government expenditures, taxation policy, and enforcement. The term *international capital markets* or *international money markets* does not refer to some supranational financial market, but rather to the linkage of these domestic markets, which allow money to move across national boundaries. The difference between the terms *capital markets* and *money markets* is that the latter usually refers only to short-term debt instruments (see chapter 11).

Interest-Rate Arbitrage

Money will tend to be attracted by the higher rate of interest in comparable risk, just as iron filings are attracted to a magnet. As a consequence, funds flow through the foreign exchange market as funds in one currency are converted to that of another to be invested in higher-yielding instruments. This is the meaning of **interest-rate arbitrage,** which can best be understood by looking at an example.

Consider a situation in which two corporate treasurers of manufacturing companies find they have surplus funds that their companies will not need for 90 days. At the end of that time, they must have the money in their account in their own currency to meet contracted purchases of equipment. One of these corporate treasurers is in the United States and has $10 million; the other is in Japan with ¥1 billion (equivalent to the dollar amount). They want to put these funds to work to obtain interest income with maximum safety during the 90 days. They are not interested in losing these funds in a high-risk investment since investing is not the principal business of their company; manufacturing is. Thus each decides to purchase only a government money market IOU. Governments cannot go bankrupt in their own currency since they have the power to tax or to print more money (although either of these has political and economic consequences).

The objective: Invest the funds for 90 days for the highest yield with maximum safety. At the end of 90 days, each investment must be converted back into its own currency.

The situation: Three-month Treasury bills issued by the Japanese government in yen yield 1.30 percent per annum; three-month Treasury bills issued by the United States government in dollars yield 6.01 percent per annum.

The options: The corporate treasurer can invest in the Treasury bills of their own government, obtain the stated return, and have no foreign exchange risk; or, they can purchase the Treasury bills of the other country, receive that rate of return, but have a foreign exchange risk.

The problem: Which will yield the higher rate of return? If the treasurer decides to purchase the Treasury bill of the other country, she must convert her local currency into the foreign exchange, invest it, and at the end of the 90 days, convert the foreign exchange back into her local currency. This means having a foreign exchange exposure for the 90 days. The exchange rates are:

Spot: $1 = ¥101

90-day forward: $1 = ¥99.8

The analysis: Both corporate treasurers might be more attracted to U.S. Treasury Bills since an annual rate of return of 6.01 percent is obviously higher than 1.30 percent. To invest in U.S. Treasury Bills, the Japanese treasurer would have to sell her yen spot for dollars and invest those dollars in the U.S. Treasury bill. At the end of the 90 days, she would receive dollars representing principal and interest and have to sell those dollars back to yen. If she wishes to be fully protected, she will hedge this by entering into a swap: buy dollars spot, sell dollars 90 days forward. To buy the dollar today, she must pay ¥101; however, when she sells the dollars in 90 days, she will get only 99.8 yen for each dollar. The Japanese treasurer is thus going to lose money on the foreign exchange swap, but she is earning the higher rate of interest on the investment.

How much is the loss versus the gain? To convert the foreign exchange swap into a percent figure, the formula is

$$\frac{\text{Forward rate} - \text{Spot rate}}{\text{Spot rate}} \times \frac{360}{\text{days to maturity}} \times 100 = \text{percent p.a.}$$

or

$$\frac{99.8-101}{101} \times \frac{360}{90} \times 100 = -4.75 \text{ percent p.a.}$$

For the Japanese treasurer, this would mean earning 6.01 percent on the U.S. Treasury bill and losing 4.75 percent on the swap, resulting in a true net rate of return of only 1.26 percent per annum (6.01 percent − 4.75 percent). This is lower than she would have earned had she invested in the Japanese government bill and not had any foreign exchange exposure. It therefore is to her advantage at the outset to do that. She also would have the choice to buy the U.S. Treasury bill and not have had the cost of a swap. She runs the risk and uncertainty, however, that the spot rate at the end of the 90 days might be ever lower.

The same basic calculations apply for the U.S. corporate treasurer, except that he would have *gained* on the swap. He would earn 1.30 percent on the Japanese government bill and gained on the swap, making his true net yield 6.05 percent per annum (1.30 percent + 4.75 percent) or a gain of 0.04 percent over investing in the U.S Treasury Bill at the outset.

Effect on Foreign Trade

Flows of money from one country to another to take advantage of higher interest rates affect the balance of trade.

To illustrate, consider two competing manufacturers of machinery who have equivalent selling prices. One is in Germany, quoting a price of DM1.5 million; the other is in the United States, with a selling price of $1 million. If the exchange rate is $1 = DM1.5 then the price to buyers in both Germany and the United States is the same. When the demand for dollars rises in Germany because investors are attracted by higher U.S. interest rates, then German investors compete and offer more deutsche marks to obtain dollars. The exchange rate moves to $1 = DM1.6. The effect of this on the two sellers of machinery is that *both a German and a U.S. buyer will find the German-made machine cheaper*. For a U.S. buyer, the cost in dollars becomes $937,500 (DM1,500,000 ÷ 1.6); for a German buyer, the U.S.-made machine would now cost DM1,600,000 ($1,000,000 × 1.6). As a consequence, the U.S. manufacturer would be unable to compete, losing potential export sales. German exports would rise, and U.S. imports would rise.

Options

A business has several choices when it is involved in buying or selling its products in another country and payment is made in a foreign currency.

For example, a U.S. company is scheduled to receive deutsche marks in three months in payment for a sale. Choice A: It can decide to do nothing now and, when the deutsche marks are received, convert them into dollars at the spot rate at that time. This could be the decision if the company were confident of its ability to analyze the trend of the exchange rate. Choice B: It could decide to eliminate all risk by entering into a forward contract, thereby fixing the rate. This would eliminate any risk exposure from the deutsche mark going up or down. Choice C: It could protect itself against just a *decline* in the value of the mark, so that if the mark goes up in value, the company will have all the benefit (the middle ground between the spot or forward choices). This third choice can be arranged by buying a **currency option**, which is one of the products now being referred to as a *derivative* (see chapter 14).

> Option contracts which can be either customized and privately negotiated or standardized give the purchaser the right to buy (call option) or sell (put option) a specified quantity of a commodity or financial asset at a particular price (the exercise price) on or before a certain date. For this right, the purchaser pays the seller (writer) an amount called the option premium.[35]

In this case, the U.S. company would purchase an option that would give it the right to sell the deutsche marks to another party (perhaps a financial institution in this case) at a specified rate in 90 days. The company would pay money for this contract. If the rate for the deutsche mark on that 90th day was lower than that option rate, it would exercise the option (sell the deutsche marks to the other party at that agreed upon rate). If, however, the rate was higher, then it would do nothing with the option and sell the deutsche marks in the spot market at the now higher rate. The other party keeps the option premium amount whether the U.S. company did or did not exercise the option. Thus the U.S. company has protected itself against a decline in the value of the deutsche mark, but has kept the benefit of any price rise. Options are, of course, also used for investment transactions.

Governments and the Market

Governments of all countries are concerned with activities in the foreign exchange markets. For those industrial countries with freely floating currencies, the objective is to maintain stable rates. For many developing countries, however, control of the use of their currency is more direct, through regulations that limit how their currency may be used.

Those regulations are usually applied in two categories: controls on current account transactions and controls on capital movements.

Exchange Controls

As the issuer of the national currency, the government, usually acting through the nation's central bank or treasury, prescribes rules for the use of the national currency by both its residents and nonresidents. The objective is to execute national policies and, in periods of economic difficulty, protect the nation's foreign exchange reserves. Each country establishes rules that are generally referred to as **foreign exchange controls** or regulations. Foreign exchange controls are often accompanied by trade restrictions, such as tariffs or quotas.

Although often extremely complex, the historic function of these controls is to restrict or prevent a resident of the country from acquiring the currency of another country or to limit the use of the nation's currency when it is owned by a nonresident. For example, when a country is experiencing balance of payments difficulties, it will want to preserve the earnings from exports to be used for essential imports, such as food or raw materials. The government does this by issuing regulations, such as: restraining banks in the country (both national banks and branches of foreign banks) from selling foreign drafts without a government permit, restricting banks from opening import letters of credit unless the buyer has obtained a government permit, prohibiting local investors from investing in other countries, limiting the amount of money a traveler may take out of the country, or requiring exporters to sell the foreign exchange they earn to the central bank rather than selling it in a free market

The government can set the rate for its purchase of export proceeds and may, in fact, have multiple rates, depending on the underlying commodity. By paying a higher rate for foreign currency earned by the sale of one type of commodity over another, the government tries to diversify a country's economy from a heavy concentration on a single export, such as coffee, copper, or sugar. Exchange controls can be imposed for political objectives, to prevent a nation's businesses from doing business with certain countries or to force them to do business with political allies.

The operation of exchange controls has an administrative cost because it requires a bureaucracy to administer and police its activities. Bankers and businesses must divert staff and time to learn and comply with the regulations. The government also has to be prepared to enforce the regulations by imposing fines or even prison sentences for violations. In some extreme situations, violations have been considered capital crimes.

Exchange controls have been used to limit all types of transactions, thereby controlling the supply available. This includes investments in a country.

By mid-1994, 93 countries, representing more than half of the membership of the IMF (including all the industrialized countries), had eliminated controls on current account transactions. A significant number of developing countries still maintain capital controls. The

trend toward liberalization of [developing] countries' capital accounts and international payments and transfer systems has reflected several factors. First, there is a growing recognition that exchange restrictions are an inefficient and largely ineffective way to protect the balance of payments. Second, greater flexibility and realism in exchange rate policies, and sounder macroeconomic policies, have enabled countries to restore viability in their balance of payments without incurring the inefficiencies of exchange restrictions. Third, there is evidence that eliminating exchange restrictions can increase capital inflows in the short run, and promote efficiency in the allocation of these inflows, if the liberalization is carried out in the context of a comprehensive adjustment strategy.[36]

U.S. Market Operations

As has been seen, central banks and governments have a goal of maintaining stable exchange rates even though they have floating exchange rates. The participants in the ERM are committed to maintain their rates within a specified band. This goal is equally important to the United States, even though it is not a participant in the ERM.

To stabilize a market, a government central bank or treasury must have foreign exchange available. The United States has the Exchange Stabilization Fund for this purpose. Maintained by the Department of the Treasury, this fund was established with \$2 billion of the profit created when the U.S. gold holdings were revalued from \$20.67 per ounce to \$35 per ounce on February 1, 1934,[37] thereby devaluing the dollar. It has been increased over the years from subsequent revaluations of gold, interest, and net profits from government foreign exchange operations. This fund was the core of the U.S. support program for the stabilization of the Mexican peso in 1995.

Since the government is the issuer of the nation's currency, it has an unlimited supply of its own money. To obtain foreign exchange, it can use the nation's reserves of gold and other currencies. Since 1962, many governments have established standby reciprocal currency arrangements, sometimes referred to as **"swap"** arrangements. The Federal Reserve has 15 such arrangements (exhibit 5.1) in addition to the Exchange Stabilization Fund. Either the Federal Reserve or the foreign central bank can request a drawing under these swap lines. The United States then credits the account of the foreign central bank with dollars and receives a credit of the foreign currency in the foreign country.

To strengthen their ability to counter disorderly market conditions, in recent years the central banks have held regular meetings and coordinated their efforts by joint interventions and policy statements that indicate what they expect the rate range to be. The joint policy statements have been attempts to influence the decisions of traders that rates should stay within certain limits. Unfortunately, by the mid-1990s, the success of governments in influencing foreign exchange rates for the major currencies had significantly diminished. Interventions by central banks—even when coordinated among several countries—have been overwhelmed by the size of the resources available to traders, which have grown greater than those available to central banks. Policy statements designed to change the thinking of market traders and thereby move the rates in a certain direction are often ignored.

"For the year [1994] as a whole, U.S. monetary authorities sold a total of \$3,500 million of marks and \$2,610 million of yen. . . . At year-end, the [Federal Reserve] System held foreign currencies valued at \$22,031 million at current exchange rates . . . . The System realized \$706 million in profits of foreign currency during 1994 and recorded a translation gain of \$1,717 million on foreign currency balances."[38] Such interventions in the foreign exchange markets also affect the balance of payments.

Artificial Currencies

To reduce the impact of changes, nations have found it advantageous to create artificial currencies for certain uses. These take two main forms: **baskets of currencies** and **clearing arrangements**.

A basket of currencies is a group of national currencies weighted by a specific formula. This combination may provide greater stability than would basing transactions on just one of the national currencies.

Special Drawing Rights (SDRs) were established in 1967 by the IMF to alleviate what was then perceived to be a problem of inadequate international reserves. Member countries of the IMF as well as some smaller, regional organizations agree to accept SDRs as payments and to count them in their reserves. The value of an SDR "is determined by the Fund each day by summing the values in U.S. dollars based on market exchange rates, of a basket of five specific currencies. The Fund's procedures require that the SDR valuation basket be revised each five years, and provide that the basket is to include the currencies of the members having the largest exports of goods and services during the five-year period."[39] The five currencies that make up the SDR are the U.S. dollar (39 percent), the deutsche mark (21 percent), the French franc (11

Institution	September 30, 1995
Austrian National Bank	250
National Bank of Belgium	1,000
Bank of Canada	2,000
National Bank of Denmark	250
Bank of England	3,000
Bank of France	2,000
Deutsche Bundesbank	6,000
Bank of Italy	3,000
Bank of Japan	5,000
Bank of Mexico	3,000
Netherlands Bank	500
Bank of Norway	250
Bank of Sweden	300
Swiss National Bank	4,000
Bank for International Settlements:	
Dollars against Swiss francs	600
Dollars against other authorized	
European currencies	1,250
Total	32,400

Source: *Federal Reserve Bulletin*, December 1995, p. 1083

percent), the yen (18 percent), and the pound sterling (11 percent). The total amount of SDRs allocated by the IMF in 1989 were 21.4 billion, unchanged since 1981.

To keep the national currencies of the countries of the European Union (EU) aligned with each other to facilitate trade and payments, these countries created the *European currency unit* (ECU) in 1979. "One European currency unit (ECU) equals a pocketful of the [EU] currencies. Its value is determined by taking a weighted average of the currencies of the European Monetary System (EMS). This weighting is based on each country's share of Community trade and GNP and is usually reviewed every five years."[40]

The ECU is used as an official currency to settle accounts between the member governments and is part of the reserves of member countries. The private sector uses it to denominate Eurobonds, syndicated bank loans, and other interest-bearing financial assets, and it is traded like other currencies in spot and forward foreign exchange markets.

A private ECU deposit, for example, can be created by a bank accepting currency and recording the value of the deposit in ECUs. The bank will generally wish to cover its newly created ECU liability by exchanging the currency deposited in a way that establishes an asset of the same value in terms of the ECU [or] the bank may exchange the currency deposited for the [individual] currencies in the ECU valuation basket in the same proportion (a process referred to as 'unbundling').[41]

The ECU (to be called the "Euro") will become the currency of Europe under the timetable set out in the Maastricht treaty (see pages 84-85). Planning is proceeding on the many practical problems this will involve. "These range from the mundane but emotive questions such as the design of the Euro-coinage to the mind-numbing complexities of the switchover from national currencies inside banks and other financial institutions . . . [adapting] up to 3.5 million cash dispensers in the European Union, minting of the coins and printing of the notes; and the legal difficulties involved in safeguarding business contracts previously valued in national currencies."[42] A forerunner of what would become a central bank, the European Monetary Institute, has been established in Frankfurt, Germany. The process will be complex and lengthy and is far from certain, since the preconditions set out in the Maastricht treaty are proving to be extremely difficult because of a considerable degree of hostility within the individual countries.

The ECU and the SDR differ in two main ways: "(i) the SDR basket contains the U.S. dollar and the Japanese yen, while the ECU basket does not but includes other currencies that are not in the SDR basket; and (ii) most of the currencies in the ECU basket are part of a mechanism designed specifically to stabilize exchange rates among the participating currencies, while the currencies in the SDR basket are generally not related by such a mechanism."[43] The deutsche mark, French franc, and pound sterling are in both baskets.

In addition to the needs of countries for such artificial currencies, companies with worldwide operations also have the problem of settling accounts between subsidiaries. Since many intracompany payments net out, it is usually impractical to settle each transaction by market trading. The companies or subsidiaries "could agree to trade in the dollar, the D-mark or yen, or for intracompany trade in an invented currency. Intraflora, for example, an international say-it-with-flowers company, has an internal currency, the fleurin (based on the Swiss franc and made up of 100 petals)." Other companies use the ECU. "This cuts conversion costs, since for internal trade each subsidiary is only dealing with two currencies, its own and the ECU."[44]

In an effort to keep their trade in relative balance with each other, often in conjunction with barter agreements, some countries have established *clearing* arrangements. These essentially require that all trade transactions between two countries are to be paid through special accounts in their central banks. The agreement specifies the maximum credit that can build up in each account.

For example, country A can buy goods from country B up to a certain amount. When that amount is reached, country A cannot buy any more until country B buys something from it. This effectively binds the two countries to trade with each other, and the trade is paid for through special accounts, not with a major currency like dollars. If country B bought goods from country A and had to pay in dollars, country A would be free to spend the dollars on purchases from country C. Country B would not be exporting and soon could run out of dollars and be unable to buy from anyone. The clearing arrangement solves this problem.

Beginning in 1949, the countries of the Soviet bloc (the USSR, the countries of Eastern Europe, Cuba, Mongolia, and Vietnam) were linked in such a clearing agreement: the Council for Mutual Economic Assistance (COMECON). Their currencies were not traded outside of this sphere and all had artificial values arbitrarily assigned to them. Thus the trade between them could be conducted only through such a clearing arrangement. The collapse of the Soviet bloc effectively ended the COMECON by 1990. This contributed to the massive shocks to the economies of the other member countries. The patterns of their trade drastically changed, and for some, their trade with countries outside of that region jumped from single digits to over 50 percent of their total trade.

Accounting

Foreign exchange contracts are reflected in a bank's balance sheet as contingent accounts. The Risk-Based Capital Guidelines specify that outstanding contracts be included in calculating the capital ratio. Contracts of fewer than 14 days are excluded. The remaining ones are then revalued based on the current market price. This is added to a factor for potential credit exposure increases by multiplying the total national value of the contracts by one of the following credit conversion factors: remaining maturity of one year or less, 1 percent; over one year, 5 percent. Contracts with the same party can be netted out under certain conditions.

Summary

The ability of money to flow freely from country to country has created massive trading markets in terms of the number of participants, volume, and values. The participants have widely varying objectives. For those whose underlying business needs would benefit from stable rates of exchange, the market can create problems with great impact on their operations. This volatility and freedom has attracted not only those who need the currency of another country for their basic business objectives, but also those who seek

to profit from the many forces affecting rates of exchange.

The foreign exchange market is described now as "an oceanic tide of 'stateless' money that broke free from national borders in the 1980s financial revolution . . . surging unanchored through integrated private financial markets across sovereign borders at lightning-fast speed and volatility, altering national interest rate levels, currency values, employment, savings and investment patterns, growth rates and everyday human lives as it came and went." [45] It is a complex situation that governments and their principal agents—their central banks—have been unable to control in recent years.

The endeavor to create a single currency in the European market to replace the multiple national currencies would reduce the risks that now exist. It is, however, being seen as an extremely difficult operational and political problem and its success is by no means certain.

Historians have noted the parallels of the goals of the Maastricht agreement of 1991 with the year 794 when Charlemagne's previous victories

had given him control of an empire stretching from modern day Austria to the Atlantic. . . . He was fascinated by economic policy and the value of his coinage. . . . 'As regards denarii . . . you should be fully aware of our decree that everywhere, in every city and every trading place, the new denarii are also the legal tender and to be accepted by everybody. And if they bear the monogram of our name and are of pure silver and full weight, should anyone reject them, in any place, in any transaction or purchase or sale, he is to pay 15 solidi [roughly the price of a cartload of wheat].' . . . For the first time since Roman days Europe's coins were minted with uniform designs. . . . The new money was widely accepted, as if some European monetary system existed.[46]

Questions

1. What is the impact of the ERM?
2. What are exchange controls and why are they used?
3. What is an ECU?
4. Why does interest-rate arbitrage occur?

Problem

You are a U.S. corporate treasurer. You have $10 million to invest for the next ninety days, after which you will need the dollars to pay the quarterly dividend. Examine the foreign exchange and U.S. Treasury bill rates in the newspaper or *The Wall Street Journal*. Consider the yen and the deutsche mark. If you were to invest in a ninety-day government bill in each of these countries on a hedged basis,

1. how much would you gain or lose in the swap?
2. what would the yield on the foreign government bill need to be to make it more attractive to you than investing in a U.S. Treasury bill?

Your objective is the highest rate of return fully hedged between these government-backed investments.

Notes

1. *Financial Times*, April 14, 1995
2. Barry Eichengreen, *Golden Fetters* (New York: Oxford University Press, 1992), p. 29
3. David Marsh, *The Bundesbank: The Bank that Rules Europe* (London: William Heinemann Ltd., 1992), p. 29
4. *The Institutional Investor*, September 1974, p. 101
5. *The Economist*, February 6, 1993, p. 51
6. Tim Hindle, *Pocket Banker* (Oxford: Basil Blackwell and *The Economist*, 1983), p. 66
7. International Monetary Fund, *Annual Report 1992*, (Washington, D.C.: International Monetary Fund, 1992), p. 46
8. *The New York Times*, January 21, 1993
9. Marsh, *The Bundesbank*, p. 15
10. Ibid., p. 25
11. Ibid., p. 269
12. Ibid, p. 206 (also chapter 8)
13. Ibid., p. 11
14. Ibid., p. 10
15. Ibid., p. 17
16. *The Economist*, January 30, 1993, p. 21
17. *Federal Reserve Bulletin*, January 1993, p. 12
18. *The New York Times*, September 19, 1992
19. See Juann Hung, "Assessing the Exchange Rate's Impact on U.S. Manufacturing Profits," *Federal Reserve Bank of New York Quarterly Review*, Winter 1992-1993, pp. 44-63
20. *The Economist*, August 15, 1992, p. 61
21. *The Economist*, April 15, 1995, p. 14 and April 29, 1995, p. 7; *The New York Times*, June 9, 1995, p. C1, *Financial Times,* October 24, 1995, p. 6
22. *The Economist*, August 15, 1992, p. 61
23. *The Economist*, December 22, 1990, p. 114
24. International Monetary Fund, *World Economic Outlook: Interim Assessment January 1993* (Washington, D.C.: International Monetary Fund, 1993), p. 1
25. Extracted from Ibid., pp. 2-3
26. *Financial Times*, September 17, 1992
27. Ibid.

28. International Monetary Fund, *World Economic Outlook*, p. 5

29. *The New York Times*, January 21, 1993

30. *The Economist*, February 20, 1993, p. 110

31. "Albania Secures $500m Debt Deal," *Financial Times*, May 12, 1995, p. 2

32. *The Economist*, July 10, 1993

33. International Monetary Fund, *op.cit.,* p. 27

34. *The New York Times*, February 5, 1993

35. United States General Accounting Office, *Financial Derivatives* (Washington, D.C.: May 1994) p. 27

36. International Monetary Fund, *World Economic Outlook October 1994* (Washington, D.C.: International Monetary Fund, 1994) p. 56

37. Milton Friedman and Anna Jacobson Schwartz, *A Monetary History of the United States, 1867-1960* (Princeton, N.J.: Princeton University Press, 1963), p. 471

38. Board of Governors of the Federal Reserve System, *Annual Report* 1994, (Washington, D.C.: Federal Reserve System, 1994), p. 41

39. International Monetary Fund *Annual Report*, 1989, (Washington, D.C.: International Monetary Fund, 1989), p. 119

40. *The Economist*, September 9, 1989, p. 120

41. International Monetary Fund, "The Role of the SDR in the International Monetary System," Occasional Paper No. 51 (Washington, D.C.: International Monetary Fund, 1987), p. 36

42. Lionel Barber, "Eurocrat Determined to Make EMU Fly," *Financial Times*, May 9, 1995

43. International Monetary Fund, "The Role of the SDR," pp. 30-31

44. *The Economist*, January 13, 1990, p. 76

45. Steven Solomon, *The Confidence Game* (New York: Simon & Schuster, 1995), p. 14

46. *The Economist*, August 14, 1993

III

GLOBAL TRADE

In 1962, President John F. Kennedy said that "trade and competition and innovation have long been a significant part of the American character. . . . The Founding Fathers—Washington, Jefferson, Adams, Franklin—were men of trade as well as men of affairs. For trade represents widening horizons." [1] More than forty years before, President Woodrow Wilson's Fourteen Points to set the goals for the post–World War I peace had acknowledged the importance of world trade. His third point contemplated the "establishment of an equality of trade conditions among all the nations." [2]

Trade is the origin of global banking. It preceded the creation of nations, laws, and money. "The evidence from anthropology now suggests that trade is one of the oldest human traits, inherent in our nature in the same way as language is." [3] Trade even in the Stone Age was not a single step that began and ended just between immediate consumers, but also was goods moving along a chain from one group to another and then to another and another with each benefitting. "Trade, specialization, the division of labour, and sophisticated systems of barter exchange were already part of a hunter-gathering life." [4]

By the eleventh century, trade was being conducted over such great distances that there was need for organization. This led merchants to develop laws and rules of procedure between themselves. "A merchant in a foreign country had no recourse to his sovereign if cheated—and no confidence that the same standards applied there as at home. So merchants began to get together and formulate the rules of the game. The *lex mercatoria* [mercantile law] was born. It had no recognition from the state. It was voluntarily produced, voluntarily adjudicated and voluntarily enforced." [5] It worked on the simple principle that if a merchant or trader would not conduct business fairly within the commonly agreed-upon rules, the other traders would not deal with him, and he would be out of business.

Since the founding of the United States, U.S. policy toward international trade has moved from protectionism toward free trade. High tariffs were initially supported to allow the development of industry and the growth of agriculture and then to protect the wages of American workers. Tariffs were important sources of revenue before the federal income tax became law in 1913, accounting in 1860 for almost 95 percent of the total federal revenue. (By 1992, customs duties were less than 2 percent of that.) The policy shifted toward lower tariffs and freer trade in the decade after the passage of the Smoot-Hawley Tariff of 1930 which has been perceived since then as having raised U.S. tariffs to an artificially high level and has become a symbol of public policy failure. "Every president from Franklin Roosevelt to Bill Clinton chose to endorse [the] liberalization agenda [of former Secretary of State Cordell Hull] that 'unhampered trade dovetailed with peace; high tariffs, trade barriers, and unfair economic competition, with war'." [6]

The U.S. government, like most other national governments, takes an active interest in the promotion of trade. It does this in two general ways, by providing financing beyond what commercial banks can do and establishing policies to support U.S. businesses in fair and equal opportunity. The former will be examined in chapter 12. The latter is accomplished through programs affecting tariffs, quotas, and terms of trade with other nations.

The U.S. Congress was the principal agency for establishing the levels of tariffs until the 1930s. After that became a domestic political quagmire, tariff negotiations moved to the State Department. In the 1960s, Congress authorized the establishment of a special trade representative, with the rank of ambassador, as part of the Executive Branch.

"Today, the occupant of the Office of the U.S. Trade Representative, or USTR, is the president's chief action officer on almost all trade matters. The decisions made by the trade representative affect the livelihoods of workers in the United States and abroad, the profits of the smallest factories as well as the multinational corporations, and competition between the United States and other major industrial powers." [7] The USTR has been the focal point for the reciprocal reduction of tariffs and trade barriers as well as the fight for equal access for U.S. business to the markets of other countries, particularly the largest industrial ones. This has sometimes involved very contentious disputes, where political forces competed with economic issues.

The expansion of trade led, as was seen in the previous section, to the development of global payments and global banking. As trade needs became greater, early in the development of global banking, traders looked to banks not only to make payments, but also to handle the transfer of documents, arrange financing, and get credit information from distant places. In this way, trade could occur between merchants and traders in various countries with different economic conditions and different financial capabilities.

In spite of the modern growth of electronic systems, much of international trade still relies on the movement of pieces of paper. This is partly due to the lag in changes in the legal systems in various countries, and also the widely differing levels of computer and electronic capabilities among trading countries. Thus, even in the late 1990s, the banker involved in global trade is moving documents between seller and buyer to convey title to the goods, protect the goods, and identify the goods.

Chapter 6, The Business of Foreign Trade, begins with an overview of the documents and principles common to a bank's participation in global trade. Echos of the history of trade appear in many ways, such as the standardization of accepted procedures through international business organizations. That chapter explores several options for linking the movement of goods with payment that rely on the growing involvement of banks. In chapter 7, The Basic Commercial Letter of Credit, and chapter 8, Letter of Credit Variations, details of the commercial letter of credit are examined. The letter of credit is possibly the most important means of conducting global trade that depends on banks committing their financial resources. Chapter 9 discusses the bankers' acceptance, a unique means of financing this trade. It, too, has origins that go back centuries, from Italian bankers through the City of London and the "bill on London." The bankers' acceptance played a vital role in the expansion of global trade, with the London banker providing the credit to the buyer and assuring the seller halfway around the globe of payment.

Notes

1. Steve Dryden, *Trade Warriors: USTR and the American Crusade for Free Trade* (New York: Oxford University Press, 1995), p. 3

2. *The New Encyclopedia Britannica*, 15th ed., s.v.

3. Matt Ridley, "Trade—Almost the Oldest Human Urge," *Financial Times*, July 1, 1995, section 2.I

4. Ibid.

5. Ibid.

6. Alfred E. Eckes, Jr., *Opening America's Markets: U.S. Trade Policy since 1776* (Chapel Hill: University of North Carolina Press, 1995), p. 282

7. Dryden, *Trade Warriors*, p. 6

6

THE BUSINESS OF FOREIGN TRADE

Learning Objectives

After studying this chapter, you will be able to

- outline alternative ways to make payment for international trade
- describe three of these methods in detail
- identify the key documents for foreign trade
- explain the use of trade terms

Overview

Within the balance of payments of nearly every country, the largest amount reflects the exports and imports of merchandise. It is not surprising, therefore, that most commercial banks commit the largest portion of their operational staff to meeting the needs of their customers in this business. Bankers have followed business overseas and developed services to meet business needs there. As commodities and manufactured merchandise move from country to country in the channels of international trade, they are being financed by either the seller, the buyer, the bank of the buyer, the bank of the seller, or by another bank. This process is sometimes called **trade financing**.

The movement of goods in international trade develops from a business transaction between a buyer in one country and a seller in another country. An integral part of the transaction is the means by which the buyer will pay the seller. Because of the distances involved, as well as differences in legal, political, and business practices, both parties need to evaluate alternative methods of payment in order to select the one most appropriate for their transaction.

Regardless of the option selected for payment, international trade involves documents. Their form, type, and number may vary, depending on the means of payment and the needs of the transaction.

This chapter introduces various alternatives for financing international trade and examines the documents of international trade. These documents are common to all trade and, as will be seen in following chapters, provide the basis on which banks enter into the trade financing process.

The Contract

Trade transactions begin with negotiations between a buyer and a seller. The negotiations can be brief, with the buyer simply ordering from a catalog, or they can be lengthy, as with the ordering of special machinery. The bank is *not* a party to this contract, nor does it participate in its negotiation.

Both the buyer and the seller have their own objectives. The importer wishes to obtain merchandise that can be sold at a profit in his business, acquire raw materials or manufactured goods for processing into his own product, or get something that is more innovative, specialized, or cheaper than can be bought elsewhere. The exporter wishes to sell her product to make a profit. Thus the completion of the transaction represented by the contract is important for both of them.

At some point in the negotiation, the buyer and seller must decide how and when the required payment is to be made. In a domestic transaction, this is simple: The buyer examines the merchandise; if he likes it, he pays for it, puts it in the truck, and drives away.

Because the international buyer and seller are a considerable distance apart, the decision about the means and timing of payment versus delivery of the goods becomes more complex. A number of factors affect this decision: the extent of competition from other sellers, availability of other buyers, payment restrictions between the two countries, reputation of the buyer and seller, and customary practices in the particular industry. Negotiations for the merchandise contract can be concluded only after the buyer and seller agree on a mutually acceptable means of payment.

The general payment options are prepayment by the buyer, open account shipment by the seller, collection, or letter of credit. There are variations within each of these categories, such as progress payments or time drafts within collections and letters of credit. Even though these payment alternatives pose different procedures and concerns to the banker, in and of themselves they are of little concern to the customer whose single interest is how to make the payment without jeopardizing the transaction, which both the buyer and seller want to complete because each benefits from it.

Prepayment (Cash in Advance)

In this case, the seller demands that the buyer pay for the merchandise in advance of the shipment. The buyer could agree to this when there is a heavy demand for the seller's merchandise from other buyers, when there is a small buyer and a large seller, or when the buyer has a poor or unknown credit reputation. Prepayment ("cash in advance") by the buyer eliminates all risk to the seller, who is in possession of the full payment before shipping the merchandise. Conversely, prepayment is very disadvantageous to the buyer, who runs the risk that the seller will not ship the ordered goods promptly, or perhaps not at all. The buyer bears the cost associated with having the use of neither the money nor the merchandise for the time it takes to complete the shipment.

The bank assists in a prepayment transaction by transferring funds on the order of the buyer to the seller through a foreign draft or some other means of money transfer. The bank may also be involved in obtaining credit information about the buyer, which may induce the seller to insist on prepayment before making the sale, or credit information about the seller, which may encourage the buyer to make the prepayment in the strong expectation that the seller will promptly make the shipment.

Open Account

In this option, the buyer insists that the merchandise be shipped and that the seller then send the buyer a bill. The buyer pays this bill after the merchandise is received and found to be satisfac-

tory. A sale on open account would be made when the credit reputation of the buyer is good, so that the seller can be confident of receiving prompt payment, or when a small seller and a large buyer are doing business. In some cases, the seller would agree to making the shipment on open account when there is considerable competition from other sellers—but even in this situation, a seller would hesitate to make a shipment on open account to a buyer with a poor credit reputation.

Of all the means of payment, a sale on open account is the most advantageous to the buyer, who does not have to pay any money until the merchandise has arrived. The risks lie with the seller, who must bear all the costs in giving up the merchandise, making the shipment, and then waiting for payment. If the buyer is slow in paying or completely fails to pay, then the seller's only recourse is legal action. This can be difficult, since it must take place in another country with differing legal standards and practices, and it can be expensive. In addition, the seller carries all risks of foreign exchange restrictions in the buyer's country. Also, an honest buyer may be restricted by his own country from making a payment to another country.

The bank would participate in an open account transaction with exactly the same services listed for prepayment: credit checks and transferring funds on the order of the buyer.

Collection and Letter of Credit

Both the collection and letter of credit means of paying for the import-export transaction require the bank to act as an intermediary in coordinating the exchange of pertinent documents for payment. A discussion of those documents is necessary before proceeding with an examination of the collection in this chapter, and the letter of credit in the next two chapters.

Documents

Banks deal only in documents and are not responsible for any disputes over the quantity or quality of the goods. While foreign trade is concerned with the movement of merchandise from one country to another, it is accompanied by a flow of documents that convey ownership of the merchandise and then record and facilitate its departure from, and arrival in, the respective countries. Foreign trade documents enable each country to compute the impact on its own balance of payments. The documents are also the means by which the banker participates in the trade transaction, either as agent or financier of the buyer or seller. The bank may also extend credit to enable the shipment to be prepared or in anticipation of the payment.

Transport Document

One of the most important documents in international trade is the **transport document** (see exhibit 6.1), which is issued by a transportation company when moving the merchandise from the seller to the buyer. Shipment may be by ocean transport (in which the transport document is called a *marine* or *ocean bill of lading*), air (*air waybill*), rail (*rail bill of lading*), truck (*truck bill of lading*), or through the mails (*certificate of posting* or *post receipt*). Each of these has different legal characteristics. The transport document may be a receipt for the goods, a contract for delivery, or a title document.

An ocean bill of lading is for the transport of the merchandise from one port to another port. A combined form may be used when the merchandise must move, for example, by truck and then be transferred to an ocean vessel. In such a case, the transport document is called a *multimodal bill of lading*. Because most foreign trade moves by ocean vessel, the ocean bill of lading

is the most common and will therefore be used as the example in this discussion. The ocean bill of lading has the means to convey title to the goods shipped. Uniformity of the law on ocean bills of lading was achieved through an international convention in The Hague in 1921; the resulting document, known as the Hague Rules, is now accepted by the leading maritime nations.

When the exporter is ready to make the shipment, the merchandise must be packed so that it will arrive in good condition, taking into account the special problems of international shipment:

> There are four problems that must be kept in mind ... breakage, weight, moisture, and pilferage. Besides the normal handling encountered in domestic transportation, an export order moving by ocean freight will be loaded aboard vessels by a sling, in a net with other items, by conveyor, chute, or other method, putting added strain on the package. In the ship's hold, cargo may be stacked on top of the crate or come into violent contact with it during the course of the voyage. Overseas, handling facilities may not be as sophisticated as in the United States; the cargo may be dragged, pushed, rolled, or dropped during unloading, while moving through customs, or in transit to the final destination. Moisture is a constant problem since cargo is subject to condensation even in the hold of a ship equipped with air conditioning and a dehumidifier. The cargo may also be unloaded in the rain and many foreign ports do not have covered storage facilities. . . . Theft and pilferage are constant threats.[1]

When the merchandise is packed, an exporter delivers it to a shipping company to be conveyed to a foreign buyer. The bill of lading is then

Exhibit 6.1   Transport Document

FORM-1212
J.T.C. 1-66-REV.

States Marine-Isthmian Agency, Inc.
AS AGENT FOR CARRIER INDICATED BELOW

DELIVERING CARRIER TO STEAMER — CAR NUMBER–REFERENCE

FORWARDING AGENT - REFERENCES — EXPORT DEC. NO.

BILL OF LADING
(SHORT FORM INCORPORATING TERMS OF LONG FORM)
(CONTRACT TERMS CONTINUED FROM OVERPAGE)

SHIPPER

Richard Sargeant Design Associates

CONSIGNED TO
ORDER OF   Happy Village Toy Shop

ADDRESS ARRIVAL NOTICE TO — ALSO NOTIFY

Happy Village Toy Shop
25 Spring Tree Lane
London   W.8

VESSEL   Garden State   VOYAGE NO.   FLAG   PIER   PORT OF LOADING   New York

PORT OF DISCHARGE (Where goods are to be delivered to consignee or on-carrier)   Southampton

PARTICULARS FURNISHED BY SHIPPER

MARKS AND NUMBERS	NO. OF PKGS.	DESCRIPTION OF PACKAGES AND GOODS	MEASURE-MENT	GROSS WEIGHT
A2 180/1-10	10	Boxes toys 2 boxes torn L.S.T	80 cu.ft.	320 lbs.

Received on Board

APR 11, 19xx

STATES MARINE-ISTHMIAN
AGENCY, INC.

By L. S. T.

SPECIMEN

ALL CHARGES EX SHIP'S TACKLE FOR ACCOUNT OF CARGO

CARRIER: *States Marine Lines, Inc.* ●   ISTHMIAN LINES, INC. ○   ○

_____ @ _____ $ _____
_____ @ _____ $ _____
_____ @ _____ $ _____
_____ @ _____ $ _____
_____ @ _____ $ _____
_____ @ _____ $ _____

(CHECK ONE OR BOTH)

In witness whereof, the carrier by its Agent has signed three Bills of Lading, all of the same Tenor and date, one of which being accomplished, the others to stand void.

Dated At: NEW YORK, N.Y.

To Be Paid At: _____

To Be PREPAID	T O T A L	$	BILL OF LADING NUMBER	DATE
COLLECT		$	3 94670	4-10-—

FOR THE MASTER *States Marine-Isthmian Agency, Inc.*

By: L. S. Tydings

prepared based on information given by the exporter (who obtained most of that information during negotiations with the importer), signed by the shipping company, and given to the exporter. This document is a receipt that the shipping company has received the goods. It is also a contract for the delivery of the goods to the foreign buyer or others, and it indicates the shipping company's terms and conditions for performing this service, specifies both the weight and dimensions of the cargo, details the charges for the shipment, and shows the shipping marks

of the crates. The shipping marks on the crates are usually specified by the buyer to facilitate identification on arrival as well as to help the shipping company identify the cargo for unloading at the proper port. To avoid pilferage en route, these marks should avoid identifying the contents. In some cases, the exporter may hire the services of a specialized freight forwarding agent to arrange many of these details. Exporters today often use various types of *containers*. These are large metal enclosures that are packed, sealed, and delivered to the shipping company.

Trade Financing in Renaissance Italy

The businessmen and bankers of northern Italy's Renaissance city-state—particularly Genoa, Florence, and Venice—developed many of the fundamental practices of modern finance. Their innovations included double-entry bookkeeping, and the provision of credit through discounted promissory notes. One of their most important innovations, however, was trade credit.

Suppose that a Florentine textile manufacturer received a potentially profitable order from Barcelona and had the means to fill it. Two things might keep him from accepting the business. First, the importer might not pay until he received the goods—perhaps not even until he had sold them. Meanwhile, the exporter would have to pay for materials, labor, storage, and shipment. Second, having produced and shipped his goods, the exporter would have to bear the risk that the importer might simply fail to pay. And there was no court to which the exporter could take the Barcelona merchant.

Commercial banks—that is, banks which specialize in financing commerce—came into being to solve such problems. By providing short-term finance (working capital), commercial banks enabled such merchants to pay for the materials and labor in advance. They solved the second problem by having trusted agents in major cities. For a fee, the bank would pay the exporter as soon as the

shipment embarked. The importer would then pay the bank's agent—adding a fee—when the shipment arrived. For an additional fee the same bank might even insure the shipment.

Over time, the Italian banks developed this vital trade-financing function. The leading Florentine banking family, the Medici, acquired agents or correspondents in Europe's trading cities and made itself indispensable in the continent's commerce. Probably in the thirteenth or fourteenth century, the bankers invented a variation that limited the degree to which their own capital was tied up over the course of the transaction. This was the "acceptance," or "four-name paper." The Barcelona agent (name 1) would sign a document "accepting" the liability of the importer (name 2) to the exporter (name 3), and the document would be conveyed to the banker in Florence (name 4). The banker would disburse (after subtracting a discount) to the exporter against this acceptance. The banker could then sell the acceptance at a discount in the Florentine financial market and thus replace most or all of the cash the banker had disbursed. After some weeks the importer would pay the agent, the agent would pay the bank, and the bank would repurchase the acceptance, concluding the operation.

Reprinted, with permission, from The World Bank, *World Development Report 1989* (New York: Oxford University Press, 1989), p. 43.

Ocean bills of lading fall into two general categories: *received for shipment* and *on board* bills of lading. The former is a receipt acknowledging that the shipping company has received the stated merchandise for transit on a specific vessel. The latter means not only that the cargo has been received but also that the goods are actually loaded on board the vessel indicated. The on board bill of lading is usually preferred because it ensures that the cargo is on the vessel, eliminating possible oversight by the shipping company.

The bill of lading specifies who is to receive the merchandise when the vessel arrives at the designated foreign port. These instructions are given by the exporter. If he directs the shipping company to deliver the shipment ("consigns") directly to the buyer, this bill of lading cannot be transferred. This is not usually desirable in a letter of credit or collection, since it would permit the buyer to obtain possession of the merchandise without regard to any bank arrangement for payment. The seller usually instructs the shipping company that the goods are "consigned to the order of the shipper." This is an example of an *order* or *negotiable bill of lading*. In this form, the bill of lading requires that evidence be presented to the shipping company at the port of unloading as to who is to receive the goods. The bill of lading is the required evidence, so that anyone in possession of an order bill of lading can obtain the merchandise. If a letter of credit instructs that the bills of lading, when issued by the shipping company, be "consigned to order of shipper," then the shipper (the exporter) can endorse them, just as one would a check. The bill is then in negotiable form, and its transfer conveys title to the goods. In these cases, title to the goods, in effect, goes with possession of the bill of lading. The shipping agent at the foreign port will release the merchandise to anyone who presents this bill of lading.

Bills of lading may be issued in multiple originals. This is a carryover from the days when sets of documents were split so that a portion went by immediate mail and the other portion by a subsequent mail, or even on board the same ship with the cargo, to ensure that at least one set would get through. Today there is strong trade sentiment to eliminate multiple originals and have only one original bill of lading. When any one of these originals is "accomplished"—that is, presented to the shipping company at the end of the voyage—the others become void. It is important, therefore, that a bank paying or negotiating under a commercial letter of credit or acting as agent in a collection have all the originals (*full set*) issued by the shipping company.

The bill of lading itself indicates the number of originals issued. In addition to the originals, the shipping company may issue any number of nonnegotiable copies of the bill of lading.

Trade transactions usually require "clean" bills of lading. This means that the merchandise was received by the shipping company in apparent good order—that is, the packing crates did not appear to be damaged, leaking, or insecurely fastened. If any of these conditions did exist, the shipping company, to protect itself against a claim for damage in transit, would note the condition on the bill of lading, and such a bill of lading would be called a "foul," "dirty," or "unclean" bill of lading. It would not be acceptable as a "clean" bill of lading.

The bills of lading described here are issued by a shipping company operating on regular routes and accepting cargo from many shippers; such ships are referred to as "liner vessels." In some cases, the exporter or other party may rent the use of an entire vessel and then specify the route. This could occur when an exporter is shipping bulk commodities such as petroleum or grain. A bill of lading issued by such a *charter party* must be especially permitted whenever a letter of credit is used, since the seller or buyer is also the issuer of the shipping contract.

It is assumed that marine bills of lading cover transportation by an engine-driven vessel. If it is under sail power, however, then a special notation is required.

Insurance

All merchandise, no matter what means of transport is used, should be covered by insurance. Depending on the terms of the merchandise contract, insurance will be obtained by either the importer or the exporter, many of whom maintain *open* or *floating policies* to cover all shipments under which they obtain certificates for specific shipments. Proper insurance coverage provides protection not only to the buyer and the seller of the goods, but also to any banks financing the shipment.

Marine insurance covers merchandise transported on an ocean vessel. This is a vast subject and has evolved over a long time. Since most international trade moves by ocean transport, the following describes marine insurance. Insurance for other transport means has different characteristics.

Marine insurance policies (exhibit 6.2) have described themselves as "covering the adventures and perils of the seas." The most obvious peril is that the ship may sink. This is a recognized risk, and all parties to foreign trade want to purchase protection against total loss of goods in this way.

Even if a vessel does not sink, there are other risks to which the cargo is exposed during an ocean voyage. Maritime law considers the diverse shippers who entrust their cargo to a particular vessel to be joined in a common enterprise. It is the responsibility of the captain of the vessel to serve that common undertaking. For example, if the ship encounters a storm at sea and is in danger of sinking, the captain must do whatever he can to save the vessel and the cargo. If, to save the vessel and most of the cargo, he has to jettison some of the cargo, he has full authority to do so. When the vessel arrives safely in port, those shippers whose cargo got through safely must reimburse those whose cargo was sacrificed to save the common venture. This charge is known as *general average* and should be prudently insured against.

The origin of this concept can be traced back to the evolution of the shipping industry. In the twelfth and thirteenth centuries, "the merchant vessel originally sailed . . . as a joint venture. It was the property of a small group of users. . . . Each one would have an allotted place on board where he could load his own merchandise. . . . On board, too, everyone took his turn, whether in navigation, watching, or chores. . . . The actual sailing was handled by three officers . . . [who were] paid a wage by the group of proprietors and placed under the command of the master who was chosen from among the co-owners." [2]

Other marine risks include damage to the individual cargo, such as that caused by water dripping on crates from pipes that leak or sweat; damage arising from a strike, riot, or similar civil commotion that could damage part of the vessel and its cargo while the vessel is in port; and cargo damage as a consequence of the vessel colliding with another vessel. Most of these can be covered in a policy against "all risks." A specific protection that requires an added premium payment is coverage for a vessel going into a war zone and for any resulting damage. It is important to the exporter, the importer, and the banker financing the transaction that the insurance be transferable and that it be written by reliable companies.

Exhibit 6.2   Marine Insurance Policy

CARGO   *POLICY OF INSURANCE*   Printed in U.S.A.

General Assurance

1256 Fifth Avenue, New York N.Y.

Nº 593598

$ 16,500.00   February 15 _____ 19--

This Policy of Insurance Witnesseth, that on 15th day of February, 19-- and in consideration of premiums as agreed to be paid, these Assurers
did make Insurance and cause Walter Division, Lark Company, New York to be Insured,
lost or not lost, for account of whom it may concern,
In the sum of Sixteen thousand five hundred and no/100 - - - - - - - - - - - - - - - Dollars
On 4000 packages cigarette paper

under deck. Valued at sum insured.

Shipped on Board S.S. International
At and From New York   via   New York
To Callao
Loss, if any, Payable to .assured   or Order,
upon surrender of this Policy, without deduction (as against purchasers or pledgees of the goods) for unpaid premiums, and when so paid
liability under this insurance is discharged.

1. Touching the adventures and perils which said Assurers are contented to bear, and take upon themselves, in this voyage, they are of the seas, fires, rovers, assailing thieves, jettisons, barratry of the Master and Mariners, and all other like perils, losses and misfortunes that have or shall come to the hurt, detriment or damage of the said goods and merchandise, or any part thereof except as may be otherwise provided for herein or endorsed hereon.
2. In case of any loss or misfortune, it shall be lawful and necessary to and for the Assured, his or their factors, servants and assigns, to sue, labor and travel for, in and about the defense, safeguard and recovery of the said goods and merchandise, or any part thereof, without prejudice to this insurance; nor shall the acts of the Assured or Assurers, in recovering, saving and preserving the property insured, in case of disaster, be considered a waiver or an acceptance of an abandonment; to the charges whereof, the said Assurers will contribute according to the rate and quantity of the sum hereby insured.
3. In case the interest hereby insured is covered by other insurance (except as hereinafter provided) the loss shall be collected from the several policies in the order of the date of their attachment, insurance attaching on the same date to be deemed simultaneous and to contribute pro rata; PROVIDED, however, that where any fire insurance, or any insurance (including fire) taken out by any carrier or bailee is available to the beneficiary of this policy, or would be so available if this insurance did not exist, then this insurance shall be void to the extent that such other insurance is or would have been available. It is agreed, nevertheless, that where these Assurers are thus relieved of liability because of the existence of other insurance, these Assurers shall receive and retain the premium payable under this policy and, in consideration thereof, shall guarantee the solvency of the companies and/or underwriters who issued such other insurance and the prompt collection of the loss thereunder to the same extent (only) as these Assurers shall have been relieved of liability under the terms of this clause, but not exceeding, in any case, the amount which would have been collectible under this policy if such other insurance did not exist.
4. This insurance attaches from the time the goods leave the Warehouse and/or Store at the place named in the policy for the commencement of the transit and continues during the ordinary course of transit, including customary transhipment if any, until the goods are discharged overside from the overseas vessel at the final port. Thereafter the insurance continues whilst the goods are in transit and/or awaiting transit until delivered to final warehouse at the destination named in the policy or until the expiry of 15 days (or 30 days if the destination to which the goods are insured is outside the limits of the port) whichever shall first occur. The time limits referred to above to be reckoned from midnight of the day on which the discharge overside of the goods hereby insured from the overseas vessel is completed. Held covered at a premium to be arranged in the event of transhipment, if any, other than as above and/or in the event of delay in excess of the above time limits arising from circumstances beyond the control of the Assured.
NOTE: It is necessary for the Assured to give prompt notice to these Assurers when they become aware of an event for which they are "held covered" under this policy and the right to such cover is dependent on compliance with this obligation.
5. Including transit by craft and/or lighter to and from the vessel. Each craft and/or lighter to be deemed a separate insurance. The Assured are not to be prejudiced by any agreement exempting lightermen from liability.
6. This insurance shall not be vitiated by any unintentional error in description of vessel, voyage or interest, or by deviation, over-carriage, change of voyage, transhipment or any other interruption of the ordinary course of transit, from causes beyond the control of the Assured. It is agreed, however, that any such error, deviation or other occurrence mentioned above shall be reported to this Company as soon as known to the Assured, and additional premium paid if required.
7. Warranted free from Particular Average unless the vessel or craft be stranded, sunk, or burnt, but notwithstanding this warranty these Assurers are to pay any loss of or damage to the interest insured which may reasonably be attributed to fire, collision or contact of the vessel and/or craft and/or conveyance with any external substance (ice included) other than water, or to discharge of cargo at port of distress. *The foregoing warranty, however, shall not apply where broader terms of Average are provided for herein or in the certificate or policy to which these clauses are attached.*
8. Notwithstanding any average warranty contained herein, these Assurers agree to pay any landing, warehousing, forwarding and special charges for which this policy in the absence of such warranty would be liable. Also to pay the insured value of any package or packages which may be totally lost in loading, transhipment or discharge.
                Additional clauses appear on the reverse side of this Policy

MARKS AND NUMBERS	SPECIAL CONDITIONS
NTC LIMA	Subject to particular average if amounting to 3%.

Provisions Required by Law to be Stated in this Policy.—This policy is in a stock corporation.

IN WITNESS WHEREOF, this Company has executed and attested these
presents; but this policy shall not be valid unless countersigned by the duly authorized Agent of this Company.
    Countersigned by
APPLETON & COX, Inc., Attorney

By _Samuel B. Cox_
           Vice-President

General Assurance Corporation

Owen E. Barker
               President
E. A. Peterson
               Secretary

F221-500-10-62   In case of loss or damage, please follow IMPORTANT Instructions on reverse side of this Policy.

ORIGINAL (ORIGINAL AND DUPLICATE ISSUED ONE OF WHICH BEING ACCOMPLISHED THE OTHER TO STAND VOID.)

Invoice

The seller prepares and presents a statement to the buyer describing what has been sold, the price, and other details. This is an *invoice* (exhibit 6.3), and it is usually prepared on a form printed with the seller's name. It includes the full name and address of the buyer and seller, any contract or order reference numbers, date of order, shipping date, description of the merchandise, price, and other information. Some countries require that invoices be presented to their consular official or some other agency in the area of the seller. The consular official examines them and then stamps and signs them. This is a *visaed* or *consularized* commercial invoice. Some countries require a consular invoice in their language to speed customs clearance at the destination and to provide statistical information.

Other Documents

Depending on the characteristics of the merchandise, the needs of the buyer, or government regulations in either the importing or exporting country, other documents may be prepared. Some of these are:

- A *certificate of origin* establishes where the goods were grown or manufactured. This is particularly necessary if the importing country has different tariffs for different countries and would therefore want to be certain that goods were not being transshipped through another country to qualify for a lower tariff rate.
- A *weight list* itemizes the weights of individual parcels or bales or, in the case of bulk commodities, covers the entire cargo. This list may be provided by shippers, but it is usually provided by other, independent companies. For packaged goods, the weight list may show the gross, tare, and net weights along with the measurements of each package. The *gross weight* is the full weight of the loaded package or container; *tare weight* is the weight of the container itself and packing materials; and *net weight* is the weight of the merchandise alone (gross less tare equals net).
- A *packing list* is usually required in circumstances in which merchandise is packed in many containers. It indicates the contents of each container, thereby facilitating an inventory for the buyer. It may also be combined with a weight list, giving weight and measurements for each container.
- An *inspection certificate* (or *certificate of analysis*) is usually issued by an independent third party and is required when outside inspection or analysis is agreed upon under the merchandise contract. It confirms that the merchandise shipped is as specified in that contract. A form of this certificate may be required for plants, to be certain they are free of pests or plant diseases.

Draft

Although not a document directly related to the movement or protection of merchandise, the **draft** or **bill of exchange** (exhibit 6.4) is an important document in letters of credit and collections. "A draft and a bill of exchange do not differ except in the way the terms are applied. In U.S. domestic trade, the instrument is called a draft. In foreign transactions, the same instrument is usually called a bill of exchange." [3]

The draft is the document by which the seller demands payment from the buyer, the buyer's bank, or some other bank. In a collection, this demand for payment is drawn on the buyer. In a letter of credit, the draft is drawn by the seller, usually on the issuing, confirming, or paying bank, for the amount of money due under the terms of the letter of credit. A draft drawn "at

Exhibit 6.3   Commercial Invoice

TRIM-MASTER COMPANY

1 Fifth Avenue

New York, N.Y. 10003

Invoice No. J 3366

Date July 17, 19____

Sold To

Fabrica Helios

Valparaiso

Chile

Quantity	Description	Price	Total
	2 cases: 48″ × 31″ × 43″ each 36.6 cu.ft. 455 #G 255#N Total: 73 cu.ft. 910 # Gross 510 # Net		
2	Trim-Master Deluxe @ $505.00 Serial No. 1023A & 1024A freight to N.Y. Pier	$1010.00 90.00	
			$1100.00 F.A.S.
		Handling	2.00
		Ocean freight	125.00
		Marine insurance	20.00
		C.I.F. Valparaiso	$1247.00

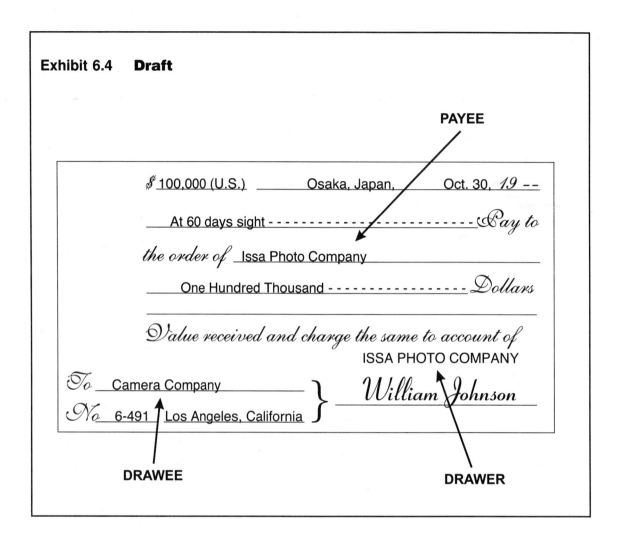

Exhibit 6.4   Draft

PAYEE

$ 100,000 (U.S.)   Osaka, Japan,   Oct. 30, 19 --

At 60 days sight - *Pay to*

the order of Issa Photo Company

One Hundred Thousand - - - - - - - - - - - - - - - *Dollars*

Value received and charge the same to account of

ISSA PHOTO COMPANY

To Camera Company

No 6-491 Los Angeles, California   }   *William Johnson*

DRAWEE

DRAWER

---

sight" is payable when presented to the drawee. The customary parties to a draft, which is a negotiable instrument, are the *drawer* (usually the exporter), the *drawee* (the importer or a bank), and the *payee* (also usually the exporter), who is also the *endorser*.

Trade Terms

Since the buyer and seller are usually quite separated, it is important that both parties understand what is included in the price quoted by the seller. For example, is the price only for the merchandise or does it include transportation? Does it include insurance?

To facilitate this understanding, international rules for the interpretation of trade terms have been agreed on. These international commercial terms are referred to by the acronym **INCOTERMS** (see appendix A).

The most commonly used Incoterms are, in brief:

- CIF (cost, insurance, and freight): The seller's price includes the cost of the merchandise, insurance, and freight to deliver the goods to the named place.
- FOB (free on board): The seller's price includes all costs through loading the merchandise on board a vessel at the named port, usually that of the seller. All other costs,

such as freight and insurance, are to be paid by the buyer directly to the shipping and insurance companies.

- CFR (cost and freight): The seller's price is for the cost of the merchandise and the freight to the named place.
- FAS (free alongside ship): The seller's price includes all the costs up to putting the merchandise alongside the vessel in the harbor or at the dock. This is used when there may be special loading required, such as the use of a lighter because the vessel must anchor in the harbor rather than at a dock.

There is a named location in all of those quotations. This means that the quoted price of the seller covers the shipment of the merchandise only as far as that location. All shipment or coverage beyond that point is the financial responsibility of the buyer.

Collection

The **collection** process provides the importer and exporter with an alternative to either prepayment or open-account financing for their international trade transactions. When the two parties cannot agree on either of the two methods, the use of a collection offers a compromise that is generally costs less than a letter of credit, but lacks the risk protection of a letter of credit. Through correspondent banking relationships, a collection uses the services of commercial banks as intermediaries and agents so that the seller has to make the shipment before demanding payment from the buyer. At the same time, the seller is afforded protection because the buyer will not get possession of the merchandise before paying or legally committing itself to pay at a future date. Nonetheless, the seller bears certain risks.

A collection is the process of presenting an item to the maker or drawee for payment. There are basically two types of collections: *clean* (financial document alone) or *documentary* (commercial documents, either with a financial document or alone). A financial document is a check, draft, bill of exchange, or promissory note; a commercial document is an invoice, bill of lading, or other shipping document. In international trade, documentary collection is the more frequent type.

The basis of collections is that banks act only as agents. A bank receives a collection from its customer, who is the principal (in a documentary collection, this will be the exporter), with instructions that must be followed exactly. Normal care must be taken to protect the collection documents from loss or damage. The customer's instructions usually cover presentation of the collection for payment, designation of who will pay the fees, statement of method for transferring payment, and procedures to be followed, if the collection is not paid, to protect the customer's goods against loss pending receipt of new instructions.

The generally accepted principles for all types of collections are covered in the International Chamber of Commerce Uniform Rules for Collections (ICC Publication No. 522—see appendix B).

Clean Collections

Checks, traveler's checks, and money orders drawn on banks or agencies in the currency of one country may be received in the course of business by individuals and companies in another country. Tourists, for example, cash traveler's checks or personal checks in the countries they visit. The hotel, restaurant, or business receiving these checks turns them over to its bank for settlement—probably a daily routine for an established business (see chapter 3).

Every check deposited in a bank is, in a sense, "collected" when it is routed to the bank of the check's writer for payment from money in the writer's account. In the United States, arrangements of the Federal Reserve System, local clearing houses, and major banks have greatly streamlined this process. A similar system for an international clearing house has not been established. Checks and other negotiable instruments drawn on a bank in one country and deposited in another country can be collected only by using the correspondent relationships established between commercial banks.

There will be other instances, particularly in documentary collections, in which the draft drawn is signed by the exporter payable to and endorsed by the exporter. Such items must be presented to the local customer, who, in turn, must separately authorize the bank to pay the draft to the debit of the customer's account.

Documentary Collections

Of far greater importance is the documentary collection by which the bank assists its clients with payment for foreign sales and purchases. Selling on open account may not be acceptable to an exporter who, while satisfied that the importer has a good business reputation, wants to be certain that he will be paid before the importer can take possession of the merchandise. Prepayment may not be acceptable to the importer, who wants to be assured that the shipment has been made before paying. The documentary collection offers a compromise (see exhibit 6.5).

Assume, for example, that a U.S. exporter (seller) has a contract order from a European importer (buyer). The U.S. exporter delivers the merchandise to the shipping company and receives a full set of ocean bills of lading consigned to the order of the exporter. The exporter endorses the bills of lading, in blank, and takes them, along with invoices, insurance, a draft drawn by the exporter on the importer, and any other necessary documents, to the bank. The exporter instructs the bank to act as its agent and to present the draft and the documents to the importer through a bank in the latter's country. There will usually be sufficient time to do this while the merchandise is in transit on a ship from the seller to the buyer.

The crux of the transaction is that in order for the importer to obtain the merchandise, he must pay the draft first. The correspondent bank in the importer's locale has both the draft and the negotiable bill of lading. As soon as the importer pays the draft, the correspondent bank will give him the shipping documents. When the vessel arrives, he can obtain the merchandise by presenting the steamship company with the negotiable bill of lading. Without the bill of lading he cannot get the merchandise: he gets the bill of lading by paying the draft drawn on him that is presented to him by his local bank. Thus both parties have been satisfied. The exporter keeps title to the merchandise until the importer pays; the importer knows that the goods have been shipped before paying. The two banks are intermediaries as agents of the exporter. The collecting bank then transfers the draft proceeds to the originating bank for payment to the exporter.

This procedure is called *documents against payment (D/P)*. The importer's bank is responsible, based on its knowledge and relationship with the importer, to assess that payment has been made in good funds.

Sight Drafts

If the exporter wishes the importer to pay immediately, the exporter draws the draft on the importer at "sight." A sight draft becomes payable when it is first presented to the importer by the collecting bank in the importer's area. In

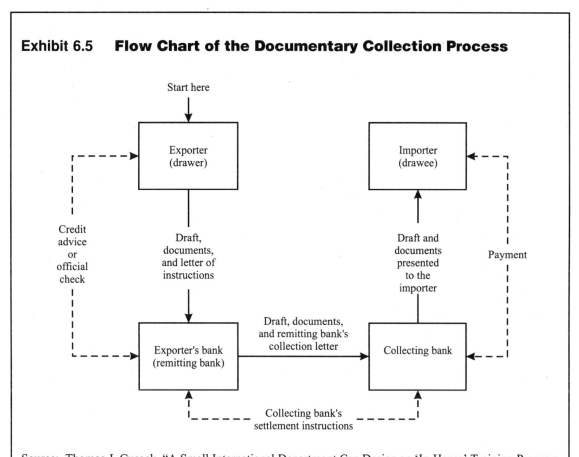

Exhibit 6.5   Flow Chart of the Documentary Collection Process

Start here

Exporter
(drawer)

Importer
(drawee)

Credit
advice
or
official
check

Draft,
documents,
and letter of
instructions

Draft and
documents
presented
to the
importer

Payment

Draft, documents,
and remitting bank's
collection letter

Exporter's bank
(remitting bank)

Collecting bank

Collecting bank's
settlement instructions

Source: Thomas J. Cusack, "A Small International Department Can Design an 'In-House' Training Program for Its Operations Clerical Staff" (Thesis, Stonier Graduate School of Banking, 1975), p. 22.

some countries, the importer is permitted to wait until the vessel arrives before paying.

To speed up the transaction, many U.S. banks furnish exporters with blank drafts and collection instruction letters; others furnish a combination draft and collection letter in snap-out form that has additional copies for the exporter and the freight forwarder. They may also be prepared through automated systems at the customer's site. These enable the exporter, who has many shipments, to prepare the outgoing collection on behalf of the bank and mail or courier it directly to the foreign bank, thereby saving days in processing at the bank. This is called a *direct collection*. The name of the U.S. bank appears as the payee, to assure that the payment is channeled back to that bank. The collection letter

serves the dual purpose of reminding the exporter of which instructions should be given to the bank and how the instructions should be worded (in banking language) to avoid misinterpretation.

The collection letter, whether filled out by the exporter, the exporter's agent, or the bank, lists documents and instructions for the delivery of the attachments (if any), for protest, for the disposition of charges, and for advice of nonacceptance, nonpayment, or payment.

Protest is the formal legal process of demanding payment of a draft from the maker or drawee who has refused to pay. This process is often a necessary step before filing a lawsuit. The legal effect of protesting varies between countries. In some countries, it may not be recognized or may be of little value. At the other extreme, it may severely damage the importer's business and reputation. The exporter should consider the impact or alternatives in the particular country before automatically requesting protest. *In case of need* is the exporter's representative, who can either be called upon to help the collecting bank in case of difficulties or is given full authority to act as that individual deems appropriate.

U.S. banks have a more or less standard set of conditions for handling collections: the right to debit the exporter's account for any charges or out-of-pocket costs, and the right to waive the requirement that the importer pay the collection fees when the importer refuses to pay such charges. Collection stipulations define the bank's role as a collector; they allow the bank to disclaim responsibility for the selection and actions of the bank's correspondents. Notwithstanding the disclaimer on the part of the exporter's bank, collecting banks are carefully selected because they control the funds given as payment for the collection from time of payment until receipt by the exporter's bank. The exporter, at the behest of the importer, often designates the collecting bank to be used unless the exporter's bank has unfavorable information about that bank. This practice deprives the exporter of the benefit of the bank's experience and deprives the U.S. bank of the opportunity of directing business to its correspondent banks.

When difficulties arise in the presentation and payment of a collection, the reports of the foreign collecting bank are relayed to the exporter for a decision.

Trade Acceptances

In some instances, the only way a buyer may be able to purchase foreign goods is on credit. The buyer wants to get possession of the merchandise before paying and then sell it, thereby generating the money to pay for the goods. The importer

has two basic options: seek financing directly from her own bank to pay the draft, or ask the exporter for credit terms. In some cases, the importer may be unable or unwilling to get the financing from her bank and instead asks the exporter for assistance. An exporter, in order to make the sale, may agree to this. Note that the exporter, not the remitting bank, is providing credit to the importer. In agreeing to release the merchandise before receiving payment, the seller wants a written promise from the buyer that payment will be made at a specific future date. The exporter draws the draft payable not at sight but at a future date, such as "ninety days after sight" or "bill of lading date."

The steps taken for the collection of such a time draft parallel those taken for the collection of a sight draft. The difference lies in the conditions under which the documents are delivered to the drawee (the buyer) and in the added operations involved in presenting the draft twice, once for acceptance and once for payment.

When a bank receives time drafts with accompanying documents, the exporter's instructions to the bank are usually to deliver the *documents against acceptance* (D/A) by the buyer. The importer's acceptance of the draft is his promise to pay on the agreed future date. This is a **trade acceptance** (see exhibit 6.6), not to be confused with a bankers' acceptance (see chapter 9). Instructions to the collecting bank are usually "for acceptance and collection," which means that the collecting bank, which is the bank in the importer's area, is to present the draft for acceptance. Upon acceptance by the buyer, the bank releases the bill of lading and other documents and then holds the accepted draft on behalf of the seller until the due date, when it is presented for payment. The trade acceptance has the characteristics of a promissory note: it is a signed promise to pay a stated sum of money on a specific future date, and there is proof that value was received by the importer, namely the merchandise.

Exhibit 6.6   Trade Acceptance

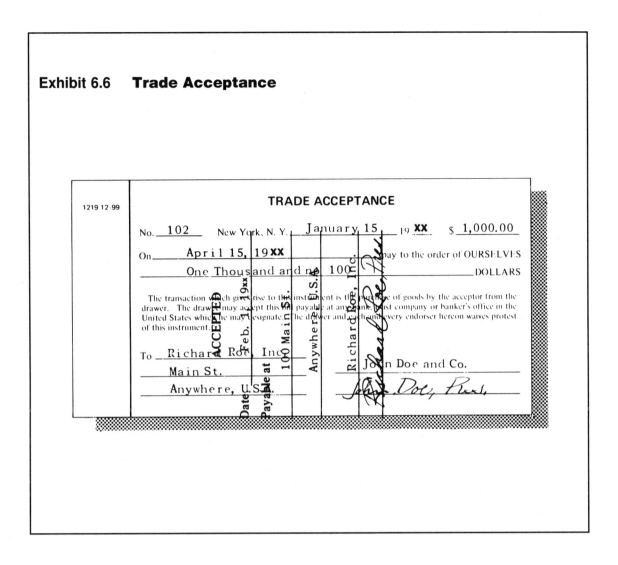

1219 12-99

TRADE ACCEPTANCE

No. __102__   New York, N. Y.   __January 15,__   19 **XX** $ __1,000.00__

On_____ __April 15, 19 XX__ _____Pay to the order of OURSELVES

_____One Thousand and no 100_____DOLLARS

The transaction which gives rise to this instrument is the purchase of goods by the acceptor from the drawer. The drawer may accept this bill payable at any bank, trust company or banker's office in the United States which he may designate. The drawer and each and every endorser hereon waives protest of this instrument.

To __Richard Roe, Inc.__
____Main St.__
____Anywhere, U.S.__

John Doe and Co.

John Doe, Pres.

On rare occasions and for various reasons, however, the instructions may read "for acceptance and return," which means that the accepted draft is returned to the seller and presented again for collection on the maturity date, with payment to be made at that time by the importer. The exporter bears the cost of the goods and shipment until the acceptance matures and the buyer pays. The bank has no obligation or commitment to pay a trade acceptance on maturity should the importer go into bankruptcy or fail to pay debts incurred. The exporter carries all the risk and thus must be confident of the moral character and creditworthiness of the buyer.

Import Collections

While the foregoing examples refer to the use of collections for U.S. exports, the same principles apply for collections covering U.S. imports. Collections for imports are the reverse of those covering exports. From the overseas exporter's point of view, the U.S. bank is the foreign collecting bank. The collections may be in the form of sight or time drafts, in U.S. dollars, or in foreign currency. The collections are usually received from a foreign bank, which conveys all instructions from the seller. Any deviations from the foreign bank's instructions and any action initiated by the collecting bank are at the risk of the collecting bank. When an incoming collection is received from a foreign correspondent bank, the international department may route it to the domestic side of the bank for presentation through the note section to the local customer. The international department may assign a control number and will act as the bank's liaison between the domestic branch, or domestic correspondent bank, and the foreign bank.

The draft amounts paid by the importer are usually credited to the Due To account of the originating foreign bank. When an account does not exist, the instructions usually request remittance to another U.S. bank for credit to the foreign bank's account. The receipt of a collection from a bank that is not a correspondent may provide an opportunity to establish a new relationship.

The handling of an incoming collection with a time draft in U.S. dollars is similar to a sight item. One presentation must be made to obtain acceptance and another to obtain payment.

Foreign Currency Collections

The handling of *foreign currency sight drafts* is similar to the handling of U.S. dollar items. To pay the draft, the U.S. importer will need to purchase the foreign exchange. The importer pays the U.S. dollar amount, and the bank remits the foreign currency amount from its Due From account to the bank that sent the collection.

The handling of *foreign currency time drafts* is a combination of the procedures for handling foreign currency sight drafts and U.S. dollar time drafts. The buyer presents the draft initially for acceptance and subsequently for payment. The buyer may also pay the foreign currency amount that is due by purchasing spot foreign exchange at the second presentation or may arrange for a forward contract at the initial presentation (see chapter 4).

Other Collections

Some exporters sell on *cash against documents* terms. This means that the collection consists of the documents alone. This procedure is the same as a sight draft sale, except that the draft does not exist. Exporters sometimes sell on such terms to avoid the stamp taxes some countries require on all negotiable instruments.

An exporter may want to send merchandise to another country in advance of a sale to have it available for prompt delivery as soon as the sale is made. This is particularly important when the foreign product is competing in that local market against a local product. The exporter may ship merchandise by the *consignment* method. In the case of a U.S. import, the foreign seller, through a foreign bank, may use the services of a U.S. correspondent bank by sending it the shipping documents along with instructions to arrange for customs entry, pay the duty, warehouse the goods, and obtain insurance for the goods. All these expenses are for the account of the exporter. Future delivery of the goods to the buyer or a local agent of the exporter may be authorized either in its entirety or piecemeal at a given price per unit. Sometimes deliveries against *trust receipt* are permitted. (In a trust receipt, the merchandise can be temporarily released to an importer while the title is retained by the bank on behalf of the exporter.)

In some countries or instances, it is not feasible or permissible to use a negotiable bill of lading. The exporter will therefore consign the merchandise directly to a third party, such as a customs broker in the importer's country, with a straight bill of lading. The collection then consists of a draft on the buyer plus a *delivery order*. This is a letter written by the seller and addressed to the third party, authorizing release of the merchandise to whoever presents the letter. The collection instructs the bank to release the delivery order when the sight draft is paid or the time draft accepted.

Financing

In collections, if the buyer wants credit, it is usually provided by the seller who agrees to draw the draft payable at a future date rather than at sight—the trade acceptance. The exporter, however, may wish to obtain financing, which can be supplied by the exporter's bank. Typically, the bank advances funds to the seller when the collection is given to the bank for forwarding. In essence, the bank finances the exporter while the collection is being forwarded in the expectation that the importer will pay the draft, either at sight or on the specified date. From that payment, the bank will retire the loan it has made to the exporter plus interest. Should the collection not be paid, then the bank will look to the exporter for the repayment.

Advantages and Disadvantages

A collection provides more protection for the seller than selling on open account and more protection for the buyer than prepaying the shipment. The seller is protected because the buyer cannot obtain possession of the merchandise without paying the sight draft or accepting the time draft. The buyer knows that when funds are paid, the merchandise has been shipped and is in transit or has already arrived. Both parties are willing to bear the slight costs involved in exchange for the advantages offered to each.

The collection, however, has some disadvantages for the seller, who can be exposed to nonpayment by the buyer who may die, go bankrupt, or refuse to pay. For example, an unscrupulous buyer may refuse to pay, hoping to negotiate better terms. While the seller still owns the goods, they are now en route to a distant point. The return of the goods will mean added shipping costs. To avoid this, the seller may try to find another buyer or even have the merchandise destroyed. An unscrupulous buyer can

anticipate this and try to get the goods by offering a lower price. Of course, such a buyer can do this only once. Forever after, the only way the seller will agree to sell goods to this buyer will be by prepayment or with a letter of credit. Before selecting the collection option, the seller must be satisfied with the credit standing of the buyer, particularly in relation to the value and nature of merchandise.

Bank Use

For the bank, too, there are advantages and disadvantages to its customers using collections. The bank's principal advantage is that collections develop business for and from its correspondent banks and are therefore important to its overall correspondent banking business and relationships. The capability to handle foreign collections can facilitate the bank's relationship with domestic customers by serving existing customers and attracting new ones. The bank does this by acting as an intermediary and agent for its customer, who is the exporter, the exporter's bank, or the exporter's freight forwarder.

The bank must handle each collection with care. In receiving a steady volume of collections from a customer or correspondent bank, the collection personnel must guard against assuming that all collections have the same instructions. Each collection must be considered and processed as an individual item. Mishandling an individual collection can result in financial loss to a bank when, because of its negligence in not following the exact instructions of that collection, the exporter suffers a loss. The bank also needs to remember that, with incoming collections, its customer is the exporter and the exporter's bank. The bank cannot take instructions from the importer, even when the importer is a local customer of the bank. The collection is the property of the exporter, and the intermediary banks are the exporter's agent.

The exporter's bank also runs certain risks if a collection is not paid. When the instructions are to protest nonpayment, in some countries the exporter's bank may experience unfavorable publicity from the local market, even when it is merely passing on its customer's instructions. There is also some risk that certain costs, such as for storage, will be charged if the bank cannot collect because the exporter has gone into bankruptcy, out of business, or disappeared. It is important, therefore, for a bank to know its customer.

Accounting

Outstanding collections do not appear in a bank's financial statement because the bank is only an agent and has no risks unless it is negligent in following the customer's instructions. Fees and operating expenses are reflected in the bank's income statement.

Summary

International trade begins with a contract between the buyer and the seller that details the terms and conditions agreed upon by the two parties. An essential element of that agreement is the method of payment. The buyer may be asked to pay in advance; the seller may bill after the goods have been delivered. When neither of these is acceptable to both the buyer and the seller, a third method of payment is the documentary collection, which has certain features like those of the other two methods. A fourth method, the commercial letter of credit, will be examined in the next chapters. This creates different responsibilities for bankers.

Regardless of how payment is agreed upon, the international trade transaction will generate certain standard types of documents to accomplish the transfer of title of the merchandise,

recording of the transaction, and protection of the shipment. The major documents are the transportation document, insurance, and invoice.

Questions

1. What is a collection?
2. Explain the difference between prepayment and open account.
3. What is the difference in procedure between documents against payment and documents against acceptance?
4. How does using a collection differ from the buyer prepaying or the seller shipping on open account?
5. If you were in New York buying merchandise from Singapore, what would be the difference between a price quotation that was US$10,000 FOB Singapore and US$10,000 CIF New York?
6. What are the functions of the invoice and transportation documents in an international trade transaction?

Problem

A manufacturer in your community has received an order from a buyer in Italy for a supply of electrical parts. The total value of the order is $7,500. The manufacturer has heard that the buyer is reputable but beyond that has no information. Discuss the advantages and disadvantages of a collection in terms of cost (use the charges applicable to your bank) and protection.

Notes

1. U.S. Department of Commerce, *A Basic Guide to Exporting* (Washington, D.C.: 1981), p. 22

2. Fernand Braudel, *The Wheels of Commerce* (New York: Harper and Row, 1982), pp. 362-363

3. Craig W. Smith, *Law and Banking*: *Applications* (Washington, D.C.: American Bankers Association, 1986), p. 2

7

THE BASIC COMMERCIAL LETTER OF CREDIT

Learning Objectives

After studying this chapter, you will be able to

- describe the basic letter of credit transaction
- identify the responsibilities of all parties to the transaction
- compare the letter of credit to collections as a means of financing international trade

Overview

Chapter 6 examined several ways in which international trade may be arranged. When the related payment is made directly between buyer and seller, either before or after a shipment, the bank's role is basically only to transfer funds. In a documentary collection, the bank acts as the seller's agent in exchanging the shipping documents for immediate or future payment. With the **commercial letter of credit** (also referred to as a "documentary credit"), the bank becomes directly involved by committing itself to pay the seller, which enables the trade transaction to take place.

"In its simplest form, a 'commercial letter of credit' involves the payment of a draft in exchange for a document of title. This payment is made through a third party—the issuer." [1] A letter of credit is an instrument issued by a bank by which the bank furnishes its credit, which is both good and well known, in place of the buyer's credit, which may be good but is not so well known. A bank issues a letter of credit on behalf of one of its customers, authorizing an individual or firm to draw drafts on the bank or on one of its correspondents for the bank's account under certain conditions stipulated in the credit.

The commercial letter of credit is widely used and highly regarded as a key bank product that enables an important amount of international trade to take place. It is perceived to be unique to international banking although, in fact, it is equally usable in domestic trade. Providing letter of credit service is central to any bank's commitment to offer international banking services to customers, and an understanding of the letter of credit is essential to the banker with customers involved in international trade. This chapter describes the basic letter of credit as issued on behalf of an importer and with the draft payable at sight. Some confusion may arise from the way in which terms are used by bankers. For our purposes, the term "letter of credit" will be used to refer to the commercial letter of credit that covers the movement of goods. Words may be inserted in front of the term to indicate other features of that particular letter of credit or the differing roles of banks.

Background

The letter of credit has been described as "the lifeblood of international commerce . . . collateral to the underlying rights and obligations between the merchant at either end of the banking chain." [2] Its ancestry can be traced back probably to the twelfth century, although today's commercial letter of credit, with its obligations on the bank, is no older than the nineteenth century: it began with the use by Finnish importers for their purchase of Brazilian coffee in 1840. "The letter of credit was first used in Anglo-American and European trade toward the middle of the nineteenth century and, in less than 100 years, it acquired guiding legal principles which hold true with a remarkable degree of uniformity across the boundaries of nations and legal systems." [3]

All letters of credit are issued at the request of and on behalf of the importer, either directly or through a correspondent bank. In discussing the financing of a transaction in which merchandise is imported from one country to another on the basis of a letter of credit, the term *import letter of credit* is often used. In fact, there is no real difference between an import letter of credit and an export letter of credit; the term used depends entirely on where the parties concerned are situated. To the U.S. buyer of Brazilian coffee, for instance, it is an import letter of credit; to the foreign seller of the coffee, it is an export letter of credit. To the party in whose favor the credit is issued (**beneficiary**), it is an export letter of credit; to the buyer on whose behalf the letter of credit is issued (**account party**), it is an import letter of credit.

Letters of credit can be either *revocable* or *irrevocable*. The overwhelming majority of letters of credit issued are irrevocable, which means they cannot be canceled or changed without the consent of all parties concerned, particularly the beneficiary. The revocable letter of credit, which can be canceled or changed solely at the buyer's request, is rarely used. Unless specifically mentioned, discussions in this book refer to the irrevocable letter of credit. An irrevocable letter of credit adds an element of credit risk for the issuing bank, since it cannot cancel its commitment should the credit standing of its customer change, even before any shipment has taken place.

While the beneficiary (exporter, seller) receives an irrevocable authority of a bank to draw drafts on it, the account party (importer, buyer) must make sure that the exporter is responsible and of good reputation. A letter of credit issued in the beneficiary's favor does not compel the beneficiary to make a shipment. The letter of credit merely provides that if a shipment is made, and if the seller wants to be assured of payment by the bank, the seller must present documents that comply with the terms and conditions of the letter of credit. The buyer relies on the seller to send merchandise of the quality and quantity described in the documents that the buyer will eventually receive under the letter of credit. Irresponsible sellers may ship inferior goods, and the shipping documents will not show this. The bank is concerned only with the documents and cannot be held responsible in such situations. However, if irregularities in the documents presented to the bank exist, the bank will not honor drafts drawn against it until those documents are in order or unless the account party agrees to accept the discrepancy.

The rules governing letter-of-credit transactions [in the United States] are derived from Article 5 of the Uniform Commercial Code (UCC), entitled 'Letters of Credit', and the *Uniform Customs and Practices for Documentary Credits (UCP)* [See Appendix C]. In contrast to Article 5, the UCP does not carry the force of law but instead is a compendium of customs and practices developed over the years for letter-of-credit transactions . . . . Frequently, the terms of the UCP are incorporated by reference into the terms of letter-of-credit transactions.[4]

The *Uniform Customs and Practices for Documentary Credits*, customarily referred to as the UCP, are the generally accepted ground rules for the myriad details in letters of credit. Since 1933, the International Chamber of Commerce (ICC), a nongovernmental association of businesses in over 130 countries, has worked with the business communities to develop a standard set of interpretations of terms and practices that will apply to everyone using letters of credit. This has reduced confusion and thus contributed to the use of letters of credit. The UCP is periodically revised; the current one (No. 500) was introduced in 1993.

The Merchandise Contract

A letter of credit transaction customarily begins after a merchandise contract or order between the buyer and seller has been made. The bank is not concerned with the details of the negotiations that led to the merchandise contract, nor is it a party to that contract. However, the bank may advise its customer as to structuring the letter of credit to implement the terms of that contract.

The terms and conditions of a letter of credit should be simple and easily understood. A letter of credit is separate and distinct from the underlying contract between buyer and seller for the purchase of the merchandise. The banks will deal only with the documents and not the merchandise. The letter of credit should be drawn in strict compliance with the provisions of the merchandise contract. Sundry details of merchandise quality and condition should not be included. The amount of credit, expiration date, shipping date, documents to be presented, tenor (maturity) of the draft, and a brief description of the merchandise shipped must be included (see exhibit 7.1).

For example, a clothing store in California learns of a firm in Scotland that manufactures women's sweaters. The California store asks the Scottish firm to send samples of and descriptive literature about its products. The store decides to buy a quantity of sweaters and negotiates a contract with the Scottish seller, covering items such as the number of each size, color, and price. Because the two parties have not done business before, the problem discussed in chapter 6 concerning the means of payment occurs. The seller may ask for prepayment; the buyer may ask for open account. The seller wants to be assured it will be paid before surrendering title to the sweaters; the buyer wants to know that the sweaters will be shipped before paying. The seller does not want to wait to be paid until the buyer receives the goods, as he would have to do in a collection or open account sale, nor does he want to risk that the buyer will change her mind. To solve this dilemma, the two parties can include in their merchandise contract an agreement that this shipment will be paid by means of a letter of credit.

Certain protections for both buyer and seller are inherent in all letters of credit. The seller knows he will be paid as soon as he complies with the terms of the letter of credit; the buyer knows no payment will be made until documents are presented showing that the shipment has been made as specified. The next step for the buyer is to approach her bank and apply for the letter of credit required in the merchandise contract.

Application for a Letter of Credit

A request for a letter of credit is similar to an application for a loan and is treated by the bank in much the same way. The bank will usually insist that the documents be in negotiable form so that it obtains title to the merchandise between the time it makes payment and the time it is reimbursed. Nevertheless, the loan officer, in considering the application, must prudently view it as if it were an application for an unsecured loan. Even though the bank may have control over title documents after making payment, the loan officer should not consider this to be sufficient security: the merchandise may have a limited market, the price may change, or difficulties may arise in getting possession of the merchandise.

A letter of credit is considered a *self-liquidating* extension of credit. This means that the loan officer expects the transfer of the merchandise from the seller to the buyer, and the subsequent sale by that buyer, to provide cash for the buyer to repay the bank. The bank may consider the collateral value of the merchandise to be shipped, although often this may not be of value to anyone other than the original buyer because many items shipped under letters of credit have a limited market.

The marketability of the goods to be imported and the integrity and financial responsibility of the importer are important to the bank. Banks deal only in documents in any letter of credit. They do not inspect the goods, although the documents may misrepresent the merchandise, particularly in case of fraud. As an added protection, the banker will usually want evidence that the merchandise is insured during shipment.

From the time the bank issues the letter of credit until the draft and documents are presented for payment, it lends only its credit. The bank

Exhibit 7.1   Irrevocable Letter of Credit

Comerica Bank, Detroit	Irrevocable Documentary Credit	Number 12865
Place and Date of issue Detroit January 2, 19--		**Expiry Date and Place of Presentation for Documents** Expiry Date: April 1, 19-- Place for Presentation: Detroit
Applicant: Harris Townley Detroit, Michigan		

Advising Bank: Reference No. Bank in London London, England	**Beneficiary:** Sylvia Beemish, Ltd. 3 Westlean Arcade London, England
	Amount: US $3,000.00 Dollars
Partial Shipments Allowed ☐ Not Allowed ☒	**Credit available with Nominated Bank:** any bank
Transhipment Allowed ☐ Not Allowed ☒	☐ by payment at sight ☐ by deferred payment at: ☐ by acceptance of draft at: ☒ by negotiation at sight
☐ Insurance covered by buyers	Against the documents detailed herein: ☒ and beneficiary's draft(s) drawn on:
Shipment as defined in UCP Article 46 From: London For transportation to: Detroit Not later than:	Comerica Bank, Detroit

Commercial invoice in triplicate covering 100 bolts of cloth CFR, Detroit

Marine bills of lading issued to order of Comerica Bank, Detroit, Michigan marked notify Harris Townly, Detroit, Michigan and freight prepaid

Documents to be presented within __12__ days of shipment but within the validity of the credit.

We hereby issue the Irrevocable Documentary Credit in your favor. It is subject to the Uniform Customs and Practice for documentary credits (1993 Revision, International Chamber of Commerce, Paris, France, Publication No. 500) and engages us in accordance with the terms thereof. The number and date of the Credit and the name of our bank must be quoted on all drafts required. If the credit is available by negotiation, each presentation must be noted on the reverse side of this advice by the bank where the credit is available.

This document consists of _1_ signed pages.

Name and signature of issuing bank
Comerica Bank, Detroit

R. Jones

makes no outlay of funds until the draft and documents are presented (see exhibit 7.2). However, the bank must be prepared for presentation of the documents and the demand for payment at any time during the life of the letter of credit. The timing of the presentation is completely at the option of the seller within the terms of the letter of credit, and only in unusual circumstances will the bank have any warning before the actual arrival of the documents with the draft demand for payment.

The application for a commercial letter of credit should identify the precise terms and conditions under which the importer wishes its bank to establish the credit and should describe the documents that the bank will receive in exchange for the payment it will eventually make. The application itself is signed by the importing customer and incorporates a *security agreement* defining the rights of the bank issuing the credit and the obligation of the customer on whose behalf the credit is issued.

The customer's agreement embodies the obligation of the customer to reimburse the bank for payments made under the letter of credit—provided, of course, that such payments are made in accordance with the terms expressed in it. This agreement covers many other eventualities, some of the most important of which are:

- The customer acknowledges the issuing bank's unqualified right to possess and dispose of all property as security under the letter of credit.
- The customer assumes all risks from the actions of the shippers or beneficiaries who use the letter of credit.
- The customer does not hold the issuing bank responsible for the validity, genuineness, or sufficiency of the documents.
- The customer does not hold the issuing bank responsible for the existence, character, quality, quantity, condition, packing, value,

or delivery of the property represented by the documents.

- The customer is obligated to pay a specified fee to the issuing bank for issuing the letter of credit. (Although this fee may be called a commission, it is, in fact, a finance charge and may be in addition to a document handling or negotiation fee. Sometimes the two fees are combined into a single all-inclusive charge.)

In addition to itemizing the documents to be delivered by the exporter, the importer must decide whether it wants all the order to come in one shipment or whether *partial shipments* will be permitted. The importer must decide whether the merchandise must come on a direct ship from the seller or whether it can be transferred from one ship to another at an intermediate port (*transshipment*). Transshipment can cause delays, or the goods may be overlooked at the intermediate port. The importer must also select the expiration date of the letter of credit so that it can receive its goods in time for their selling season or for its need of them. The banker can advise the buyer on many of these points in preparing the application.

The application will be the basis for the details that the bank will include in its letter of credit. The bank must screen the application to be certain that the exporter will be able to obtain all of the documents that facilitate payment under the letter of credit (for example, the transportation document from the shipping company, insurance from the insurance company, and an inspection certificate from an inspection company in its area). Any requirement, for example, that the buyer would have to approve that the shipped merchandise was satisfactory before the exporter could be paid would be unacceptable in a letter of credit. All of the conditions in the letter of credit must be able to be met by some document; there cannot be any nondocumentary conditions.

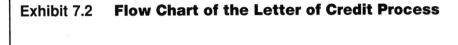

Exhibit 7.2 Flow Chart of the Letter of Credit Process

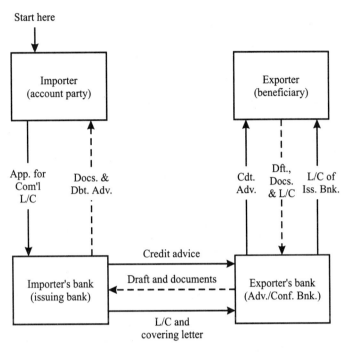

Source: Thomas J. Cusack, "A Small International Department Can Design an 'In-House' Training Program for Its Operations Clerical Staff" (Thesis, Stonier Graduate School of Banking, 1975), p. 29.

Once the bank is satisfied with the credit responsibility of its customer and the credit risk, it will approve the formal application for a commercial letter of credit. The issuing bank sets up bookkeeping entries in its general ledger. Although no outlay of funds has occurred, the bank has made an irrevocable extension of credit, on which it is earning income, and which can be converted into a demand for cash without any further option for the bank.

The Exporter's Responsibilities

Issuing a letter of credit involves more than a bank's statement to honor a beneficiary's drafts and documents upon presentation. The benefici-ary is in a foreign country and consequently wants to be able to negotiate the draft and docu-ments with a bank in its own country. Therefore, a bank issuing a letter of credit must have already established its name and responsibility in the commercially important cities of the world. Many banks that are not recognized throughout the world and are not equipped to handle letters of credit will use a correspondent bank in open-ing letters of credit.

A letter of credit is sent either directly to the beneficiary or indirectly through a correspondent bank in the exporter's locale. Routing the letter of credit through a correspondent bank enables that bank to verify the signatures: thus, the exporter knows that it is a bona fide commitment and that the issuing bank is, in fact, a reputable organization. Upon receiving the credit, the beneficiary examines its terms and conditions to see that they conform to the contract and that the beneficiary is able to perform under the credit. If an *amendment* to the original terms and conditions in the letter of credit is necessary, it contacts the buyer directly or through the bank and asks for an amendment covering the changes. Changes may refer to the amount, documentary requirements, expiration date, or shipping date. Any changes must be agreeable to all parties concerned—the beneficiary, the buyer, and the bank opening the credit.

When the beneficiary is satisfied that the terms of the credit agree with the contract with the buyer and can be complied with, the shipment is made. In the example of the Scottish sweaters, the manufacturer packs the sweaters in crates for marine shipment and delivers them to a shipping company in exchange for bills of lading that meet the terms of the letter of credit, as for example when it requires them to be in negotiable form ("to order of shipper, blank endorsed"). Insurance certificates or policies, if required, are obtained to cover the cargo, and customs invoices and any other documents are prepared. The beneficiary then prepares a commercial invoice, draws a draft on the specified bank, and presents these documents in the required number of copies with the letter of credit to its local bank for negotiation. The draft can be drawn on the issuing bank or another bank, as stated in the letter of credit.

The expiration date on the letter of credit is the final date on which drafts may be presented for negotiation. Unless otherwise stipulated, letters of credit usually expire in the city in which the beneficiary is located. The reason for this provision is that generally a beneficiary can control when documents are presented to the local bank for negotiation. If the beneficiary needed to have those documents delivered by a stated date to the country of the buyer, however, the timing of that delivery would be entirely at the mercy of the mails. If the documents were delivered after the expiration date, the buyer could refuse to authorize payment.

Once the shipment has been made, there is another time limit on the seller—the *presentation date*. Documents must be presented to the bank not later than 21 days after issuance of the bill of lading, unless otherwise stated in the letter of credit, and before the expiration date. This *presentation date* allows time for the bills of lading to be processed and delivered to the importer before the arrival of the ship. Bills of lading that reach the importer after the ship has arrived are considered *stale*, which could result in unexpected expenses for the buyer, since the unclaimed merchandise incurs storage charges.

Frequently, in an international sale of goods, the merchandise arrives at the importer's (buyer's) port before the arrival of correct and complete bills of lading. In such instances, it is customary for the importer (buyer) to obtain immediate possession of the goods by providing the shipping company with a bank guarantee, often called a *shipside bond*,* which holds the shipping company blameless of damage resulting from release of the goods without proper or complete documents. Usually the bank's guarantee relies on a counter-guarantee issued by the importer to the bank.[5]

These transactions are reflected as contingent items in the bank's financial statement.

_____

* Other terms for this include steamship indemnities, steamship release, or bill of lading guarantee.

Negotiation

An important function of a bank issuing a credit arises when it must honor its obligation expressed in the letter of credit. The bank must examine the documents presented to verify that, on their face, they conform to the conditions of the letter of credit.* This process of comparing the documents to determine whether they comply with the terms and conditions of the letter of credit is known as *negotiation*.

Negotiation involves checking the documents to make sure that

- the documents have been negotiated or presented on or before the expiration of the credit or presentation date
- the amount drawn does not exceed the amount available under the credit
- the documents comply with the stated requirements of the letter of credit and all amendments
- the documents conform to each other and are compatible with the UCP
- each individual document appears to be properly prepared

The negotiator takes the bank's record of the letter of credit with all the presented documents and methodically examines them, comparing the documents to the letter of credit and to each other.

If *discrepancies* are noted, they are referred to a discrepancy officer. Some discrepancies,

such as an insufficient number of copies of an invoice, may be minor and can be remedied in the bank. The bank cannot alter the documents as presented. Other discrepancies, such as a different description of the merchandise, will be sufficient cause for the bank to refuse payment. Any deviations will be referred to the account party who requested the opening of the letter of credit. This customer has the right to refuse to permit any deviation from the original application. In practice, however, the customer may agree to accept trivial discrepancies in order to receive the goods. The bank will ask for a written concurrence and then will make the payment. However, if the customer refuses to waive the original requirements, the bank will refuse to pay the draft, and it will be up to the seller to correct the discrepancy before payment can be made.

In the sweater transaction, the Scottish beneficiary may present the documents to a local bank. Because the letter of credit represents an irrevocable obligation of a known U.S. bank to honor drafts and documents in conformity with the terms of the credit, the beneficiary's local bank has the assurance that it may make its payment if it wishes to. The issuing bank becomes liable to this negotiating bank. The negotiating bank, therefore, usually will choose to buy the draft or advance the funds, and give the shipper its money immediately, making allowance for the time until it can expect to be paid. It then sends the draft and documents to the issuing bank.

Each party in the letter of credit process examines the documents on its own behalf. Even if the first negotiating bank pays the seller, the issuing bank will itself examine the documents to see that they are in accord with the letter of credit it issued. Negotiation of the documents and payment of the draft by the bank do not commit the buyer to pay until she has examined the documents and is satisfied. If the banks have been careless and overlooked discrepancies, the buyer can refuse to pay. This could result in a

---

* The importance of this examination is demonstrated by the landmark decision on November 13, 1942, of the British Court of Appeals, Civil Division, in the case of *J.H. Raynor & Company, Ltd. v. Hambros Bank, Ltd.* (Times Law Reports, vol. LIX) that a bank is not bound to honor drafts presented to it under a letter of credit unless those drafts, with the accompanying documents, are exactly as stipulated in the letter of credit.

financial loss for the bank that has made the payment.

The issuing bank pays the sight draft and credits the Due To account of the negotiating bank or transfers the money to it. The bank is then reimbursed either by charging the buyer's account or by refinancing with a line of credit for the buyer. However, if the buyer is no longer able to repay the bank, the bank's obligation to pay the exporter under the letter of credit remains. This is the essence of the letter of credit as a means of financing international trade. In practice, the bank will usually simultaneously pay the seller and debit the account of the buyer. The knowledgeable banker must recognize that these are two distinct and unlinked functions. The bank carries the risk in letters of credit, just as in any other extension of credit, that it will not be repaid. The only difference is in the timing of when it disburses its own funds.

The documents are then delivered to the importer, who signs a receipt, and the letter of credit transaction is complete. The importer arranges with a customs broker for the formal entry and payment of duty on the goods, if necessary. In the sweater example, the California buyer now has the merchandise for subsequent retail sale.

If the importer is unable to pay the bank, the bank has the bills of lading in negotiable form. The bank can take possession of the merchandise and collateralize its loan for whatever value the merchandise represents. This is why the bank requires that bills of lading be in negotiable form and that the goods should not be consigned directly to the buyer.

Besides benefitting the buyer and seller, the letter of credit benefits the banks involved. They collect fees for opening letters of credit, amending, advising the credit, confirming (see chapter 8), and negotiating the documents when presented. In the example, the Scottish bank also benefits from an increase in its account balance at the California bank when that bank pays the letter of credit draft. The Scottish bank has the option of purchasing the draft from the seller, thereby earning transit interest and foreign exchange profit from converting the U.S. dollar draft into pounds sterling. Even if it does not purchase the draft in advance of being reimbursed, the Scottish bank can earn the foreign exchange profit when it pays the Scottish seller against the dollars in its account. This illustrates the benefits of correspondent banking through such short-term relationships.

Fraud

Fraud, usually by the seller of the merchandise, is a disturbing problem for banks. The UCP states that "all parties concerned deal with documents and not with goods" (Article 4) and, if there are irregularities, the "bank must determine, on the basis of the documents alone" (Article 14) not to make payment (see appendix C). The dilemma, however, arises when the bank knows or strongly suspects that the documents, when presented, do not describe the actual merchandise or fraudulently misrepresent the facts. In several instances, banks have refused to pay. The resulting court decisions have analyzed the conflicting responsibilities of the banker, including the banker's role in issuing a letter of credit.

> It is well established that a letter of credit is dependent on the primary contract of sale between the buyer and the seller. The issuing bank agrees to pay upon presentation of documents, not goods. This rule is necessary to preserve the efficiency of the letter of credit as an instrument for the financing of trade. . . . Where the seller's fraud has been called to the bank's attention before the drafts and documents have been presented for payment, the principle of the independence of the bank's obligation under the

letter of credit should not be extended to protect the unscrupulous seller.[6]

A later decision in another case stated:

> An exception to the strict rule exists. The bank ought not to pay under the credit if it knows that the documents are forged or that the request for payment is made fraudulently in circumstances when there is no right to payment.[7]

Another case concerned a shipment from the United Kingdom to Peru on the vessel *American Accord*, in which the bills of lading were presented showing that the merchandise had been loaded on board on the last permitted shipping date under the letter of credit. The loading, it turned out, had actually been done on the day after and the bills of lading were fraudulently prepared by an agent of the shipping company.

> [The document] is not a genuine or valid document entitling the presenter of it to be paid, and if the banker to which it is presented under a letter of credit knows it to be forged he must not pay . . . . [T]he bank owes no duty to the beneficiary to pay and, I would say, owes a duty to the customer not to pay.[8]

These court decisions span almost 40 years, making it obvious that the bank must proceed with caution in selecting a course of action when the issue of possible fraud comes to its attention. Some bankers feel that when fraud is suspected, the most appropriate procedure is that the account party, who is usually the first one to uncover it, should apply for a court restraining order rather than put the burden on the bank to decide not to pay.[9] A judge in one of the cases discussed above summed up the continuing dilemma for the banker: "[T]he fewer the cases in which a bank is entitled to hold up payment the better for the smooth running of international trade. But I do

not think that the courts have a duty to assist international trade to run smoothly if it is fraudulent." [10]

Collections Versus Letters of Credit

One of the many decisions an exporter must make is whether to insist on having a letter of credit opened in its favor or to ship on a collection, or sight draft, basis. Such a decision depends on the exporter's past relationship and experience with the buyer as well as on the political and economic circumstances in the importer's country, which may hinder transfer of payment despite his ability and intent to pay. It is important, therefore to review the differences between these two means of effecting payment or financing.

An irrevocable letter of credit is an obligation of the issuing bank. Drafts are drawn on a bank, either the issuing, confirming, advising, or reimbursing bank, depending on the characteristics of the letter of credit. Exporters can be certain that if they ship in compliance with the stated terms and conditions, their drafts will be paid regardless of any calamity or act of the importer. The exporter looks to the bank for payment and knows payment is forthcoming on presentation of the appropriate documents.

In a collection, the exporter must wait until the documents are presented to the buyer to be paid. The exporter's draft is not drawn on a bank; it is drawn on the importer. The bank's role is to present the draft to the importer for payment or acceptance, as the case may be. An importer might not pay an exporter for many reasons. Importers may change their minds or go out of business; the goods shipped may be claimed to be inferior; restrictions on imports may be imposed after the shipment has been made. The danger of nonpayment is particularly great for certain types of perishable commodities for which market price fluctuations can be severe and sudden. If the market price of a shipment should decline sharply, the importer may refuse to pay when the draft is presented. If the exporter has already shipped the commodity and the importer refuses to pay, the exporter may be forced to renegotiate the sale at a lower price to avoid a complete loss on the shipment. The exporter's other options include having the goods returned, storing them until a new buyer is found, or destroying them, all of which incur substantial expense to the seller.

When a letter of credit calls for drafts to be drawn at, for example, 180 days after sight, the draft is drawn by the exporter on a bank that accepts it (see chapter 9). In the United States, the accepting bank must pay such an acceptance at maturity, regardless of any change in the financial existence or condition of the importer. The active market for bankers' acceptances allows exporters to easily discount the document for cash without consideration of their own credit lines.

In a collection, a draft payable at a future date is drawn on the buyer, not on a bank; the buyer accepts the draft and undertakes to pay it at maturity. But there is always the chance that the buyer may go into bankruptcy or that some other difficulty may arise before maturity. In addition, the exporter is providing the financing during this period, since no active market exists for trade acceptances. Usually the only way exporters can discount a trade acceptance for cash before maturity is by using their own credit lines at their bank on a "with recourse" basis.

When the amount involved is relatively small, the cost to both importer and exporter to use the collection method is generally lower than the cost of opening a letter of credit. The collection method also has the advantage of avoiding the use of bank credit (something the importer may be unable or unwilling to do).

When a shipment involves merchandise that is not subject to sudden market fluctuations, the exporter often considers using the collection method. This ensures a degree of protection because the exporter obtains payment or at least acceptance of a draft before the buyer can take possession of the merchandise. In the same circumstances, the collection method may also help an exporter make a sale in a competitive market, as the cost to the importer is lower than the cost of obtaining a letter of credit.

If, however, the exporter has once used a collection for a sale to a particular buyer and had difficulty in obtaining payment from the buyer, then the exporter will probably insist on a letter of credit before undertaking further orders.

Accounting

The amount of the letter of credit appears as a contingent account in the bank's financial statement as soon as it is issued. When the documents are negotiated and the draft is paid or accepted, or if no drawing takes place by the expiration date, the amount is taken out of the contingent account. If financing is provided, then the appropriate loan category would be charged.

For the risk-based capital calculation, the amount of the outstanding letter of credit is first multiplied by a credit conversion factor of 20 percent and then assigned to the appropriate risk category of the account party (the bank's customer, for whom it is issued). For a business importer, the risk category would be 100 percent. Therefore, this sample calculation would be the amount of the letter of credit × 20% × 100% = the amount against which capital would be required.

The bank has to maintain capital for its outstanding letters of credit, so it is important to remove any unused balances promptly after the expiration date.

Summary

The commercial letter of credit is one of the most important instruments in international banking. It is indispensable in banking and financing international trade and a most important activity for most countries.

The letter of credit substitutes a bank's credit for that of a customer and thereby ensures payment from buyer to seller. The transaction rests on documents that prove that the shipment has taken place as agreed. Buyers are assured that the shipment has been made before they are called on to pay, and sellers know that they will be paid as soon as they ship regardless of any change in the buyer's financial standing.

This instrument in international trade has been a major banking activity for many years. Its continued widespread use after more than a century is testimony to its vitality and usefulness in international trade— particularly in times of economic difficulty, when its use has increased. The letter of credit is an important and unique service that banks provide in international banking.

Questions

1. What is a letter of credit?
2. What does negotiation mean?
3. What is the responsibility of the importer?
4. What is the difference between a collection and a letter of credit?

Problem

A customer of your bank wishes to purchase toys from a seller in Hong Kong. The seller does not know anything about the credit standing of your customer and is, therefore, willing to make the shipment only if a letter of credit is opened in its favor. What will be your bank's responsibilities, and what should you consider in making your decision?

Notes

1. Craig W. Smith, *Law and Banking: Applications* (Washington, D.C.: American Bankers Association, 1986), p. 109

2. *Harbottle (Mercantile) Ltd. v. National Westminster Bank Ltd.*, (1978) Q.B. 146, 1955

3. Boris Kozolchyk, "Letter of Credit," *International Encyclopedia of Comparative Law*, 1983

4. Smith, *Law and Banking*, p. 105

5. U.S. Department of the Treasury, *Comptroller's Handbook for National Bank Examiners* (Englewood Cliffs, N.J.: Prentice-Hall, Inc.), Section 812.1. National banks are restricted in issuing such guarantees from U.S. offices that differ from foreign branches. See also Board of Governors of the Federal Reserve System, *Commercial Bank Examination Manual* (Washington, D.C.: November 1993), Section 714.1, for similar provisions relating to state member banks.

6. *Sztejn v. J. Henry Schroder Banking Corporation*, 31 N.Y.S.2d 631 (1940)

7. *Edward Owen Engineering v. Barclays Bank International Ltd.*, Q.B. 159 (1978)

8. *United City Merchants (Investments) Ltd. v. Royal Bank of Canada* (1977 V No. 111)

9. Interview with Anthony Ruggiero, *Letter of Credit Update* (Arlington, Va.: October 1985), pp. 24-27

10. *United City Merchants (Investments) Ltd. v. Royal Bank of Canada* (1977 V No. 111)

8

LETTER OF CREDIT VARIATIONS

Learning Objectives

After studying this chapter, you will be able to

- describe the letter of credit that provides for time drafts
- explain specialized types of clauses
- describe the use of export letters of credit
- identify the special features of standby letters of credit

Overview

One of the great strengths of the letter of credit is its flexibility. The basic sight import letter of credit can be varied to accommodate the particular needs agreed to between buyers and sellers, while maintaining the fundamental principles and procedures already discussed.

Letters of credit can provide additional financing for the buyer or advance funds to the seller or permit a large international bank to provide financial support to smaller banks or customers. This flexibility is what makes the letter of credit the principal means of bank financing for international trade.

Export Letters of Credit

Because every foreign trade transaction is both an export and an import, every international commercial letter of credit is both an export credit and an import credit. To the beneficiary (the seller) and to the advising, confirming, or negotiating bank, it is an export credit; to the buyer and to the opening (issuing) bank, it is an import credit.

Regardless of whether the underlying transaction is a U.S. export, a U.S. import, or trade between any two countries, all letters of credit are opened at the request of the importers to their bank.

Confirmed Letters of Credit

The letters of credit issued by many foreign banks may not be acceptable to U.S. sellers. The ability of some banks to honor their obligations has been affected in the past by foreign government exchange restrictions, local political situations, economic crisis, and wars or the threat of war. In addition, many foreign banks that issue letters of credit on behalf of their customers are small and not known to the U.S. exporter. Even though a U.S. exporter insists on receiving a letter of credit, she may feel that a letter of credit from a small foreign bank does not provide the desired protection.

The U.S. exporter consequently may insist not only that the buyer's local bank issue a letter of credit but also that a U.S. bank add its commitment to pay to that of the foreign bank. This requirement is met by a letter of credit that is an irrevocable obligation of the issuing bank (in this case, the foreign bank), which is **confirmed** by a U.S. bank (usually by adding a cover letter that states "we hereby add our confirmation to this credit in accordance with the stipulations under UCP No. 500, Article 9"). In other words, the U.S. bank adds its obligation to that of the foreign bank to honor drafts and documents presented in accordance with the terms of the credit.

The confirming bank "has acted as an intermediate, has assumed the risk of default of the foreign bank, and has assured the draft's holder of payment."[1] The U.S. bank will do this because of the established correspondent relationship with the foreign bank and because the U.S. bank is willing to extend credit to the foreign bank. If the credit risk of the requesting bank or the country risk of that country is not satisfactory to the bank asked to add its confirmation, it is under no obligation to do so. By adding its confirmation, the U.S. bank is able to facilitate foreign trade, particularly U.S. exports. The draft in a confirmed letter of credit will usually be drawn on the confirming bank so that it can to pay the exporter immediately. The fee collected represents the credit risk the confirming bank is assuming and is similar to interest.[2]

The exporter now has a letter of credit that bears the promise of two banks—the issuing foreign bank and the confirming U.S. bank. The U.S. exporter is thus relieved of any concern about whether the foreign bank will be able to obtain dollars to pay; this risk is borne by the confirming U.S. bank.

If an exporter receives a letter of credit that has not been confirmed and wants it to be confirmed, she must request the importer to have his bank ask the U.S. bank to confirm. This may seem cumbersome, but the U.S. bank is looking for reimbursement from the foreign bank that is its customer. No one else can ask the U.S. bank to provide credit to the foreign bank. The U.S. bank must be careful to distinguish between its responsibilities to its customers in such a transaction. Although the exporter may be a bank's customer for many types of business, the foreign bank is the party to whom the bank is extending credit when it confirms a letter of credit. The U.S. bank should not get into a situation where it is attempting to respond to the demands of both parties.

Although this example has referred to a U.S. exporter, the procedure is the same when the trade transaction takes place between two foreign countries. A U.S. bank will add its confirmation at the request of a bank issuing a letter of credit in favor of a beneficiary anywhere in the world. Similarly, the confirmed letter of credit can be in U.S. dollars or another currency. Confirmation does not indicate what type of letter of credit is being issued.

When a U.S. bank adds its confirmation to a letter of credit issued by a foreign bank, it charges a fee to the foreign bank that is ultimately passed on to the foreign buyer. This fee, which may be called a commission, represents the bank's charge for extending credit.

Advised Credits

As foreign exchange conditions in many countries have become regularized and as business competition has become greater, many exporters have been willing to forgo confirmation of letters of credit by U.S. banks. Many of the larger foreign banks have become well known around the world; consequently, exporters have been willing to accept their letters of credit directly. As a result, banks often are not asked to confirm a foreign bank's letter of credit but merely to *advise* it. This is sometimes called an *unconfirmed* letter of credit. The U.S. bank states that this "is solely an advice of a credit opened by the mentioned correspondent and conveys no engagement by us." In the example given of a U.S. export, the U.S. bank, after verifying that the signatures on the foreign letter of credit are authorized signatures of a bona fide bank, advises the beneficiary of this fact and volunteers its services in general. Because such letters of credit are often in U.S. dollars, they usually provide that drafts can be drawn on the advising U.S. bank. When such drafts are negotiated, the U.S. bank earns a commission as well as activity through the Due To account of its correspondent.

Sometimes an exporter receiving an advised letter of credit may ask the advising bank to "confirm" the letter of credit. This is not to be confused with the confirmed letter of credit arrangement described above. The issuing foreign bank is not requesting it, has not authorized it to be carried under its line of credit, and is not assuming any responsibility to pay any confirmation fee. The exporter is willing to pay that fee to obtain a "silent confirmation." In essence, the exporter is paying the U.S. bank to assume, in advance, responsibility that the issuing bank will be in business when the exporter presents the documents and that there will be no restrictions on the payment of the currency of the draft (usually dollars) either from government controls or changes in the issuing bank's financial capabilities.

Letters of Credit Available by Time Drafts

In addition to letters of credit available by drafts payable at sight, a frequently used letter of credit is the **time** or **usance letter of credit**.* This letter of credit specifies that drafts are drawn on the issuing or other designated bank, depending on the currency or other conditions, and that payment is to be made at some future time. When the draft is in dollars, this means up to six months after sight. In such a letter of credit, the seller draws the draft and presents it with all the shipping documents to the designated bank, which "accepts" the draft. This means that the bank promises to pay the full face amount of the draft, not when the documents are presented but on a specified future date. The accepted draft is returned to the seller, who holds it to maturity and presents it to the bank on the future date to receive the full amount, regardless of whether the buyer has paid the bank or not. Such time drafts may be drawn, for example, "X days after sight," "X days after date," or "X days after date of bill of bill of lading." In these cases, the specific maturity date must be indicated when the draft is drawn. The accepted draft is a bankers' acceptance to be examined in detail in chapter 9.

The procedure for using the time letter of credit is similar to that for the sight letter of credit. The importing customer submits an application to the bank for the letter of credit that identifies the documents to be presented, amount of the credit, expiration date, and other information. The bank establishes the letter of credit, following the procedure previously described. The shipper provides the documents stipulated and the draft to the issuing bank for examination, honor, and eventual release of the documents to the importer.

The similarity between sight and time letters of credit ends with the routine of issuance and negotiation. A sight letter of credit is payable upon presentation of documents to the issuing bank, as long as those documents conform to the terms of the letter of credit. The bank is obligated to make such payment regardless of the ability of the importer to pay and will release the documents when payment is made to it by the importing customer. A time letter of credit, on the other hand, implies an extension of credit by the issuing bank beyond the date on which the documents are presented. The seller has to agree to a letter of credit providing for a time rather than a sight draft. In essence, the seller agrees to wait the period of time—for example, 90 days—before receiving full payment. The seller may be willing to wait for various reasons: a highly competitive market in which other sellers of similar goods are offering buyers 90 days before having to pay, or the need for a delay because otherwise this particular buyer would be unable to complete a purchase contract at all. In any event, the seller surrenders title to the merchandise in return for a promise of the issuing bank to pay for it at a future date. The seller might quote a slightly higher price for the goods for a 90-day delay in payment, even though a bank is obligated to pay at that time.

An importer's primary reason for requesting a time letter of credit is to have time to obtain and sell the goods in order to pay the draft. But the bank issuing the time letter of credit has a different credit consideration than exists with a sight letter of credit. The bank must release the goods to the importer immediately, thereby losing possession of the title documents to the goods, but will not receive payment from the importer until the end of the 90 days. At the same time, the bank must honor the obligation whether or not its customer, the importer, pays. The banker, therefore, considers to what extent the bank is willing to fulfill the customer's request in such a situation, because the banker will be releasing the bank's collateral in trust to the customer. In other words, how much of a credit line will the

---

* The *Oxford English Dictionary* traces the origin of *usance* to the seventeenth century: "the time or period (varying in respect of different countries) allowed by commercial usage or law for the payment of a bill of exchange, etc., especially as drawn in a foreign or distant land."

bank give its customer on **trust receipt**? "This is an arrangement in which the lender retains title to the goods that are held by the borrower. The borrower holds the goods in 'trust' for the lender." [3] (Factors to be evaluated in extending a line of credit are covered in chapter 10.)

Note that the exporter has a bank commitment to pay throughout the transaction, whether the letter of credit provides for a sight draft or a time draft. The exporter ships, in either case, against a bank's commitment to pay upon presentation of specified documents under certain stated conditions. With a sight draft, the exporter surrenders title to the merchandise for a cash payment. With a time draft, the exporter surrenders title against the bank's unconditional commitment to pay on a stated future date. Once the shipment is made in accordance with the letter of credit, the exporter never loses the protection of the bank's credit standing and is never exposed to the importer's credit capabilities. The bank stands in place of the importer in both sight and time letters of credit until the drafts are paid in cash.

A trust receipt is a document signed by a buyer in which a bank retains a security interest in the goods while the buyer has possession of them. It is intended to be used for short periods of time. The buyer is obligated to maintain the identity of the goods or the proceeds from the sale of those goods distinct from other assets and subject to repossession by the bank. Depending on the law in a particular state, the U.S. bank may wish to have greater protection by taking a lien on the inventory or some other form of collateral. In spite of these legal obligations, the bank does not have possession of the goods and may not be able to find them to repossess. In fact, the goods may have been sold to a third party without the bank's immediate knowledge. The bank must consider these realities when making its decision.

In most cases, when the bank issues a time letter of credit it presupposes that the merchandise will be released on trust receipt at the time the draft is presented for acceptance. However, a bank may elect not to release the shipping documents to its customer. In such circumstances the issuing bank itself, holding documents giving title to the goods, may decide to store these goods in a public warehouse and hold the warehouse receipt as collateral. Releases may then be made against payment or as otherwise determined by the bank. This, however, will not be the usual case. Thus the essential differences between a sight letter of credit and a time letter of credit are the added credit risk assumed by the issuing bank and the technical procedure of creating a banker's acceptance liability.

Time letters of credit will be used when the draft is drawn payable within six months, the maximum term permitted for eligible U.S. dollar bankers' acceptances, which is what the draft becomes after it has been accepted by the bank. (See chapter 9 for the conditions of a bankers' acceptance.)

Deferred Payment Letters of Credit

The seller of the goods may be willing to extend credit to the buyer for longer than six months. This **deferred payment** may be particularly suitable in sales of heavy equipment. To do this the letter of credit may specify that sight drafts are to be presented not at the time of shipment but, for example, one year later. The shipping documents and all other documents will be presented at the time the shipment takes place. The bank acknowledges their correctness to the seller and forwards them to the buyer. A year later, the shipper presents the sight draft to the bank; the bank pays it and looks to the buyer for reimbursement at that time.

The bank's direct commitment to pay at the end of the deferred payment period is assumed at the time the bank receives the documents in order and acknowledges their receipt to the beneficiary.

Therefore, issuance or confirmation of such a letter of credit must take place only after full evaluation of a credit exposure for this longer time and after the merchandise has been delivered to the buyer (at the time of presentation of the documents to the bank, which is before the time of payment). The actual financing is made by the seller, who, in this example, is willing to wait a year before payment. Deferred payment letters of credit may also provide for a series of payments over a number of years.

In summary, the difference between a time letter of credit and a deferred payment letter of credit is that the former will provide for a draft payable no more than six months later. In a deferred payment letter of credit, the draft will not be presented until sometime in the future, usually much more than six months.

Other Letters of Credit

The letter of credit is a flexible document. Clauses may be added to the basic letter of credit or may be changed to meet the special needs of a bank's customers and thereby broaden the uses of this document.

Red Clause Letters of Credit

The buyer of goods may be willing to make cash advances to the seller before shipment. The need for advances can arise when the seller is an agent of the buyer and needs cash to buy a crop from farmers in the interior of the country. For example, a letter of credit for the shipment of copra from the Philippines to the United States might contain a **red clause** to permit advance payments that will enable the seller to buy the commodity from planters who insist on cash. When the crop moves to the port and is shipped, the shipping and allied documents are presented to the negoti-

ating bank; the payment to the seller would be the difference between the invoice amount and the amount already advanced.

The term "red clause" derives from the red ink in which such clauses were originally written. A typical red clause would read as follows:

The negotiating bank is hereby authorized to make advances to the beneficiary up to the aggregate amount of X dollars or the remaining unused balance against the beneficiary's receipt stating that the advances are to be used to pay for the purchase and shipment of the merchandise covered by this credit and the beneficiary's undertaking to deliver to the negotiating bank the documents stipulated in the credit. The advances with interest are to be deducted from the proceeds of the drafts drawn under this credit. We hereby undertake the payment of such advances with interest should they not be repaid by the beneficiary prior to the expiration of this credit.

The buyer assumes the risk that the seller might draw the advance and not ship the goods. The bank will issue a letter of credit with such a red clause only when it knows that it can obtain reimbursement from the buyer if the shipment is not made. The buyer, in requesting a red clause, should be aware of the exposure on the interest cost. The rate of interest varies substantially in various parts of the world. A drawing in U.S. dollars can be converted into the local currency and re-lent by the beneficiary at many times the interest rate in the United States. If the foreign bank honors a drawing, it can either establish a loan on its books to the exporter using the red clause as its source of repayment if the exporter fails to repay or it can immediately negotiate the draft to provide the exporter with the funds. In either case, the drawing will be subsequently charged to the account of the importer. An unscrupulous seller can thus profit at the expense of the U.S. buyer.

This is sometimes called a *packing credit* "meaning that the beneficiary is to buy from different sources, consolidate the purchases, and pack and ship the purchases to his principal, the real buyer." [4]

A *green clause* letter of credit is a variation of the red clause. It is used in a few countries, such as Australia for the wool trade. It permits advances to the seller but requires that the merchandise be stored under the bank's control until it is shipped.

Transferable Letters of Credit

A letter of credit may be used only by the addressed party, normally the seller of the merchandise. In some cases, however, this party may be an agent who wants to transfer the letter of credit to the actual seller. At the request of its customer, the issuing bank addresses the letter of credit to the beneficiary as before, but states in the letter of credit that it is **transferable**. The credit may be transferred only once, and the new beneficiary cannot transfer it again. The original beneficiary must give the issuing bank the name of the new beneficiary *(transferee)*, from whom documents will then be accepted. This letter of credit can be transferred for the entire amount or for a partial amount.

Such letters of credit are also useful for a business representative making a buying trip. The representative can carry a letter of credit and transfer portions of it from time to time as purchases are made from manufacturers.

Assignment of Proceeds

A beneficiary of a letter of credit may seek financing from another supplier or third party in order to prepare the shipment. As collateral the beneficiary may agree to pledge to the supplier the proceeds of the draft drawn under the letter of credit. This is done by instructing the bank to pay a portion or all of the letter of credit payments to the third party. Called an **assignment of proceeds**, it is of value only if the beneficiary presents documents in compliance with the letter of credit. If no draft is drawn under the letter of credit, then the bank has no obligation to honor the assignment of proceeds.

A bank can also advance funds to the beneficiary and takes the assignment of proceeds as repayment, called *discounting a letter of credit*. If the letter of credit's beneficiary does not make the shipment and present the documents, the bank that discounted the letter of credit cannot make the shipment or present documents to recover the money it has advanced. To permit anyone other than the beneficiary to do so would make the letter of credit transferable, which cannot be done unless the letter of credit so states.

An assignment of proceeds differs from a transferable letter of credit. In the latter, the beneficiary authorizes another party to make the shipment, present the documents to the bank, and be paid. In the assignment of proceeds, the beneficiary in the letter of credit is the one who makes the shipment and presents documents to the bank. He has, however, authorized the payment to be made to another party.

Back-to-Back Letters of Credit

Back-to-back letters of credit are two letters of credit with identical documentary requirements [5] except for a difference in the price of the merchandise and, possibly, curtailed expiration dates. This is appropriate when an agent acts between buyer and seller and uses the creditworthiness of the ultimate buyer as the agent's own. The agent agrees to purchase the goods against a letter of credit. The agent then asks the buyer to open a letter of credit at the buyer's bank in favor of the agent, and having identical documentary requirements except for the draft amount. This credit is lodged with the agent's bank, which issues a new credit for account of the agent in favor of the seller.

The documents differ only in the amount of the draft and the invoices, providing profit for the agent. The agent's invoices and the draft for the higher amount are given to the agent's bank when it issues its credit. When documents are presented under the credit opened by the agent's bank, that bank can pay the seller and can present to and collect from the bank that issued the credit for the ultimate buyer in favor of the agent.

If the agent dies, the presigned draft and invoices may not be usable. Of greater concern is the possibility of discrepancies in the documents. The second bank might find the documents to be in order; the first bank may not. As a consequence, any bank issuing the second letter of credit in a back-to-back transaction must carefully evaluate the transaction and all the involved parties.

The agent may prefer to use a back-to-back letter of credit instead of a transferable letter of credit because this may prevent the buyer from knowing the identity of the seller. A buyer who had this information might elect to deal directly with the seller instead of using the agent.

Revolving Letters of Credit

When a series of identical shipments for the same amount with the same parties involved are to be made over a period of time, and when the total value is greater than the amount the bank or the buyer is willing to have outstanding at any time, a letter of credit may be issued for a smaller amount, with the provision that after a shipment takes place and an amount is drawn, the credit will reinstate that amount. This is a **revolving** letter of credit. It has the advantage of using one

letter of credit instead of issuing a new one each time, which may be less costly for the customer. After each shipment is made, received by, and paid for by the buyer, the bank notifies the beneficiary that the letter of credit has been reinstated with a new expiration date.

Revolving letters of credit provide some means of control over the bank's credit exposure and ease administration tasks. A letter of credit may be established with a fixed amount and a provision that only a certain amount of merchandise may be shipped each month. This provision restricts the exposure of buyers so that they cannot be faced with a larger shipment than expected. Such revolving credits may be cumulative or noncumulative; that is, any amount not drawn in one month may or may not be added to the shipment made in the following month. The revolving letter of credit usually requires notification to the seller that it has been reinstated for the next shipment, or it may be automatically reinstated at specified periods. It can be issued for the amount of each transaction or for the full amount of all of the shipments but be available only in specified increments.

Straight and Negotiation Credits

The letter of credit will indicate where it expires. If it specifies that documents must be presented at the office of the issuing bank by the expiration date, the letter of credit is a *straight credit*. If the letter of credit specifies that documents are to be presented to another bank by the expiration date, then it is a *negotiation* credit.

The straight letter of credit may state: "We hereby agree with the beneficiary that all drafts drawn under and/or documents presented hereunder will be duly honored by us provided the terms and conditions are complied with and that presentation is made at this office on or before [the expiry date]." The negotiation letter of credit could state: "We hereby agree with the drawers, endorsers, and bona fide holders of drafts/documents drawn under and in compliance with the terms and conditions of the Credit that such drafts/documents will be duly honored on due presentation if negotiated or presented at this office on or before [the expiry date]."

The negotiation credit is usually more convenient for the exporter since it allows her to present documents at a bank in her locale by the expiration date and thus comply with the terms of the letter of credit. The varying reliability of mail service might make it difficult for the exporter to get the documents to the issuing bank by the expiration of a straight credit.

When a straight letter of credit is used, the issuing bank is only committed to pay the beneficiary when the beneficiary presents draft and documents. Under a negotiation letter of credit, the issuing bank is committed to pay either the beneficiary or another bank that has negotiated the documents.

For example, a negotiation letter of credit issued by a U.S. bank in favor of a beneficiary in Argentina would state that documents are to be presented to an Argentine bank by the stated expiration date. On that date, the exporter presents the draft and documents to her local bank. The Argentine bank examines the documents, finds them to be in order, and pays the exporter. That bank is now a "holder in due course." As such it has certain legal protections. When the issuing bank receives the draft and documents, it will negotiate them, and assuming they comply with the requirements in the letter of credit, will pay the Argentine bank. The Argentine bank is not required to negotiate the draft and documents if it does not wish to, unless it has confirmed the letter of credit.

If, however, this had been a straight credit, then the beneficiary would have been responsible for seeing that the draft and documents arrive at the issuing bank by the expiration date. While an

Argentine bank could still have negotiated the documents and paid the exporter, it would have acquired no rights against the issuing bank, which has no commitment to protect any other bank that purchased the draft. In the normal course of business, however, it is not unusual for the exporter's bank, in fact, to negotiate the documents and purchase the draft from an exporter— its customer. It will need to protect itself with some legal legal agreement from the exporter to receive the proceeds when the issuing bank pays, as it has a credit relationship with the exporter.

Revocable Letter of Credit

A letter of credit that can be canceled by the buyer or the opening bank without the concurrence of the seller is a **revocable letter of credit**. Because such an instrument negates one of the main advantages of a letter of credit for the seller, it is rarely used for general trade. The only protection for the seller is that, if the documents are presented and the seller is paid before cancellation by the buyer, the issuing bank will honor the draft and documents if they are in order.

Authority to Pay

A similar but less frequently used type of letter of credit is the **authority to pay**. This document is not really a letter of credit but merely an advice of a place of payment, carrying neither the U.S. bank's nor the foreign bank's obligation to make such payment. In effect, it is only as good as the foreign buyer and provides payment in advance of arrival of the documents in the foreign country, provided that revocation does not take place before presentation. It therefore acts merely as a guide to the shipper in the preparation of shipping documents.

Authority to Purchase

An **authority to purchase**, used primarily in Asia, is similar to a letter of credit except that the draft is drawn on the foreign buyer. It can be either irrevocable or revocable. In revocable form, it should call for drafts drawn with recourse on the beneficiary, meaning that the beneficiary must return the funds if payment is not made by the buyer. Irrevocable drafts are without recourse to the beneficiary. The use of authorities to purchase has decreased in recent years.

Reimbursement Arrangements

In some instances, a bank will issue its letter of credit in favor of a beneficiary in a country where it does not have a correspondent bank. For the letter of credit to be payable at a bank near the beneficiary, the paying bank will be authorized to draw on another bank to reimburse itself for the payments it makes. Usually this third bank (reimbursing bank) will be a correspondent of both the issuing and advising banks. This is a **reimbursement arrangement**, which is basically a paying mechanism. The reimbursing bank will receive a letter or telecommunication from the issuing bank with information about the letter of credit and authorization from the issuing bank to honor the request for payment by the paying bank. All shipping documents go directly from the paying bank to the issuing bank. The arrangement can also provide for usance drafts. The letter of credit will provide for the seller to draw a usance draft on the reimbursing bank, which accepts it for the account of the issuing bank. The negotiating bank has to supply the necessary details of the transaction so that the reimbursing bank can complete the acceptance.

Letters of Credit Payable in Foreign Currency

Letters of credit issued by U.S. banks may be expressed not only in U.S. dollars, but also in the currency of the seller or in a third currency. An example would be a letter of credit expressed in pounds sterling under which drafts are drawn on the London correspondent of the U.S. bank issuing the credit. (A U.S. bank that has a branch in London would, of course, use that branch instead of a correspondent bank.)

An importer may request that a letter of credit be denominated in another currency to meet the demand by the seller for payment in the seller's currency, thereby eliminating the foreign exchange risk. After negotiating the documents, the bank makes payment through its Due From account and charges the importer the U.S. dollar equivalent. When the letter of credit provides for a time draft, the U.S. bank will make arrangements for a bank in the country where that currency is legal tender to accept the draft under the credit responsibility of the U.S. bank. Forward foreign exchange contracts will often be used (see chapter 5).

Government-Sponsored Letters of Credit

International development agencies, such as the World Bank, and U.S. government agencies, such as the Commodity Credit Corporation and foreign-aid servicing entities, often use the commercial letter of credit as the vehicle for disbursing funds.

Once the government agency has approved a loan, it will issue a letter of commitment to a commercial bank. This permits the foreign borrower to send applications to that commercial bank to open letters of credit in favor of suppliers of specific items authorized as part of a multimillion-dollar loan. The individual letters of credit may be for only a few thousand dollars or for a very much larger amount. The commercial bank issues the letter of credit. The essential documents will include some specialized ones required by the government entity. When the shipment is made, the documents and draft are presented to the bank as in any other trade transaction. When the documents are in order, the bank pays the seller. However, instead of then looking to the importer for payment, the bank requests reimbursement from the government entity under its letter of commitment. In this way, the government entity can disburse its large loan without becoming involved in the technical trade requirements that are routinely handled in any major bank's letter of credit section.

Traveler's Letter of Credit

Before worldwide use of traveler's checks, banks issued a special document for travelers. This was the **traveler's** or **circular letter of credit**. Its purpose was to enable a traveler to draw money at any of a bank's correspondents anywhere in the world. The letter of credit was issued with a separate letter that contained the specimen signature of the traveler. When the two documents were presented, the correspondent bank would advance cash up to a stated limit. Each drawing was noted on the letter of credit so that subsequent correspondent banks could know how much was still available to the traveler.

The use of the traveler's letter of credit has almost disappeared. It is a cumbersome document requiring safeguarding by the traveler, and it is inconvenient because it could be used at a bank only during banking hours.

Domestic Letters of Credit

Use of a U.S. bank's commercial letter of credit is not confined to financing the importation or exportation of merchandise. Whether it is available at sight or at any number of days up to six months, the letter of credit is applicable in the financing of merchandise transactions within the United States and within the Uniform Commercial Code. Time can be saved and many troublesome credit problems eliminated by the domestic use of the letter of credit.

A seller of goods, for instance, may request such a letter of credit and thereby eliminate much credit investigation, knowing that it will receive a bank's irrevocable obligation to pay against stipulated documents. The seller need not worry about payment or extension of credit; rather, he should be concerned with his own ability to perform under the terms of the credit and within the time limit stipulated in that credit. Furthermore, the seller is protected against cancellation of an order by a buyer because the bank cannot cancel its irrevocable obligation without the seller's consent. The financial position of the seller with his own bank is strengthened when he can show that his sales are made against commercial letters of credit.

Use of the letter of credit also has many advantages for the buyer of goods. When there is a heavy demand for a particular commodity, a buyer offering her bank's obligation to pay in the form of a letter of credit may receive more favorable consideration from possible suppliers because those suppliers are, in effect, selling on a cash basis. At the same time, the buyer does not necessarily have to pay cash until delivery of documents to her bank. Furthermore, the buyer may fix an expiration date on a letter of credit to provide that seasonal merchandise is received on time. The cost of such letters of credit is nominal.

Standby Letter of Credit

What has been discussed thus far is the commercial letter of credit, a document issued by a bank stating that payment will be made when something is done, usually when a shipment of merchandise from a seller to a buyer is completed. A **standby letter of credit** is a document also issued by a bank, but payment is made when something *does not* happen. In further contrast to the commercial letter of credit, neither the issuing bank nor applicant nor beneficiary of a standby letter of credit expect that any payment will ever be requested. The banker, however, should not be deluded by this, since there is considerably more risk in issuing a standby letter of credit than a commercial letter of credit. There is also greater risk to the beneficiary.

U.S. banks generally are not legally allowed to issue their own guarantees to back the performance or financial commitments of their customers,[6] as banks in some countries may do. A U.S. bank may provide comparable support for its customer by issuing a standby letter of credit. This differs from a letter of guarantee because it conspicuously states that it is a letter of credit (issued in accordance with the Uniform Customs and Practices for Documentary Credits), has a specified expiration date, is limited in amount, permits payment to be made only against draft and documents that do not require the bank to determine any questions of fact or dispute, and the bank's customer has the unqualified obligation to reimburse the bank for any payments.[7] Some foreign banks prefer to issue standby letters of credit rather than issue their own letters of guaranty in order to get the protections of the UCP.

As with a commercial letter of credit, the bank receives a written application from its customer on which it will make a credit judgment. A standby letter of credit usually covers the performance of the applicant or the financial commitment of the applicant to the beneficiary or other third party.

A *performance standby letter of credit* may be used in the construction business, where it is customary for a contractor to post a bond or other financial support to ensure that it will complete the project within the specified terms of the contract. If it does not, then the standby letter of credit payment will enable the contracting party (the beneficiary) to complete or correct what was not done properly. A *financial standby letter of credit* is issued to back the applicant's obligation to repay a debt to the beneficiary. In such an instance, the bank's customer may have borrowed money from another source with a more favorable interest rate or conditions than it could have gotten from the bank. The lender, however, wants to have the backing of the bank to repay if the borrower does not.

The documentation required for drawing is usually very simple: a draft (usually drawn at sight or a few days after sight) and the beneficiary's statement that the applicant has failed to perform in accordance with a contract or terms of the debt. As with the commercial letter of credit, the banker deals with documents and will not investigate whether that statement is true or not.

Risks

The banker must be alert to the particular risks of a standby letter of credit. The bank's exposure to loss begins as soon as the standby letter of credit is issued, and even though no bank funds are disbursed at that time, the risk of loss is exactly the same as if the bank had disbursed money. The transaction needs the same ongoing financial supervision of the borrower's financial conditions. When approving the issuance of a performance standby letter of credit, the banker must be satisfied that the contractor is financially and technically capable of meeting the obligations under the contract. An important consideration for the party awarding the contract, the bank, and the contractor is the reputation of the contractor and the awareness that failure to perform under this contract will impair that reputation and future of his firm. Before approving an application for a financial standby letter of credit, the banker must be satisfied that the applicant has the financial capability to meet the scheduled debt repayment to the third party.

Even though no one expects any drawing will ever take place, when one does it usually is after a dispute that the two parties have been unable to resolve. The banker probably will find that the applicant's financial conditions that prevailed at the time of issuance have drastically deteriorated. The bank must honor the drawing and can find itself making an actual disbursement of funds for a borrower to whom it would not have been willing to grant credit based on the present conditions.

The standby letter of credit has a stated expiration date. However, the bank may have to agree to extend the standby letter of credit if the underlying transaction is not yet completed. Failure to do so would trigger an immediate drawing since the beneficiary will not want to continue without that protection from the bank.

The beneficiary of the standby letter of credit has the risk of the creditworthiness of the issuing bank. The U.S. Supreme Court has ruled that a standby letter of credit is not a deposit.[8] If the U.S. bank fails, its commitment to pay a drawing under a standby letter of credit does not become an obligation of the liquidator, which is the FDIC. By contrast, in the case of a commercial letter of credit, the beneficiary would still have control over the merchandise, which presumably would limit her exposure to total loss.

Using the Services of a Correspondent Bank

The procedure involved in successfully completing a letter of credit transaction requires a trained staff thoroughly familiar with all the ramifications of the letter of credit instrument. In addition, the procedure presupposes that a bank with an established reputation has placed its authorized signatures on record with banks located in commercially important centers throughout the world.

Relatively few U.S. banks are equipped to handle letters of credit. Nevertheless, the lack of trained personnel and of an international reputation need not deter a bank when it is asked to assist a customer in opening a letter of credit. The facilities of a domestic U.S. correspondent bank capable of handling all phases of letters of credit are available. For a bank without a full international department to operate effectively, however, an official in the bank should have at least a rudimentary knowledge of the subject to discuss intelligently the various phases of the business. The actual mechanics of the procedure can be turned over to the correspondent bank maintaining an international department.

An active correspondent bank is usually eager to cooperate with its correspondents in other cities. It solicits letter of credit business and may share the fees, making the cooperation attractive to both banks. The correspondents are supplied with the necessary forms, including the application blank. This application differs from the form the larger bank receives from its own commercial customers in two respects:

- Addressed to the correspondent bank in the form of a request, it asks the correspondent bank to act as agent for the small bank.
- It bears the signatures of both the bank without the international department and its customers.

Otherwise, the forms of the letter of credit agreement are substantially similar. The customer's agreement included in the form is, under appropriate circumstances, a protection for both banks involved. Banks operating without an international department do not necessarily have to prepare complicated forms to bind their customers.

The smaller bank using the facilities of a correspondent bank assumes the credit risks involved in accommodating its customer. This emphasizes the importance of bank officers having at least a basic understanding of what is needed to appraise the risks properly.

When it receives an application for a commercial letter of credit from one of its correspondents, the larger bank looks to that correspondent for payment. In most cases, all details involved in establishing the credit, handling documents, handling foreign exchange operations, advising of payment, and preparing forms and trust receipts are taken care of by the correspondent bank.

In each letter of credit transaction, regardless of whether the bank is issuing, advising, or confirming, the bank must be aware of and comply with any rules or restrictions of its own government.

Letter of Credit Limitations

The discussions in this chapter and chapter 7 have described how the commercial letter of credit furthers international trade and protects the different parties. There are, however, important limitations.

First, the letter of credit does not require the exporter to do anything if he does not want to. Some importers mistakenly believe that once a letter of credit has been issued, the exporter must comply with it. That is not so. If the exporter does not want to make the shipment, she does not have to. This may cause, or be the result of, a

dispute with the merchandise contract. But the letter of credit itself does not force a shipment to be made. All it says is that if the exporter wants to be paid by the bank, then she must comply with the terms and conditions of it.

Second, no advance notification is required by the exporter to the bank prior to presenting documents nor that the exporter is not going to make any shipment. If partial shipments are permitted, the exporter may only make that partial shipment. Again, this may create a dispute under the merchandise contract between the buyer and seller, but the bank is not a party to that.

Third, and this emphasizes points made several times here, banks deal with documents in a letter of credit—not merchandise.

Fourth, the fact that a bank has issued its letter of credit on behalf of an importer should not be taken to mean that the importer has impeccable creditworthiness that can be applied to other transactions. Bank standards differ, and some banks will issue a letter of credit solely against a deposit of cash without any other credit assessment.

Accounting

The letters of credit described in this chapter are reflected in a bank's financial statement as contingent accounts in the same manner as described in chapter 7.

The risk-based capital calculations for standby letters of credit differ from those for other letters of credit. Standby letters of credit that back "repayment of financial obligations such as: commercial paper . . . commercial or individual loans or debt obligations" are called financial standby letters of credit. These have a credit conversion factor of 100 percent. Standby letters of credit that back "the performance of nonfinancial commercial contracts or undertakings . . .

[such as] construction bids" are called performance standby letters of credit. These have a credit conversion factor of 50 percent.[9]

Summary

The great strength of the commercial letter of credit is its flexibility. This perhaps is why it is used so widely and has been used for so long. To meet special needs, clauses may be added or items changed.

A particularly important characteristic of the letter of credit is that it makes it easy for major international banks to back the transactions of smaller banks around the world, thus facilitating the movement of international trade. This occurs when a letter of credit is confirmed.

While most commercial letters of credit require that someone do something (usually ship goods) in order to obtain funds, the standby letter of credit is drawn against the *failure* of someone to do something. This has become important for construction bids, performance guarantees, obtaining local market financing for a corporate subsidiary, or supplying a credit backing for outside funding.

Questions

1. What is the difference between an import letter of credit and an export letter of credit?
2. What is the difference between a usance and a sight letter of credit?
3. What is the difference between a confirmed letter of credit and an advised letter of credit?
4. How does a standby letter of credit differ from a commercial letter of credit?

Problem

Your bank's customer has an order to sell machinery to a company in Singapore. He has received a letter of credit from a bank in Singapore to which a major California bank has added its confirmation. Explain to your customer what he must do in order to be paid for his shipment.

Notes

1. *Bank of America v. United States*, 680 F.2d 142 (Ct. Cl.1982).
2. Ibid.
3. Jay M. McDonald and John E. McKinley, *Corporate Banking: A Practical Approach to Lending* (Washington, D.C.: American Bankers Association, 1981), p. 228
4. William S. Shaterian, *Export-Import Banking* (New York: The Ronald Press Company, 1956), p. 437
5. Henry Harfield, *Bank Credits and Acceptances*, 5th ed. (New York: Ronald Press, 1974), p. 193
6. See note 5, chapter 7
7. U.S. Department of the Treasury, *Comptroller's Handbook for National Bank Examiners*, (Englewood Cliffs, N.J.: Prentice Hall, Inc., 1977-1981)
8. *Federal Deposit Insurance Corporation v. Philadelphia Gear Corp.*, U.S. Supreme Court 84-1972, May 27, 1986
9. Board of Governors of the Federal Reserve System, Federal Reserve Regulation Y, Appendix A, Section III D

9

BANKERS' ACCEPTANCES

Learning Objectives

After studying this chapter, you will be able to

- define the bankers' acceptance
- outline what a bankers' acceptance can finance
- describe the role of the various parties in the transaction
- examine typical transactions using the bankers' acceptance

Overview

In the United States, a **bankers' acceptance** is a means of providing financing, primarily associated with international trade, by creating a unique standardized financial instrument that is attractive to money market investors. It facilitates and expands the sources of credit funds beyond what is available directly from a commercial bank.

The bankers' acceptance is separate and distinct from the letter of credit, although many arise from it. It is a **time draft** (or **time bill of exchange**) drawn by one party (the drawer) on a bank (the drawee) and accepted by the bank as the bank's commitment to pay a third party (the payee) a stated sum on a specified future date (see exhibit 9.1). The bank's acceptance of this draft is a formal acknowledgment of its irrevocable, unconditional promise to pay the draft at its maturity.

Section 13 of the Federal Reserve Act permits banks to discount such an acceptance at a Federal Reserve bank when the acceptance finances specified types of commercial transactions, mostly relating to foreign trade. Because there is an active investors' market for bankers' acceptances, such discounting at the Federal Reserve is rarely necessary. It does, however, define the characteristics of the product in which the market deals. Through the bankers' acceptance, banks can provide credit to their customers without using their own funds. This is done by creating a negotiable instrument with a specified maturity date that is attractive to investors seeking a short-term, non-interest-bearing note sold at a discount that will be redeemed by the accepting bank at maturity for the full face amount. The bank creating an acceptance thus becomes primarily liable for the payment on the maturity date.

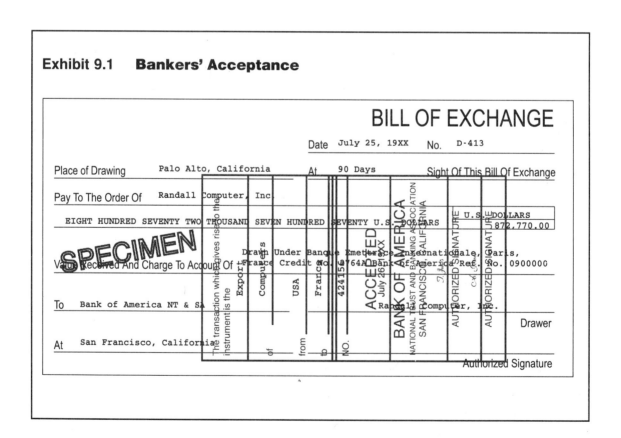

Exhibit 9.1   Bankers' Acceptance

While bankers' acceptances exist in varying forms in other countries and currencies, this chapter is concerned only with what is permitted to banks in the United States and in U.S. dollars. The expression "prime bankers' acceptance" is sometimes used and refers to the stature of the accepting bank. What constitutes a "prime" U.S. bank is a matter of investor judgment.

Background

The bankers' acceptance or time bill of exchange is a financing instrument with origins as far back as the twelfth century as a means of financing international trade.

> When in the second half of the eighteenth century, the entrepôt trade of Amsterdam deteriorated . . . [it] brought new prominence to another "branch" of Dutch commercial activity, the so-called acceptance trade. . . . Thus Amsterdam remained the "cash box" and the Dutch "the bankers of Europe". . . . The acceptance trade related to the countless bills of exchange which had long been the vehicle of credit throughout Europe. . . . Transfers, endorsements, discounting, drafts and deposits made the bill of exchange an indefatigable traveller from one center to another, one merchant to another, . . . from a businessman to his correspondent or to a discounter (as he was known in Holland).[1]

It was essential then because of the time needed between production, sale, and final payment.

> For the two centuries before the creation of the Fed, world trade was denominated and financed primarily in sterling, and a market in sterling bankers' acceptances flourished in London. The founders of the Federal Reserve System, created in 1913, felt that a

domestic bankers' acceptance market patterned after the London market should be developed to enhance New York's role as a center of international trade and finance, to promote U.S. foreign trade, and to improve the competitive position of domestic banks. The Fed's founders thus empowered national banks to accept time drafts, which these banks were previously unauthorized to do. They also took other actions to support the growth of this infant market, including permitting the Federal Reserve to rediscount and purchase eligible acceptances.[2]

While the global banker will consider the risk between a trade acceptance and a bankers' acceptance as considerably different, the two have a structural similarity.

> So far as the legal incidents are concerned, one acceptance is like another. The distinctions . . . between trade and bankers' acceptances . . . have no legal significance that is related to the form or the effect of the instrument. A "bankers' acceptance" is a draft or bill of exchange that is drawn on a bank or banker and has been accepted by the drawee. If the drawee-acceptor is not a bank or banker, the instrument is called a "trade acceptance".[3] (see chapter 6)

Acceptances have had an important role in the development of international trade. The acceptance's

> principal purpose is to provide current financing. . . . The principal use of an acceptance is to permit one person to use the credit of another person to facilitate the acquisition of money. Historically, the credit of a bank or banker has been preferred to that of merchants, with the consequence that the market for bankers' acceptance has developed virtually independently from the market in which mercantile obligations are traded

and entirely distinct from the securities market.[4]

Foreign Trade

In a typical foreign trade transaction, a U.S. bank issues its letter of credit on behalf of its customer, the importer. As seen in previous chapters, the letter of credit may provide for drafts to be drawn on the bank payable at sight, at a specified number of days after sight, or on a specific future date. The latter two are time letters of credit. When the importer knows at the time of negotiating the merchandise contract that she cannot pay for the merchandise when it is shipped, she must arrange for credit. This can be done in several different ways. For the use of the bankers' acceptance, it would be as follows:

The importer may ask the exporter to agree to wait for payment until she can take possession of the merchandise and sell it. If the exporter agrees—in order to make the sale—it will make the shipment against a time letter of credit. The exporter agrees to give up the title documents to the goods (for example, the bill of lading) in exchange for a continuation of the bank's promise to pay. To enable importers to possess and sell the merchandise before paying for it, the letter of credit will provide for the exporter to draw a draft on the bank payable at a future date. This draft is formally accepted in writing by the bank as its obligation to pay. The exporter may hold this bankers' acceptance to maturity and then present it to the accepting bank for payment of the full amount.

If, however, the exporter wishes to receive cash immediately, the accepted draft may be sold prior to maturity to an investor at a discounted amount. (Since the bankers' acceptance does not provide for the payment of interest, the investor will buy it for less than the face amount. He will receive the full face amount at its maturity; the differential representing the return on his invest-

ment.) The investor will hold it until it matures, at which time he will present it to the bank for payment. It is the bank's commitment to pay that enables intermediaries to hold or trade the draft so that the bank's customer may have the needed financing. In periods of tight money, this feature becomes vitally important, since it is a means by which banks can obtain funds for their customers from outside the bank's own resources by selling bankers' acceptances to investors.

The following example of a foreign trade financing transaction illustrates the parties involved in using bankers' acceptances and demonstrates options that each may have.

- *The borrower.* The importer needs financing to make a purchase. She may obtain a loan from the bank, pay the seller in full, and then repay the bank upon selling the goods. On using the bankers' acceptance, the importer still obtains credit from the bank and is still obligated to pay the bank cash at maturity. What differentiates the bankers' acceptance from a direct bank loan or other financing options the buyer may have, such as commercial paper or various types of Eurodollar financing, is the type of instrument used to obtain financing and the manner in which the financing costs may be calculated or paid.

- *The seller.* To make the sale, the exporter agrees to ship merchandise against a letter of credit that stipulates that the draft will be payable at a future date up to six months. The exporter required a letter of credit initially because of unwillingness to make the shipment relying solely on the buyer's credit. The exporter is willing to wait for payment, provided that he retains the bank's commitment to pay. The exporter therefore surrenders title to his merchandise in exchange for the bank's promise to pay on a future date. If the exporter insisted instead on a sight letter of credit that would require payment at the time of presentation of documents, the burden would be on the importer to get a loan from her bank. Once the exporter receives the bankers' acceptance, he may opt to hold it until maturity and then present it to the accepting bank for payment in full. In essence, the exporter has invested his manufacturing and other costs in the merchandise until the date of payment. The other option is to sell the bankers' acceptance before maturity and receive a lesser amount of cash immediately instead of the full draft amount on the future date. When the exporter does this, he usually is finished with the transaction, although he remains secondarily liable to the investor should the bank default when the bankers' acceptance matures and payment is due.

- *The bank*. The bank's customer, the importer, requests credit. The bank must evaluate that request. Once it has determined that its customer is creditworthy for the requested amount, it then must determine how to fund the request. The bank may use its own money and make a direct loan, or it may decide that it wishes to carry only the credit risk but let some other party provide the funding. In this case, it structures the credit to use the bankers' acceptance.

The creation of a bankers' acceptance is an extension of credit by the bank to its customer. "The use of the bankers' acceptance . . . cannot mask their essence. The essence of the transactions, like that of a direct loan, is the use of [the bank's] credit." [5] The bank is committing itself to pay the obligation at a stated future date, thereby inducing a seller of goods to surrender the goods to the buyer in exchange for the bank's commitment. The bank does this by stamping "accepted" across the draft, indicating on the draft the underlying purpose that is being financed, signing it with authorized signatures, and indicating the date the acceptance begins or matures. Because the bank has committed itself

in writing to pay, investors are willing to furnish their funds during the interim period. The bank is irrevocably committed to pay the acceptance when it is presented on the maturity date, regardless of whether the bank has been paid by its customer.

A bank's decision to extend credit to any customer is based on its judgment of the conditions and risks involved (see chapter 10). The fact that a bank is lending its credit and not its funds cannot exempt the proposed financing from a thorough credit analysis. However, the bankers' acceptance is used basically to finance transactions that are self-liquidating, an important feature in the decision to extend credit. The expected source of repayment will be from the importer's sale of the financed merchandise to another party or parties. If the bank were to cease payment of its obligations, however, the holder of the acceptance would become a general creditor and not be reimbursed from the sale of the merchandise. The holder could seek reimbursement from the drawer of the draft or prior endorsers.

- *The broker*. A broker acts as a centralized distributor who puts persons wishing to sell bankers' acceptances in contact with those wishing to buy them. The broker may be a company specializing in this function or a commercial or investment bank providing the service as part of its overall money market activities. Because of the large size of the U.S. money market, the broker will usually quote a price to the seller of the acceptance, buy the instrument, and then find an investor who would be interested in buying the acceptance. The broker sells the acceptance at a slightly higher price than was paid for it and thereby earns a profit. This is the broker's spread.
- *The investor*. Corporations, banks, municipalities, money market funds, foreign central banks, domestic and international institutions,

and individuals have temporary surplus funds on which they wish to earn a return. In the United States, they can select from a wide range of money market instruments. The safest such investments are the obligations of the U.S. government. However, the investor may determine that short-term obligations of a U.S. bank are almost as safe as government obligations; the investor may be attracted to purchase of bankers' acceptances because they offer a higher rate of return. The investor may perceive that the bankers' acceptance offers greater security than a bank's certificate of deposit, since there is an underlying commercial transaction that should generate the source of repayment to the bank. On the other hand, the certificate of deposit may qualify for FDIC insurance.

The term "discounting an acceptance" means that the holder of the bankers' acceptance is selling it prior to its maturity date and receiving money at the time of the discounting. In the illustration above of the foreign trade transaction, the exporter may have agreed to a time letter of credit in order to assist the importer and to make the sale. There is a time value to money. The exporter has costs such as labor, raw materials, and so forth, and may need a reduced amount of money immediately rather than the full draft amount in six months. The exporter may have reflected this in his original export sale price.

As indicated above, the investor may be an entity outside of the accepting bank. However, the investor may also be the accepting bank itself. When a bank acts as the investor in discounting its own bankers' acceptance, it pays the holder (the exporter in the above illustration) the discounted amount and receives the full face amount at maturity from the importer. The bank may discount its own acceptance for various reasons: the amount is too small for other inves-

tors (each bank determines that limit for itself), the bank may not be well enough known to attract outside investors, it considers the rate to be attractive, or it wants to assist its customer (the importer) by financing at a lower rate than if it had made a direct loan. The bank discounting its own acceptance is, essentially, making a loan to its customer that is reflected as part of its legal lending limit. If subsequently, before maturity, the bank decides to sell that bankers' acceptance to an outside investor, this is described as "rediscounting."

In summary, after the bank accepts the time draft and creates the bankers' acceptance, there are three sources of funding: the exporter holds the bankers' acceptance to maturity, the bankers' acceptance is discounted to an investor other than the bank, or the bank discounts its own bankers' acceptance and holds it to maturity.

Eligible Bankers' Acceptances

Bankers' acceptances drawn in accordance with Section 13 of the Federal Reserve Act are eligible for discount or purchase by a Federal Reserve member bank at any of the Federal Reserve banks. Although seldom necessary as long as an active private trading market exists, this practice does protect the bank. (In fact, the Federal Reserve has not discounted bankers' acceptances for a number of years.) Nonetheless, the criteria for Federal Reserve discounting or purchasing define the instruments the market will readily trade. The following are the permitted underlying purposes for which a bank may create a bankers' acceptance that can be discounted at a Federal Reserve bank:

- importation or exportation of goods
- domestic shipment of goods within the United States
- storage of readily marketable staples

Member banks are also permitted to accept drafts for the creation of dollar exchange (see below), although this is not widely used.

Bankers' acceptances may be created for a maximum term of six months. This term is calculated on the basis of the underlying transaction. In the case of a foreign trade shipment, the acceptance term will begin to be calculated, in general, from the time the shipment takes place. If the bankers' acceptance will be used for the creation of dollar exchange, the maximum permitted term is three months.

Section 13 of the Federal Reserve Act permits the creation of bankers' acceptances for a maximum of six months. Any acceptances created for a longer term and discounted to an investor are interpreted under Regulation D to be a "deposit" for which a bank is subject to the usual reserve requirements. The Federal Reserve banks are permitted to discount only acceptances "which have a maturity at the time of discount of not more than 90 days' sight," or six months in the case of acceptances drawn for agricultural purposes.[6]

Drafts may be accepted by banks in the United States, including the U.S. agencies and branches of foreign banks and U.S. banks, or by overseas branches of U.S. banks, provided that the acceptance is payable at the bank's head office. Bankers' acceptances that meet the requirements of the Federal Reserve Act to be *eligible for discount* are exempt from reserve requirements. Acceptances are also not subject to assessment for deposit insurance.

State and private banks had been allowed to engage in acceptance financing before enactment of the Federal Reserve Act in 1913, but such financing was not extensive. Although the impetus for the development of a discount market and banking system that would be similar in many respects to that in the United Kingdom was strong, the enactment of the Federal Reserve Act was in keeping with the existing U.S. banking structure.

The Federal Reserve Act governs only member banks. State banks may have broader acceptance powers under their respective state laws. Notwithstanding, practically all bankers' acceptances follow the Federal Reserve guidelines in order to be readily marketable to investors.

A national bank may have bankers' acceptances outstanding up to 150 percent of the bank's capital and unimpaired surplus unless it receives permission from the Board of Governors of the Federal Reserve System to go up to 200 percent. The limitations on the maximum lending to any one customer apply.

International and Domestic Trade

The shipment of goods categories include the financing of goods imported into the United States, exported from the United States, shipped between two foreign countries, or shipped within the United States. Neither the importer nor the exporter must be in the United States. At the time that the bank is asked to accept a draft, it must have evidence that the shipment has in fact taken place, when the shipment was made, and what the merchandise was. The bank usually has a copy of the bill of lading or invoice for this purpose. The bankers' acceptance may also extend over the preshipment period needed to assemble the merchandise; however, this cannot include any manufacturing, processing, or growing. The bankers' acceptance should cover a current shipment, which generally means that it has taken place within 30 days of the creation of the bankers' acceptance. Exceptions to this occur when a reasonable explanation exists, such as the acceptance financing beginning after the use of normal trade credit.[7]

Although most bankers' acceptances evolve from letters of credit, they need not necessarily do so. A collection can be refinanced by a bankers' acceptance, as can a sight letter of credit or even a shipment made on open account or prepaid. In such cases, the importer pays the exporter and then draws a time draft on the bank, which the bank accepts and discounts in the market, giving the importer the net amount. On maturity, the importer repays the bank just as if it were a direct loan.

The creation of bankers' acceptances under letters of credit is discussed in chapter 8. In instances where the client has already signed a letter of credit agreement, that agreement usually suffices. For transactions not covered by such a letter of credit agreement, the bank may ask the customer to sign an acceptance agreement.

An acceptance covering shipments between two foreign points is similar to acceptances financing both U.S. imports and exports. The acceptance may be made under either a letter of credit or an acceptance financing arrangement. If the transaction is executed on behalf of a commercial customer, the documents may have been released against trust receipts, but if the drawer of the bill is a foreign bank, the accepting bank is unlikely to have received the controlling shipping documents. The bank creating the acceptance must retain evidence showing the nature of the underlying transaction, such as a non-negotiable copy of the bill of lading.

Although domestic U.S. shipments can be adapted easily to acceptance financing, buyers and sellers alike generally resort to the more usual forms of industry financing because they are not familiar with acceptance financing.

Storage

Merchandise that has been put into storage may be financed by means of bankers' acceptances. This practice is widely used, particularly in the agricultural areas of the United States. A wheat farmer, for example, may deliver wheat to a public warehouse, which will issue its **warehouse receipt** to the farmer. The warehouse receipt is a title document and, in essence, states that the

warehouse company is holding a certain quantity of a stated commodity and that the company will continue to hold these goods until the warehouse receipt is presented. At such time, the merchandise is returned in exchange for the warehouse receipt. The wheat farmer can endorse the warehouse receipt and deliver it to the bank, thereby providing security for the bank's creation of the bankers' acceptance. If the farmer fails to repay, the bank can take possession of the wheat and sell it to repay the acceptance. Since there is no seller to draw a draft on the bank, the acceptance is created by the wheat farmer drawing a draft on the bank to pay him- or herself the stated sum at the future date and endorsing the draft. The bank accepts this draft, sells it to an investor, and gives the farmer the discounted proceeds. On the maturity date, the farmer repays the full draft amount.

Public warehouses are private companies that maintain buildings for the storage of goods for third parties. Such buildings are referred to as *terminal warehouses*. In addition, private companies set up *field warehouses* on the premises of a farmer or manufacturer. In a field warehouse, the warehouse company takes possession of the customer's warehouse building or part of a building, puts its own locks on the doors, and puts its own warehouseman in charge. The warehouse receives the merchandise and issues warehouse receipts just as though the building were owned by the company. In this way, farmers and manufacturers have the benefits of a public warehouse on their own premises without having to go to a distant terminal warehouse. Banks insist that warehouse companies obtain insurance against various types of calamities, including fraud by the warehouse companies' employees.

Banks may create acceptances to cover the storage of goods in the United States or to cover storage in other countries, provided a valid warehouse receipt comparable to those in the United States can be obtained that will secure the bank during the life of the transaction. This is possible in relatively few foreign countries.

This type of financing enables the farmer or manufacturer to store goods pending their sale. The costs associated with manufacturing, growing, or processing require interim financing, and these costs are expected to be recovered when the final sale is made. In general, the kinds of stored goods eligible to be financed by bankers' acceptances are commodities (such as wheat, sugar, corn, coffee, copper, or silver) and processed goods that have a ready market. However, if the goods have been processed to such a degree that only one company can buy them, then the bank is not secured: if that company does not buy the goods, they cannot otherwise be sold.

Regardless of whether the bankers' acceptance has covered preshipment, shipment, storage, or any combination of these, the maximum term for the financing is six months. The maturity of the bankers' acceptance should match the completion of the transaction being financed.[8]

It is important to note the difference between acceptances arising from a time letter of credit and those created for other purposes. When establishing letters of credit calling for a beneficiary's draft to be accepted by the bank, the bank expects the customer for whom it opened the letter of credit to reimburse the bank at maturity. When creating acceptances for other types of financing, the bank looks to the drawer of the draft for reimbursement at maturity.

Dollar Exchange

Although bankers' acceptances for the purpose of creating dollar exchange are now rarely requested, they were a way for foreign countries to raise U.S. dollars needed for purposes of trade. The procedure was cumbersome, since it required the foreign government, in essence, to request eligibility for these acceptances. Once this was done

and the country was on the Fed's list of approved countries (the last list was published in the *Federal Reserve Bulletin* in 1922)[9], designated foreign banks could request acceptance financing solely for the purpose of obtaining dollars for a short term for the needs of trade. Such countries generally had a single crop to export, and this financing was to advance foreign exchange to the country pending the sale of its crop, which would then provide the export earnings to repay the banker's acceptance.

The Market for Acceptances

A *money market* is a center where the demand for short-term funds meets the supply. A leading international money market has been established in New York City. The facilities there attract and redistribute funds from all over the United States and the world. This general market comprises many different clearly defined markets, each of which deals in a different type of credit.

> The U.S. money market is a huge and significant part of the nation's financial system in which banks and other participants trade hundreds of billions of dollars every working day. . . . *The money market is a wholesale market for low-risk, highly liquid, short-term IOUs.* It is a market for various sorts of debt securities rather than equities. The stock in trade of the market includes a large chunk of the U.S. Treasury's debt and billions of dollars worth of federal agency securities, negotiable bank certificates of deposit, bank deposit notes, bankers' acceptances, short-term participations in bank loans, municipal notes, and commercial paper. . . . The money market . . . provides a means by which the surplus funds of cash-rich corporations

and other institutions can be funneled to banks, corporations, and other institutions that need short-term money.[10]

The market trades in "eligible" acceptances and therefore is limited to specific transactions. The skills needed for marketing bankers' acceptances are the same as those needed for marketing other short-term obligations. Dealers who handle bankers' acceptances generally are part of the active market in a wide range of government paper—federal, state, and municipal.

The bankers' acceptance is an attractive short-term investment since its rates, while usually moving in concert with those of U.S. Treasury bills, offer a slightly higher yield. In normal circumstances, most investors will find that the higher yield compensates for what is not, in many judgments, a significantly higher risk. As of December 1994, there were $29.7 billion of bankers' acceptances outstanding, of which 57 percent represented financing for trade to and from the United States.[11] This total represented a level of usage that had declined to almost half of the usage of five years before.

Mechanics

There are usually two charges for an acceptance: the accepting bank's commission for creating the acceptance and the market price for discounting the bankers' acceptance if it is traded. These are two separate and distinct functions. Accepting a draft provides the credit backing of the bank. Discounting is a money market funding. In the nineteenth century when the sterling "bill on London" (the predecessor and model for today's U.S. dollar bankers' acceptance) was providing financing for world trade, there clearly were two different groups of banks doing this: the so-called accepting houses and the discount houses.[12]

The bank's commission for accepting the draft is determined by its credit relationship with its client and is analogous to a portion of the interest rate on a loan. The acceptance commission is collected at the time the draft is accepted and is paid by the bank's customer. For example, a U.S. importer for whose account the letter of credit was opened pays the acceptance commission to the bank. The foreign exporter can ask that the acceptance be returned to it so it can be held until maturity. At maturity, the exporter presents the acceptance either through her bank or directly to the accepting bank for full payment. In essence, the exporter invests her costs for the period from the time of exportation until the maturity date of the acceptance. Though an acceptance has been created, it does not mean that it has to be sold in the market.

In practice, most exporters want funds as soon as their draft becomes a bankers' acceptance and will instruct the accepting bank to discount the acceptance immediately at the prevailing rate of other short-term money market instruments. Exporters are willing to receive less than face value immediately rather than the full face amount in the future. The discount charge, therefore, is generally borne by the exporter, who may have adjusted her selling price to anticipate this charge. For the importer to have acceptance financing, the exporter has an option of requiring the importer to pay for this discount. This is called "discount for buyer's account."

The bankers' acceptance has no provision for any interest payment, so the investor receives a rate of return by buying the bankers' acceptance at a discount. The dollar price and yield are calculated as follows:[13]

$$\text{Dollar price} \atop (\% \text{ of face amount}) = 100 - \frac{\text{Discount rate} \times \text{Days to maturity}}{360}$$

To convert a discount rate on a bankers' acceptance to the equivalent simple interest basis, the formula is[14]

$$\text{Interest rate} = \frac{\text{Discount rate} \times 360}{360 - (\text{discount rate} \times \text{days})}$$

Having created an acceptance, the bank, on instructions of the holder, can sell it to a dealer at the dealer's discount rate. The proceeds are credited to the account of the holder of the acceptance—the exporter, in the previous example. The exporter has now completed the transaction; the importer will not be required to pay until the acceptance matures. The dealer, in turn, recovers the funds by selling the acceptance to an investor, usually taking a small spread. Upon maturity of the acceptance, the investor presents it to the accepting bank for payment. The bank pays, and then its customer, the importer, pays the bank. The failure or inability of the customer to pay does not relieve the accepting bank of its commitment to pay. Likewise, if the investor delays in presenting the acceptance after the maturity date, no further interest will be paid. The bank is obligated to pay only the face amount.

Bankers' acceptances may be created for other types of transactions, such as storage of commodities, in which the entire purpose of creating the acceptance is to obtain funds immediately; thus the discount is automatic. The customer receives the net amount after deduction of the acceptance commission and the discount. When the purpose is to finance goods in storage, the bank's customer is the only other party. The customer draws the draft on the bank, which accepts it and then discounts it with a dealer. The net proceeds go to the bank's customer, who is obligated to repay the full face amount of the acceptance on maturity.

Since the acceptance is a short-term prime obligation of a U.S. bank, it is very attractive to many investors. Dealers are able to establish a highly liquid market for acceptances. Established dealers quote rates at which they will buy and sell acceptances. These rates change in accordance with the supply and demand for short-term

investments and the investor's perception of the creditworthiness of the accepting bank.

Between the original discounting and the final maturity, the original investor may no longer wish to hold the acceptance. Because of the liquidity of the market, the investor can readily sell the acceptance to a dealer at the prevailing discount rate, having earned a rate of return for the number of days the bill was actually held. Thus an acceptance can pass through many hands without the knowledge of the accepting bank.

Because the bankers' acceptance is a liquid and competitive investment, an accepting bank may want to hold some of its own acceptances, or a bank may hold other banks' acceptances as part of its own portfolio. None of the bank's clients are aware of this because the same discount rates apply.

Advantages of Acceptance Financing

The U.S. bankers' acceptance has become established in the financial market as an instrument by which banking institutions lend their name as part of the process of granting credit to their customers. Its particular advantage to commercial banks comes at those times when great demands are made on banks for the use of their loanable funds—demands that are often greater than their ability to make loans. If certain customers can be financed with bankers' acceptances, a bank will be eager to do so, since the funding is obtained when the bankers' acceptance is sold to an investor. In essence, the bank uses someone else's money to make loans to its customers.

A customer with a transaction that can be financed by bankers' acceptances may find that the overall cost of the acceptance commission plus market discount is less than borrowing on a promissory note at a bank's prime interest rate.

The bankers' acceptance competes with other money market instruments for both the customer seeking financing and the investor. The borrower will consider the available financing options. It may be cheaper or more convenient to borrow directly from the bank through a loan, arrange with the seller for delayed payments, issue commercial paper that is placed with investors, or utilize a Eurodollar short-term borrowing. "Bank loans become an attractive alternative to [bankers' acceptance] financing when spreads are reasonable and the borrower is unsure how long he will need financing. If a borrower repays a [bankers' acceptance] early . . . no proportion of the bank commission on the [bankers' acceptance] is repaid to him. He does get a pro-rata rebate on the discount fee, but minus ¼ or so." [15] The investor likewise has options about where to place funds to obtain the most favorable rate of return commensurate with personal standards of safety. Banks creating bankers' acceptances need to be mindful of these alternatives.

Ineligible Acceptances

This discussion so far has dealt with bankers' acceptances created in compliance with Section 13 of the Federal Reserve Act and therefore eligible for discount at the Federal Reserve bank. These acceptances can be discounted without making the bank liable for the creation of any reserves.

Banks, however, may also create bankers' acceptances for any underlying purpose or for terms longer than six months, but such acceptances are not eligible for discounting at a Federal Reserve bank. A bank may choose to use this instead of a promissory note as a financing instrument. As long as the bank retains such ineligible acceptances, it has merely made its customer a loan, using bank funds to do so, just as if it had made the loan against the customer's

promissory note. If the bank wishes, it may use this as a means of making a loan at a financing rate lower than the bank's prime rate. It does this by charging the borrower an acceptance commission and a market discount rate as if it were an eligible acceptance.

Banks sometimes find this useful when their prime rate is maintained at a higher level for competitive reasons. In some cases, the bank may be able to sell such ineligible acceptances to investors. Such sales are usually based on direct negotiations between the bank and the investor. Sometimes a broker may be involved. However, discounting ineligible acceptances incurs a reserve requirement to the creating bank. "Thus a borrower who requires ineligible as opposed to eligible [bankers' acceptances] financing pays a higher rate." [16]

Syndicated Acceptances and Participation

A number of banks have at times formed syndicates to meet the credit needs of some large borrowers, often foreign governments. Sometimes these borrowers wish to use bankers' acceptances. The pattern of operating such a syndicate is the same as for loans. The mechanics of drawdown require the borrower to supply, either in advance or at the time of drawdown, a quantity of signed drafts. The agent bank advises each bank of its prorated drawdown. Each participating bank then fills in the draft, accepts it, discounts it at an agreed common rate, and remits the net proceeds after deducting its acceptance commission to the borrower through the agent bank.

To preserve the short-term character of the bankers' acceptance, with its limited exposure of exchange and country risks in syndicated facilities that are basically created for long-term financing needs, the Federal Reserve applies a two-year maximum on syndicated commitments. "The 2-year limit on bankers' acceptance syndicates is complied with if each syndicate bank has the right to withdraw from the syndicate, without restriction, every 2 years. . . . The Federal Reserve Bank of New York maintains that syndicated bankers' acceptances should be liquidated at maturity from sources of funds independent of the creation of new acceptances." [17]

A variation occurs when a bank sells a participation in a bankers' acceptance to another bank. This occurs when a bank creates a bankers' acceptance and then decides to sell part of its liability to another bank. The creating bank may need to stay within its legal lending limit to the borrower or reduce its total outstanding acceptances. A legal document is signed by both banks, and the second bank thereby commits itself for a portion of the liability to pay the acceptance on maturity and receives a proportionate share of the acceptance commission. The borrower's commitment is unchanged. When the borrower repays the bank that accepted the draft, that bank will pay a portion to the participating bank.

For the accepting bank to reduce its liability, documentation between the participating and accepting banks must clearly transfer the liability to the participant in the event the borrower does not pay and thereby give the participant the right to take legal action directly against the borrower. The participating bank must also satisfy itself of the creditworthiness of that borrower.[18]

Accounting

Once the bankers' acceptance has been created, it appears on the bank's financial statement. The outstanding acceptance is listed as a liability ("Acceptances Outstanding"); the customer's liability to pay the bank at its maturity is shown as an asset ("Customer's Acceptance Liability"). If these result from a time letter of credit, the contingent balance for the letter of credit is reduced when the negotiation takes place and the acceptance entries are made.

The holder of the bankers' acceptance may decide to discount it. This may be done outside the accepting bank and therefore would not appear in any of the bank's accounting. When the discounting is done by the bank itself, the transaction may be reflected only in transit to the investor.

The letter of credit will have been reflected as a contingent account in the bank's balance sheet since it is not certain at the time of issuing the letter of credit whether it will be drawn down in whole, in part, or not at all. The bankers' acceptance, however, represents the actual drawdown of the letter of credit and is a specific amount due to be paid at a specific date.

Summary

The bankers' acceptance in the United States is a means of financing certain transactions, generally related to international trade. It is a negotiable credit instrument that readily attracts short-term investors. Because of this, the bankers' acceptance provides an alternative source of funds to a bank and its customers that can be important in periods of tight money. In addition, its rates reflect yields in the money markets and, at times, offer the banks' customers a preferential rate of return.

Questions

1. What is a bankers' acceptance?
2. How is a bankers' acceptance different from a trade acceptance?
3. What is the role of the Federal Reserve in bankers' acceptances?
4. What is the attraction of bankers' acceptances to an investor?

Problem

A processor of foodstuffs in your area, who is a good customer of your bank, must purchase wheat when it is harvested in Canada and the Midwest of the United States in order to have a supply during the year. Explain how she can use the bankers' acceptance to finance and store the wheat purchases.

Notes

1. Fernand Braudel, *The Wheels of Commerce* (New York: Harper and Row, 1982), pp. 243-244

2. Marcia Stigum, *The Money Market*, 3d ed. (Homewood, Ill.: Dow Jones-Irwin, 1990), p. 995

3. Henry Harfield, *Bank Credits and Acceptances*, 5th ed. (New York: Ronald Press, 1974), p. 118

4. Ibid., p. 119

5. *Bank of America v. United States*, 680 F.2nd 142 (Ct. Cl. 1982)

6. Federal Reserve Act, Section 13, Paragraph 6

7. Walker F. Todd, "An Introduction to Bankers' Acceptance in the 1980's," in *International Banking: U.S. Laws and Regulations* (Washington, D.C.: American Bankers Association, 1984), Section 1-24

8. Ibid.

9. *Published Interpretations of the Board of Governors of the Federal Reserve System*, paragraph 1500, p. 80B (6-78). The approved countries were "Australia, New Zealand, and other Australasian dependencies, Argentina, Bolivia, Brazil, British Guiana, British Honduras, Chile, Colombia, Costa Rica, Cuba, Dutch East Indies, Dutch Guiana, Ecuador, French Guiana, French West Indies, Guatemala, Honduras, Nicaragua, Panama, Paraguay, Peru, Puerto Rico, Salvador, Dominican Republic, Trinidad, Uruguay, and Venezuela."

10. Stigum, *The Money Market,* pp. 1-3

11. *Federal Reserve Bulletin*, November 1995, p. A24

12. See Gillett Brothers Discount Co., *The Bill on London* (London: Chapman and Hall Ltd., 1952). A uniquely illustrated, detailed description of an important product.

13. Marcia Stigum, *The Money Market: Myth, Reality and Practice* (Homewood, Ill.: Dow Jones-Irwin, 1978), p. 542

14. Ibid., p. 474

15. Marcia Stigum, *The Money Market*, 3d edition, p. 1009

16. Marcia Stigum, *The Money Market, Myth, Reality and Practice*, p. 467

17. Todd, *"Introduction,"* pp. 1-23

18. Ibid., pp. 1-21

IV

GLOBAL FINANCING

Financing consists of two distinct elements: first, the decision to allow another party to obtain something of value now, but to pay for it at a later date for a fee (interest), and second, the form of the payment between the two parties. The usual financing transaction is a bank loan—the borrowing of money now that is to be repaid at specified later dates with interest. In modern global financing, the transaction can have many complex variations.

The credit decision pervades most facets of global financial activities. It has been essential to the development of global trade for centuries, underlying letters of credit, foreign exchange trading, money transfers, and the mobilization of funds from one country to another for both short-term and long-term development.

The linkage between the ability to conduct trade with the availability of credit was evident in the great thirteenth-century fairs of Champagne, France. These were held at regular times and lasted for many weeks. The primary purpose of the fairs was the exchange of goods: fabrics from northern Europe were traded for spices, pepper, silks, and drugs from Italy, the entrepôt between Europe and the Levant.

The originality of the Champagne fairs lay less however in the super-abundance of goods on sale than in the money market and the precocious workings of credit on display there . . . the money-changers [usually Italians] came into their own . . . [setting] up shop on a fixed date. . . . Their equipment consisted simply of a table covered with a cloth, a pair of scales and several sacks filled with ingots or coins. All compensatory payments balancing sales and purchases, all deferred payments between one fair and another, all loans to lords and princes, the settlement of bills of exchange which expired at the fair, as well as the making out of new ones to be sent elsewhere passed through their hands. As a result, all the international and above all most modern aspects of the Champagne fairs were controlled, on the spot or at a distance, by Italian merchants whose firms were often huge concerns, like the *Magna Tavola* of the Buonsignori, the thirteenth-century Rothschilds of Siena.

Italy was the banker for the trade, leading the world in business techniques: she had introduced to Europe minted gold money, the bill of exchange and the practice of credit.[1]

The first element of any financing is the credit decision, the prospective lender's analysis of the borrowing party to evaluate the latter's ability to make the payment at the agreed-upon future date. Centuries of experience have led to certain procedures and forms of analysis. This process is discussed in chapter 10, Principles of International Credit, and generally follows the procedures of the commercial bank, but is equally applicable to any other lender or investor in a bond.

The second element in global financing is the funding decision—how to implement the credit decision. This can be accomplished in many different ways and from many different sources besides the commercial bank. Regardless of the form, the lender faces exactly the same risk, namely that the borrower will not repay. In one basic sense, it may be said that a good loan is one that is paid back when it is supposed to be; a bad loan is one that is not. The key factor is that the credit decision is separate from the source or means of funding. The source of funding does not change the credit risk.

The sources of funding are discussed in chapter 11, Funding Global Finance, and chapter 12, Government Agencies. When the credit decision is made by the commercial bank, the bank can provide funds to the borrower from the deposits that it has received from its customers, or it may borrow the funds from a domestic or international source. Either of these can be in the bank's local currency or in funds obtained in a foreign exchange transaction. The commercial bank does not have to make actual money available, but may provide credit by merely lending its name with its commitment to disburse funds in the future, if called upon under certain specified conditions. This is the basis of the commercial letter of credit and the standby letter of credit, where the bank will pay out money to a third party on behalf of its customer if or when certain specified events take place. It is also describes the banker's acceptance in which the amount and date of payment by the bank is definitely stated.

Financing from the investment or merchant banker will likewise begin with a credit assessment, but not for the risk of their own funds or responsibility as in the case of a commercial banker. The investment or merchant bank will seek transactions that can be sold as bonds to investors, who in turn will provide the funds, earn the interest, and be repaid. In some cases, these bankers do not rely exclusively on their own credit assessment but use those of credit rating agencies, who categorize borrowings based on the financial strength and earning power of the borrower. Notwithstanding the fact that someone else is providing the funds and carrying the risks of nonrepayment, the investment and merchant bankers are concerned about these risks because they want their investors to succeed and be available for other future such transactions.

Global financing may also be provided outside any banking structure when a corporation makes funds available to a foreign subsidiary, either for the long-term construction of a factory or mine or merely delays in receiving payment for merchandise or services provided by the parent company.

The credit and funding elements of global financing are also considered when governments make loans and when governments are borrowers. In the former case, the decision may be as much political as economic. (Government lending agencies and their objectives are discussed in chapter 12.) When governments are borrowers, the credit decision may be different than for financing a business and can be basically a country risk assessment (see chapter 13).

Notes

1. Fernand Braudel, *The Perspective of the World* (New York: Harper and Row, 1984), p. 110

10

PRINCIPLES OF INTERNATIONAL CREDIT

Learning Objectives

After studying this chapter, you will be able to

- apply the fundamentals of international credit analysis
- detail the types of credit
- outline the special factors in making international loans
- recognize the types of borrowers and their differing needs

Overview

Through banks, the United States makes a major contribution to the growth of international trade and development by providing credit facilities to its customers throughout the world. This is also a major source of income for banks.

The principles of international and domestic credit are the same. The international banker's customers have specialized needs: importers or exporters who need to finance international trade; correspondent banks that need to finance their customers in international trade and for local economic development; multinational businesses that want to build manufacturing plants, open mines, and control interest and foreign exchange rate exposures; and foreign governments that need to facilitate all of these.

Fundamentals of Credit

When a bank extends credit, it contemplates the riskless rental of money. But no bank loan is completely without risk. Bank lending officers must assess the degree of risk in each application and, exercising prudence, should not make any loan if repayment seems unlikely. Bank lending officers must remember they are lending depositors' and stockholders' money. A commercial banker lending money differs from an investor who uses his own funds. If the business fails, both will lose their money. If a business succeeds, however, the investor can expect great profit from dividends and appreciation in equity value. The bank, on the other hand, can only expect repayment of the loan and an agreed amount of interest earnings and fees. Thus credit risk and equity risk offer different rewards.

Arriving at a credit judgment involves gathering and analyzing certain facts and making a decision based on those facts. The first step in considering an application from a customer for credit is to determine answers to four basic questions:

1. *How much money do you want?*
   This question sets the framework for the entire credit consideration. The lending officer can begin to determine how much thought potential borrowers have given to their proposal. Surprisingly, some applicants do not have a clear idea of exactly how much money they need. Vagueness on this point is often a prelude to more confusion as the loan discussion continues.

2. *What do you want the money for?*
   Banks will want to provide credit for worthwhile or productive purposes, such as financing imports and exports, the production or growing of goods that will enter into international trade, or the development of foreign economies to increase the market for imports and exports through establishment of new manufacturing plants or mines.

3. *How long do you want the money?*
   The term of the requested financing should bear a relationship to the purpose of the loan. For example, an importer of toys for the Christmas season needs financing to cover the time of shipment from the foreign manufacturer, time to sell it, and time to give customary credit terms to the store buyer through the Christmas selling period. This calls for a letter of credit and financing to last up to six months. A request for financing to build a new manufacturing plant, however, would normally require an extension of credit lasting several years. The international department does not usually engage in foreign mortgage financing. In recent years, banks have been willing to make international loans for as long as 10 years, but the general preference is not to exceed 7 years.

4. *How will you pay the money back?*

The source of repayment for the imported toys would come from their sale. This illustrates self-liquidating financing, an important characteristic of letters of credit. The financing for the movement of goods that will ultimately be sold to another party is repaid from the proceeds of the sale. The financing is short term (less than one year). Repayment for long-term loans (more than one year) for purposes such as factory expansion is often based on the increased production capacity of the enlarged plant. This increased production is expected to lead to increased sales, and hence to larger profits. The revenue from these sales represents a part of the company's cash flow.

Financial Risk

Once these basic questions have been answered, the bank lending officer will ask for additional information to clarify the loan request. The international lending officer, like the domestic lending officer, analyzes and evaluates the factors commonly known in the United States as the Cs of credit: *character*, *capacity*, and *capital*. In other words, the lending officer evaluates the integrity of the borrower, the ability of the borrower to repay, and the soundness of the borrower's financial position.

In gathering information about a borrower's character, the lending officer is seeking to determine whether the applicant is a serious individual or company that will recognize debts as obligations and make every effort to honor these obligations despite possible adverse developments; whether the borrower is experienced in the business; and whether there is a demonstrated capability to run the business profitably. The basis for character evaluation includes the lending bank's own experience with the borrower, other banks' experiences, and the borrower's business

reputation. When the borrower is a company, the character of management is evaluated. Companies such as Dun and Bradstreet in the United States provide some credit background data on businesses.

The global banker, however, deals not only with local importers and exporters, about whom it is relatively easy to obtain information, but also with foreign borrowers, including banks, corporations, and individuals. It is often more difficult to obtain detailed credit information from foreign sources. However, banks around the world customarily and confidentially share with other banks their lending experiences with particular customers.

A bank establishes a credit file for each borrower. This file contains a complete history of its credit experiences with that customer. By reviewing this file, the loan officer can assess the bank's past relationship with the borrower, have a record of the financial statements and previous borrowings, and determine how well the borrower has adhered to the terms and conditions of previous loans, including repaying on time. The bank maintains credit files primarily for its own use, but these files can also furnish its clients with credit information about prospective purchasers abroad. This information in summary form is available only in accordance with certain well-established customs and is confidential.

Capacity refers to the borrower's ability to repay. Will he have enough income to make the payments to the bank on this transaction as well as all his other obligations: normal business costs of wages, operating expenses, taxes, and other debts. *Capital* means the amount of money that the owners have in the business. For a company, this centers on the equity the owners or shareholders have already invested. Capital is the financial cushion against future problems or losses.

To evaluate capacity and capital, the banker asks for the customer's financial statement, which is "a written record of a firm's financial position at a point in time, as well as that firm's performance over a period of time. Financial statements include an income statement, balance sheet, and statements of cash flow."[1] The balance sheet is a snapshot showing the financial position of the company on a given day; the income, profit-and-loss, or operating statement is a history showing the income and expense for the year or over some other period. Ideally, these documents should be prepared and signed by independent auditors. To analyze financial trends, the banker wants these statements for the past three years and for the same day of the year. Although such statements are usually easily obtainable from U.S. clients, they are often not so readily available from foreign clients. Their format varies from country to country, they may be recorded in another currency that has fluctuating value to the dollar, and often they are not audited.

The financial statement customarily reflects the company's situation as of the end of its business year. This year-end statement may be December 31, whatever date the company designates as its year-end, or a date customary for the particular industry. Some industries—for example, department stores—find that December 31 is not a suitable date because they have not yet concluded their major selling season. For department stores, a date such as the end of February is usually better, since by that time they have received payment for their Christmas sales. In Japan, banks report their fiscal year ending March 31. Whatever the date, the banker wants to see the condition of the company at the same time each year.

By comparing various items on the balance sheet, the banker can draw conclusions about the operation of the firm. Comparison of the balance sheet over several years may reveal a trend. In the United States, comparison of these figures industrywide may be possible, because specialized firms such as Robert Morris Associates summarize such figures from time to time. Comparable figures are less available outside the United States.

The banker must also be aware of the way this information has been prepared. The company keeps its financial accounts daily during the year. At regular intervals, perhaps monthly, it prepares a summary, which is called a statement. For the year-end, the company may hire an independent firm of auditors to verify the company-prepared statement. These auditors or accountants will examine the records, verify parts of them by making certain tests, and compare the company's procedures and allocations with what are known as "generally accepted practices." These practices vary from country to country. In the United States, the interpretations and practices are generally set forth by accounting industry groups. At the end of the audit, the accountants state in writing what they have examined and give an opinion of the accuracy of the company's financial statement. The banker should read this opinion very carefully to know how much the independent auditor agrees or disagrees with the company's numbers.

For international businesses with subsidiaries in many countries, the banker wants financial statements from all subsidiaries as of the same date in order to interpret the global operations. This may be difficult when accounting practices in different countries have different annual close-off dates. Sometimes the borrower may deliberately attempt to confuse the banker about inter-subsidiary transactions.

Currency Risk

All the factors discussed so far are equally applicable to an analysis of giving credit to a borrower in the bank's own community or country as to one in another country. The global banker considering an extension of credit to a borrower in another country has additional factors to analyze. One of these is the fact that the currency that the bank will disburse is different from the currency that the borrower uses to conduct business. Cross-border lending usually means that one party has a currency conversion risk.

U.S. banks generally prefer to grant loans to foreign borrowers in U.S. dollars. The bank also wants to be repaid in dollars, thereby avoiding exposure to changes in the rate of exchange. If the proceeds of the loan are used in the borrower's own country or in a third country, the borrower will convert the loan money into local or some other currency. Even when financing imports from the United States, the borrower sells these goods in another country and receives payment in the currency of that country. While the borrower may be successful in selling the imported goods and have the local currency to pay the U.S. bank, the country may not have the dollars available to sell. Thus the borrower is at the mercy of the central bank of the country and may be unable to repay in dollars.

When considering whether to make a loan, the bank not only must assess the current position of the borrower's country with regard to international liquidity, but also must anticipate what this position may be when the loan matures. The possibilities of devaluation in times of financial and political stress must be considered. The impact of devaluation can be severe. In the early months of 1995, the Mexican peso fell in value by almost 100 percent in just weeks. As a consequence, Mexican companies that had borrowed in dollars were faced with having to repay those loans in dollars that now cost twice as many pesos as they had received when the loans had been made—even if the loan had been made just a few months before.

At times, some countries require the borrower to obtain approval from local foreign exchange control authorities to borrow abroad and also to obtain permission to pay interest on the loan and repay the principal at maturity. Such requirements arise from these nations' efforts to control foreign expenditures as part of a program to improve their balance of payments.

Country Risk

Country risk includes all the risks other than credit that a bank takes on in making loans to a borrower in another country. Such risks include the currency risk discussed above and also the risk that economic or political conditions in the borrower's country might change to such an extent that they jeopardize the borrower's ability to repay the loan or even to survive as a business. This topic is examined in detail in chapter 13.

Borrowers

The global banker deals with four general categories of borrowers: governments, banks, businesses, and individuals. Sometimes it is difficult to classify a particular borrower. Is the government-owned corporation a business or a government agency? Is the sole proprietorship an individual or a business? It is difficult to analyze all borrowers against the same basic criteria. The banker is influenced by the characteristics and capabilities of each borrower in making a credit decision based on the borrower's particular needs as well as the goals of the bank. For some classes of borrowers—the international business or the individual—the credit officer may take a different perspective than for a domestic transaction.

Governments

A foreign government normally represents the best credit risk in that country. The borrower may be a government bank that needs the same type of facilities as correspondent banks, government corporations that seek financing for specific projects (as do private corporations), or the government itself for the financing of infrastructure development (roads, ports, electricity distribution, and so forth) or balance of payments deficits. Regardless of the actual type of borrower, the banker considers that this is lending to a foreign government, often referred to as **sovereign risk** lending. This group of borrowers usually represents the bank's largest credit exposure in a developing country.

Sovereign risk lending may be the safest loan in a foreign country because the government is often the strongest financial entity in its country and has certain unique characteristics as a borrower. One prominent banker observed that even "LDCs [lesser-developed countries] don't go bankrupt . . . the infrastructure doesn't go away, the productivity of the people doesn't go away, the natural resources don't go away. And so their assets always exceed their liabilities, which is the technical reason for bankruptcy." [2] A government has the power to tax, it has access to substantial external financial resources by its membership in the IMF and various international development banks, and it has the capacity to set the rules by which all business in a country is conducted.

But a government can also be a risky borrower precisely because it is a sovereign entity; history is replete with monarchs who decided not to repay their bank loans, suffering little or no penalty as a consequence. Even the modern banker may find it difficult to force a sovereign borrower to adhere to repayment schedules, particularly when the country encounters financial problems. While the statement that a country cannot go bankrupt because its assets always exceed its liabilities is technically true, it may not be helpful in the immediate repayment of a loan since the assets may not be salable. The power to tax is unique, and it will produce revenue in the local currency, but that revenue will not necessarily generate the foreign currency needed to repay foreign borrowings. There have been a few, rare circumstances in this century in which a government (dominated by a brutal dictator or because of war) has forced all earners of foreign income to surrender it for application to pay the country's foreign debt or purchases—with devastating consequences to the country's domestic economy.

In dealing with a foreign country, a banker may be interacting with a *state-owned enterprise* (SOE), sometimes called a *para-statal*. This term "covers all state-owned industrial and commercial firms, mines, utilities, and transport companies as well as financial intermediaries." [3] These are prevalent either because a country lacks a private sector capable of running or developing an essential industry or because the political environment dictates public ownership of certain activities. The quality of management varies widely, may be subservient to government policies and interference, or may even be run by civil servants with no competitive business experience. The SOE is sometimes used for internal political purposes to the detriment of its financial success. The record of SOEs has been mixed, and when they are unprofitable they look to the government for financing, which adds to the internal national budget deficit. Because of this, the trend since the collapse of the Soviet Union has been for countries to *privatize* many of these companies— that is, to sell them to private domestic and foreign investors. The global banker evaluates each one separately and determines whether to treat it as a borrower that can be expected to meet its loan obligations from its own resources and activities, or to finance it only with a guarantee of that government.

Correspondent Banks

As has been seen in previous chapters, the foreign correspondent bank is important to the U.S.

bank's ability to conduct many international banking functions. Similarly, the U.S. bank is important to many foreign correspondent banks, particularly those in developing countries, as a source of credit that enables the foreign bank, in turn, to provide credit to its own customers. For example, an African importer needs a letter of credit to make a foreign purchase of tools from the U.S., but his local bank is not well enough known to have its letter of credit accepted by the foreign seller. The foreign bank needs to have its letter of credit confirmed by a U.S. bank. This confirmation, which is an extension of credit to the foreign bank from the U.S. bank, permits the transaction to be done, and the foreign bank is thereby able in turn to provide credit to its local customer.

Having opened an account with a U.S. bank does not automatically mean a foreign bank will be given credit. The U.S. bank provides financing to a correspondent bank based on its credit assessment of the foreign bank, the country risk, and the transaction being financed. Usually the U.S. bank does not know who the foreign bank may be relending to or the financial capability of that customer. The U.S. bank may be asked for seasonal financing to enable the foreign correspondent bank to finance local farmers to buy seed, fertilizer, and tools for an export crop that otherwise might not have been possible because of a shortage of capital in that country. The U.S. bank thereby facilitates international trade through financing the production of a crop that will move through the channels of world trade. This same type of financing can provide working capital through the correspondent bank to the foreign manufacturer to produce goods for export. In some cases, these exports may be to the U.S. bank's local customer.

The U.S. bank may provide financing to the foreign correspondent bank by opening a Due From account with it and keeping a certain balance in that account. The foreign bank then has deposits that are the source of funds for its loans. The risk to the U.S. bank, in the event of difficulties, is that its legal relationship to the foreign bank is now as a depositor rather than a lender. Each has a legal position that can be significantly different when the foreign bank is facing liquidation.

The banker analyzes several risk factors in deciding to extend credit to a foreign correspondent bank. The transaction is expected to be not only self-liquidating (the goods being financed provide the ultimate source of repayment), but also short term, which limits the time during which something can go wrong. The primary source of repayment is the commodity or product being financed as it moves through the international trade cycle. The secondary source of repayment is the financial capacity of the correspondent bank—its balance sheet. Additionally, the banker must be knowledgeable about the legal or implied backing from the government to banks in that country, the degree of examination, and any controls on loan concentration to one borrower or to the owners. Few countries have deposit insurance, so depositor panics can result in sudden withdrawals and the collapse of the bank. In some countries, on the other hand, the government has a policy of not permitting local banks to fail, but instead will take them over. As with any international borrower, the banker will evaluate the quality of the bank's management, its capital strength, and the country risk.

Businesses

The types of businesses that the global banker finances vary from the small importing and exporting company to the large multinational corporation with factories and operations in many countries. Businesses often demand the greatest sophistication in structuring financial solutions to their needs. These solutions may include traditional trade financing, term loans for building a new plant, risk management programs through foreign exchange hedging and sophisticated derivatives (see chapter 14), complex financings for developing mineral resources, and a variety of capital market products.

To analyze the business credit risk, the international banker examines the financial condition of the company, the cash flow projections of the future sources of repayment, collateral, quality of management, and other factors, much as the domestic banker does. The business's future operations may also be particularly vulnerable to country risk changes. As with other types of borrowers, the bank expects the company's cash flow to be the primary source of repayment and its capital and other assets to be a secondary source of repayment.

A global business that manufactures in different countries for assembling in another country may manipulate the **transfer pricing** between subsidiaries. This refers to the setting of a price at which one subsidiary sells to another. Each subsidiary's price, for example, can be set so as to accumulate profits in a particular country, usually one with low taxes. Individual countries are usually alert to this as it can affect their tax revenues. The banker should be, too, particularly when lending to just one subsidiary. The multinational corporation may find an overall advantage having some subsidiaries operate at a low, or even nil, profit. A banker therefore must be certain that the bank will have access to a profitable subsidiary in the chain, either by direct lending or through a guarantee.

Individuals

The individual is the smallest of the four categories of borrowers, both in numbers and in monetary amount. Generally, the international department does not make loans for retail purposes (for example, buying a car), except through a branch in that country.

Lending to individuals may be part of a **private banking** relationship or what has been called "specialist banking for the rich" [4] (that is, high-net-worth or upscale individuals). These individuals have different backgrounds and financial objectives. Those with inherited wealth are often most concerned with preserving the value of their capital. Successful entrepreneurs seek lines of credit for new ventures and investments, and capital flight is another source of activity (see chapter 13).

International private banking views capital and money markets on a worldwide scale. The individual customer of private banking is comfortable investing in different currencies and domestic capital markets in a variety of countries. The banking products vary from investment management to unsecured lending; these individuals' accounts are often handled by specialized account officers.

Basic Considerations

Having assembled and analyzed the basic Cs of credit (character, capital, capacity [cash flow], and the international C of country risk), the banker must now apply what could be called the "banker's Cs" of credit—*competence* to evaluate the information and *courage* to make a decision. The banker has a responsibility not only to the bank but also to the customer. For the bank, there is the obvious responsibility to avoid loss from a bad loan as well as the responsibility to earn the profits that a successful loan can bring. Then, the banker is equally responsible to the customer to make available the resources that can develop a business to the benefit of a community. In international banking, this can also include the opportunity to raise the standard of living in other countries, increase the food supply, and encourage economic and environmental development. Balancing these responsibilities is neither easy nor automatic. This is where the banker's courage must enter the picture.

In the early twentieth century, bankers lent only to the rich, the successful, and the powerful. They made loans based on collateral, which gave rise to the complaint that bankers extended credit only to those who did not need it. At most banks today, this pattern has changed. Every community has stories of the business that was saved or an idea that developed into an industry because a banker had the courage to stand by a customer when the need was great. This has been the foundation for many profitable long-term relationships, both international and domestic.

While a primary function of a bank is to make loans, it is not easy to make a credit decision, particularly when considering international credit. Business today is global and all countries, including the United States, depend on international economic growth. The courageous banker will assess the risks and seek a way to make a loan; the timorous banker, too often hiding behind an imagined reputation for high credit standards, will seek to rationalize turning down that same loan request. Whatever decision the banker reaches after evaluating the facts and risks, the customer is entitled to a prompt reply. Such promptness is especially important if the banker intends to decline the request, since clients often consider a long delay to be a favorable omen. A delayed negative response may create difficulties for them in seeking alternative sources of financing.

Facts, common sense, and experience form the basis of a credit decision. Notwithstanding the many books and courses available on the various facets of banking, most credit officers learn how to make credit decisions primarily through on-the-job experience.

Lending Policy

Every credit decision begins with the bank's written lending policies. These are senior management's instructions to loan officers on the types of credit the bank wants to make, its terms and requirements, and geographic and industry distribution, and they usually include a statement of the bank's overall objectives in extending credit.

After deciding to grant a loan, a lending officer must obtain internal approval. Each bank establishes its own procedures to be followed before committing the bank. U.S. banking regulations limit the aggregate amount a bank may extend to any single borrower to a percentage of the bank's unimpaired capital and surplus. This is the bank's **legal lending limit**.

> The maximum dollar amount of an unsecured loan to any single borrower is legally restricted to a percentage, depending on state laws, of the bank's capital and surplus. Capital is the shareholder's investment in the bank; surplus is the funds paid for stock in excess of par value. Fifteen percent is a common maximum. If the loan is fully secured, this limit becomes 25 percent. This legal restriction forces banks to diversify their loans, avoiding the problem of concentrating too heavily in a single customer.[5]

Lending to foreign government entities can pose a particular problem in defining what constitutes a single borrower. "Generally speaking an agency of a foreign government that can be demonstrated to stand alone, having its own assets and revenue base, may be regarded as an entity apart from the government itself for lending limit purposes while agencies that derive their current funds from general tax revenues will be counted as part of the government." [6] Thus a bank's unsecured lending to all of these entities would be *aggregated*, that is, counted together and limited as though they were one borrower.

Within the bank, each lending officer may be given a lending limit based on that officer's experience. For large amounts, the bank's senior credit officers or directors may become involved; it is the responsibility of the lending officer who has direct contact with the customer to make the necessary presentations within the bank to obtain approval of the application. Once a loan is approved, the customer must be informed in writing of the terms and conditions of the bank's willingness to extend credit.

Structuring of Credit

Thus far, the terms *credit* and *loan* have been used interchangeably. The lending officer must be careful to evaluate the credit risk separately from the means of funding the loan. Credit is credit; funding is funding—and the experienced loan officer does not confuse the two. Whether an extension of credit is to be funded by the use of domestic dollars (that is, from the bank's own pool of deposits [see below]), Eurodollars, a standby letter of credit, a bankers' acceptance, foreign currency, or any other means, the bank has the same credit risk: If the bank's borrower does not repay, the bank may suffer an actual loss of money. The rate or fee is intended to compensate the bank for its risk.

Interest Rate

A loan in U.S. dollars may be funded by drawing on the pool of deposits that a U.S. bank will have from individuals, businesses, and governments.

These may be referred to as *domestic dollars*. Or the bank may borrow dollars or obtain a specific deposit to match the loan. One source of such funds is *Eurodollars* (see chapter 11). For loans that will be funded domestically, each bank establishes its own **prime rate**—a commonly used reference rate established by that bank for pricing loans. Each bank's prime rate (sometimes called *base rate*) is set at a level that covers the bank's cost of funds, its operating expenses, and a margin of profit. The cost of funds recognizes that interest is paid to depositors on time deposits; commercial accounts have certain maintenance costs seldom fully recoverable through service charges. It also reflects the competitive forces of alternatives from active and sensitive domestic and global money markets. Banks must hold minimum reserves against deposits in the form of interest-free deposits at their Federal Reserve bank for their domestic office deposits. Banks also may have to pay an insurance premium for those deposits at domestic offices that are insured by the FDIC.

The degree of risk assumed by the bank must be reflected by and compensated for in the rate of interest: the higher the risk, the higher the rate. A longer-term loan has a greater risk than a short-term loan. To attempt to compensate for added risks, the bank will add a margin over its prime rate. No precise mathematical computation determines how these elements can be evaluated to arrive at an interest rate. Rather, the rate is established by the judgment and experience of the lending officer and the bank. They must also be aware of rates offered by competing lenders in the market. An interest rate for a loan will be quoted as "our prime rate + X percent per annum." When a bank changes its prime rate and the interest rate on the loan also changes, this is known as a **floating rate**. When a bank does not change its interest rate during the life of the loan regardless of any change in the bank's prime rate, this is known as a **fixed interest rate**. Because of the volatility of the cost of funds to banks in recent years, the trend has been to quote floating rates on most international loans.

As mentioned above, the second means of funding a dollar loan is with Eurodollars. Such loans are traditionally quoted as "LIBOR + X percent per annum." **LIBOR**, the acronym for London Interbank Offered Rate, is the interest cost to the bank to obtain a deposit in this market. The bank borrows Eurodollars, pays the LIBOR, and then lends these dollars to its customer. Eurodollars are time deposits; for a term loan the bank will usually borrow Eurodollars for six months at a time at LIBOR and then replace it with another deposit for successive six-month increments. The borrower's interest rate is fixed for each six months and will change according to what LIBOR is at each renewal of the deposit.

Even though an interest may be quoted based on LIBOR, the bank may elect not to actually use Eurodollars to fund the loan. This could occur for several reasons, such as the bank having surplus domestic dollars available at the time of disbursement or rollover.

It is important to note the substantial difference in earnings to the bank in an interest rate quoted as prime + X percent per annum or LIBOR + X percent per annum. A prime rate has built into it the cost of funds to the bank, plus an amount to cover the bank's overhead, plus an amount to provide the bank with a return on its equity. LIBOR covers only the cost of funds. Thus the increment charged over LIBOR, usually referred to as the **spread**, provides the only source of earnings to the bank. From the spread, the bank must pay its expenses, earn a profit, and be compensated for the credit risks.

Bankers may price loans as a spread above the interest rate paid on certificates of deposit (CDs) in the United States. This practice reflects the current domestic money market rates with greater sensitivity than does a bank's prime rate. It is often used to compete with the rate a multinational company can obtain by issuing commer-cial paper (one company borrowing from another one by means of unsecured promissory notes).

When the means of extending credit is a letter of credit or bankers' acceptance, the bank quotes a rate, often inaccurately called a commission, to compensate the bank for the credit risk in the transaction. The bank may make other charges, such as commitment fees, structuring fees, and so forth, as part of its overall compensation.

Secured and Unsecured Financing

A loan may be either *secured* or *unsecured*. In granting an unsecured loan, the bank relies solely on the financial strength and reputation of the borrower. The financing is based on the signing of a promissory note or other debt instrument. In secured financing, the bank requires not only evidence of the financial and moral integrity of the borrower and the signing of the note, but also possession of, or title to, outside value as protection. For example, the borrower may have marketable securities in negotiable form pledged to the bank. The bank could sell these if repayment for the financing does not come from the transaction itself. Internationally, the title to marketable goods in warehouses and the title to goods moving in trade under a letter of credit are examples of **collateral** or security (sometimes referred to as the fourth C of credit).

Such collateral provides additional protection for the bank and reduces its risk in the transaction, which may result in its being willing to charge a lower interest rate. In marginal cases, a bank may lend only if collateral is pledged, but a banker should never lend solely on the basis of collateral. Other than cash deposits in the currency of the loan, collateral values change. The values of securities and commodities change, based on the supply and demand expressed in the market price. The value of fixed assets (such as buildings) and capital goods (such as airplanes and ships) may change as a result of the demand for their use. The cost of building a vessel, for example, may not be the price that a buyer would pay. The value of the vessel is based on the amount of cash flow its use will bring. In past years, the substantial oversupply of ships resulted in low shipping rates and declining collateral value of the ships. Buyers were willing to purchase them only at a price that would enable owners to earn profits at prevailing shipping rates.

The amount that can be realized by the sale of collateral will be affected by many factors, such as the collateral's location. A paper mill, for example, is not easily moved. Its value to buyers in another country will be restricted to those who wish to own a mill in that particular location. The value of such fixed-asset collateral is also affected by the political stability of the country in which it is located, availability of raw materials supply, proximity of competitors, and general business outlook for the product. If the borrower was unable to make a profit operating a manufacturing plant in a particular location, the banker must consider whether this was due to other problems of the borrower or inherent problems in the plant itself. If the latter, then the realized value can be adversely affected. Poorly located or inefficient oil refineries, for example, have attracted little interest even in times of high demand for their product.

Guarantor

In some instances, the banker may not consider it prudent to lend to a potential borrower solely on the basis of that borrower's financial strength, which may be inadequate, and the borrower may not have adequate collateral to pledge. Another person or corporation, however, may be willing to guarantee repayment to the bank in the event of the borrower's nonpayment. This other party serves as **guarantor**, and the banker makes the credit decision by evaluating the capacity, character, and capital of the guarantor. Requiring a guarantor is common for new businesses, because the owners or parent companies may be willing to provide a guarantee to enable the new company to obtain the bank financing it needs. International lenders may ask a foreign government to guarantee the borrowings of the government's development agencies or a parent company to guarantee the debt of an overseas subsidiary.

Depending on the laws of the country, this guarantee may be evidenced by a separate document, an endorsement, or *aval*. The aval is accepted in some countries (not the United States) and by signatories to the Geneva Convention on Negotiable Instruments. It permits the guarantor to sign on the promissory note with the statement *por aval* or *bon pour aval* and be legally bound as the guarantor of that document.

In international transactions, the country risk of the guarantor must be specifically considered. If the guarantor is in the same country as the borrower, then the same country risks associated with the borrower will apply to the guarantor. However, if the guarantor is in another country, as when a parent company in an industrialized country guarantees the bank's credit to a subsidiary in a developing country, then the bank will base its decision on the country risk of the guarantor. This may change an otherwise unfavorable assessment of the borrowing request. The banker must be certain that a guarantee can be legally enforced in that country if it needs to be. This is not an automatic process, and there are many legal ways a guarantor can delay or even seek to annul its commitment if it does not wish to pay. In some countries, there must be proof that there was some benefit to the guarantor when it provided backing for the borrower. Thus the documentation of the guarantee, the character of the guarantor, and the financial capabilities of the guarantor must be carefully evaluated.

Lines of Credit

Many borrowers have a series of transactions to be financed over a period of time. For these customers, the establishment of a **line of credit** is more suitable than a one-time loan. Importers, for example, need to have letters of credit established regularly as they make purchases; foreign banks need lines of credit for confirmation of letters of credit and other short-term financing of international trade. The bank determines the maximum amount of credit it will allow that customer to have outstanding at any one time. Then it establishes a revolving line of credit that permits the importer to request any number of individual transactions within the credit limit. As transactions mature and are paid, the cycle may recur. Such an arrangement enables the bank to serve the customer more quickly and easily.

Term

A loan scheduled to be repaid in less than a year from the time it is disbursed is described by the commercial banker as *short-term*; one that has a schedule for final repayment of more than a year is a *term* loan or a *long-term* loan. Investment bankers and governments often refer to a loan as *medium-term* when the maturity is between one to five years and as *long-term* when the maturity is more than five years.

Short-term financing may be used for international trade transactions. A term loan is usually needed when a new manufacturing plant or mine is being constructed in one country and it will result in expanded exports from that country. In such an example, the bank commits to the financing before construction begins. Disbursements of funds will take place at certain established stages of the completion of construction. Between the time it approves the loan request and the disbursements, the bank will charge a *commitment fee* which will be replaced by interest when the funds are actually disbursed. A *grace period* is the time between the last disbursement and the first due installment of repayment.

Government Support

Certain international credit transactions may qualify for financing or other credit support under programs of national or international governmental agencies. The Export-Import Bank of the United States, for example, provides support for some transactions that finance U.S. exports (see chapter 12). The global banker should consider the availability of such programs, which can offer their customer reduced interest costs, reduced risks, and other credit enhancements that benefit both the customer and the bank. Some agencies have programs to support long-term financing.

Types of Financing

Banks may extend credit in a variety of ways. The purpose and the type of transaction often govern the method of financing. Some of these techniques are also used in domestic banking, but others are special to the international transaction. The nature of the transaction usually determines the selection of the debt instrument. If several means exist, the customer may indicate the choice.

Direct Loan

A promissory note is the most commonly used borrowing instrument in banking. The borrower signs a document acknowledging receipt of the money and making a commitment to repay this money with interest. The note may provide for interest to be paid at stated intervals—for example, quarterly between the time of disbursement and the date of maturity. Similarly, repayment of principal may be due in installments or in full on a stated date. Generally, banks allow full repayment in one installment at the end of a specific period only for short-term loans.

When a borrower is in a foreign country, the bank must be certain that the promissory note is in a form enforceable not only in U.S. courts but also in courts in the borrower's country. Sometimes the promissory note must be bilingual, and a bank active in such types of financing must have legal counsel in that country. Some banks assume that, because such financing occurs in the United States, they can use basic domestic note forms. If the foreign borrower has no U.S. assets, however, a judgment obtained in a U.S. court may not be enforceable.

Trade Financing

An exporter's objective is to be paid promptly in cash for the full amount of her sale. In many instances, this fails to happen because of constraints on the exporter's own cash flow or conditions in its country, or because it is offered delayed payment terms by other sellers who are competing to make the sale. The exporter then must decide what alternatives she is prepared to accept to make the sale. If there is a large demand for her product, the exporter may be able to find other buyers who can pay cash, or she may be able to insist that the buyer obtain bank financing and pay promptly. Otherwise, the exporter will examine the means of payment the buyer can offer and then decide whether to accept them. The following are some of the alternatives.

The importer wants to pay at a future date. He expects to generate the cash by selling the merchandise before paying the exporter.

For example, a U.S. seller shipping on a collection draws a draft on the foreign importer due 90 days after sight. The documents are released upon acceptance of the draft by the importer, who commits to pay 90 days from the date of acceptance. (The draft has become a trade acceptance for which the exporter expects to receive the full amount at its maturity in 90 days.) If the exporter wants funds before then, the bank can assist by discounting the trade acceptance with recourse to the exporter. The exporter receives less than the full face amount, and the bank will present the trade acceptance to the importer for full payment in 90 days. The differential is the bank's income for the financing. If the trade acceptance is not paid by the importer, the exporter will be expected to pay the bank and then seek repayment from the importer. The bank's decision to discount will depend on its analysis of the credit capacity of the exporter. If it is satisfied with the importer's credit capacity, the bank may discount the trade acceptance *without recourse*. In this case, if the importer does not pay, the exporter has no obligation to repay the bank.

If the importer can obtain a guarantee from a government export agency or commercial bank on this trade acceptance or similar obligation to pay, the exporter can then sell the debt *à forfait* (a French commercial term meaning "outright" or "by contract," which has become anglicized to "forfeiting"). This is a means of financing that developed in Europe originally for financing East-West trade and is available in the United States through specialized finance companies and banks that buy trade obligations of importers at a discount without recourse to the exporter. The financing entity is relying on the credit strength and country risk of the guarantor. The guarantor is usually better known and financially stronger than the importer, which makes financing easier to obtain than relying on only the credit strength of the importer. This guarantee is often evidenced by endorsing the note by aval. "Although it may be used for all export transactions, in practice it has been applied mainly to exports of capital goods with credit terms of five to seven years maturity." [7]

When the importer opens a U.S. dollar time-letter of credit, the exporter will receive a bankers' acceptance (see chapter 9) after presenting the specified documents evidencing shipment. The exporter can discount this immediately and be paid. The importer will not have to pay the bank until the bankers' acceptance matures. If it is a deferred payment letter of credit, the exporter will be paid by the issuing bank at specified future dates when the buyer also pays the bank, although in some circumstances arrangements can be made by the seller to discount these payments with a third party before the due date.

The importer cannot pay in money. There are many situations today in which an importer cannot obtain any, or can obtain only a part, of the foreign exchange from its government in order to pay for the purchase. This situation usually occurs when a country has a balance of payments problem, but it may also develop when a government wishes to force the sale of some of its country's goods that might not otherwise be easily sold internationally.

The exporter will be told that the sale can be made only if she agrees to accept merchandise as payment or if she commits to purchase merchandise at a future date. These compensatory trade arrangements are referred to as **countertrade**. The exporter will receive merchandise in payment, which she must then sell in some other country for cash. This may not be simple and can result in delays. The price ultimately received will, in effect, be the payment for the original sale.

Some countries require that trade between themselves or within a bloc of countries be balanced. An exporter may find that her ability to make an export sale will depend on the other country having made sales in the exporter's country—*clearing agreements* (see chapter 5). The exporter is paid in her own currency by her own government from a "clearing account."

The exporter may need to obtain the financing herself. This can be done by using programs offered by her country through a government export agency. Many countries have such agencies to encourage and promote exports that provide employment and income to the nation. In addition, the exporter may ask her bank to provide financing to the buyer. When the bank does this, she will then consider the buyer as the borrower and make a credit decision based on the creditworthiness of the buyer. If this is not sufficient, then the bank may require a partial or full guarantee from the exporter.

In many foreign banks, financing by overdrawing a commercial account is a customary means of extending credit to a customer. Both custom and law make this method unacceptable in the United States. Therefore, to provide flexibility of financing in a manner comparable to that provided abroad, a bank may enter into an agreement with a customer that, from time to time when the customer requests funds for certain purposes, the bank will make the disbursement without any promissory note. The client's obligation to repay is contained in the agreement. In this way, each disbursement retains its identity without the customer's having to prepare a promissory note each time.

Syndicate Loans

When a borrower seeks a large loan, a single bank may be unwilling or unable, because of its lending limits, to make the entire loan itself, even though the proposal is sound. To make the loan, a bank may seek to attract other banks to make the loan jointly as a **syndicate**. Each bank determines whether the proposal is creditworthy and how much it is willing to lend.

The basic principle behind syndicating loans is diversification of the loan portfolio—spreading the risks. As one banker has described it, "There's never anything so good . . . that we want to have a hundred percent of it." [8] The size of a single transaction or the total number of transactions from the same borrower may have grown so large that banks feel it is almost a necessity to syndicate most large loan requests, considering their impact on each bank's legal lending limit.

One bank or a small group of banks is given the mandate by the borrower to raise the funds, and it serves as the syndicate manager to locate enough banks to make the loan. The syndicate manager has many responsibilities to the participating banks. This lead bank may bring in other banks to be comanagers. This is partly in recognition of their willingness to take a large portion of the loan and partly to gain expert help in the long, often tedious, process of convincing a number of banks to join the syndicate, negotiating the details, and providing the documentation. Basically the manager must represent the borrower to the group of lenders and represent the lenders to the borrower. The lead bank will be paid a fee by the borrower, and that bank may offer a portion of the managing fee to other banks to become co-managers.

Syndicates can comprise both U.S. and foreign banks. Since many foreign banks do not have a source of U.S.-based dollars, international syndicates are usually funded in Eurodollars. The borrower and all participating banks write and sign the loan agreement. One of the managing banks is the *agent* and assumes the responsibility for coordinating disbursements, repayments, and dissemination of other documents such as financial statements and progress reports.

Many smaller banks have come into syndicated loans, thereby providing an added source of funds. In exchange they earn the interest, have a chance to diversify their loan portfolio, and gain introduction to the senior officers of the borrower—or in the case of a foreign government as borrower, the senior financial ministers. This is usually done at the loan closing. The participating banks will all be listed in the financial press advertisements announcing the loan (referred to as *tombstones*). Thus even the smallest partici-

pating bank will be identified as being an international lender, which may attract new business for that bank. The smallest bank in a syndicate must recognize, however, that it must evaluate the credit risk for itself, since a foreign borrower seeking to reschedule its repayment in times of trouble presents the same problem to the small bank as to the large bank.

Leasing

In a typical leasing transaction, the bank, either directly or through a special subsidiary, purchases a piece of equipment, such as a machine. The borrower enters into an agreement with the bank to lease this machine for a stated number of months and to pay the bank a certain sum each month as rent. At the end of the term, the customer may have the option of buying the machine for the remaining depreciated value.

An advantage of leasing for a customer in some countries is that the entire monthly payment may be treated as an expense for tax purposes. If the customer had purchased the machinery directly or had obtained a bank loan, only a portion of each monthly payment would be a taxable expense. The bank's advantage in a lease is that, as the owner of the equipment, it is entitled to all the depreciation and investment tax credits in computing its overall taxes. These are *direct leases*. A *leveraged lease* is basically the same, except that the bank locates other investors to become joint owners of the equipment and receives, in turn, a pro rata share of the tax benefits.

Documentation

The bank protects itself by having the borrower sign certain legal documents. In these documents, the borrower acknowledges receipt of the funds and makes a commitment to repay them.

In addition, the borrower provides the bank with the means of recourse if repayment does not occur. When the loan is large and other lenders are involved, such documentation may be extensive and include controls on the borrower while the debt is owed, as a means of protecting the bank.

For syndicate loans, the principal legal document is a *loan agreement*. This document may be very long and have many supporting certifications detailed. It must be legally enforceable in the borrower's country, which requires special knowledge of the laws of different countries. Besides serving to commit the borrower to repay, the loan agreement should remove any confusion between the borrower and the lender or among the lenders about the procedures of disbursement and repayment. The document defines relevant procedures and terms. Most loan agreements detail what violations of the agreement constitute a *default* by the borrower as well as cross-default provisions. A *cross-default* provision means that if the borrower defaults on any other loan, this loan becomes immediately due and payable. This protects the bank by giving it equal standing with any other lenders. The loan agreement also requires the borrower to submit interim financial and operating reports. Thus the lender can detect any adverse development at an early stage. The experienced banker, however, is aware that the imposition of conditions in any loan agreement can have limited effectiveness when the borrower encounters financial problems. The borrower may be unable to maintain loan agreement conditions, and the banker can be faced with the choice of either waiving a condition or having the loan go into default, with all the problems that will ensue with a potential loan loss.

Although loan agreements in international syndicate loans greatly depend on work by lawyers, the banker must ensure that the document reflects banking needs. The banker, not the lawyer, makes credit or business decisions.

Managing the Credit

The decision to extend credit is only a part of the banker's task. Equally important is to see that the credit is repaid. The banker's responsibility does not end until final repayment has been made. This means that the banker must stay involved with the customer during the disbursement of the credit, in the course of its utilization, and as the borrower's business is conducted.

During the actual disbursement of the loan, the banker will monitor that the funds are being delivered to the borrower in accordance with the agreed use. In a term loan, the funds may be released as certain stages in the construction are reached. In a trade financing, the credit may go through a series of transactions as the goods move. It is the banker's responsibility to know what is happening.

The banker needs to stay informed about the financial condition of the borrower and be alert to warning signs that the borrower may be encountering unanticipated difficulties. These can show up in such things as late payments of interest or principal installments, information from trade sources of other slow payments, or further unexpected requests for short-term financing. The experienced banker knows that it is important to be aware of developing problems and to discuss these with the borrower as soon as possible, since early attention can often prevent major problems that could later lead to a loan loss.

When a borrower is unable to repay, the banker can anticipate spending considerable time and effort to assess what has caused the borrower's difficulties, what can be done to correct these problems, and what must be done to protect the bank's commitment and minimize any loss. This is equally true whether the borrower is a company or a country. Often this must be done in conjunction with other banks that have also lent money to the borrower as part of a *creditors' committee*. Working out problem loans is not an easy task, and it requires all the skills and experience of the banker.

Accounting

Loans are assets in the bank's balance sheet regardless of how they are funded. Loan commitments are contingent accounts until a drawdown occurs, then the amount of the drawdown is reduced from the contingent account and becomes a loan asset.

Before the effective date of the Risk-Based Capital Guidelines, all international loans are given the same weight in calculating the primary capital-to-asset ratio. However, the Risk-Based Capital Guidelines change this, and different risk weightings are applied depending on the borrower, guarantor, or collateral as follows:

- A distinction is drawn in the risk percentage for a bank's loans to borrowers in differing groups of countries, for example, countries that are members of the Organization for Economic Cooperation and Development (OECD) and those that have concluded special lending arrangements with the IMF associated with the Fund's General Arrangements to Borrow.

  Loans to central and local governments in countries belonging to the above groups are assigned the same risk percentage as comparable U.S. government entities. For the central government, this is 0 percent; for local governments, it is 20 percent. Loans to the governments in all other countries are risk weighted at 100 percent. In effect this means that loans to national and local governments in most of Latin America, Africa, and Asia will require banks to use more capital than for financings to governments in Western Europe, North America, and certain industrialized countries of Asia. However, as countries join the OECD, the lower rating

percentages become applicable to their outstanding loans as well as new ones.

- Loan commitments with an original maturity date of less than a year are excluded. Loan commitments of more than a year require that 50 percent of that commitment be counted and then given the risk weighting of the borrower or guarantor.

- The collateral securing a credit can alter the risk weighting. For example, a loan to a foreign corporation would be weighted 100 percent in calculating the risk-weighting formula. However, if that loan is collateralized by a government bond issued by the United States or any of the above countries, then the loan instead will be risk weighted based on the percentage applicable to that foreign government, which may be 0 percent for central governments or 20 percent for state or municipal governments.

Summary

This chapter has examined the many facets of international credit. These have included the facts the lending officer needs to know about the transaction, how to evaluate the information, and how to apply all this to creating the proper combination to meet the borrower's needs as well as to protect the bank.

Examination of an international transaction begins with the same considerations as for a domestic one. The decision must be founded on the bank's lending policies and objectives, the constraints established by law, and the dispassionate assessment of the risks involved. The fundamental question the banker is seeking to answer is, "If I make this credit available to this customer, will I be paid back?" The banker knows that the funds being used are primarily those of the bank's depositors and therefore the credit must be viewed differently than if the banker were an investor using exclusively his or her own funds. To approach an answer, the banker filters the available information through the Cs of credit:

- *Character.* "Am I dealing with an honest, responsible, experienced borrower?"
- *Cash flow.* "Will the borrower have a stream of income sufficient to meet the interest and principal repayment schedule?"
- *Capital.* "Does the borrower have other assets that could be used to pay interest and principal if his cash flow falls below expectations and is not enough?"
- *Collateral.* "If the cash flow and capital are not enough, are there other assets that I can convert to cash?" (These four are common questions asked of all transactions, but for international credit, the banker must add another query.)
- *Country risk.* "Will there be political or economic events in the borrower's country that could affect the ability to repay?"

The banker has traditionally relied heavily on the borrower's financial statement as the source of most of these answers. Most loans are structured so that the "full faith and credit" of the borrower are behind the loan. This means that the banker expects that any borrower will use, if necessary, all of his or her available cash flow from all sources to meet the interest and principal repayments of a particular loan. However, some loans, such as for developing mineral resources have been structured so that only that particular project is the source of repayment. This involves a comprehensive evaluation of the financial and economic factors.

An international credit decision involves all of these factors plus the awareness that the bank's customer is functioning in the global business community with its unique considerations. These basically focus on the characteristics of an international borrower as well as assessing the risks for a domestic borrower with an international transaction. The customer expects to have a banker who is able to understand and evaluate these situations. The banker cannot become panic-stricken by international risk. By carefully detailing and assessing the risks of global business, the domestic credit officer can comfortably make a credit decision for an international transaction using the skills and experience gained from having made domestic credit decisions.

Questions

1. Why do U.S. banks lend to foreign borrowers?
2. What is currency risk?
3. How does extending credit to a correspondent bank differ from credit to a foreign government?
4. What are financial statements, and how are they used to evaluate international credit?

Notes

1. American Bankers Association, *Banking Terminology*, 3d ed. (Washington, D.C.: 1989), p. 153
2. Walter Wriston in *The Way it Was: An Oral History of Finance* (New York: William Morrow and Co., Inc., 1988), p. 25
3. World Bank, *World Development Report 1983* (New York: Oxford University Press, 1983), p. 75
4. "Survey of Private Banking," *The Economist*, June 24, 1989, p. 3
5. Paul A. Carrubba, *Principles of Banking* (Washington, D.C.: American Bankers Association, 1994), p. 143
6. William H. Baughn and Donald R. Mandich, eds., *The International Banking Handbook* (Homewood, Ill.: Dow Jones-Irwin, 1983), p. 730

7. International Monetary Fund, *Exchange Arrangements and Exchange Restrictions*, Annual Report 1986, p. 33

8. Anthony Sampson, *The Money Lenders* (New York: Viking Press, 1981), p. 19

11

FUNDING GLOBAL FINANCE

Learning Objectives

After studying this chapter, you will know how

- to examine the characteristics of funding with domestic dollars and Eurodollars
- Eurodollars are created
- bonds are a source of global funding
- interest rate swaps are used to lower financing costs

Overview

After the credit decision has been made, the banker and the borrower must consider how it will be funded—that is, they must determine the source of the funds to be lent and the operational structure.

A commercial bank may use the funds it has attracted into the myriad types of accounts reflected as deposits in its balance sheet. For some accounts, the money deposited can be withdrawn on demand of the depositor. Other accounts pay fluctuating interest, and still other accounts are established for a fixed period and a fixed interest rate. Alternatively, the bank may obtain Eurodollars. These are funds the bank has bid for in the market for a fixed term (usually three to six months), with a fixed interest rate for that period. Such dollar funds are deposited in banking offices outside the United States. *Eurodollar* is a term that describes a particular kind of time deposit; the actual accounts are in U.S. dollars and are interchangeable with any other dollar accounts. Other Eurocurrencies exist when marks, yen, pounds, francs, and so forth are deposited outside their home country.

Other sources of funds, generally available outside the commercial banking system, are the assets of institutional investors: pension funds, insurance companies, personal trusts, and wealthy individuals. These entities may provide the funding to a borrower by purchasing the borrower's bonds which constitute the promise to repay principal and interest directly to the owner of the bonds.

The source of the funds to be used may be dictated by the existence of other money and capital market capabilities that can enable the borrower, after receiving the proceeds of a bank loan or bond, to lower the cost of that borrowing through various types of separate financial agreements—for example, to swap with another borrower its commitment to pay interest.

All of these alternative funding sources and considerations compete and are inextricably linked with each other in today's global capital and money markets.

The credit decision must be made separate from the determination of how the transaction will be funded. Only after the banker has decided to make the loan to the borrower should the funding alternatives be considered.

The U.S. commercial bank, lending dollars, has two basic alternatives: domestic dollars or Eurodollars.

Domestic Dollars

The majority of the loans that a commercial bank makes are funded with the deposits on their balance sheet and, to a lesser extent, the bank's capital (shareholder's equity, retained earnings). Most such deposits are checking accounts, savings accounts, and time deposits from local individuals, businesses, and governmental entities that maintain them with the bank for convenience, earnings, and safety. These are primarily domestic customers, and consequently these funds may be referred to as *domestic dollars* to distinguish them from Eurodollars (see below). Due To accounts from foreign banks as well as deposits from foreign firms are included in such accounts. These balance sheet deposits are operated as a pool of funds when the bank is funding its loans and are not segregated as to the country of the depositor or to match any particular loan. The bank manages these liabilities to ensure that its liquidity is protected. This means that the bank will have sufficient funds available to meet withdrawals. The bank knows from experience the normal day-to-day cycle of withdrawals, new deposits, loan disbursements, loan repayments, and other flows of funds.

There are costs to the bank associated with this pool of deposit funds in addition to any interest payment. First, only a percentage of the deposits is available for the bank's use in funding loans or investing in debt securities because the

Federal Reserve requires that a portion of these deposits be maintained as a reserve in a noninterest-earning account at the regional Federal Reserve bank. Second, deposits are required to be insured within the protection provisions of the FDIC or otherwise collateralized.[1]

Eurodollars

A **Eurodollar** is a U.S. dollar deposited in a banking office outside the United States. The bank does not have to be a foreign bank; it may be an overseas branch of a U.S. bank. It may also be an International Banking Facility (IBF) (see chapter 2). Eurodollars, which are basically a wholesale market, are a phenomenon of the post-World War II financial world. They are unique in having become a major world currency without existing in either banknote or coin form and without a central bank for regulation.

Today, the Eurodollar is traded in financial centers around the world. Like foreign exchange, the Eurodollar market is conducted by telephone and telecommunications rather than in a central physical location.

A number of names have been used for Eurodollars to denote special ownership. When the rapid increase in the price of petroleum occurred in the early '70s, the oil-producing countries began to acquire large amounts of Eurodollars from their sales; these dollars were often referred to as *petrodollars*. In fact, these were simply Eurodollars owned by oil producers and indistinguishable from any other Eurodollars. *Asian dollars*, another form of Eurodollars, are traded in such Asian money centers as Singapore.

Operations

All Eurodollar transactions are time deposits for a stated fixed term, even if that term is just one business day or requires only one business day's notice to cancel (*call money*). The interest rate quoted depends on the term of the deposit.

A Eurodollar may be created in many ways. When a U.S. business pays for an import, the U.S. dollars move from the importer's account to the account of a foreign exporter. The exporter may choose to sell the dollars in exchange for his local currency or to keep the dollars and put them on deposit in a bank or banking office outside the United States for a fixed term, thereby earning interest. Upon such deposit, the U.S. dollars become Eurodollars.

There are several fundamental differences between a Eurodollar and a "domestic" dollar. All Eurodollar deposits are for a fixed term, anywhere from one day to as long as five years. In the domestic dollar market, there are demand accounts. All Eurodollar deposits earn interest, and the rate of interest varies, depending on the supply and demand for any given maturity. Eurodollar deposits are free of any reserve requirement, and therefore all the funds deposited are available for use. Federal Reserve Regulation D may require a U.S. bank to hold reserves against its net borrowing of Eurodollars, regardless of whether this is done through a branch or a foreign bank, and when it lends Eurodollars to a domestic borrower for domestic use from a foreign branch. Eurodollar deposits are not insured by the FDIC.

It is important to recognize that, even though the money has now become Eurodollars, *it has never left the United States*.

Exhibit 11.1 describes the important accounting features of Eurodollar creation and use.

As the Eurodollar has developed into a worldwide monetary unit, it has become closely linked to changes in the U.S. money market and the rates for domestic money transactions. Holders of dollars have the option to place them in U.S. or Eurodollar instruments and will make such decisions based on yield, safety perceptions, and possible tax consequences. Instead of redepositing with another bank, the dollars can be

Exhibit 11.1   Important Accounting Features of Eurodollars

The following describes changes in the balance sheets of each of the banks involved in the transaction. The left column shows the changes in the accounts of the U.S. banking system; the right column shows the changes in the accounts of the banks outside of the United States. C/A = checking account; DD = demand deposit; D/F = Due From account; D/T = Due To account; TD = time deposit. The transfers from one U.S. bank to another are shown only at the end of any Fedwire or CHIPS entries (see chapter 3).

EXAMPLE: CREATING EURODOLLARS

1. California Oil Company buys crude oil from Middle East Country for US$10 million. The company pays by instructing San Francisco Bank to debit its checking account and credit the Due To account of the Middle East Central Bank at San Francisco Bank. No Eurodollar is created because the funds are on deposit only in the United States.

San Francisco Bank

Assets	Liabilities
	− C/A Calif. Oil Co. [DD]
	+ D/T Middle East Cent. Bk. [DD]

2. Middle East Central Bank deposits the funds at London Bank, which offers to pay interest. London Bank establishes the time deposit at its head office. This is now a Eurodollar transaction.

San Francisco Bank

London Bank

Assets	Liabilities
	+ D/T Middle East Cent Bk. [TD]

3. To make the funds transfer, Middle East Central Bank instructs San Francisco Bank to debit its Due To account and, in accordance with instructions from London Bank, transfer the funds to New York Bank A for credit to the Due To account of London Bank at New York Bank A (via Fedwire). When this is done, London Bank now shows that it has $10 million in its Due From account in New York Bank A. London Bank's assets and liabilities have now increased by $10 million. It is paying interest on the Eurodollar deposit; it is not earning interest on its demand deposit in New York Bank A.

Exhibit 11.1 Important Accounting Features of Eurodollars (continued)

San Francisco Bank

Assets	Liabilities
	− D/T Middle East Cent. Bk. [DD]

New York Bank A		**London Bank**	
Assets	Liabilities	Assets	Liabilities
	+ D/T London Bank [DD]	+ D/F New York Bk. A [DD]	+ D/T Middle East Cent. Bk. [TD]

4. London Bank took the deposit as part of its money market trading activities. It now decides to place these funds in another bank to earn interest. It negotiates with Zurich Bank and accepts their offered interest rate. Zurich Bank shows that it has a $10 million time deposit from London Bank; London Bank shows that it has a $10 million time deposit in its Due From account at Zurich Bank. To transfer the funds, London Bank instructs New York Bank A to transfer the funds from its Due To account to New York Bank B for credit to the Due To account of Zurich Bank at New York Bank B. When this is done (via CHIPS), London Bank's financial statement shows that it no longer has the money in its Due From account in New York Bank A. Zurich Bank shows that it now has $10 million in its Due From account at New York Bank B on which it is not earning interest.

New York Bank A		**London Bank**	
Assets	Liabilities	Assets	Liabilities
	− D/T London Bank [DD]	− D/F New York [DD] Bk. A + D/F Zurich Bank [TD]	+ D/T Middle East Cent. Bk. [TD]

New York Bank B		**Zurich Bank**	
Assets	Liabilities	Assets	Liabilities
	+ D/T Zurich Bank [DD]	+ D/F New York Bk. B [DD]	+ D/T London Bank [TD]

Exhibit 11.1 **Important Accounting Features of Eurodollars** (continued)

5. Australia Bank needs $10 million to fund its loan to India Construction Company. Through its Cayman Islands branch, Australia Bank bids for the funds from Zurich Bank, paying the current LIBOR. Zurich Bank's financial statement shows it has a Due From time deposit with Australia Bank; Australia Bank shows it has a Due To time deposit for Zurich Bank. It obtains the actual funds when Zurich Bank instructs New York Bank B to debit its Due To account and transfer to New York Bank C for credit to the Due To account there of Australia Bank (via CHIPS).

New York Bank B		**Zurich Bank**	
Assets	Liabilities	Assets	Liabilities
	− D/T Zurich Bank [DD]	− D/F New York Bk. B [DD]	+ D/T London Bank [TD]
		+ D/F Australia [TD] Bank	

New York Bank C		**Australia Bank**	
Assets	Liabilities	Assets	Liabilities
	+ D/T Australia Bank [DD]	+ D/F NY Bk. C [DD]	+ D/T Zurich Bank [TD]

6. To disburse its loan, Australia Bank instructs New York Bank C to debit its Due To account and credit the checking account at Chicago Bank of India Construction Company (via Fedwire). India Construction Company can now pay its suppliers.

New York Bank C		**Australia Bank**	
Assets	Liabilities	Assets	Liabilities
	− D/T Australia Bank [DD]	− D/F NY Bk. C [DD]	+ D/T Zurich Bank [TD]
		+ Loan: India Const. Co.	

Chicago Bank	
Assets	Liabilities
	+ C/A India Co.

Conclusion: The financial statements of all the banks in these transactions show that London Bank, Zurich Bank, and Australia Bank have each grown their assets and liabilities by $10 million for a total growth of $30 million. The total change in the U.S. banking system has been *zero* because the overseas banks have set up time deposits; the U.S. banks have merely moved demand deposits. The entire pattern will reverse when the loan or time deposits mature and are paid back.

invested in U.S. Treasury bills, bankers' acceptances, or any other money market instrument.

A Eurodollar is indistinguishable from a domestic U.S. dollar and, consequently, it is easy to move from one market to another. As in foreign exchange, money will move to the higher interest rate, and when rates for short-term investments are higher in the United States, money is attracted there. The Eurodollar rates, as a consequence, must likewise increase. The historical pattern has been that both markets tend to move up or down in tandem. The main impetus comes from changes in the U.S. domestic market simply because it is the larger market.

Interbank Trading

A bank has two basic sources of Eurodollars—its customers and the interbank market. As the Eurodollar market grew, fewer instances arose in which a participating bank would have a deposit offered to it for precisely the same amount for which it had a borrower seeking a loan. A bank would often find itself paying interest on a Eurodollar deposit from one of its customers, but with no borrowers seeking loans. To put these deposits to work and receive interest income to offset the interest expense, an interbank trading market developed. Banks redeposit Eurodollars with another bank that might be seeking the money to fund a loan. Because of the size of the market, interbank trading now encompasses most Eurodollar activity. Deposit of Eurodollars with another bank is referred to as a *placement* of funds and . . . the receipt of Eurodollar deposits from another bank as a *taking* of funds. Other people in the U.S. money market are likely to use the jargon of the Fed funds market, referring to placements of Euros as *sales* of funds and to takings of Euros as *purchases* of funds." [2]

As in any money market, Eurodollar rates fluctuate with supply and demand. In the course of a business day, a bank's trader is offered deposits by brokers or other banks and offers to place deposits with another bank. For example, a bank trader may have a $1 million Eurodollar deposit, for which the bank is paying 6 percent annual interest, committed to remain with the bank for six months. The trader may have an opportunity to redeposit that money with another bank for 30 days for $6^{1}/_{16}$ percent annual interest. Anticipating higher rates at the end of the 30 days, when another short-term placement of the deposit will be sought, the trader may be able to obtain a greater spread (profit) on the $1 million on deposit. The renewing of a deposit or a loan is called a *rollover*.

As each transaction is made, settlement instructions are sent to a U.S. bank to debit the Due To account of the seller and credit the Due To account of the buyer. Most of this is done through accounts maintained in New York City banks. To facilitate the prompt processing of this enormous volume of daily payments, a computerized communications network was established by the member banks of the New York Clearing House and certain other active Edge Acts in New York City. This is the Clearing House Interbank Payments System (CHIPS). The CHIPS system and S.W.I.F.T. (see chapter 3) have been designed to provide a computerized interface, thereby eliminating clerical handling.

Lending

A loan funded in Eurodollars is made at a banking office outside the United States or through the separate IBF accounts at a bank's domestic office. Most Eurodollar borrowers are outside the United States.

A Eurodollar loan requires exactly the same credit criteria as any other loan. It differs only in the means by which the loan is funded. In essence, a Eurodollar loan is made with borrowed funds. If a Eurodollar loan is not repaid, a bank suffers the same loss it would from a loan made in the United States funded with depositors' money. This fact has been overlooked by too many bank credit officers in recent years.

A foreign borrower applies to a U.S. bank for a loan in the same manner, whether the loan is to be funded in Eurodollars or domestic dollars. If the bank decides to use Eurodollars, then it must take several additional steps:

1. *The bank must domicile the Eurodollar loan outside the United States.* Regardless of whether the foreign borrower made the loan request to an overseas branch of the U.S. bank or to the head office in the United States, the bank must select an overseas location for making the loan. It may be a foreign branch of the U.S. bank, one of the offshore financial centers, such as The Bahamas or the Cayman Islands, or an IBF (considered to be outside the United States for purposes of Eurodollar lending). The selection depends on the management policy of the U.S. bank.

2. *The interest rate must be fixed for a given period.* A Eurodollar loan is quoted to the borrower at an interest rate of a stated percentage over the cost of obtaining the Eurodollars. When the actual disbursement is made, the bank obtains a Eurodollar deposit for the stated amount from another bank in the interbank trading market. The rate at which these funds are obtained is the bank's cost, to which is added the additional stated percentage to determine the borrower's exact interest cost. The entire deposit can be used to fund the loan. This differs from the use of domestic dollars in which the bank may have to put a part of the deposit into its reserve account at the Federal Reserve.

Eurodollar deposits are placed for a stated period of time, usually six months. If the loan is for a longer period, such as a term loan of five years, then the bank takes the deposit—borrows the funds—for six months at a time. At the end of every six months, the bank must pay back the deposit and obtain another one. The loan interest rate for the borrower thus changes every six months.

The cost to the bank of the deposit is referred to as the LIBOR. This is the interest rate it will pay the depositor and will be the bank's sole cost for these funds. (Because the Eurodollar interbank trading has been concentrated in London, London rates have become the usual base quotation.) The use of LIBOR does not mean that the loan must be domiciled in London, only that the price for the funds is that at which a bank obtains a deposit in the London Eurodollar interbank market. The funds may be obtained in another market—such as Asia or New York—and the interest rate can be stated based on any of these interbank markets rather than London. In legal documents, many banks refer to the rate simply as the Interbank Offered Rate.

3. *Advance notice must be given for a disbursement.* The Eurodollar market has the characteristics of the foreign exchange market. Settlement on a trade will occur two business days in the future. To make a disbursement on a Eurodollar loan, the bank must buy a deposit in the market. The money will be available only in two days, at which time the loan can be disbursed. The bank must also take into account that at least two days are also needed in a foreign market. For example, considering international time differences, a borrower in Latin America may have to give three days' notice to a lender in Asia.

Syndicates

Many large loans are syndicated by the managing banks. Most such loans are made in Eurodollars in order to attract a large number of potential participating banks, particularly non-U.S. banks that do not have a source of domestic dollars. The syndicate loan made in Eurodollars requires that the base cost of funds be set by the managing banks. This cost is usually determined by taking the average cost of a Eurodollar deposit as quoted by three or more major banks as of the agreed-upon time three or more days prior to disbursement.

Eurocurrencies

In addition to dollars, a smaller international market exists for certain other major currencies, including deutsche marks, Swiss francs, and yen. When these currencies are held by nonresidents and deposited in banks outside the respective countries, they have the characteristics of Eurodollars and are referred to as *Eurocurrencies*. "The conventional definition of the Eurocurrency market includes deposits and loans booked outside the country in whose currency they are denominated." [3]

Liability Management

Banks manage their liabilities to ensure that they have liquidity (that is, funds available to disburse loans, invest in securities, meet deposit withdrawals) and an interest rate spread between the cost of such funds and the earnings of their assets (loans, securities). The Eurodollar market offers bank treasurers an added source of funds and different interest rate opportunities than would be available solely in the U.S. money market. This is done through either foreign branches or an IBF.

Although Eurodollar deposits are free of reserve requirements when taken in an overseas branch or IBF, Federal Reserve Regulation D can require reserves when a bank is, in essence, a net taker of Eurodollar deposits to use for the bank's domestic funding. Nonetheless, the level of interest rates and the availability of fixed-term deposits may make Eurodollar liability management operations advantageous for a bank.

On every Eurodollar loan a bank makes and funds, it has three potential sources of profit. First, there is the spread the bank gets over LIBOR, which compensates it for operating expenses and the credit risk it is assuming. Second, there is the extra $1/16$ or $1/8$ percent that the bank may be able to make if its dealers can pick up the needed funds a little below LIBOR, for example, through astute timing of the purchase. A third way a bank can profit from a loan is through mismatching its book.[4] (The term *book* refers to the assets and liabilities of a bank's balance sheet.)

Mismatching means, for example, charging interest on a loan based on the rate for a six-month LIBOR deposit, but actually taking only a one-month deposit that has a lower interest rate payment and then rolling that deposit over for each of the six months. As long as the one-month rate stays below the initial six-month rate, the bank will have an extra profit. The borrowing customer does not know this and is not concerned, since the loan rate is set assuming that the bank took a six-month deposit.

Many strategies and techniques are available to a bank when it runs a single global book.[5]

Global Capital Markets

Companies and governments may fund their borrowings by issuing **bonds**. A bond is a long-term debt instrument generally with an original maturity of 5 years or more, issued in standardized format, that bears interest and promises repayment of the principal. A bond is issued under an indenture that specifies the issuer's obligations to the bondholder and the manner in which the debt is secured. The indenture provides for a trustee who is responsible for the bondholders' rights.[6] A bond differs from a bank loan in a number of ways, such as documentation. The funds from a bond are disbursed to the borrower at one time, while term loan disbursements can be made in increments to match the borrower's needs.

By issuing a bond, a borrower can attract sources of funding other than a bank loan: insurance companies, pension funds, trusts, individuals, and even other banks. Funding a transaction by means of a bond creates different relationships between borrower, lender, and the owner of the funds. When a bank makes a loan, it is funded with depositors' money (from either the pool of domestic dollars or Eurodollars). The bank is responsible for returning those funds to the depositor regardless of whether the borrower repays the loan. With a bond, the lender and depositor are one; if the borrower does not repay, then those funds are lost to their owner. There is no intermediary. The provider of the funds (the investor) would therefore expect a higher rate than for a bank deposit; the borrower, however, may find that rate to be lower than the bank's loan rate.

A **Eurobond** is a bond issued by a company or government in a market other than that of its currency of denomination and is traded internationally. Some of these are informally described as a *Yankee bond* (a dollar-denominated bond issued in the United States for a non-American borrower), a *Samurai bond* (a yen-denominated bond issued in Japan by a non-Japanese borrower), and a *Bulldog bond* (a sterling-denominated bond issued by a non-British borrower).

The investment or merchant banker structures the transaction to meet the needs of the borrower and with the term, yield, and other features that will attract investors. Banks collect a fee for this service but usually do not invest any of their own funds in the bonds.

Bonds may be issued at a fixed or floating interest rate. A *fixed rate* means that the amount of interest the borrower will have to pay semiannually or quarterly will not change during the life of the bond. The interest rate is sometimes referred to as the *coupon*, reflecting that all bonds were originally issued as bearer bonds with a series of coupons attached, each of which had to be cut from the bond and presented to a designated paying agent in order to collect the interest when due. Bonds now are also issued as registered bonds—the name of the owner is registered with the issuing company, who then makes interest payments directly. A fixed-rate bond can be very attractive to borrowers. It can be difficult for a bank to make a term loan at a fixed rate, since its deposits are received for a short term and the interest rate the bank has to pay will fluctuate. However, the institutional investor, such as an insurance company or a pension fund, can take a fixed interest rate for a long-term bond because it has a different source of funds. It receives funds that it can calculate, based on actuarial tables, it will not have to pay out for many years.

Bond investors, unlike a bank lending, will rarely make their own credit evaluation of the borrower's financial statement, cash flow, and so forth. They rely on rating agencies, which will classify the bond issuer into a small number of categories using alphabetical letters and numbers. This rating summarizes all the borrower's financial conditions and, based on this simple designation, the investors can make their decision as to suitability for the investor's needs and expected interest rate.

The principal and interest are usually paid in the same currency, but depending on the outlook for various currencies, dual currency bonds (principal in one currency, interest in another) have at times been attractive. Bonds may also be issued that pay no interest. Such *zero-coupon* bonds have been used, for example, in the refinancing of some sovereign risk debt from the 1980s debt crisis. The foreign government borrower bought such U.S. Treasury Bonds maturing at the end of 10 years, paying about 20 percent of the face amount. These were pledged as collateral for some bank refinancing so that, at maturity, the bond would pay the face amount matching the principal due on the bank loans. The price at which these are sold is discounted to yield an implied annual interest rate when they mature.

Well-organized markets exist for most bonds so that the original purchaser of the bond can readily sell it. This liquidity can also be an attractive feature of a bond in comparison to a bank loan. Bonds will often pass through many owners. The price of the bond being traded will reflect the market interest rates at the time of the trade.* This does not affect the borrower whose obligation remains unchanged as to the amount and schedule of interest and principal payments. A *private placement* concerns bonds that are sold directly to a small group of sophisticated investors who will hold those bonds until maturity. This eliminates certain legal costs and restrictions that some countries impose on securities traded in their market.

Past Experiences

The financing of foreign governments and businesses through the issuance of bonds has had a long and checkered history. In the nineteenth century, use of bonds was customary in international financing. Large-scale global lending by

commercial banks for their own risk and with their own funding did not become widespread until the 1960s.

Foreign bond investors mostly financed the dramatic growth of the American railroad system from 1870 to 1913 (an increase from 53,000 miles of track to 380,000 miles).

> Foreign investments in American railroads were awesome. . . . Foreign savings flowed into U.S. railroad bonds and shares, more to the former than to the latter. . . . Banks helped the railroads to decide in what currency it should be denominated (dollars, pounds, or francs). If denominated in dollars, bonds could have a fixed exchange rate specified for interest and principal, or just for the interest payments. Some bonds were specified as gold-backed. There were first and second mortgage bonds and general mortgage bonds. Some were convertible [into equity]. Bonds were issued on divisions of particular railroads, or subsidiaries of railroads. There were "serial debentures," "first collateral trust mortgage gold bonds," "refunding and extension mortgage gold bonds," "first consolidated mortgage gold bonds," and numerous other types of securities.[7]

While most international investors profited from owning bonds, there were also spectacular cases where things went wrong.

> Between 1822 and 1825 seven Latin American nations . . . issued over £20,000,000 in bonds in the City of London. . . . After discounts and deductions the borrowing nations received approximately only 60 percent of the face value of the loans they had contracted. The first Latin American lending boom, however, assured high profits at

---

* For the mathematics of calculating prices for yield to maturity on coupon bonds, zero-coupon bonds, and so forth, see Marcia Stigum, *The Money Market*, 3d ed. (Homewood, Ill.: Dow Jones-Irwin, 1990), Chapter 4.

little risk for the selected financiers and merchants who organized the credits. Unlike their post-World War II counterparts, the early loan contractors did not keep any significant portion of the bonds on their own books, and passed the risk of non-payment on to more gullible investors in the form of bearer bonds. Unfortunately by 1829 nearly £19,000,000 of the bonds issued in 1822-5 were in default. Thousands of investors suffered . . . and [their] attempts to recover their investments provoked frustrating cycles of renegotiations, reschedulings, litigation and further defaults which lasted throughout much of the nineteenth century.[8]

In the early twentieth century, political revolutions and economic depressions left many investors holding beautifully engraved and solemnly worded, but now defaulted bonds. ("Only two governments—the Imperial Russian Government and the State of Mississippi—have actually repudiated their debt and said they will never pay. Many others have simply defaulted, leaving bondholders with paper whose value is uncertain at best."[9]) Decades later many of these could be purchased at less than 1 percent of their face value and ended up as ironic framed curiosities on the walls of the homes of bankers.

Short Term

In addition to investors in bonds, other nonbank sources of funding are available for short-term borrowings. The major one is *commercial paper*, which is basically one company borrowing directly from another company by means of unsecured promissory notes. In the United States, this is limited to 270 days, but most are for a much shorter time. This led to the development of a similar market elsewhere, *Euro commercial paper*.

Interest Rate Swaps

A bond or loan will have a designated interest rate, either fixed or floating. In some cases, the borrower may be able to change that rate by a separate transaction, such as an **interest rate swap**. This is an agreement between two parties (such as borrowers) to pay each other's interest obligation over an agreed period of time, with the result that each has less interest cost than if the swap had not been made. In some cases this may be negotiated between the two parties in advance (either directly or with the assistance of a banker) and form the basis for their loan request or bond creation. This can best be understood with a "plain vanilla" example:

Two companies need to borrow money. Company A has a strong financial condition and is considered to be a very good risk. If it wants to borrow for the long term, it can do so by issuing a five-year bond and pay a fixed rate of 6 percent per annum; or it can borrow for the short term from its bank at a variable interest rate of LIBOR + ¼ percent per annum, with LIBOR reset every six months. Company B has a good financial condition, but it is not as strong as company A. If it wants to borrow for the long term with a five-year bond, it will have to pay a fixed rate of 7 percent per annum; borrowing for the short term would cost LIBOR + ½ percent per annum—also reset every six months.

Company A's borrowing is for the carrying of its inventory, which is constantly turning over. It wants to borrow short term so that its interest costs will reflect changing market costs. Company B wants to borrow long term at a fixed rate so that it can build a new factory.

They may reduce their cost with an interest rate swap. Company A borrows long term (five years); company B borrows short term (and agrees to roll it over for five years). They agree to pay each other's *interest costs*—not the principal, as each retains its full responsibility to repay what it has borrowed. Thus company A is paying LIBOR + ½ percent; company B is paying 6 percent per annum. This appears to be a perfect arrangement for company B because it is effectively getting its long-term loan at a fixed rate cost of 6 percent per annum. If company B had borrowed without the swap, it would have had to pay 7 percent per annum, so it has gained 1 percent per annum. But why would company A agree to pay LIBOR + ½ percent when it could have borrowed on its own at a cost of only LIBOR + ¼ percent per annum?

Company B agrees, in the swap, to split its gain of 1 percent per annum with company A and thus transfers ½ percent per annum to company A. The final cost to company B: 6 percent per annum interest and ½ percent per annum to company A, for a total interest cost of 6½ percent per annum. The final cost to company A: LIBOR + ½ percent per annum, but receives ½ percent per annum from company B, making its final cost LIBOR. Both have gained (see exhibit 11.2).

Operational Matters

Such swaps would be constructed using a *notional* amount. This is the amount of principal upon which the calculations are based and is often reported by banks as a means of reference in financial statements. It is not meaningful in considering any credit exposure because the two parties to the swap remain solely responsible for their own borrowings.

Exhibit 11.2   Summary of the Swap

Company A		Company B
6 percent p.a.	LT Bond rate	7 percent p.a.
LIBOR + ¼ percent	ST bank rate	LIBOR + ½ percent
	Wants to borrow	
Short Term		Long Term
	How it borrows to do swap	
LT Bond @ 6 percent p.a.		ST loan @ LIBOR + ½ percent
LIBOR + ½ percent	Swaps and pays the other's interest of	6 percent p.a.
	Company B pays to company A	½ percent p.a.
LIBOR + ½ percent p.a − ½ percent p.a	Final effective interest cost	6 percent p.a. + ½ percent p.a.
LIBOR		**6 ½ percent p.a.**

Standardized documentation has been created to facilitate the use of such swaps. While the example would suggest that there are payments back and forth between the two firms, *netting* is used instead, in which the calculations are made and then only a single payment is made. Because the LIBOR is a floating market rate, it can be higher or lower than the fixed rate at any settlement date.

Variations

The swap can be arranged between the two firms by a bank acting as an intermediary (for which it would collect a fee). The bank may also be one party when a company wants to do a swap but there is no counterparty borrower available. The bank may enter into the swap with the intention of merely warehousing it until the other counterparty can be found, or it may keep it as part of its own funds management.

The basic swap can be constructed in many ways to meet the needs of the participants. Instead of the fixed-to-floating swap described above, it can be floating-to-floating, in which case two different types of markets—such as commercial paper to LIBOR—would be used.

Cross-Currency Swap

The examples of swaps given above involve the use of the same currency. The borrowers did not have to be in the same country as long as they used the same currency. An interest rate swap can also be done with different currencies. "In a cross currency swap, each party exchanges one currency for another on day 1 on some notional principal amount, with an agreement to service the interest payments on the counterparty's debt and to reverse the initial exchange at a specified time and at the original exchange rate." [10]

For example, a financially strong German company has a subsidiary in the United States and a comparable U.S. company has a subsidiary in Germany. Each wishes to obtain three-year financing for the subsidiary. Each parent company is better known in its own country than in the other. The German company has long-standing relationships with several German banks, one of which is a large minority shareholder in that company. It can therefore borrow deutsche marks at the best possible rate. The U.S. company also has good relationships with its commercial and investment banks, although under U.S. law there are restrictions on banks having ownership of the company. It can borrow in the United States at the most favorable rates.

The two companies arrange for a cross-currency swap. The German company borrows three-year deutsche marks, then swaps them for dollars that its subsidiary can use. The U.S. company borrows dollars, which it swaps for deutsche marks with the German company and then uses those funds for its German subsidiary. Each subsidiary pays in the currency it has obtained. Thus each subsidiary is able to obtain the funds it needs, in the currency it needs, and pays a lower interest rate than if the parent company had done the borrowing in the foreign currency.

The global capital markets are so large and sophisticated that complex variations of swaps can be structured to meet the particular needs of borrowers.

Accounting

All deposits that a bank takes are carried on the bank's financial statement as liabilities; Eurodollar placements are assets. In the Risk-Based Capital Guidelines, short-term Eurodollar placements generally have a 20 percent risk weighting.

Swaps are reflected in the contingent ("off-balance sheet") category of a commercial bank's financial statement when the bank is one of the parties in the swap. Bonds appear as assets only if the bank is acting as an investor.

Summary

There are a number of different sources of funds that can be used in any global lending. The commercial bank, making the loan on its own risk, can use the pool of funds it has in deposits, or it can obtain a Eurodollar deposit to match the amount of the loan. Eurodollars are dollars deposited outside the United States and are used as funding sources as well as for bank liability management.

Other sources of funds are available from sources such as insurance companies, pension funds, and wealthy individuals. These are accessed by the borrower issuing a bond, which the investor buys. The credit obligation runs directly from the borrower to the bond-holder, who can be exposed to loss if the bond goes into default or, in rare cases, is repudiated.

The price of the interest in borrowings can be modified through the creation of a variety of financial contracts, such as interest rate swaps.

Questions

1. What is a Eurodollar?
2. What is the difference between funding a bank loan using domestic dollars and Eurodollars?
3. How does funding a loan by means of issuing a bond differ from a bank loan?
4. What are the advantages of an interest rate swap?

Notes

1. Paul A. Carrubba, *Principles of Banking* (Washington, D.C.: American Bankers Association, 1994), pp. 58-59
2. Marcia Stigum, *The Money Market*, 3d ed. (Homewood, Ill.: Business One Irwin, 1990), p. 205
3. *Federal Reserve Bulletin*, October 1982, p. 565
4. Marcia Stigum, *The Money Market*, p. 246
5. Ibid., chapter 7. See also: Marcia Stigum and Rene O. Branch, Jr., *Managing Bank Assets and Liabilities* (Homewood, Ill.: Dow Jones-Irwin, 1982).
6. American Bankers Association, *Banking Terminology* (Washington, D.C.: American Bankers Association, 1991), pp. 40-41
7. Mira Wilkins, "Foreign Banks and Foreign Investment in the United States" in *International Banking 1870-1914*, ed. Rondo Cameron and V.I. Bovykin (New York: Oxford University Press, 1991), pp. 235-236
8. Frank Griffith Dawson, *The First Latin American Debt Crisis* (New Haven: Yale University Press, 1990), pp. 1-2
9. *The New York Times*, June 4, 1995, p. F5
10. Carl L. Beidleman, *Cross Currency Swaps* (Homewood, Ill.: Business One Irwin, 1992), p. 7

12

GOVERNMENT AGENCIES

Learning Objectives

After studying this chapter, you will be able to

- describe the financing support from the principal U.S. government agencies for furthering national exports
- describe the major international financial organizations run by national governments
- provide an example of how these agencies work in concert during a financial crisis

Overview

Commercial banks and private investors are not alone in financing world trade and economic development. Governments participate in these activities, both directly through their own national entities and indirectly through their membership in a variety of international economic organizations. When using its own national entities, a country's primary objective is to support and expand exports to benefit its balance of payments, which creates jobs domestically. This is done through programs that offer foreign buyers a subsidized preferential rate of interest for loans, guarantee commercial banks in export lending, insure national exporters against commercial and country risks, and make aid grants as an inducement to purchase national goods. Through these means, a country hopes to encourage domestic exporters and foreign importers to expand that country's foreign trade. Because so many countries today have these objectives, national entities continue to be active, allowing each country to be competitive in certain types of international business.

Multinational organizations have also been established jointly by countries whose goals are to maintain orderly financial conditions globally or to provide long-term development capital in amounts and at rates that could not be supplied by the commercial or investment banking system. These organizations are increasingly important as many borrowing countries and their creditors become enmeshed in debt-servicing problems, which reduced the availability of private-sector financial resources. For several years during the 1980s, such organizations were the only net lenders to many developing areas.

The specific programs of each organization, as well as their requirements, undergo constant modification. To remain up to date with the current policies, the banker working with domestic and international clients must be in regular contact with the organization and be on its announcement mailing list. Some of these organizations directly affect U.S. business, whereas others influence conditions in other countries. U.S. business, for example, is affected not only by the programs of U.S. government entities but also by those of international organizations and the programs of other governments.

The term *official financing* describes the support from those entities created by a national government to meet the needs of its residents as well as entities created by many governments to meet broader goals. This funding is differentiated from *private financing*, which refers to sources such as commercial banks and investors.

National Export Agencies

Many countries have established programs to encourage the export of their products. The competition between manufacturers, particularly of capital goods (for example, large machines and aircraft) is very intense. As a consequence, a manufacturer's success in making a sale often depends as much on the conditions of financing that a foreign buyer can obtain (rates, terms, down payment) as it does on the competitive quality of the product. Because a successful sale can mean jobs in a country, governments are actively involved in providing attractive terms to foreign buyers as an inducement to purchase their country's product instead of another country's. This competition between nations can be so intense that governments have periodically attempted to agree to a floor on interest rates and a ceiling on maximum terms. But international agreements to limit export credit terms have been difficult to maintain, particularly when economic activity in a country slows and unemployment rises.

Governments often believe that the cost of the subsidy they give for the export is offset by the internal employment created. In addition to offering attractive interest rates and repayment terms on financing, governments may combine the financing with a *grant*, which is a nonrepayable gift of funds as part of a foreign aid program. These tied aid-credit export subsidies, referred to as *mixed credits*, have the overall effect of lowering the total financing cost to the buyer.

Exact terms and conditions of national export agencies change, and the banker will need to have the current rates, policies, and programs, which can be obtained from the agencies themselves. Some changes may be made on short notice because of internal political and budgetary considerations. The existence of these programs enables the bank's customers—such as exporters and investors—to remain competitive with businesses in other countries. Importers likewise may find that they can benefit from the programs of other countries.

The programs are generally one of two types: **supplier credit**, in which the exporter permits the buyer to pay over a period up to five years, or **buyer credit**, in which the foreign importer arranges financing with a bank and pays the exporter immediately. The export agency provides financing or guarantees to either the exporter for supplier credit or the importer for buyer credit.

Organizations wholly owned by the U.S. government follow policies established by Congress and the Executive Branch. The government provides financial support through the provision of initial capital, annual appropriations, or the organization's authority to draw on the government, if needed, to meet its guarantees. The organizations' operations are subject to periodic review, and from time to time many have undergone changes in their authorized activities. Some of the programs may be conducted with private business and state government programs. The features of programs offered by other countries have many similarities to those of U.S. organizations.

Export-Import Bank of the United States

The principal U.S. government agency in this field is the **Export-Import Bank of the United States** (*Eximbank*). Its basic mandate is to assist in financing U.S. exports of goods and services by providing credit support for those transactions that cannot be made in the private sector. It does this through direct credit, insurance, loan guarantees, working capital guarantees, leasing guarantees, and other programs for hundreds of U.S. exporters, both large and small. It supplements rather than competes with private financing. In spite of its name, it does not provide support for imports into the United States.

In general, Eximbank has interpreted its legal mandate "to mean that private capital should play the leading role in financing U.S. exports, and Eximbank's programs should not be used unless private financing is not available on competitive terms. Eximbank has viewed its role as encouraging greater participation by private financing, but not displacing private capital that is available to provide the necessary financing." [1] Eximbank does not cover the full 100 percent exposure, it covers political and commercial risk. In past years, Eximbank's total authorizations for all programs represented only about 5 percent of total estimated U.S. exports. It usually covers 90 percent of working capital exposures and 85 percent of all other exposures. Eximbank also works with export programs of state governments and the U.S. Small Business Administration.

Eximbank was established in 1934, originally to finance trade between the United States and the Soviet Union. In 1945, the bank was reorganized to concentrate on its present activities. Eximbank is an independent agency wholly owned by the U.S. Treasury and has capital along with the right to borrow from the U.S. Treasury. Its liabilities are considered to be "general obligations of the United States backed by its full faith and credit." [2] Its charter must be regularly renewed by Congress, and its programs are affected by U.S. global policies. Operating funds come from loans from the U.S. government, repayments on outstanding loans, and net income. Eximbank activities are included in the federal government's consolidated budget.

Loans are made to governments or private borrowers with or without the guarantee of private banks, substantial stockholders, or governments, depending on the nature and size of the transaction. Eximbank is required by law to make loans that "shall generally be for specific purposes, and, in the judgment of the Board of Directors, offer reasonable assurance of repayment." [3] Its variety of programs includes direct domestic loans and international loans through banks for a percentage of the contract value to overseas buyers of U.S. exports, U.S. exporters themselves, and banks, which usually are in U.S. dollars and have maturities from 5 to 10 years. Other programs provide for commercial guarantees and insurance, also from 5 to 10 years; medium-term credits to exporters, up to 5 years; and a working capital guarantee to assist exporters.

Eximbank performs its own credit analysis based on the information supplied by the banks. Collateralization is done in a manner similar to the procedures used by commercial banks. Applications for assistance come directly from customers or banks.

"Many of the bank's transactions involve high technology and specialty goods and services from smaller companies. The products include CAT scanners, telecommunication ground stations, air navigation equipment, computer software, wood products and even soft-shell crabs shipped daily by plane to Tokyo from the Chesapeake Bay. Nearly 30 percent of Export-Import Bank transactions help small and medium sized companies." [4]

To assist its customers, a U.S. bank may be able to obtain access to other governments similar programs for their customers by working through its correspondent banks in those countries.

Agency for International Development

Beginning with the Marshall Plan after World War II, the U.S. government established a series of programs to make funds available to other countries for economic development. These funds, usually given as nonrepayable grants or on concessionary terms, were to be used to alleviate disease and famine or to help countries that could not do so on their own raise their standard of living. The **Agency for International Development** (AID), funded by annual appropriations from Congress, now administers these programs. When these grants are used in conjunction with Eximbank programs, they are mixed credits.

Over the decades that these programs have been in existence, their focus has shifted as economic and political conditions have changed. The goal is "not simply to keep people alive for the next 12 months. Rather, it is to give people the tools to be self-sufficient economically and to pursue more advanced levels of economic growth in an atmosphere of political stability." [5]

Others

Other U.S. agencies have programs to provide funding or guarantees to expand U.S. trade and foreign investments. For example, the *Commodity Credit Corporation*, a part of the U.S. Department of Agriculture, finances the sale of U.S. agricultural products. This is in addition to private exporting companies.

International Organizations

Governments working together have established organizations to maintain orderly international financial conditions and provide capital and advice for economic development, particularly in those countries that lack the resources to do it themselves. The U.S. government is a participant in these, providing a minority portion of the capital and exercising a share of the management and policy guidance.

The impetus to found such organizations came toward the end of World War II as part of an overall spirit of international cooperation. The Allied countries emerging from the war were determined to avoid the economic conflicts that many believed had contributed to the outbreak of that war. On July 22, 1944, Articles of Agreement were signed by delegates from 16 nations at a conference at Bretton Woods, New Hampshire, to create two major international organizations: *the International Monetary Fund* (IMF) and *the International Bank for Reconstruction and Development* (IBRD), commonly known as the *World Bank*. They came into existence on December 27, 1945.

These international organizations obtain funds for their lending activities from two basic sources. The first is the contribution of capital that each nation makes when it becomes a member. The amount of this contribution varies with the financial capacity of the country; from time to time, member countries have been asked to contribute additional capital. The second source of funds is through borrowing.

Although the IMF and the IBRD were created at the same time, their purposes are different. In general, they operate independently of each other, although a degree of informal cooperation and information sharing occurs. Each has its own organizational structure, with management by representatives of all the member countries.

There are, however, similarities in the two organizations. Both have headquarters in Washington, D.C. They have the same membership, which now includes almost all countries, and their staffs reflect that global membership. Most of the capital comes from the industrialized countries; the borrowing is usually done by developing countries. Voting is weighted so that the countries providing the greater capital have a proportionately greater vote. They hold a joint annual meeting each fall, which is widely attended by bankers.

World Bank Group

The World Bank group encompasses the **International Bank for Reconstruction and Development (World Bank)** and three subsidiary organizations: the **International Development Agency**, the **International Finance Corporation**, and the **Multilateral Investment Guarantee Agency**. Each has a specific mission within a common objective "to help raise standards of living in developing countries by channeling financial resources from developed countries to the developing world."[6]

The World Bank obtains its funds from the capital subscribed by its members, issuing bonds in world capital markets, retained earnings, and repayments on previously made loans. Loans "generally have a grace period of five years and are repayable over fifteen years or fewer. They are directed toward developing countries at more advanced stages of economic and social growth. . . . It must lend only for productive purposes and must stimulate economic growth in the developing countries in which it lends."[7] The World Bank does not lend to the industrialized countries. These loans are made at market rates of interest to governments or are guaranteed by governments. The World Bank has also supported programs for easing a debt crisis by making loans for the purposes of principal reduction or interest support, or to enable a country to buy back its commercial bank debt at a discount.

Such economic development is a complex problem, much like a wheel—each part needs another and is closely interrelated with other parts. For example, a country may aim to raise the standard of living of its people by creating the industrial capacity to process a natural resource rather than by merely exporting the raw material, a situation that many countries view as exploitive. To develop industry requires electric power and therefore hydroelectric dams or coal-burning power stations. The power must be transported from its source to its users, and this requires a power transmission system. To get people to work in industry, they must be encouraged to leave agriculture, with the result that those who remain in farming must become more efficient to feed those in the cities. This requires all-weather roads to markets, fertilizer, and increased irrigation. The health of the populace must be improved to reduce infant mortality, conquer disease, and increase longevity, which means improving the water supply, building more efficient sewer systems, and establishing public health programs. To export its product, the country may need more efficient transportation and port systems.

Obviously all of these goals cannot be accomplished at one time. The role of the World Bank has been to advise and help a country finance the individual components. Since 1948, the World Bank has done this through project loans. A project is a separate "package of investments, policy measures, and institutional and other actions designed to achieve a specific development objective . . . within a designated period." [8] The Bank is involved from the identification stage through the construction and completion phase, not only with financing but also by providing technical advice and supervision.

In the 1980s, the Bank began to shift toward policy-based loans, "which differ from standard project loans in being disbursed in as little as one year rather than the customary five to eight; they are also targeted not at building another highway or housing complex but at fostering far-reaching structural reforms, such as an end to import restrictions or the establishment of market prices for agricultural goods." [9] These are of two types: structural adjustment loans, for economic policy changes such as covering a balance of payments shortfall caused by a structural economic shock (for example, the collapse of commodity prices); or sector adjustment loans, for a specific economic category such as agriculture (for example, to allow a government to meet the foreign exchange costs of reducing an import tariff). "Sector adjustment loans address an issue specific to one part of the economy. . . . Structural adjustment loans aim to support economy-wide policy changes." [10] As such loans have increased, project loans have declined.

Loans are made in major world currencies and are to be repaid in such currencies. The interest rate is based on the World Bank's cost of funds. Because the Bank has the highest credit rating, it can borrow easily in many national private capital markets at the lowest rates.

A number of countries, however, are unable to meet the repayment criteria of a World Bank loan. Countries that have the lowest annual per capita gross national product (below $865) receive development funds from the IDA. These are called *credits* to distinguish them from the loans made by the IBRD. Credits are made only to governments and have 10 year grace periods, 35- to 40-year maturities, and no interest. Such loans are often called *soft loans*, which refers to the repayment terms. The projects themselves meet the same criteria as the IBRD loans and are managed by the same staff. These credits are made in major world currencies, but may be repaid in the currency of the borrower.

The International Finance Corporation (IFC), another part of the World Bank group, was established in 1956. Its function is to make equity investments and loans to the private sector of developing countries and serve as an adviser. The IFC assists these private companies by acting as a catalyst to attract more capital from domestic and foreign sources.

The emphasis is on combining equity for privately owned companies with term loans. The IFC will subscribe for a minority of the shares of the company, but its presence, including its advice, helps to attract local investors with the long-term effect of expanding private enterprise in developing countries. After a project succeeds, the IFC sells its equity shares. In recent years, IFC projects have "ranged from farm privatisation in Russia to capital market developments in Zambia, privatisation of telecommunications systems in eastern Europe, investment in the first leasing company in Romania, and the formation of private pension funds in Peru and Argentina." [11] It has been active in establishing new stock exchanges in developing counties, principally in Africa.

The Multilateral Investment Guarantee Agency (MIGA) was established in 1988 with the specialized mandate of encouraging the flow of direct foreign investments to developing countries by reducing the risks to the investor through issuing guarantees for noncommercial risks, primarily political risks. It also offers advisory services. In the decade before the MIGA's establishment, direct foreign investment in the developing world was less then 15 percent of the total worldwide flow of such direct investment.

The World Bank group also assists the flow of foreign investment with the *International Centre for Settlement of Investment Disputes* (ICSID), established in 1966 to provide facilities for the conciliation and arbitration of disputes between governments and foreign investors.

By tradition, the United States nominates the President of the World Bank, who has always been from the United States and in most cases has had extensive experience in commercial or investment banking.

Following the pattern of the World Bank, regional development banks have been established to focus on the needs of particular regions: the European Investment Bank (1958), the Inter-American Development Bank (1959), the African Development Bank (1964), the Asian Development Bank (1966), and the European Bank for Reconstruction and Development (1991, concentrating on Eastern Europe). The United Nations Development Program (1965) provides financing to low-income countries.

International Monetary Fund (IMF)

The basic purpose of the IMF is to "oversee the international monetary system in order to ensure its effective operation." [12] It does this by providing interim financing to member countries experiencing balance of payments difficulties and assisting them in correcting the conditions that brought about these difficulties. The IMF also exercises surveillance over the exchange rate policies of member countries, monitors developments in the field of international liquidity, manages the Special Drawing Rights (SDR) system (see chapter 5), and provides guidance for the standardized presentation of national balance of payments data.

Each member country subscribes capital, which is used as the primary means to fund the lending activities of the IMF.

When countries join the Fund, they are assigned a quota that fits into the structure of existing quotas considered in the light of the member's economic characteristics relative to those of other members of comparable size. The size of the member's quota determines, among other things, the member's voting power, the size of its potential access to Fund resources, and its share in allocations of SDRs. . . . Subscriptions are equal to quotas. Initial subscriptions, and normally subscriptions associated with increases in quotas, are paid mainly in the members' own currencies, and a smaller portion, not exceeding 25 percent, in reserve assets (SDRs or currencies of other members acceptable to the Fund).[13]

"The principal way in which the Fund makes its resources available to members is by selling to them the currencies of other members or SDRs in exchange for their own currency."[14]

Throughout its existence, the Fund has provided assistance to countries experiencing balance of payments difficulties. These are usually developing countries. In 1976, however, the United Kingdom had to seek assistance.[15] The general pattern has been for a country to request assistance, then the Fund sends a team of experts to that country to examine the magnitude of the problem and determine its cause. This may be internal inflation, unrealistic exchange rates, or high government deficits, and the Fund will make recommendations for corrections. The government concerned will then sign an agreement with the Fund to implement these recommendations, and the Fund makes a loan (usually for a term of two to three years) to assist during the transition period. While this procedure may seem simple, it has led to great strains and political turmoil in some countries with severe international debt problems.

The IMF Managing Director has customarily been a European with extensive governmental financial experience.

Other Global Organizations

Several other international organizations provide specialized assistance to meet particular needs of global finance and business.

Bank for International Settlements

The oldest multinational financial institution still functioning and possibly one of the least understood is the **Bank for International Settlements (BIS)** in Basel, Switzerland. It has been inaccurately described by financial journalists as "the central bank's central bank" (which it is not), or as "establishing the rules for commercial bank capital adequacy" (which it does not). The BIS is not a long-term lender and has practically no official authority, but its long experience has given it considerable influence. Over the decades, it has survived several challenges that questioned whether it retained a meaningful purpose—particularly the recommendation of the Bretton Woods conference that it be liquidated because it was being replaced by the IMF and IBRD.[16]

It was established in 1930 as the operating agency for transferring the reparations payments that Germany was required to make for World War I (hence its name). The following year, there was a moratorium on those payments. In subsequent years, the BIS took on a series of transitional intra-European payments tasks.

Today it is has a membership of 33 central banks, mostly European. "Some 84 percent of the 473,125 shares . . . are owned by central banks; the remainder are held by private shareholders, mainly in Europe."[17] These privately owned shares are listed over the counter on the Basel stock exchange. The American shares are among those privately held, since the U.S. government and the Federal Reserve declined to subscribe at the time the BIS was established. Ownership of shares, however, carries no voting rights at the general annual meetings. "The right of voting and representation, in proportion to the number of shares subscribed in each country, is exercised by the central bank of that country."[18] The Chairman of the Federal Reserve has, since September 1994, been a member of the Board of Directors and votes approximately 8 percent of the total outstanding BIS shares. The bank regulatory agencies in the United States participate in BIS activities. Its financial statements are in gold francs, a currency that no longer exists (1GF = $208).

Its importance in global banking today is in providing facilities for central bankers to meet regularly (10 times a year) for informal discussions, the results of which were described by a former head of the BIS as "some sort of monetary cooperation by intellectual osmosis. How these decisions get made no one really knows."[19] The BIS also provides the secretariat for various committees of bank regulators from many countries that meet to formulate common policies (such as the risk-based capital guidelines for commercial banks). It has been a vehicle for interim short-term financing during certain global currency crises, and it has certain operational activities, such as acting as an agent for private ECU clearings and settlements.

Paris Club

This is an informal name for the confidential meetings needed when a debtor country is unable to meet the repayment terms of some of its borrowings. "The debt to be rescheduled is limited to officially guaranteed export credits and straight government loans."[20] Officials of the country in difficulty will meet with officials of the lending countries in a group, which usually leads to a rescheduling of the borrowings. The name Paris Club is applied to these meetings because they were organized by the French.

World Trade Organization

The World Trade Organization (WTO) was established in 1994 as the successor to the *General Agreement on Tariffs and Trade (GATT)*. The Bretton Woods conference 50 years earlier had expected that an International Trade Organization would be created to complement the IMF and World Bank, but for political reasons, the 1948 Havana conference failed to agree on it. GATT was created as an interim measure in that same year to maintain some means of negotiating the reduction of trade barriers. As a result of what was called the "Uruguay Round" of GATT negotiations from 1986 to 1993, an agreement was reached among 117 nations to move toward freer world trade. "Its 28 separate accords extend fair trade rules for the first time to agriculture, textiles, services, intellectual property and foreign investment. Tariffs on industrial goods will be cut by over a third, and farm export subsidies and import barriers will be substantially reduced. GATT, the new accords on services and intellectual property, and the various GATT codes such as those on government procurement and anti-dumping will all come under the umbrella of a World Trade Organization."[21] The WTO will have stronger powers to resolve trade disputes.

Role of U.S. Commercial Banks

U.S. commercial banks actively cooperate with the various national government and international lending agencies by participating in loans (usually the shorter maturities), interim financing, or cofinancing. Disbursement procedures for the loans of these agencies frequently provide for establishment of commercial letters of credit, which are processed by banks since the government entities are not equipped to provide the necessary technical operational support. When a lending agency approves a loan for a development project, the borrowing country and its agencies then issue individual contracts and purchase orders to suppliers. To pay these suppliers, the foreign country requests banks to issue letters of credit. After shipment is made and documents are presented to the commercial bank, letter of credit negotiation is done and payment is made to the supplier. The U.S. bank involved then receives reimbursement from the national government or international lending agency.

When commercial banks provide financing to exporters using any of the guarantee or insurance programs offered by national agencies, the bank has a credit with the added backing of the government entity. Because of this strength, the bank can often offer credit to its customers on better terms than if it had to rely solely on the company.

Cooperating for Crisis Management

Each of these national and international official organizations has its own objectives, policies, and procedures. At times of crisis, they readily cooperate because of their common interests in maintaining the stability of the global financial system. An example of this was the debt crisis that began in the early 1980s and dominated, and ultimately reshaped, banking for the next decade.

The current use of the term **debt crisis** generally refers to the inability of a developing country to meet its debt repayments on the original schedule. In the 1980s, the term specifically referred to the problems of a number of countries, primarily in Latin America, in repaying their governments' borrowings from commercial banks.

The events of 1982 were perceived as a crisis because they were unexpected by both borrowers and lenders, the amount of debt was huge, and so many countries eventually were affected. This crisis was unique because it predominantly involved commercial banks. Before this, from the nineteenth century to the late 1940s, term lending to developing foreign governments and for projects such as building railroads had been done by merchant banks and investors who knew from the outset that their own money was at risk. Previous debt crises had meant that these bondholders were the ones who were exposed to losses.

The Situation in the 1970s

The 1970s saw a great spurt in the projects that the developing countries wanted to build and, at the same time, a tremendous interest by bankers in lending. With the sudden rise in the price of oil, some petroleum-exporting countries acquired massive surpluses of funds, which they deposited in banks through the Eurodollar market. The banks put these funds to work in a process that came to be called *recycling*. This meant simply that banks assumed the risk of putting these dollars back into the developing countries by making more loans. It was not a coincidence that the great increase in international loans for new manufacturing plants, infrastructure, and mineral development came at the same time that a huge surplus of funds was being deposited in the global banking system.

There were warning signs that trouble could come. Zaire, for example, had borrowed heavily in the early 1970s. When the world price for copper, almost its only major export earner, dropped, Zaire found that it could not earn enough dollars to pay its foreign debts, which accounted for 40 percent of its gross domestic product. In 1973 and 1974, when Zaire was borrowing, copper prices ranged from $0.80 to

$0.93 a pound. In 1976 and 1977, when it asked for rescheduling of its debt, the price ranged from $0.59 to $0.63 a pound.

Concerns also developed that some countries were borrowing so fast that new borrowings were being used to pay the installments that would have been past due on old loans rather than being used for their stated purposes of specific developments. Banks had only incomplete information about the total amount some countries were borrowing in both the public and private sectors and how much foreign exchange was going to be needed in the future to service this debt. Sometimes even the countries themselves did not have accurate and complete information.

The Crisis

Mexico triggered the international debt crisis in 1982. Although Brazil was the largest international borrower at the time, Mexico was not the first large-debtor country to have problems. This had come the year before, when Poland had requested a moratorium on its debt repayments. Mexico, however, was very much a customer of the United States, with two-thirds of its exports and imports going to its northern neighbor. U.S. commercial banks had made substantial credit available to both the public sector (the government and government-owned companies) and the private sector (privately owned corporations) in Mexico. When Poland had encountered problems, German banks suffered; with Mexico, it was the U.S. banks. Poland had owed more than $25 billion to all its creditors; Mexico owed more than $70 billion.

Mexico had discovered huge new reserves of oil in the 1970s. It decided to export at a level of 1.1 million barrels a day. This came at the same time that the Organization of Petroleum-Exporting Countries (OPEC) forced the increase in oil prices and as the industrialized countries projected an upward trend of future consumption.

Thus Mexico anticipated a rising income for years. Faced with a need to create new jobs and a need to maintain momentum to keep the standard of living rising, which were politically important as the middle class grew, Mexico decided to build the new manufacturing plants and government projects. To do this, it borrowed principally from banks. With its projected future oil income, neither Mexico nor its bankers anticipated any cash flow problems when these loans came due.

Other countries made similar decisions based on similar projections. What went wrong was that neither the demand nor the price for oil continued to rise. They stabilized, and then actually fell. Basic economic tenets were proved once again: rising supply and falling demand will result in falling prices. Mexico had less-than-expected income when it came time to repay the money it had borrowed to make its big industrialization push.

The shock of an oil producer running out of foreign exchange caused bankers around the world to hesitate to lend to any developing country. Brazil was the next to be affected; it could not borrow what it needed to continue its plan for creating export industries. Bank syndications virtually stopped. Country after country found itself unable to borrow at long term for any purpose, unable to complete development projects, and unable to repay the loan installments coming due.

These countries' problems can be understood by looking at Nigeria. "Much of the $20 billion in debt was incurred in the early 1980s after economists predicted that the $26 billion Nigeria earned from oil in 1980 would swell to $40 billion in 1986. But oil revenues, which account for almost all of the country's export earnings, were crippled when world prices plummeted and are . . . just $5 billion [in 1986]." [22]

In August 1982, some thought the problem was only a short-term cash flow shortage that could be easily corrected. They were wrong.

Many countries had to ask for new repayment schedules and assistance. They had over-borrowed; the banks had over-lent. Within each country there continued to be many borrowers and projects that were maintaining their profitability, but when they went to the central bank for foreign exchange, they became part of the crisis.

The Search for Solutions

In the months following Mexico's announcement on August 20, 1982, of its repayment problem, a series of steps were initiated. The banks extended the loan installments that were immediately falling due. Mexico sought a loan from the IMF of $4.65 billion. The United States advanced money against future oil purchases and made credit available through the Eximbank. Central banks of the industrialized countries, coordinated through the BIS, made an interim (*bridge*) loan. The World Bank provided financing. The commercial banks formed a creditors' committee to begin work with the Mexican government: first, to define the size of the problem, then to assess the causes, and finally to develop a program to resolve it. During 1982, Mexico's international reserves dropped from over $4 billion to $800 million.

Mexico was to be the prototype program for other developing countries who subsequently announced their difficulties in meeting their current loan repayments. Between 1982 and 1985 "some $210 billion of third-world debt has been rescheduled or rolled over." [23]

Eventually, the IMF made its loan in return for Mexico's agreement to cut inflation, restrain imports, reduce the government's deficit, and devalue its currency. A condition of the IMF's agreement was that all the commercial banks would participate by agreeing to extend the repayments of their existing loans and make new loans based on a percentage of what each had

outstanding. *Rescheduling* or *restructuring* means taking loan installments that are now due but are not being paid and creating a new schedule for these to be repaid in installments over a number of years, such as five or seven, providing new grace periods, and often lower interest rates. To obtain the commercial banks' agreement, the IMF went to the central bank of each country and asked them to prevail upon their commercial banks. The central banks thus exercised one of their classical powers—moral suasion. This describes the ability of a central bank to influence management decisions of commercial banks by persuasion and the reality that commercial banks will need approvals and other agreements in the future from their central bank.

It soon became apparent that there was not one major problem but two, and within each of these there were other complexities that needed to be addressed. The first major problem was the ongoing need to reschedule repayments from previous term loans as they fell due. The goal was to ease the strain on each country's balance of payments so that current account earnings would not be completely consumed by repayments of principal and interest. Lenders however, could continue to expect that the full amount of the loans would eventually be repaid. New syndicated bank loans were unavailable, which meant that each country was now heavily dependent on its own capacity to generate foreign earnings. The commercial banks recognized the necessity for short-term trade financing to be extended to give a country the capability to have export earnings. Analyzing a country's balance of payments was discovered to be inadequate, since it did not show the timing of the actual foreign exchange receipts or payments. This meant developing a greater capacity within each country to capture this data so that recovery plans could be made.

The second major problem was that almost no new net capital was coming into these countries to complete development programs or start new ones. Economies stagnated, unemployment rose, and standards of living fell. In Latin America from 1980 to 1985, a period spanning the onset of the debt crisis, per capita output declined 8 percent overall, with some countries suffering a drop of 10 to 15 percent, while unemployment was 10 percent higher than it was before the crisis. Although many of the restructurings included what was described as new money, in many instances this money turned out to be what was needed by the country to pay the interest on its existing bank loans. More money was being returned to the industrialized countries and official agencies than the developing countries were receiving! In addition, there was an indeterminate amount of capital flight that added to the burden.

By the late 1980s, the term *debt fatigue* was being used. Negotiating teams and senior officers from the commercial banks were exhausted from several years of searching for formulas to solve both the problems. Many banks that had participated in syndicated loans disposed of or otherwise wrote off their outstandings at a loss and withdrew from any further activities. Whereas official creditors in 1980 accounted for only 18 percent of the $172.8 billion long-term debt Latin America, by 1990 official creditors had grown to account for 34 percent of the now $339 billion debt.

The governments of developing countries were likewise exhausted and their people were angered by the decline in living standards without any apparent resolution of the crisis. Some governments simply stopped paying the interest due or restricted the amount paid to a percentage of their export earnings. De facto debt moratoriums occurred.

Over the years, proposals were made by senior government officials in the industrialized countries, including one by U.S. Treasury Secretary Nicholas Brady, seeking to break the stalemate of the crisis. The "Brady Plan" was intended to help both borrowers and lenders recognize that they had to compromise. The banks would charge off part of their loans and restructure the remainder; the countries would collateralize or guarantee that the remaining loans would be repaid on the new schedule. This became the basis for the end of what had come to be seen in many developing countries as the lost decade for economic development. This prompted new rounds of negotiations between the banks and the debtor countries that were centered on reducing the debt-servicing strain through forgiving part of the debt, reducing the interest rate on existing debt, or making new loans, usually accompanied by some external guarantees for the repayment of some of the remaining debt. Such an agreement for Mexico, for example, achieved the effect of a reduction of "about $14.5 billion in the present value of [its] debt to commercial banks,"[24] which had been about $48.5 billion in medium- and long-term debt. (Mexico's total foreign debt was about $90 billion at this time.) The reduction was achieved through the actual forgiving of loan principal and lowering the interest rate on the remaining principal.

Debt Reduction Techniques

The resolution of the debt crisis spawned a market for trading the debt of these countries, usually involving the Brady Bonds that had been created from the renegotiations. The source of these loans were many banks who wished to dispose of their loans. Purchasers included various types of investors and speculators, aware that, historically, some defaulted bonds eventually had been redeemed at or near their face value. The debt was traded at discount, which in some cases was in excess of 75 percent. This market was occasionally used by a borrowing country as a way of buying back its debt at a discount or by debtor country residents as a way to repatriate flight capital.

Accounting

Bank accounting practices have been an important factor in the debt-restructuring negotiations.

Interest. Banks use the accrual method of accounting for earnings. Interest income is recorded when earned, although it is not collected in cash on the daily balances of the principal amount outstanding throughout the life of the loan. When the cash payment is not made within 90 days after the due date, the general practice is to stop accruing, reverse from the bank's earnings what has been accrued but not yet collected, and then report the interest as earnings only when it is actually paid. This can cause considerable distortion in a bank's overall earnings. Banks were willing to make new loans to a number of countries so that interest payments could be made and thus protect the bank's earnings. This had the same basic effect as capitalizing the interest.

Allowance for loan losses. As the debt crisis stretched over years, the likelihood of full repayment of many loans became questionable. Banks increased their *allowance for loan losses* from each year's income so that when any loss would be recognized, it would not all have to be charged to that one year's earnings. It became an important criterion for outside investors to see how much allowance a bank had built up. Until the loss was actually realized, the bank could count this loan loss reserve, except an *allocated transfer risk*, as part of its capital, although the Risk-Based Capital Guidelines limit this.

Loss. In addition to the normal practice of charging off a loan when it has been determined to be uncollectible, banks had a loss whenever they sold a loan at a discount. Thus a bank that sold a loan in the market, agreed to a debt-for-debt swap at a discount, or forgave some debt under a Brady Plan negotiation, had to recognize that amount below the face amount as a loss.

Summary

Governments actively compete to expand their own country's exports. The major industrial countries and a number of developing countries have created government agencies to provide preferential financing rates and terms for loans to foreigners who buy from that country's exporters. In the United States, this is done principally through the Export-Import Bank of the United States.

International agencies such as the World Bank and the International Monetary Fund were created to provide financial assistance and advice to member countries in their needs to meet balance of payments difficulties and long-term developmental needs. Both of these entities affect U.S. banks by the direct and unique contributions they can provide to meet the urgent needs of many countries, thereby providing a more orderly and stable international financial environment.

Questions

1. What does the Eximbank do?
2. What does the World Bank do?
3. What does the International Monetary Fund do?
4. How was the debt crisis of the 1980s resolved?

Notes

1. Charles E. Gaba, "Export Finance and the Role of the Export-Import Bank of the United States," *International Banking: U.S. Laws and Regulations* (Washington, D.C.: American Bankers Association, 1984), pp. 6-11

2. Ibid., pp. 6-12

3. Export-Import Act of 1945 § 2(b)(1)(A), 12 U.S.C. § 635

4. *The New York Times*, February 6, 1990, p. C7

5. Peter McPherson, "We Weren't Looking for a Quick Fix," *The New York Times*, November 23, 1986, § 3, p. 2

6. The World Bank, *Annual Report 1990* (Washington, D.C.: World Bank, 1991), p. 3

7. Ibid., p. 3

8. Warren C. Baum and Stokes M. Tolbert, *Investing in Development* (New York: World Bank/Oxford University Press, 1985), p. 8

9. *Institutional Investor*, September 1986, p. 88

10. *The Economist*, September 27, 1986, p. 33

11. *Financial Times*, September 21, 1994

12. International Monetary Fund, *Annual Report* (Washington, D.C.: 1986), p. 31

13. International Monetary Fund, *International Financial Statistics: Supplement on Fund Accounts* (Washington, D.C.: 1982), p. iii

14. Ibid.

15. For a full analysis of the background, see Kathleen Burk and Alec Cairncross, *'Goodbye, Great Britain' The 1976 IMF Crisis*, (New Haven, Conn: Yale University Press, 1992)

16. *The New Encyclopedia Britannica*, 15th ed. s.v. "International Settlement, Bank for"

17. *Federal Reserve Bulletin*, October 1994, p. 904

18. Edwin M. Truman, Staff Director, Division of International Finance, Board of Governors of the Federal Reserve System, letter to author, July 3, 1995

19. Steven Solomon, *The Confidence Game: How Unelected Central Bankers Are Governing the Changed Global Economy* (New York: Simon & Schuster, 1995), p. 113

20. "Survey," *The Economist*, March 20, 1982, p. 27

21. *Financial Times*, December 16, 1993

22. "Nigeria, Rich in Oil, Juggles Its Huge Debt," The New York Times, December 22, 1986, p. 28

23. "Debtors Hope for Growth, Yearn For Cash—And Fear the Worst," *The Economist*, October 12, 1985, p. 75

24. International Monetary Fund, *Annual Report 1990* (Washington, D.C.: International Monetary Fund), p. 28

GLOBAL RISK MANAGEMENT

The business of banking, according to Federal Reserve Board Chairman Alan Greenspan,

> has always been the measurement, acceptance, and management of risk. In the past, commercial and investment banks performed these basic functions with quite different tools and strategies. Today, the tools and strategies increasingly overlap, blurring traditional distinctions between commercial and investment banks. . . . It is sufficient to say that a strong case can be made that the evolution of financial technology alone has changed forever our ability to place commercial and investment banking into neat, separate boxes.[1]

Unlike the products of a factory production line, the banker's products are not something physically produced that can be held in the hand or touched. Generally, the banker provides services directly related to the movement of money. This is done by people making judgments, either as an individual doing a transaction, a small group reaching a consensus, or a larger, yet competing, group called a market.

The global banker has all the same risks as the banker who is dealing with a domestic transaction. The global banker has added risks because the customers are moving between different countries with different laws, practices, and currencies. Unfortunately, to many domestic bankers those risks are incomprehensible and even dangerous. That view can dominate a bank's decisions, since virtually every bank is primarily a domestic bank, and its global activities are only a small part of its total activities.

This conflict between domestic and global banking became evident during the debt crisis of the 1980s (discussed in chapter 12). A number of regional banks joined in international loan syndications in the late 1970s and early 1980s without fully understanding the risks. Later, when the foreign borrowers encountered difficulties, some of these bankers retreated, acknowledged their losses, and determined that their bank would never return to international lending. Thus in the mid-1990s, the landscape of commercial bank participation in global business is drastically reduced from what it had been a decade and a half before. Today's banker must overcome the legacy of past mistakes when global risks were not properly managed.

Managing risks means balancing the different responsibilities of the bank: to the customers who need the services to conduct their business, to the owners (shareholders) who have invested their funds in the expectation that they will receive a reasonable return on their money; to the communities the bank serves (both local and national) who need the catalyst to economic prosperity and employment; and to all those in the bank who contribute their skill and expertise for the benefit of all the other groups.

Thus the global banker must not only understand the risks but also be able to structure the means to manage those risks and protect all those who depend on the bank, its resources, and its skills.

The greatest risk in global banking arises from its nature—*the business is global*. Political or social events in a country halfway around the globe can suddenly increase a bank's exposure to loss, or a bank's branch far away can slip out of control of the head office and damage the entire bank. Both such external and internal risks grow greater, the farther the distance from the head office.

Certain kinds of risks have been discussed in previous chapters: credit risk—that borrowers will not repay the loan or meet their commitments on trading contracts; market risk—that rates for money or capital market purchases or sales will change adversely to the trader's expectations, for any number of reasons beyond the bank's control. There are great similarities in how these risks are managed by both domestic and global bankers. There is, however, another category of risk: establishing, applying, and monitoring the bank's policies as they are applied by the personnel of the bank. The global manager has a considerably greater problem in doing this than does her domestic counterpart because it must be done at a great distance.

These final two chapters serve as a review of all the procedures and skills that have been detailed in each of the preceding chapters. However, the perspective is not on the individual products themselves but on the common features that make up the risks of global banking. Chapter 13, Country Risk Assessment, concentrates on the basic risk that underlies all the external risks of global banking—namely, the risks from doing business from one country with a customer or market in another country. Chapter 14, Global Financial Risk Management, considers the internal problems and risks of managing units of a bank from abroad.

Risk can be managed, but it can never be eliminated—the only way that a banker can eliminate risk is to do nothing. To put it more simply, the secret of the success of a dealer in the City of London at the end of the nineteenth century was described like this: "It was uncanny the manner in which he could steer clear of trouble." [2]

Notes

1. Statement of June 6, 1995, *Federal Reserve Bulletin*, August 1995, p. 778
2. David Kynaston, *The City of London Vol. II: Golden Years 1890-1914* (London: Chatto & Windus, 1995), p. 14

13

COUNTRY RISK ASSESSMENT

Learning Objectives

After studying this chapter, you will be able to

- use the basic analytical elements in developing a country risk assessment
- review the effect of political, cultural, and social factors on a country's business environment
- describe how to manage country risk exposure

Overview

Country risk is the exposure to loss that a lender or investor has when doing business with an entity in another country. The lender may be a commercial bank making a short-term or long-term loan, it may be an investment bank arranging financing, or it may be a person, institution, or pension fund that owns a bond. The investor may be a corporation with a factory or source of raw materials in another country, or it may be a mutual fund or individual owning shares in a foreign corporation.

The essence of global business is dealing with customers in another country—subject to the consequences of changes in that country's economic conditions, social structures, and political events. The effect of such changes represents a risk in addition to all of the customary business risks: credit risk for the lender; yield, competition, marketing; and management risks for the investor.

Country risk assessment begins with an analysis of a country's economic information: the internal elements, such as inflation and government deficits, and particularly the country's international payments and receipts as expressed in the balance of payments. The assessment also considers the effect of political, social, and cultural factors on the business. Such risk analysis may have several elements: the risks associated with cross-border lending and investing, that is, from one country to another; the transfer risks associated with repayment, which will require the borrower to be able to transfer funds from one country to another for the remittance of dividends to the investor; and the risks associated with the general factors that would affect a currency.

Country risk assessment is done in a series of analytical steps: What are the conditions in that country now? What is the likelihood of change? What effect would such change have on a borrower's ability to repay the lender in the future or on the investment's chance to succeed?

Country risk analysis is not only a defensive assessment to identify problems that may have a negative effect; it can also be an offensive strategy for business development. This process can identify the markets the lender or investor would want to grow in and where to find new customers. Trade follows the flag—it is equally true that financial business follows trade.

While country risk assessment is normally done only by the lender or investor, it may also be a self-assessment tool for a country seeking to attract investment. It enables a country to see how it compares to others and how to improve its competitive position.

Background

Each time a bank extends credit to a foreign borrower, it is exposed to country risk regardless of whether the borrower is a government, private company, or bank. It incurs country risk whenever it finances a local business that, in turn, depends on a foreign source of repayment. A bank also experiences country risk when it has funds on deposit in another country, buys or sells foreign exchange, or establishes a branch in another country. **Country risk** is defined as the risk that changes in economic, political, or social conditions in a country will adversely affect repayment of a loan, access to foreign funds, or the safety of an investment. Although this definition focuses on adverse change, bankers should also consider the effects of favorable changes. These can offer opportunities for developing new business or commencing business in a previously unsatisfactory area.

The risk that a banker has in doing business in another country is not new. In 1867, Walter Bagehot, a distinguished British economics writer, stated the problem:

Many persons have not a distinct perception of the risk of lending to a country in a wholly different state of civilization. They can hardly imagine the difficulties with which such a country struggles, and the dangers to which it is exposed. They forget that national good faith is a rare and recent thing . . . [or] how little do facts . . . prove that a debt will be paid, or that interest on it will be paid when new borrowings cease to be possible.[1]

Country risk assessment is difficult because it is an attempt to forecast the future. Banking and investment decisions are made today, but their success depends on conditions in the future, which is ultimately unpredictable. The banker must evaluate not only the credit risks of the borrower's future business prospects but also how changes in political and economic conditions in that country may affect the borrower's business and ability to pay debts as scheduled. The conclusion of a banker's country risk assessment can be only an evaluation of probabilities. If, for example, 10 countries in the past exhibited an economic ratio or characteristic of A, and three years later the economic or political condition in 8 of those countries had changed to X, then the banker could infer an 80 percent probability that the same could happen to the country being analyzed.

The banker financing a local customer, who in turn is selling to a foreign buyer, would likewise apply a country risk assessment to consider the harm to the local customer's overall financial health if that foreign buyer could not make timely payments. What would be the effect on the local customer dependent on buying materials or goods from a foreign source if that supplier fails to deliver at the agreed-upon price or even fails to deliver at all? The failure of the foreign supplier may affect the profitable operation of the local customer, who may not be able to replace those supplies at a comparable price or availa-

bility. This could then make that customer uncompetitive in his own markets. A local bank's customer has only one financial statement, and any problems that customer has with country risk will affect all his commitments with the local banker.

Projecting such future events is done by analyzing the present and the past and examining each component separately to come to an overall conclusion. The major components of this analysis are economic and political.

Country risk analysis requires an historical perspective to project what might happen in a country by comparing it with the past experience of other countries. It should begin with this question: If the conditions presently existing in a country were unchanged during the life of the loan or investment, would you be satisfied with the risk? If the answer is no, then the entire decision process should stop. Reevaluate why the loan or investment is being considered, since its success would seem to depend on only favorable changes in the future.

When the answer is yes, then the country risk assessment is based on analyzing the possibilities of only adverse changes to the present economic, political, and social status. Favorable changes would be expected to make the satisfactory present even better.

Analyzing the Economic Component

A nation's economy is made up of domestic and international activities. The latter are reflected in the balance of payments (see chapter 1) which is a single interconnected report. Stanford University Professor Paul Krugman said in a book review:

Some of [the author's] confusions involve elementary accounting. . . . [He] offers the straightforward prediction . . . that in the years to come the newly industrializing economies will both run massive trade surpluses and attract massive inflows of capital. He is clearly blissfully unaware that a country's current account and capital account necessarily sum to zero—that a country which runs massive trade surpluses cannot help being a net exporter of capital.[2]

International Analysis

Loans are repaid from cash flow. Trade finance transactions are considered to be self-liquidating, which means that the cash flow is expected to come from the sale of the goods being shipped. Working capital and term loans are expected to generate that cash flow from the sale of inventory or the earnings of new manufacturing plants or mines. The international repayment of any financing from a cash flow is complicated by the reality that borrowers also need access to the currency required by the lender—usually the currency that was lent. The borrower may have its own exports, which generate foreign currency earnings, or have access to a foreign exchange market, or obtain the money from the government's holdings. Borrowers in the major industrial countries may not have to pay in a foreign currency because a lender is willing to accept the borrower's domestic currency. This will affect the currency transfer portion of the overall country risk assessment.

A favorable national balance of trade indicates that the country is earning more from its exports than it is spending for its imports. A borrower in that country should be able to obtain foreign exchange with little difficulty. The banker needs to analyze what is causing such a favorable trade balance. As was seen in chapter 12, Nigeria, Zaire, and Mexico all borrowed with favorable trade balances that rested on the assumption that the price for a single commodity would continue to rise, thereby maintaining a trade balance surplus in future years that would service their debt. In fact, when the commodity price dropped, all three countries faced serious problems that prevented repaying their debt.

National export earnings may have to service all of a country's foreign debt.

As a rule of thumb any country with outstanding [foreign] debt worth more than 200 percent of the present value of its exports is in trouble. This measure is, in effect, an indicator of how close it is to bankruptcy. Another measure, the debt-service ratio, gauges a country's liquidity rather than its solvency by showing how much a country spends on paying creditors instead of on, say, investing in health or education. Any country that spends more than 40 percent of its annual export revenue on servicing its debt is likely to face big problems.[3]

The banker may also consider the level of a country's reserves in relation to its imports: How many months of imports would the reserves cover if all other sources of income stopped.? (Reserves may be considered to be comparable to a corporation's capital [see chapter 10] as a backup cash source for repaying debt when the cash flow is inadequate.) While such a circumstance will not happen, this ratio provides a means of comparing the adequacy of the level of the country's reserves to the reserves of other countries. From 1987 to 1993, this ranged from 3.5 months to 5.8 months for all developing countries. There were, however, significant variations by geographic area (see exhibit 13.1).

The capital and financial account information in the balance of payments may disguise risks because it shows only transactions made during the reporting period and not the sum total of all previous years. In the past, this was generally not considered to be a major risk because it was presumed that investments were made for the long term and, in the case of manufacturing

Exhibit 13.1 **Number of Months Reserves Would Cover Imports of Goods and Services**[4]

	1987 – 1993
All Developing Countries	3.5 to 5.8
Sub-Saharan Africa	1.5 to 2.2
Middle East & North Africa	4.1 to 5.4
Latin America & Caribbean	3.1 to 5.8
Europe and Central Asia	2.6 to 10.3
Severely-Indebted Low Income Countries	1.2 to 2.2

plants or development of natural resources, could not depart the country. Analysts and investors tended to become concerned only if the level of annual capital flow significantly dropped, which suggested that there was a problem elsewhere in the political or economic perception of foreign sources of capital. The events of the 1990s highlighted how the current account and the capital and financial account influenced each other, and how the investment categories decidedly differed in influencing economic trends.

The sources of capital and financial resources going to the developing countries changed in the period from 1987 to 1993 (see exhibit 13.2). Total debt grew, but the percentage of long-term debt from banks dropped in absolute and percentage terms (mostly as the residual consequence of the losses banks had taken in the 1982-1985 debt crisis). Debt from bonds, which generally were held by institutional investors (pension funds, insurance companies), went up. The annual flow of capital and financial resources showed that debt declined in importance. Direct investment (factories, mines) became a larger percentage of the annual resource flow to those countries, while portfolio investment exploded from 1 percent to

22 percent of the total resource flow.

As was seen in chapter 5, investments made in factories and mines, even in industrialized countries, could create concerns for the investors if there were a major currency crisis within the European Union. To protect the value of their investment from translation losses, the investors could be forced into taking a foreign exchange position, which tends to magnify the immediate market speculation and its subsequent effects on the country's current account (immediate rise in the cost of imports offset by possible longer-term gain in expanding exports).

A Case of Crisis

The Mexican crisis in December 1994 starkly revealed the volatility of portfolio investment. Stocks in **emerging markets** (developing countries) had been attracting investors, largely from the United States, into mutual funds that were rapidly being formed to specialize in such markets by either country or region. There was a perception that such stocks offered higher returns than were available in the U.S. and European

Exhibit 13.2 External Financing for All Developing Countries[5]

in US$ billions	1987	1993
Total Debt Outstanding	1,128	1,423
Owed to Commercial banks	366 (32%)	232 (16%)
Bonds	46 (4%)	193 (14%)
Year's net resource flows	68	213
From		
Net long-term debt	53%	32%
Foreign direct investment (net)	21%	31%
Portfolio equity	1%	22%

stock markets. Mexico saw such total portfolio equity flows jump from $563 million in 1990 to over $14 billion in 1993. The same was true for its bond market, which was financing the government deficit and development projects.

The government securities market is large (294 billion pesos), with foreign investors accounting for 28 percent of outstandings. . . . Most of the market is short-term instruments, namely Tesobonos and Cetes. Tesobonos, dollar-denominated securities with peso returns, provide investors currency protection. Because of this feature, Tesobonos gained popularity among foreign investors in 1994, and the market share of these securities rose from 15 percent at the end of 1993 to 65 percent at the end of 1994. Foreigners held 34 percent of outstandings in December 1994.[6]

The peso was unexpectedly devalued in December 1994. Mexico's current account had been heavily in deficit: As a result of a turbulent presidential election campaign in 1994, during which the government tried to maintain the exchange rate, the reserves had been depleted to

less than one month's imports (from $25 billion to $5 billion). In essence, the trade deficit had been financed through the inflow of portfolio investment; two-thirds of the government borrowings were in pesos, whose value was linked to the U.S. dollar.

The individuals and companies that had invested in those mutual funds (or in some cases, directly) were faced with sudden losses. They wanted to get their money out of these investments and out of Mexico before they lost more. To meet those demands, the mutual funds had to sell their holdings of stocks and bonds. The Mexican stock market plunged 35 percent in December, mostly in the second half of the month. Those shares were in pesos, which had to be sold to get dollars. The exchange rate plummeted, losing half its value in a month. When the Tesobonos matured, the government had to pay them off in pesos at a rate linked to the current exchange rate, which meant that pesos to be sold for dollars flooded into the foreign exchange market and caused the rate to fall even faster. Foreign investors were not the only ones to flee from pesos into dollars; Mexican investors likewise sought to preserve the value of their assets by selling pesos and buying dollars.

With the flow of capital and financial account funds virtually stopped and the reserves gone, the government had to take drastic measures to restore the current account.

Investors and those specialized mutual funds then became fearful about the value of their holdings in other countries. The result was heavy selling in many other stock markets. One index of Latin American markets "lost 16.9 percent in December and 21.5 percent for the [fourth] quarter. Especially hard hit were Argentina and Brazil, with December declines of 13.4 percent and 6 percent respectively."[7] Not only did mutual funds specializing in Mexico fall, but so did those specializing in Russia, Turkey, Indonesia, China, and other countries.

Domestic Analysis

International economic events are not separate from domestic activities. A high rate of internal inflation will influence a country's foreign exchange rate. Internal prices will be rising, which will make its exports less competitive, and imports will become cheaper unless there are compensatory changes in the exchange rate. Inflation can be fueled by an extensive government deficit when the government puts more money into the hands of the populace or provides subsidies to enable certain products to be sold below their cost.

For decades a number of countries, both developing and industrialized, had political policies that encouraged government ownership of basic industries. These policies led to heavy government spending to support such companies, many of which continued to operate at a loss. By the end of the 1980s, a large number of these governments reversed their policies and began to sell their basic industries to private ownership (*privatization*). As a consequence, their national budgets show income from those sales as well as elimination of the government subsidies, both of which tend to reduce the government's overall deficit.

In summary, the economic element of country risk analysis requires understanding the various parts of the balance of payments, knowledge of what is within each of those categories, and awareness of the forces that can cause rapid changes with resulting effects on the projections being made. The analysis also needs to include an examination of the domestic economy and how it will effect changes in the balance of payments.

Analyzing the Political Component

The political outlook for a country is assessed not because of the banker's preference for one political side or another, but to evaluate the likelihood of political change and its impact on economic policy or a change in the rules for doing business in that country. Such assessment of future political events is very difficult. Bankers have sought to assess political risk as best they can, even hiring political scientists and professed experts. Unfortunately, the banker makes loans today, and no one can accurately predict tomorrow. Neither the economic nor the political future forms a trend line from the past. "In politics," as a retired British cabinet minister summed up, "the only really useful guide is history."[8] In political analysis, there are not even numbers that the economic analyst can use.

The banker, when considering a term loan, is concerned with those political events that might change a country's or business's ability to repay the loan. In actuality, the banker cannot know. All that can be done is to attempt to evaluate the known data to arrive at a degree of probability about a country's political future while recognizing the lessons of history and expecting that the unexpected will happen. Some of the factors to consider are discussed below.

Political Change

Political change in any country can alter that country's economic outlook. Political decisions may result in new taxes, new support for a particular industry, withdrawal of support from other industries, or changes in attractiveness to investors. A government nearing an election might undertake economic policies to maintain its popularity, or launch a military adventure to distract an unhappy electorate.

It is a fact of politics that in at least 90 percent of countries, some group is plotting to take over the government. In a democracy, the plotting would be an open plan to win the next election. In other societies, it may be a clandestine plan for revolution, either from within or by exiles. Many of these changes will never take place, but some will succeed and, in doing so, will lead to changes that can affect business and the country's economic situation—some for better, some for worse.

The analyst should consider these questions: What is the country's political tradition? Is it one of regular elections and orderly, nonviolent transfers of power? Is revolution likely? Some countries have a history of dictatorships, whether by an individual, family, tribe, or political party. In such countries changes do not come regularly. History has shown that dictatorships, whether benign or repressive, tend to be stable for a while but are almost always followed by violence that has the capacity to tear apart the fabric of the society and with it the economy. In other countries, there is a tradition of regular intervention by the military, usually the army. Changes in these situations tend to be decided by a small group of power brokers. In recent years, such military control has not been demonstrated to be particularly successful, and there have been a number of instances of the military losing the support of the people and returning government to civilian control. Labor unions, having developed their positions from the policies of past governments who sought their support in domestic political confrontations, may also be important political power centers.

Memory and Nationalism

The identity of a nation is its collective memory, as the late President Mitterrand of France pointed out. How this memory is applied can have widely varying consequences. Abraham Lincoln appealed to it in his first inaugural address to evoke the common goals and hopes of those citizens whose ancestors had come to settle America in the seventeenth and eighteenth centuries. Trying to avert the fury that was about to lead to civil war, President Lincoln said, "We are not enemies, but friends. . . . Though passions may have strained, it must not break our bonds of affection. The mystic chords of memory . . . [in] every living heart and hearthstone, all over this broad land will yet swell the chorus of Union, when again touched, as surely they will be, by the better angels of our nature." [9]

Unfortunately, today in other places in the world, such an appeal to memory is a raging scream against the grievances perpetuated by other nationalities and defeats, sometimes recent but most often centuries old—the battle of Kosovo in 1389 or the battle of the Boyne in 1690, to cite just a few.

"John Stuart Mill, a great nineteenth century English liberal, picked out two defining elements to nationality (1) the wish to be governed together; (2) the common sympathy created by shared language, history, and beliefs. Ignoring one half or the other of this definition has caused grief among nations ever since." [10] A modern scholar of nationalism adds another important element to the meaning of the term: ". . . nationalism locates the source of individual identity with a "people" which is seen as the bearer of sovereignty, the central object of loyalty, and the basis of collective solidarity. The 'people' is the mass of a population whose boundaries and nature are defined in various ways . . . common territory or common language, statehood or shared traditions, history or race." [11]

It is nearly impossible for an outsider (the banker or the investor) to understand why some appeals to nationalism turn violent and others do not. A few countries are states with a single nationality, which usually developed within a clearly demarcated physical area. The boundaries of most other countries are arbitrary and developed over time, having been established as a consequence of military events. Within some of these, the various nationalities have developed a way to live together through balancing of political powers or other peaceful agreement. Many of the countries of Africa and Eastern Europe have borders that were arbitrarily imposed by colonial powers or victors in wars. The 1919 Versailles Treaty was intended to settle the world after World War I. The borders it created in Eastern Europe were literally drawn by a few statesmen in Paris, each of whom had his own separate agenda, and most of whom had never even seen the areas in question. Using inaccurate data, they formed some countries of peoples who had long histories of conflicts with each other, or divided nationalities between neighboring states. The grievances this caused created conflicts for the rest of the twentieth century. Even 75 years after the 1920 Treaty of Trianon carved up prewar Imperial Hungary, it was still described on the front page in the press of several countries as poisoning relations in the region and a great catastrophe.

The 1990s have seen the violence that such conflicts between antagonistic nationalities in a single country can create. A few countries (such as the former Czechoslovakia, now the Czech Republic and Slovakia) peacefully divided themselves. In other regions, such as Chechnya and the former Yugoslavia, ancient ethnic hatreds have led to war. But whether violently or peacefully, this political conflict gave rise to economic dislocations.

In assessing a future trend, the banker must be aware of history, both the actual events and how different groups perceived those events. The history (and the historical myths) learned by generations of schoolchildren and accentuated by art, literature, and music, may be a significant catalyst or restraint to a government's selection of policy options. It can quantify "moral geography" and establish what a nation's people accept as standards. The childhood literature of the Dutch, for example, centers on tales of seagoing captains triumphing against shipwrecks and disasters in far-off areas. "This was frontier literature, as much as the Wild West stories that fed another young republic's sense of courage, sin and virtue." [12]

Corruption can be a factor. In some parts of the world, petty corruption is more readily accepted than in others. Other countries are completely intolerant of any level. But even in the more relaxed societies, the people can suddenly express their anger when the generally accepted level is breached. This can lead to street demonstrations, political unrest, and even a change of government. "Corruption seriously undermines the effectiveness of government. . . . Some corruption is on such a scale that it has major economic consequences: it may stimulate the illegal export of capital or result in large projects being awarded to contractors . . . according to the size of their bribes rather than the quality of their performance." [13]

Political alliances, including former colonial and mother-country relationships, can affect future political events. Colonial relationships have been more than just political.

The trouble with calling all . . . regions
"colonial" economies is that the term . . .

suggests that if alien domination of some sort is thrown off, a stunted, narrow economy will no longer remain stunted and narrow, will proceed to become better rounded and capable of producing amply and diversely on its own behalf as well as for others. To be sure, there are often good reasons for throwing off alien domination or influence: reasons that are politically, socially, culturally and emotionally important and sometimes economically important as well. Yet, it should be clear by now, the stultification of . . . regions and the fragility of their economies are not so simply or easily corrected as the epithet "colonial" suggests. When Fidel Castro disposed of American influence in Cuba he did not throw off Cuba's servitude to sugar.[14]

Political change can affect not only the way business is conducted, it can also so involve a populace that the economy itself becomes a victim. When civil wars or invasions become all-consuming, with everyone struggling merely to survive or fleeing a battle zone, foreign loans and investments are lost in the melee.

Political Evaluation

Political assessment is likely to differ, depending on the bank making it. Banks in two countries may tend to view risk in a third country differently. For example, West Germany and France were prepared to extend more credit to the countries in Eastern Europe after the political changes of 1989-1990 than were U.S. banks. Similarly, U.S. banks were more committed to Mexico and Latin America than were European banks. Such differing perceptions are not surprising. A country does more business with its neighbor and has perhaps a better, or more comfortable, feeling because of proximity.

Bank Regulation

U.S. bank supervisors assess each bank's country risk exposure because it may affect the overall condition of that bank. The assessment includes a review of "three basic components in every bank's country risk management system: (a) evaluation of economic, political, and social trends in countries where the bank has asset exposure; (b) country exposure limits established by executive bank management; and (c) current, accurate, and complete internal reporting systems to monitor and control country risk."[15]

To coordinate the assessment of country risk between the various regulatory agencies in the United States, the *Interagency Country Exposure Review Committee (ICERC)* was established in 1979 by the Comptroller of the Currency, the Federal Reserve, and the FDIC. It meets at least three times a year to assess information from a number of sources. These include a statistical analysis prepared by the Federal Reserve Bank of New York of the ability of countries to service their external debt, country studies prepared by the Federal Reserve System, other U.S. government information, and information and analyses prepared by major U.S. banks for their own country assessments.

ICERC then categorizes countries on the basis of economic-social-political conditions that may affect the country's flow of foreign exchange necessary to repay U.S. banks' cross-border exposures in that country. ICERC may determine that one category may apply to all U.S. bank loans in a country, or that several categories apply depending on the type of maturities of cross-border exposures U.S. banks have in the country. ICERC distributes its country evaluations to the federal bank examiners who regularly examine the international activities of U.S. banks.[16]

As a practical matter, the regulators tend not to be concerned with small exposures that a bank might have. These ICERC categories are, in descending order, substandard, value impaired, and loss. If a country's debt is categorized as value impaired or loss, which means that the chances of repayment are small, then banks with loans to these countries will be expected either to establish specific loan loss reserves or to recognize the losses. When a country's debt is put in less severe categories of other transfer risk problems or transfer risk warranting special comment, banks with loans to that country may not be required to establish reserves. The examiners will, however, consider such loans when assessing the quality of the bank's portfolio and the adequacy of its capital.

Assessing Country Risk

Beginning with the foundation of the balance of payments, the banker tries to determine the risk in making a loan or an investment in a foreign country. Unfortunately, no one has found a foolproof formula; but this does not mean that the banker must give up. The assessment is a serious concern. All credit evaluations about a specific borrower will come to naught if the borrower's country encounters difficulties from economic, social or political causes. When that happens, foreign exchange to repay a loan, remit a dividend, or pay for foreign trade may not be available. Changing economic conditions, perhaps triggered by political events, may make it no longer possible for a borrower even to stay in business. Political events can completely disrupt a market or so completely change the economy as to make any analysis derived from even recent economic data meaningless. For example, the political upheavals in Eastern Europe and the former Soviet Union suddenly changed centrally planned economies—that had been conducting most of their international trade through intrabloc

barter—into market-oriented countries forced to compete in global markets where payments were required in convertible currencies. This led to considerable internal economic anguish.

Notwithstanding the uncertainties of the future, the banker must make decisions. Country risk assessment begins with a study of the most recent balance of payments elements. This must be more than just a superficial answering of the question "Is it favorable or unfavorable?" Not all the necessary information to answer a banker's questions may be detailed in a balance of payments, but it may be readily available from other international and national sources.

Certain events in the past can give a hint of the future: heavy incoming investment in past years will almost certainly mean steadily increasing expenses for dividends in the future. A nation that has been dependent on the export of a single commodity in the past is not likely to lessen that dependency in the immediate future. (Australia, however, provides an example of a shift in dependency on export products, from wool up to the 1950s, then to beef, and then to iron ore and coal.) Ores and minerals are subject to fluctuating demand, competitive sources, and technological changes. Long-term global commodity price trends can suggest future levels of export income. Sudden changes in prices, such as those seen since the 1970s with oil, can tremendously affect, both those countries that have the commodity and those that do not have it.

Some countries, such as The Bahamas, depend heavily on tourism as a major contributor to their balance of payments. Their ability to import goods and service their debt is heavily dependent on the continued attractiveness of the country to foreign tourists.

Income from remittances of nationals working in other countries has been a major source of income to some countries. Bangladesh, described by the World Bank as one of the poorest countries in the world, for a number of years has earned the equivalent of 28 percent of its imports from such workers. In 1993, this amounted to over $1 billion—44 percent of what the country earned from merchandise exports.

Ratios from certain key items in the balance of payments and from other economic sources can be meaningful guides for assessing country risk. Such ratios highlight trends and facilitate comparisons between countries of comparable levels of economic development. Examples of some of these ratios can be seen in the report prepared by the Federal Reserve Bank of New York for the ICERC that ranks countries by their ability to service external obligations. "The rankings are based on five basic ratios: current account deficit to exports; cumulative current account to exports; net external interest payments to exports; net external interest payments to international reserves; and total current debt service requirements to receipts from exports of goods and services."[17] This illustrates the importance of certain categories of data selected to meet a particular analytical need. Another comparison often studied by analysts is the number of months a nation's reserves would finance the country's imports (see the discussion of Mexico [page 237]). Good ratio analysis is only the beginning of the evaluation.

Each bank is responsible for making its own evaluation of the risk of doing business in another country. After making the economic and political assessments described, how does a bank come to a conclusion?

There is no one solution. Each bank does its own analysis and comes to its own assessment. Different banks may review the same data and come to different conclusions. Overall, each bank is seeking to answer the question of whether it can expect that any credit extended to a borrower in a country will be repaid. Part of this is the credit assessment of the borrower, whether it be a corporation, a bank, or an entity of the government. Beyond the normal credit assessment process, however, the bank is also concerned that conditions in a country may change.

Changes may impair a borrower's ability to obtain foreign exchange to repay the credit or the ability to continue to operate in the same environment that existed when the credit was extended.

The investor will make a similar analysis whether making a direct investment in a new factory, investing in a bond or other form of long-term debt, or making a portfolio investment. Each of these will be affected by changes in the economic, political, or social conditions in a country.

Based on its experience, the bank will examine economic trends and project these into the future when the credit is due to be repaid. It will assess political and social trends, the likelihood of changes, and their impact, in turn, on the economic environment. Whether the bank does this by relying on the experience of a few key individuals or through a structure of committees, it must arrive at a decision. On the basis of that decision, it will develop a business plan for that country, which then must be communicated to all those in the bank responsible for credit, foreign exchange, or investments.

Country Risk Assessment of New Countries

After the political breakup of the Soviet Union and other countries in Eastern Europe, U.S. banks faced unusual difficulties in evaluating country risk exposure. For example, if a local business needs financing to make an export sale to one of these countries, how can the bank assess its credit risk when the source of repayment is from an importer in the new country? Some larger banks may be asked to provide longer-term financing for new industrial investments.

The Soviet Union divided into 15 separate republics and Czechoslovakia divided into 2, and Slovenia split off from Yugoslavia without being drawn into the violence that other parts of that country suffered. As these new countries are created, there is little if any record upon which to analyze the balance of payments, total reserves, total foreign debt, and annual servicing (interest and principal) of that debt. Even where data are available, interpretation may be difficult. For example, 1993 data on Ukraine's trade with the countries of the former Soviet Union show either a trade deficit of US $1.9 billion or US $16 billion, depending on whether the official or market implicit rate of exchange is used.[18] Additionally, there is a lack of meaningful information on those internal factors that affect a nation's economy: inflation, budget deficit, gross national product, labor costs, and so on. The inability to get accurate data to answer such basic questions is proving to be an obstacle for many banks and investors, which reduces the availability of the financing that the new countries need.

It is not surprising, therefore, that many financial decisions are being based on political rather than economic objectives. "Germany is the biggest creditor [to the former Soviet Union], partly because German reunification resulted in the amalgamation of an estimated DM 12 billion loans extended or guaranteed by former East German enterprises. Germany has also provided grants and other transfer payments in connection with the resettlement of Soviet troops and reunification."[19]

The political division of an established nation not only disrupts former internal business links, but also completely changes the basis of analysis of the old country. Domestic transfers now become international ones. In the Soviet Union, cotton was grown in Uzbekistan to supply the textile mills in Russia. When the Soviet Union dissolved, this cotton flow became foreign trade. It raised new questions of international payments, pricing, and dependability of supply, since Uzbekistan was now free to sell its cotton to other countries for payment in hard currencies. Even if all the cotton continues to go to the Russian textile mills, it represents foreign trade

and affects the balance of payments for both countries.

The now-independent republics of Uzbekistan and Kazakhstan produce two-thirds of the former Soviet Union's output of copper.[20] The latter republic "also has 90 percent of the former Soviet Union's chrome, 60 percent of its silver, 20 percent of its coal, half its tungsten and lead, 40 percent of its zinc . . . 25 percent of its bauxite . . . [and] a third of the grain of the former Soviet Union."[21] Many of these had been major exports of the Soviet Union. The export earnings now belong to just the one republic. The other new republics are clearly poorer as a result.

Overall, comparing the 15 new republics with the former Soviet Union showed significant balance of payments consequences. "Over the period 1990-93 recorded trade of the new independent states fell by more than 60 percent. Trade among these states bore the brunt of the decline. . . . Exports to the rest of the world fell from $105 billion in 1989 to $58 billion in 1993 or 46 percent. Imports shrank even more, from $121 billion to $45 billion or 63 percent."[22]

Political analysis of dividing countries becomes almost impossible as different forces vie for prominence. The populace itself often seems to be unsure of what they want.

Government funds in foreign bank accounts, holdings of gold, foreign debt that the country contracted in the years before the breakup, annual repayment of principal and interest—these are all matters to be resolved by the new countries.

Business Development

Although country risk assessment is usually done to identify, and thereby avoid, risks that may cause a future loss, it can likewise indicate (but not guarantee) those countries with an outlook for political stability and economic growth. Used in this way, it becomes a business development tool for the banker to identify nations and businesses with factors of strength that would lead to their success—precisely those which a bank would want as its customers.

Every nation possesses what economists have termed *factors of production*. Factors of production are nothing more than the inputs necessary to compete in any industry, such as labor, arable land, natural resources, capital, [knowledge], and infrastructure. . . . A nation will export those goods which make intensive use of the factors with which it is relatively well endowed. The United States, for example, has been a substantial exporter of agricultural goods, reflecting in part its unusual abundance of large tracts of arable land. A nation's endowment of factors clearly plays a role in the competitive advantage of a nation's firms, as the rapid growth of manufacturing in low-wage countries such as Hong Kong, Taiwan, and more recently Thailand, attests. . . . The factors most important to competitive advantage in most industries, especially the industries most vital to productive growth in advanced economies, are not inherited but are created within a nation, through processes that differ widely across nations and among industries. Thus, the stock of factors at any particular time is less important than the rate at which they are created, upgraded, and made more specialized to particular industries.[23]

. . . . A nation's competitive industries are not spread evenly through an economy but are connected in . . . *clusters* consisting of industries related by links of various kinds. In Italy, for example, over 40 percent of total exports are due to clusters of industries all connected to food, fashion, or the home. In Sweden, over 50 percent of total exports are industry clusters in transportation, forest products, and metals."[24]

With this type of analysis of a country, the banker and investor can fashion a business development plan. The information needed for the country profile—that is, the country risk analysis—provides detailed data about the investment sources, the nation's commodity trade, and the countries that are its customary markets. It should be a short step then to match this information with the market in which the bank and investor are interested. This type of application is equally suitable for both small and large banks.

Accounting

When ICERC requires a bank to establish a specific reserve against its outstandings in that country, the bank may either charge off the amount (which may be a percentage of all their outstandings in that country) as it would any other loan loss, or it may establish a specific reserve account: *allocated transfer risk reserve*. "Such reserves shall be charged against current income and shall not be considered as part of capital and surplus or allowances for possible loan losses for regulatory, supervisory, or disclosure purposes."[25] This means the amount is excluded in calculating the bank's capital adequacy or risk-based capital ratios.

Summary

Country risk analysis is the assessment of future probabilities based on historical interpretations. It is essential for global banking, investment, and business. To do this requires attention not only to the economic factors that can put financial deals in jeopardy, but equally to the political and social possibilities that can change financial expectations. Using the tools of country risk analysis, the banker and investor can assess the risks in another country and decide whether to accept them. The country risk decision, credit evaluation of the borrower, analysis of the requested transaction, and the transactions objectives are the elements of managing a bank's international credit portfolio.

Questions

1. What is country risk?
2. If a country has a deficit balance of payments in one year, how can it correct it?
3. What is the role of the ICERC?
4. What are the objectives of political analysis in the overall country risk assessment?

Notes

1. Walter Bagehot, "The Danger of Lending to Semi-Civilized Countries" (November 23, 1867), *The Collected Works of Walter Bagehot,* ed. Norman St. John-Stevas (London: *The Economist*, vol. X, 1978), p. 419
2. *The Economist*, April 29, 1995, p. 99
3. *The Economist*, May 6, 1995
4. The World Bank, *World Debt Tables 1994-5*, vol. 1 (Washington D.C.: World Bank, 1995), pp. 192-220
5. Ibid.
6. The World Bank, *Financial Flows and the Developing Countries: A World Bank Quarterly*, February 1995, p. 6
7. Ibid, p. 10
8. Review quoting from *The Time of My Life*, by Denis Healey, *The New York Times Book Review*, September 23, 1990, p. 9
9. Abraham Lincoln, *Speeches and Writings 1859-1865* (New York: The Library of America, 1989), p. 224
10. *The Economist*, March 6, 1993, p. 89
11. Liah Greenfeld, *Nationalism: Five Roads to Modernity* (Cambridge: Harvard University Press, 1992), pp. 3,7
12. Simon Schama, *The Embarrassment of Riches* (New York: Alfred A. Knopf, 1987), p. 30
13. The World Bank, *World Development Report 1983* (New York: Oxford University Press, 1983), p. 117
14. Jane Jacobs, *Cities and the Wealth of Nations* (New York: Random House, 1984), pp. 69-70
15. Robert Bench, "International Lending Supervision," *International Banking: U.S. Laws and Regulations* (Washington, D.C.: American Bankers Association, 1984), § 4, pp. 4-32
16. Ibid., § 4, p. 27
17. Ibid., § 4, p. 26
18. The World Bank, *Trade in the New Independent States* (Washington, D.C.: The World Bank, 1994), p. 5
19. The World Bank, *World Debt Tables 1992-93*, vol. 1 (Washington D.C.: The World Bank, 1993), p. 32
20. International Monetary Fund, The World Bank, Organization for Economic Co-operation and Development, and European Bank for Reconstruction and Development, *A Study of the Soviet Economy*, vol. 3 (Paris: International Monetary Fund et. al., 1991), p. 278
21. *The New York Times*, March 2, 1993, p. A3
22. The World Bank, *Trade in the New Independent States*, (Washington D.C.: The World Bank, 1994), pp. 2-3
23. Michael E. Porter, *The Competitive Advantage of Nations*, (New York: The Free Press, 1990), pp. 73-74
24. *Ibid.*, pp. 131-132
25. International Lending Supervision Act of 1983 (97 Stat. 1278) § 905: (a)(2)

14

GLOBAL FINANCIAL RISK MANAGEMENT

Learning Objectives

After studying this chapter, you will be able to

- identify the risks of global banking activities
- describe how such risks can be managed
- formulate guidelines for analyzing risks in global banking

Overview

Risks for the global banker fall into three broad areas. The first area is risk arising from activities unique to the global rather than the domestic side of a bank, such as foreign exchange trading, cross-border money markets, and the operational aspects of letters of credit. (Trading in general, however, is not confined to international activities; it is also a major business within the U.S. domestic market for short-term investments, bonds, and equities.)

The second area is risk that arises from banking business in general. This may include credit, payments, deposit accounts, collections, and so forth. With these, the global banker differs from the domestic banker only in that the customer is doing business outside, or is actually outside, the United States.

The third area of risk management overrides the first two and can be a greater problem for the global banker: how to manage these risks at a distance. When any bank has a single location for conducting all its activities, it is easier for senior management to know what is happening. Managers can visit all the units easily and be available promptly to make decisions. In a large trading operation, the senior manager may actually stay in the trading room to provide advice, guidance, and authority for decisions. It is considerably more difficult when the decisions are being made several time zones away.

When risks are not properly managed within a bank, losses often can result. For U.S. banks, the view of the Comptroller of the Currency is not in doubt: "the lack of an adequate risk control function . . . [is] an unsafe and unsound banking practice." [1] Some of these unsound practices involve spectacular amounts of money, and the magnitude of their consequences has resulted in considerable public interest. The post-mortems likewise become public, regardless of whether they are done by internal auditors, investigative journalists, regulators, or courts. In many of these situations there is a depressing similarity in how the risks of the business failed to be managed. "Those who cannot remember the past," said American philosopher George Santayana, "are condemned to repeat it." [2] Paying close attention to failures can teach lessons that lead to programs for identifying risks and establishing proper risk management procedures for all bankers.

The various products of global banking and the practices associated with each have been discussed individually in previous chapters. Overall risk management for a bank begins with the separate product risks and then recognizes that these many risks are interconnected and consequently require an overall risk management program. This chapter will apply another perspective to the individual products already discussed that make up global banking. The reader may wish to review the previous chapters as part of this overall topic.

Rather than cataloging the risks that the global manager confronts, this chapter examines these interconnected risks primarily within the framework of the failure of a specific international bank—Barings. The focus is not on whether anybody committed any criminal action (that is a matter for the courts), but rather on how this bank failed to manage its risks and what can be learned from that.

The Barings Lessons[3]

Background

The firm of Barings was established in 1762 as wool merchants. As with the history of so many such firms that became merchant banks, it moved within a few years into financial activities. Barings was represented among the directors of the East India Company, raised funds for the British government's war against the American colonies, led the financing of the Louisiana

Purchase, and by early in the next century was the premier banker for a number of European countries (see chapter 2). It was considered so important that when it faced bankruptcy in 1890 because of its international financing, it was saved by a consortium of banks led by the Bank of England.

The picture in 1995: "In London, Barings was respected as the city's oldest merchant bank but was in truth no more than middle-sized. In Asian markets from Tokyo to Singapore and Hong Kong, it carried much more weight. That Asian clout had paid off handsomely. On Wednesday [February 22] the Barings board had met to consider the 1994 draft accounts. They showed a small rise in profits. . . . And one big contributor to those results, as in the year before, had been a very profitable operation in Singapore. That Friday morning [February 24] then, Barings looked in good shape—the bluest of blue-chip merchant banks, coping well with the new international financial order." [4] Yet by Sunday (three days later) at 10:10 P.M. following a frantic weekend, the Bank of England announced that Barings had failed because of that Singapore operation, where trading losses (which were ultimately found to be £830 million) exceeded the Barings capital of £541 million (US$750 million).

What risks had not been managed?

Trading Risks

For a bank, trading—whether of foreign exchange, Eurodollars, derivatives, or securities—inherently has greater risks of financial loss than most of its other banking activities. It is precisely because of those greater risks that bank managements establish units for such trading. The risks may be greater, but so is the possibility for meaningful earnings. The decision to trade may be made by a bank's management to provide better service to customers or to benefit the bank's own earnings (proprietary trading). Success in trading relies on the skill and experience of the trader, who must make decisions quickly in a time span measured in minutes. The trader is basically a risk taker. As was seen in section 2, trading is done in a high-pressure, intensely competitive atmosphere. It is not an activity that can be done by committee, and thus it requires a different structure for managing the risks.

Management supervision of a trading operation cannot control the trader's decisions. There is not enough time for that. What management can do is control the framework within which the trader works by setting "fences," and then ensure through supervision that the trader stays within that fence.

Fence one. Bank management determines—as a credit matter—which banks or companies the trader may trade with and establishes a dollar or other monetary limit for the total amount in trades that may be outstanding at any one time. This applies a credit judgment on the counterparty risk. This decision will also establish a settlement limit. "Settlement risk is the loss exposure arising when a bank performs on its obligation under a contract prior to the counterparty performing on its obligation . . . [and] frequently arises in international transactions because of time zone differences." [5] This was not a factor in the Barings collapse because the counterparty credit risk of the trades was borne by the Singapore International Monetary Exchange, as is often the case in trading in contracts through commodity exchanges. In essence, the trader buys or sells contracts on the Exchange, which has approved the credit capability of those permitted to do such buying or selling, and which, as a safety feature, will require *margin*—a percentage of the contract value covered by a cash deposit with the Exchange.

Fence two. Management establishes the limit of **market risk** it is prepared to take. "Market risk is the exposure arising from adverse changes in the market value [the price] of an instrument or portfolio of instruments. Such exposure occurs with respect to derivative instruments when changes occur in market factors such as underlying interest rates, currency rates, equity prices, and commodity prices or in the volatility of these factors."[6] Barings management had intended for the unit in question to trade only in low-risk, clearly defined, fully hedged, specified arbitrage between the Japanese and Singapore exchanges with no overnight open exposure.

> The product . . . was a financial one: a futures contract on the Nikkei 225, the main Japanese stock market index. The underlying value of such contracts is dictated by the performance of the shares that make up the index. If the shares rise in value, your futures contract is worth more; if they fall it is worth less. But the magic of futures is leverage: to buy a futures contract you have to put up only a small proportion of the value of the underlying shares. That greatly magnifies any swings in the value of the index. A big one will pay off hugely; a big fall will wipe you out. Buying a block of Nikkei futures—taking a long position—is thus a risky bet on the future direction of the Japanese market. But Barings did not plan to do that. Instead, it took advantage of the fact that there are, in fact, two main markets for Nikkei 225 futures: one traded on the Osaka Stock Exchange, one on Simex, the fast-growing Singapore financial futures exchange. Both exchange contracts are based on the same basket of stocks, so their fundamental value is the same. But from moment to moment, differences appear between the price quoted at one exchange and the price quoted at the other. A dealer with a link to both exchanges can buy in the market where the price is lower and sell simultaneously in the other where it is higher. Result: a risk free profit.[7]

What the Barings trader actually did, however, was to trade unhedged, very speculative open positions. As his losses mounted, he took on more and more contracts in an attempt to recoup his losses. When an earthquake caused widespread damage in Kobe, Japan, the stock markets fell rapidly, accelerating Barings' loss. At the same time, the Barings trader was reporting to London profits that generally were the option premiums he was receiving as new contracts were opened (see chapter 5).

Fence three: Management ensures the absolute separation of trading from settlement. This can be the most important control for any trading activity. The trader's job is to trade. Once a trade has been made with another bank or company, the transaction is reported to a separate unit for the settlement. Settlement involves reporting the trade in the record of the position, sending confirmation to the other party, and giving the instructions to the operating units to transfer the funds on the settlement date and to receive the offsetting funds (if trading foreign exchange) or the money market or investment documents. As soon as a trade is done, the trader is responsible to report this to the settlement unit—often on a simple piece of paper. If the trading is particularly active, some firms may actually have a clerk sit near the trader to do the reporting of all the transactions. If this method is used, that clerk must be supervised and held accountable by someone other than the trader. The concern here is not that the trader is dishonest. (If that is the fear, management should never have hired him in the first place.) The concern is rather that in the often frantic tension and activity in dealing in the market, the trader will become involved in a losing position that she will hold, expecting the market to turn around. In the unusual situation at Barings in Singapore, the trader was also in charge of settlement. When his positions were losing money, he hid this from the bank's management by creating a special "Error Account No. 88888." In his capacity as head of the settlement unit, he ordered the internal computer reporting system to be reprogrammed to exclude this account or to report it so as to appear as a routine temporary operational settlement error with a customer. Eventually, however, the losses became too big to hide.

Product Risk

Every product the banker uses carries risks. Many of these are discussed in previous chapters. For example, the risks in extending credit are covered in chapters 10 and 11; some of the risks in foreign exchange trading are described in chapters 4 and 5; and trade finance risks are discussed in chapters 6, 7, and 8. When the bank is conducting these activities from many separate global units, it must control its total exposure to its customer. For example, while a borrower may use several different units of the bank, the bank will have a single credit limit for that customer and be able to manage this risk to ensure that the total of all the units does not exceed it. The same would be applicable to the bank's foreign exchange limit for a customer.

Derivatives

The product that the Barings trader was using is a type of **derivative**. This is an ill-defined term that covers a wide range of financial products. Although the term has been used often in the financial press or by companies as if, in and of itself, it were the explanation for a large loss, a derivative can be used to reduce risk as well as to try to increase earnings from another product.

A derivative is a financial contract whose value is "derived from a reference rate, index, or the value of an underlying asset . . . [such as] stocks, bonds, commodities, interest rates, foreign currency exchange rates, and indexes that reflect the collective value of underlying financial products." Four basic types of products fall within that definition: forwards, futures, options, and swaps. Each of these is either a "standardized contract traded on exchanges . . . [or] customized contracts that include negotiated terms such as amounts, payment timing, and interest or currency rates. When contracts are not traded on an exchange, they are called over-the-counter (OTC) derivatives." [8] (see exhibit 14.1)

The use in global banking of some of these derivative products has already been discussed: interest rate and cross-currency swaps in chapter 11 and foreign exchange swaps and options in chapter 5. Not all of these are new products. The legality of options, for example, was argued in the London Stock Exchange in 1802. The Exchange tried to ban them in 1821, but the use of options had become so widespread by that time that the ban itself was lifted in 1822. Likewise, contracts for future delivery and settlement were being accepted reluctantly by the 1890s.[9]

A derivative contract can be entered into to reduce risk (as seen with the foreign currency option) or to reduce the interest rates (interest rate swap). It can also be used as a means of speculation to increase earnings. The huge losses, and law suits and countersuits, that have resulted from some of these uses by multinational corporations have been highly publicized. A bank may play two roles in derivatives. In one role, as a dealer developing a product it sells to a customer, or as a middleman between two customers. In the other role, it may function as the investor for its own account in which it carries all the risks and presumably will earn all the rewards.

The risks posed by derivatives use include (1) credit risk . . . (2) market risk

Exhibit 14.1 The Four Major Types of Derivatives

Derivatives	Market	Definition	Example
Forwards	OTC markets for customized contracts	Forwards and futures obligate the holder to buy or sell a specific amount or value of an underlying asset, reference rate, or index at a specified price on a specified future date.	A U.S. importer promises to buy machinery at a future date for a price quoted in German currency. The importer can use a forward contract—or a futures contract, if one is available that meets the firm's needs—to fix the dollar cost of converting to German currency at that future date. Thus the importer avoids a loss if the dollar cost of deutsche marks increases between the purchase and delivery dates.
Futures	Organized exchanges primarily for standardized contracts		
Options	OTC and exchanges	Options contracts grant their purchasers the right but not the obligation to buy or sell a specific amount of the underlying at a particular price within a specified period.	A mutual fund buys an option on a given amount of Treasury bills. The fund will benefit if the price of the Treasury bills moves in a favorable direction. If the price moves in an unfavorable direction, the fund will not recover the option's price.
Swaps	OTC	Swaps are agreements between counterparties to make periodic payments to each other for a specified period. In a simple interest rate swap, one party makes payments based on a fixed interest rate, while the counterparty makes payments based on a variable rate. The contractual payments are based on a notional amount that for interest rate swaps is never actually exchanged.	A bank has portfolio of loans whose floating rates must be adjusted frequently because they are tied to changes in market interest rates. The bank also has deposits that pay customers at rates that are adjusted infrequently. This bank has interest rate risk, because a decline in interest rates reduces the interest receipts on its loans but not the interest payments the bank must pay depositors. The bank may enter into an interest rate swap with another financial institution to hedge its interest rate risk.

Source: U.S. General Accounting Office, *Financial Derivatives*, pp. 3-4 (adverse movements in the price of a financial asset or commodity); (3) legal risk (an action by a court or by a regulatory or legislative body that could invalidate a financial contract; and (4) operations risk (inadequate controls, deficient procedures, human error, system failure or fraud). These general types of risks exist for many financial activities, but the specific risks in derivatives activities are relatively difficult to manage, in part, because of the complexity of some of these products and the difficulties in measuring these risks. For example, because derivatives might be used in conjunction with other assets and liabilities, measuring the extent of market risks of derivative products alone is not sufficient to understand firms' total market risk.[10]

The basic problem for Barings was that the senior management thought all the contracts were being bought on behalf of a customer who would pay the bank and thus carry all the risks. In fact, however, almost all the contracts were solely for Barings' proprietary risk and responsibility.

It was the use of such a derivative that led to the Barings situation. Note, however, the previous description of the actual product the trader was using. It was not the product that was the cause, but rather how the trader used it in contravention of his management's policy. "The quality of the risk isn't in the deal" said one top Barings executive later. "It's in the management of the deal."[11]

Operational Risks

At the heart of banking are the multitude of transactions broadly referred to as *bank operations*: passing entries to transfer funds, posting deposits to accounts, making debits in customer or bank accounts, recording transactions to report profits and losses accurately. All of these are done in accordance with the objectives of the bank's management and in compliance with all regulations.

One of the most basic of these in any financial institution is the control of cash. In any bank, the movement of cash is monitored with utmost care. Tellers have to balance each day; cash flow from the vault is usually accomplished with double checks.

This should be equally true at every level of a bank. A British senior corporate executive summed up the problem of cash control from that level: "If you think you make a profit it is reassuring to see it in the form of money [that is, cash in the bank]. When people think they are making a profit but not making money, we have learnt to become suspicious."[12] This would have been even more apparent at Barings since at the same time that huge profits were supposedly being made in Singapore, there was a heavy flow of cash *from* the parent in London to Singapore to cover the margin requirements of the trading.

Banks rely on computer systems to keep track of most operational activities. Another recent case in which the bank ultimately failed showed the difference between "profit" and "cash" as well the need to understand what the computer system is reporting.

"[The firm's] daily P&L-inventory report showed [the trading] department with a three-month year-to-date profit of more than $51 million. . . . An examination of . . . transactions by a special accounting team concluded . . . that the firm really had $350 million of 'unrecognized losses' as the result of . . . trading activities over the past two years."[13]

This loss occurred as a result of the daily trading. "The computer automatically booked the trade, then informed [the trader] whether his purchase or sale had given him a profit or a loss."[13] The problem was that the computer had been misprogrammed to report "profit" instead of "discount" and to calculate that profit as of the date the trade was made rather than when it was settled. This continued for several years. The computer system kept reporting profits, but apparently there was no internal bank procedure to link this with any cash showing up.

Common sense should have made the trader and supervisors sense that something was wrong.

Where could [the trader] have acquired common sense? In the old days traders were not let loose with the firm's money until they had spent some time in the cage, watching operators make deliveries and payments and handling physical bonds, coupons, and money. But today there is no real world; everything is in the computer—instruments, financing, delivery, payment even the P&L. . . . [It] does not provide a cash register with greater or lesser contents at the end of the accounting period. [He] had been trained at the Massachusetts Institute of Technology and at Harvard Business School to accept information from computer screens and to act on it. . . . If the computer got it wrong, he was going to get it wrong . . . [and] see no reasons to ask questions even when the thing got silly.[13]

The postmortem revealed that the levels of supervisors above the trader did not understand how he was making so much profit, but were content to bask in the glory of it.

Contrast this with the system that U.S. commercial banks use for reporting profit on their loans, in which there is recognition that earnings have to be evidenced by the actual receipt of money. Under the accrual system, a bank reports income for each day that a loan is outstanding, not just when it is paid. However, if the interest is not actually paid within 90 days after the due date, then the bank stops accruing interest as income, reverses all uncollected interest from its income statement, and shows income only when the cash is actually received.

Compliance

Banks must comply with their government's laws and banking regulations for their operations in their home country as well as their units in other countries. The global bank must further comply with the laws and regulations of the country in which it has branches or other units. In 1995, a Japanese bank's New York branch discovered a decade-long fraud by a bond trader that had resulted in a loss of over $1 billion. The bank notified the Japanese banking authorities but failed to notify the U.S. regulators as required. The loss, while large, did not jeopardize the solvency of the bank. For failure to comply with U.S. laws and other regulatory infractions, however, the U.S. government ordered the Japanese bank to close all its banking offices in the United States in 90 days. This caused a cascading erosion for the parent bank, causing it to lose major Japanese corporate customers in its home market because those customers had extensive business needs in the U.S. and needed a bank who could meet their worldwide needs.

Personnel Risks

Banking is a business that relies on people. There are very few phases of banking in which there is anything resembling an automated production line. Personnel are the bank's greatest resource as well as the greatest risk to be managed. This begins with the selection of employees who can perform to reach the bank's goals, the compensation to retain those with the best skills, a full training program to build those skills

the bank needs, and an assignment program that matches that training with experience working with those who already are proficient. Much of banking, whether trading, credit, or operations, is learned by one person teaching another person and passing on the knowledge gained from experience. One of the more difficult judgments made by managers at any level is knowing when an employee has enough experience and training at her present job and is ready to be promoted and assume more responsibility.

A single trader in Singapore brought down the Barings bank. He had begun work at Barings in London in mid-1989. In 1992, he was sent to Singapore as a clerk, and by the end of the year, he had become a trader. A year later, he was General Manager of the Barings subsidiary. By 1994, he was hiding trading losses in Account 88888, and in February 1995, the firm collapsed from his losses.

The organization of personnel so that the work can be done is fundamental to the business of banking. This requires supervision through a management structure. At the basic level, every employee must know what his or her job is. In the report on the causes to the Barings collapse, the Bank of England noted one of the lessons for bank management:

> Each individual in the institution should have a job description which clearly identifies his or her responsibilities and to whom and for what he or she is accountable. . . . All institutions should maintain an up-to-date organizational chart which shows clearly all reporting lines and who is accountable to whom and for what. There must be no gaps and no room for any confusion so that the situation of one manager believing another manager has responsibility for an issue, and vice versa, is avoided.[14]

These were problems for Barings. The trader in Singapore reported to three people, each for a different part of his work. One was in Singapore, one in Tokyo, and one in London. Thus none of his supervisors knew everything he was doing. This made it easy for him to hide losses and operate outside of his instructions. The Barings organization was also undergoing constant reorganization, with periods when confusion existed.

Language is a particular problem for global banking. Does the manager in a foreign branch speak the same language, and with the same fluency, as those he is supervising? In the Japanese bank crisis cited above, the manager did not. This meant that the trader, who was fluent in both English and Japanese, was able to conduct telephone trades with other bankers using colloquialisms and slang that the manager could not understand and, therefore, could not monitor.

Banks with global branches customarily rotate officers' assignments to enable them to gain experience. A branch in another country will have a local staff and a few managers from the head office who are rotated regularly to other posts. The local staff knows the banking and general business practices of that country, has background knowledge of local businesses, and has contacts for business development. The manager, transferred from another country, relies on this local knowledge to maintain the unit. While this arrangement has many benefits for the bank and the individual manager, it also has risks. Changing managers every few years weakens the continuity of operational knowledge and makes effective supervision more difficult.

Managing at a Distance

Ensuring that personnel have the ability to make quality decisions based on knowledge, experience, and judgment is a difficult problem even when the entire hierarchy of the bank—from the president to the newest clerk—is in one location. This problem is even more complex when decisions are being made an ocean away from the

head office and senior management. In the era before the computer and the communications satellite, and even before the telegraph, the management of a bank had to know that the person in charge of an overseas branch was able to carry out all the responsibilities of the parent bank. Sending out a member of the owning family or a director to take charge was a common practice. The history of the Rothschild banking family exemplifies that practice—each merchant bank in a different country was headed by a brother. Because of the difficulty of distant control, many banks chose to conduct their international trade financing activities through correspondent banks or by an investment in a foreign bank rather than their own branches. In the late nineteenth century, many of the major British merchant banks chose to do all their activities and make all their lending decisions in London, where they relied on their knowledge of foreign customers and foreign markets rather than working through a foreign branch. This risk remains today, and bank management must avoid succumbing to the illusion that instantaneous communication has preserved control of personnel working at great distances from headquarters.

The Bank of England noted that "neither the top management of Barings nor the relevant members of the derivatives group understood the business that [the trader] was supposed to be undertaking despite large profits and funding requirements. Barings' experience shows it to be absolutely essential that top management understand the broad nature of all the material activities of the institution for which they are responsible." One of the trader's supervisors rather amazingly admitted that "there is no doubt in my mind that my lack of experience in the area was a contributing factor in what has happened here." [15]

The Bank of England's report pointed out that management must visit the bank's foreign units to see what they are doing and talk to the staff, other participants in the market, regulators, and any other sources that can tell them what their unit's reputation is in that market.

There were public reports, such as the weekly report from the Osaka Securities Exchange, showing that Barings' trader had built up a position on his contracts that was eight times greater than that of the next-largest bank and accounted for 20 percent of the total outstanding contracts. There were many rumors and concerns among other market participants—warning signals that could have alerted the senior management well in advance, had they been listening.

Management must have the means to supervise what is happening in its organization. The Barings episode clearly shows that a bank is at risk from activities at any level of its organization. This risk requires that the bank have a rigorous internal audit system. Experienced personnel not in the regular management chain of the organization should be assigned to examine the activities of every unit. The examiners should report directly to the top level of management and the Board of Directors. It is incumbent on those senior managers, then, to pay attention to what is reported. There were many indications that something was amiss at Barings months before the collapse actually happened.

The importance of prompt action in managing risk was painfully revealed after Barings collapsed. At the end of 1994, the cumulative hidden loss built up over several years was about £200 million. "Had the unauthorized positions been discovered at that time, [the situation] might not have brought about the collapse of Barings, although it would have placed Barings in a serious financial position. Over the . . . next two months the losses grew . . . to a final balance of £827 million at February 27. This included a £278 million deterioration [in the last four days]." [16]

Accounting

Most derivatives are reported in the "off-balance sheet" (contingent) section of a bank's financial statements. They are usually shown at the notional amount—that is, the face amount of the contract. This greatly overstates the bank's true exposure to loss since the cost of replacing a contract in the event the counterparty fails to perform is a small fraction (sometimes 1-2 percent) of that notional amount. That exposure may be further reduced if legally enforceable netting agreements exist, which would permit all the offsetting transactions with one party to be calculated at their market value in the event of the bankruptcy of the counterparty.

Summary

Managing risk begins at the top of a bank. Policies must be clearly defined, procedures must be established, supervisors must supervise, products must be understood, and a separate line of audit must be established that reports directly to senior management, who must listen.

After the Bank of England report, the *Financial Times* commented:

> If a business seems too good to be true, it probably is. Two other recent British financial disasters—the collapse of Barlow Clowes and the closure of Bank of Credit and Commerce International— also featured above-market returns with no obvious explanation. For many people, indeed, there is an intriguing element to above-average returns: they feel as if they've found a way to buck the market, and perhaps the rules too. The

The ICE Analysis Formula

Managing risk at any level requires a process for the orderly assessment of the details. One simple formula can be summarized in three steps:

- *Identify* the risk. Exactly what is the one major thing that you must be concerned about?
- *Catalog* all the specific events that could cause that to happen.
- *Evaluate* the likelihood of each of those events happening.

Applying this to a trade finance transaction, for example, a manufacturer in Trinidad receives a first-time order from a buyer in the United States:

- *Identify.* The single overriding concern of the exporter is that she will make the shipment and not be paid on time.
- *Catalogue.* This could happen if:
  — the buyer refuses to pay
  — the buyer goes bankrupt
  — the vessel sinks en route to the U.S.
  — the U.S. government imposes exchange controls that prevent the payment
  - the buyer claims he never got the goods or did not get them in time
- *Evaluate.* Some of these are of more concern than others. The exporter then has to decide about each. How much of a risk is there? The exporter can *accept* the risk, *reject* it, *reduce* it, or *replace* it.

For example, the risk of the United States imposing exchange controls would be so remote in this case that the seller can accept it without any further action. However, the vessel could sink, and the exporter may want to substitute that risk with an insurance policy. Note that the exporter has not eliminated risk; the risk of the vessel's sinking has been replaced with the risk that the insurance company will not be financially able and willing to pay a claim. The risks the seller confronts can be reduced or replaced by selecting the means of payment. Requiring prepayment or a letter of credit would either eliminate any risk (prepayment) or replace it (letter of credit). Both of these options will incur expenses to the buyer, who might not be willing to incur them and place the order with another seller. Using open account or documentary collection would be cheaper for the buyer, but still exposes the seller to risks. Whether the seller will accept those risks could be determined by obtaining information about the buyer's credit and business reputation. If this information is not satisfactory to the seller, she might reject the order because the risks would be greater than the rewards from the sale.

If the transaction concerned a bank financing such a transaction, the bank's ICE assessment would begin with the risk that the bank would not be paid back.

truth is that miracles—and miracle workers—should be regarded with as much suspicion as admiration.[17]

It is interesting to note that, in the Barings collapse and many other recent losses purportedly from types of derivatives, that senior management

did not understand how the trader was making all that profit. Management was reluctant to challenge the source of those profits for fear that the trader would leave and they would lose their bonuses.

The Bank of England summarized its review as follows:

Management and directors of all financial institutions will draw lessons for themselves. However, we would emphasize the following five significant lessons of the Barings case . . .

(a) Management teams have a duty to understand fully the businesses they manage;

(b) Responsibility for each business activity has to be clearly established and communicated;

(c) Clear segregation of duties is fundamental to any effective control system;

(d) Relevant internal controls, including independent risk management, have to be established for all business activities;

(e) Top management and the Audit Committee have to ensure that significant weaknesses, identified to them by internal audit or otherwise, are resolved quickly." [18]

Questions

1. What are the risks involved in a bank having a trading department?

2. What is trading settlement, and why should it be separate from trading?

3. What is a derivative?

4. What are the three steps in the ICE formula for risk management?

Notes

1. Comptroller of the Currency, *Risk Management of Financial Derivatives* (Washington, D.C.: Comptroller of the Currency, October 1994), p. 6

2. John McCormick, *George Santayana* (New York: Alfred A. Knopf, 1987) p. 144 (quoted from *Santayana, Reason in Common Sense,* p. 218

3. The general details of the Barings crisis are derived from the extensive series of articles published in the *Financial Times* from February 27, 1995, until October 18, 1996, and Bank of England, *Report of the Board of Banking Supervision Inquiry into the Circumstances of the Collapse of Barings* (London: HMSO, 1995)

4. "The City's Lost Weekend," *Financial Times*, March 3, 1995, p. 3

5. Comptroller of the Currency, *Risk Management*, p. 20

6. Ibid., p. 10

7. "The City's Lost Weekend," p. 10

8. U.S. General Accounting Office, *Financial Derivatives* (Washington, D.C.: U.S. General Accounting Office, 1994) pp. 3-4

9. David Kynaston, *The City of London Volume I: A World of Its Own 1815-1890* (London: Chatto & Windus, 1994), p. 49; idem, *Volume II: Golden Years 1890-1914*, p. 20

10. General Accounting Office, *Financial Derivatives*, p. 9

11. Richard W. Stevenson, "Breaking the Bank," *New York Times*, March 3, 1995, p. C13

12. Nicholas Denton and John Gapper, "Probing to Find if Incompetence Became a Cover-Up," *Financial Times*, July 7, 1995, p. 10

13. Martin Mayer, "Joe Jett: Did the computer make him do it?" *Institutional Investor*, March 1995, pp. 7-12

14. Bank of England, *Report*, § 14.13

15. Nicholas Denton, "Managers Did Not Understand the Business," *Financial Times*, July 19, 1995, p. 7

16. Bank of England, *Report*, § 14.11

17. Peter Martin, "Triumph of Optimism," *Financial Times*, July 22, 1995

18. Bank of England, *Report*, § 14.2

SUGGESTED READING LIST

Those interested in more information on a particular topic may find it in the various sources cited in the notes at the end of each chapter. The following are other publications that can increase one's knowledge and depth of the world in which international banking takes place.

Baughn, William H., and Donald R. Mandich, eds. *The International Banking Handbook.* Homewood, Ill.: Dow Jones-Irwin, 1983.

Braudel, Fernand. *Civilization and Capitalism, 15th-18th Century.* 3 vols. New York: Harper and Row, 1981. A fascinating and readable economic history in which the reader can see the origin of many activities of international banking. For the specifics of international trade and finance, see Vol. 3, *The Perspective of the World.*

Harfield, Henry. *Bank Credits and Acceptances*, 5th ed. New York: The Ronald Press, 1974. A key book on the legal underpinnings of bankers' acceptances and letters of credit.

International Monetary Fund, Washington, D.C., has published a series of publications offering detailed current data and information on international finance. These include statistical series on *Balance of Payments*, *International Finance*, and *Direction of Trade.*

Kynaston, David, *The City of London.* A projected trilogy covering the history of the London-based banks from 1815 to 1986 (when they dominated international banking). The reader can see the beginning of modern global financial practices that have shaped today's U.S. commercial and investment banking. Two volumes have been published to date: *A World of Its Own 1815-1890*; and *Golden Years 1890-1914.*

Porter, Michael E. *The Competitive Advantage of Nations.* New York: The Free Press, 1990. An original insight into the relationship between successful global industries and their national base. One reviewer's comment: He "has done for international capitalism what Marx did for the class struggle."

Shaterian, William S. *Export-Import Banking.* New York: The Ronald Press, 1956. Although this is an older book, it continues to be a basic guide to letters of credit.

Stigum, Marcia. *The Money Market*, 3d ed. Homewood, Ill.: Business One Irwin, 1990. The latest edition of a series describing the money market instruments used by international bankers. There is simply nothing better nor more readable on this topic.

World Bank, Washington D.C., has published a number of studies on the finance of developing countries. These include an annual *World Development Report* focused on a single topic, an annual *Debt Tables* providing statistics on the external debt of developing countries, and a quarterly *Financial Flows and the Developing Countries*, which emphasizes capital and equity market fundings.

GLOSSARY

These terms are particularly associated with global banking activities. For terms used in banking in general, refer to the American Bankers Association's *Banking Terminology*.

acceptance—A time draft (bill of exchange) on the face of which the drawee has written the word "accepted" and the date it is payable, and that the drawee has signed, thereby acknowledging a commitment to pay at the future date (see **bankers' acceptance, trade acceptance**).

affiliate—A business organization sharing with another organization some aspect of common ownership and control.

agency—A banking office of a foreign bank in the United States that is restricted to accepting deposits in its own name.

American Depository Receipt (ADR)—A certificate representing shares of a foreign stock that is issued by a U.S. depository bank.

arbitrage—A technique for buying and selling of the same currency in different markets to take advantage of price differentials.

authority to purchase—An instrument similar to a letter of credit, except that the draft is drawn on the foreign buyer. Authorities to purchase are used primarily in Asia.

aval—A form of guarantee established by signing on a promissory note, which is acceptable in some countries.

back-to-back letter of credit—A letter of credit with identical documentary requirements and covering the same merchandise as another letter of credit, except for a difference in the price of the merchandise as shown by the invoice and the draft. The second letter of credit can be negotiated only after the first is negotiated.

balance of payments—A statement that shows all of a country's receipts from and payments to foreign countries during a given period of time.

balance of trade—The difference between a nation's merchandise exports and imports over a given period of time.

bankers' acceptance—An acceptance drawn on and accepted by a bank that thereby becomes primarily liable to pay on the maturity date. In the United States, it must cover certain specified underlying transactions in accordance with Federal Reserve requirements to be eligible for discount at a Federal Reserve bank.

barter—The trade of goods without an exchange of money.

beneficiary—The person in whose favor a letter of credit is issued.

bilateral net credit limit—The maximum dollar amount a bank participating in a U.S. payment network (for example, CHIPS) will permit in net transfers during a day (value of receives in excess of value of sends).

bill of exchange—See **draft**.

bill of lading—A document issued by a transportation company that acknowledges the receipt of specified goods for transportation to a certain place, sets forth the contract between the shipper and the carrier, and provides for delivery of the goods.

branch—A separate banking unit that is part of a U.S. or foreign bank.

capital account—1) The net worth, capital investment, or owner's equity of an enterprise. Capital account is the difference between an entity's assets and liabilities. 2) The account used to record the flow of investment (long-term) capital to and from a nation.

capital flight—A transfer of money from one nation to another as a hedge against poor economic or political conditions.

cash letter—The cover letter used by banks in sending checks to a correspondent, sometimes in another country, for clearance.

certificate of analysis—See **inspection certificate**.

certificate of origin—A document that certifies the country of origin of the goods.

CHIPS—Acronym for New York's Clearing House Interbank Payments System, an automated large-item payments system.

clearing agreement—An agreement between two or more countries that the payment of all trade between them will be passed through special accounts in their central banks and will be kept generally in balance.

collateral—Value, such as securities, that is pledged as an alternate source of repayment of a loan.

Collection—The process of presenting a negotiable instrument to the maker for payment.

confirmed letter of credit—A letter of credit issued by the importer's local bank and to which another bank, usually in the country of the exporter, has added its commitment to honor drafts and documents presented in accordance with the terms of the credit.

consignment shipment—A shipment for sale that is available to the importer in his location, at which time payment is made to the exporter.

consular invoice—An invoice for merchandise shipped from one country to another, prepared by the shipper and certified at the shipping point by a consul of the country of destination.

correspondent bank—A bank with which a second bank in another area has an account relationship and that helps the second bank to conduct business.

cost and freight (C&F)—A shipping term under which the seller quotes a price, including the cost of transportation to the named point of destination.

cost, insurance, and freight (CIF)—A shipping term under which the seller quotes a price including the cost of the goods, insurance, and all transportation charges to the named point of destination.

counterparty—The entity with which a trade, such as for foreign exchange, has been made.

countertrade—A term for barter between countries.

country risk—The risk that borrowers within a country will not be able to repay their obligations to foreign creditors because of political or general economic factors, such as lack of foreign exchange, prevailing in their country.

cross-rate—The exchange rate between each pair of three or more currencies.

current account—The value of all invisible and visible trade between nations (goods, services, income, and unilateral transfers).

customs invoice—A document that contains a declaration by the seller, the shipper, or the agent of either as to the value of the goods covered.

deferred payment letter of credit—A letter of credit under which the seller agrees to full or partial payment over six months or more after shipment.

derivative—Financial contract whose value is based on some underlying asset value, such as reference interest rate, commodities, foreign exchange rates, or stock index.

developing country—An ill-defined term that identifies those countries that have not attained a high degree of industrialization, sometimes referred to as less-developed countries (LDC) or the Third World.

direct investments—Investments in foreign corporations where the investors have a controlling interest in the overseas firm.

documents—Items presented along with the draft under a letter of credit. These may include the bill of lading, invoice, customs invoice, marine insurance policy or certificate, certificate of origin, weight list, packing list, and inspection certificate (or certificate of analysis).

documents against acceptance (D/A) draft—A time draft to which title documents are attached. The documents are surrendered to the drawee when the drawee has accepted the corresponding draft, acknowledging the obligation to pay at the future date.

documents against payment (D/P) draft—A sight draft to which title documents are attached. The documents are surrendered to the drawee only when the drawee has paid the corresponding draft.

draft—A signed order by one party, the drawer, addressed to another, the drawee, directing the drawee to pay a specified sum of money to the order of a third person, the payee.

drawback—Rebate of U.S. customs duty for imported goods that are subsequently exported.

dual currency account—An account kept by a bank with a bank in a foreign country in the foreign currency (Due From account).

Due From account—A deposit account maintained in another bank.

Due To account—A deposit account maintained by another bank.

Edge Act corporation—A national chartered U.S. corporation established under section 25(a) of the Federal Reserve Act to engage in international banking and investment.

emerging markets—Stock and bond market exchanges in developing countries.

Euro—1) Informal name for Eurodollars. 2) Name agreed upon by European Union governments for common currency to replace national currencies under terms of the Maastricht treaty.

Eurodollars—U.S. dollars deposited in a banking office outside the United States.

Exchange Rate Mechanism (ERM)—An agreement between member countries of the European Union to stabilize the value of their currencies with each other by central bank interventions or interest rate adjustments.

export trading company (ETC)—A company established under the Export Trading Company Act of 1982, which permits banks to function as agents in international trade.

exports—Goods and services that a nation sells abroad.

Fedwire—Automated system for effecting payments between banks through their accounts at a Federal Reserve bank.

floating rate—The absence of fixed rates of exchange. Each currency rate is determined by supply and demand.

foreign currency—The money of another country.

foreign draft—A draft drawn by a bank on a foreign correspondent bank.

foreign drawings and remittance service—A service through which major banks make their Due From accounts available to their correspondents for use in arranging money transfers overseas.

foreign exchange—1) The money of another country. 2) The process of converting the currency of one country to that of another country.

foreign exchange rate—The price relationship between the currencies of two countries.

foreign exchange trading—The buying and selling of the currency of one country for that of another.

foreign trade—The exchange of goods between nations.

forward delivery—Contracting for the transfer of foreign exchange at a specified future date.

free alongside (FAS)—A shipping term under which the seller quotes a price including delivery of the goods alongside the ocean vessel and within reach of its loading tackle.

free on board (FOB)—A shipping term under which the price quoted applies only at shipping point, and the seller is responsible for all charges only until the merchandise is loaded on the vessel.

general average—A marine insurance concept whereby all the shippers on a given voyage reimburse those shippers whose cargo was jettisoned in bad weather—for example, to save the ship.

Giro—An automated payment system between banks and post offices, used primarily in Europe.

Global Depository Receipt (GDR)—Similar to an American Depository Receipt, except that it is issued and traded on international exchanges (see **American Depository Receipt**).

gross national product (GNP)—The total value of the goods and services produced in a nation during a specific period, also comprising the total of expenditures by consumers and government plus gross private investment plus exports minus imports.

guarantee—A written promise by one party to be liable for the debt of another party.

guarantor—One who extends a guarantee.

hedging—The purchase or sale of foreign exchange, usually on a forward basis, to avoid any loss in the event of a change in the foreign exchange rate.

imports—Goods and services that a nation buys from abroad.

incoterms—Commonly accepted definition for trade price items.

inspection certificate—A certificate issued by an independent third party when outside examination is called for in the merchandise contract in international trade.

interest rate arbitrage—The movement of funds from one money market to another through the foreign exchange market to obtain a higher rate of interest.

international banking facility—A separate set of asset and liability books established within a banking office in the United States that domiciles Eurodollar loans and deposits.

investments—The flow of funds, usually for a long term, to build or acquire assets.

invisible trade—The foreign trade of services, such as travel and transportation, and interest from investments abroad.

invoice—A statement prepared by the seller, addressed to the buyer, showing the details of the sale.

letter of credit—An instrument issued by a bank to a seller by which the bank substitutes its own credit for that of the buyer.

LIBID—Acronym for London Interbank Bid rate for Eurodollar time deposits of a given tenor (see **tenor**).

LIBOR—Acronym for London Interbank Offered Rate, which is the interest rate a bank agrees to pay on a Eurodollar deposit to another bank.

LIMEAN—Acronym for the average of LIBOR and LIBID of a given tenor.

Maastricht—A city in The Netherlands; the name is used as a synonym for the agreement—

signed there by the leaders of the European Community in December 1991—establishing a timetable to create a common currency by 1999.

market risk—The possibility of a change in the price of a specific traded security or other asset.

merchant bank—The European form of an investment bank.

most favored nation—A convention in foreign trade treaties that a designated nation will not be charged a tariff rate any higher than the most preferential rate the granting nation gives to anyone else.

negotiation credit—A letter of credit that expires at the location of the exporter, thereby permitting drafts to be negotiated through any bank.

netting by novation—Trading contracts, such as in foreign exchange, by which agreement may be amalgamated with all other contracts with the same customer of same value, date, and currency and legally substitute a single net amount for the previous gross obligations.

North American Free Trade Agreement (NAFTA)—Treaties negotiated between the United States, Canada, and Mexico to eliminate tariffs, quotas, and other barriers to imports and exports among the three countries.

nostro account—An old term from Italian meaning "our account with you" (see **Due From account**).

option—The right, but not the obligation, to buy or sell a security, foreign exchange, or commodity at a specified price (exercise or strike price) during a specified period.

option contract—A foreign exchange contract that matures not on a stated date but on any date between two specified dates at the option of the one party.

par value—The basic value of a country's currency, declared by that country in accordance with the requirements of the IMF.

para-statal—A government-owned corporation.

position—A bank's net balance of purchases and sales in a foreign currency at the end of a business day.

premium—The fee paid for an option in advance, which is nonrefundable.

prime rate—A bank's base lending rate of interest.

promissory note—A written promise that commits the signer to repay a certain sum to the payee at a fixed future date, usually with interest.

protest—The legal process of demanding payment of a negotiable item from the maker or drawee who has refused to pay.

quota—A restriction on the quantity of an import.

red clause letter of credit—A letter of credit that provides for payments before the presentation of documents.

reserves—1) Profits of a business that have been set aside for a specific purpose, for example, reserves for depreciation, bad debts, and contingencies. 2) Cash on hand or deposited with the Federal Reserve, used by depository institutions to meet legal reserve requirements. 3) A nation's holding of gold, special drawing rights (SDRs), convertible currencies, and other foreign assets.

revocable letter of credit—A letter of credit that may be withdrawn from the beneficiary at any time without prior notice to the beneficiary.

revolving letter of credit—A letter of credit that provides for renewed credit to become available as soon as the opening bank has advised the negotiating or paying bank that the drafts already drawn by the beneficiary have been reimbursed to the opening bank by the buyer.

sender net debit cap—The maximum dollar amount a bank participating in a U.S. payment network (for example, CHIPS) will permit in daylight overdraft (the value of all sends in excess of the value of all receives).

settlement—1) A transfer of funds to complete a transaction. 2) The conclusion of a transaction: completing all necessary documentation, making the necessary payments, and, where appropriate, transferring title.

sight draft—A draft payable upon presentation to the drawee on sight or on demand.

signature book—A book containing facsimiles of the signatures of the authorized bank officers who may commit that bank.

sovereign risk—The risk that a foreign government (as distinct from a business in that country) may default on its borrowings (see **country risk**).

special drawing rights (SDRs)—An international reserve asset created by the IMF, the value of which is based on a basket of currencies.

spot delivery—The transfer of foreign exchange within two business days.

spread—The difference between the buying rate and the selling rate of a foreign currency.

standby letter of credit—A letter of credit that can be drawn against only if another business transaction is not performed.

straight credit—A letter of credit instrument under which the beneficiary is paid by a bank in the beneficiary's area that has been designated by the bank opening the credit.

subsidiary—A company owned by another company, either wholly or by holding a majority of the stock.

swap—1) The purchase or sale of foreign exchange for delivery on one date, with the offsetting simultaneous sale or purchase of the equivalent exchange for delivery on another date. 2) An agreement between two parties exchanging the obligation to pay interest on each other's debt.

S.W.I.F.T.—Acronym for the Society for Worldwide Interbank Financial Telecommunications, a cooperative for a standardized, automated international funds transfer information system between banks.

tariff—A customs tax on goods being imported.

tenor—The time between the date of issue or acceptance of a note or draft and the maturity date.

test key—A code established between banks for authenticating telecommunication messages, usually for the transfer of funds.

time draft—A draft payable at a fixed or determinable future time.

trade acceptance—A draft drawn by the seller of goods on the buyer and accepted by the buyer for payment at a specified future date.

transferable letter of credit—A letter of credit that enables the beneficiary to transfer the credit to another party, thereby authorizing the other party to present documents and a draft.

traveler's check—A special check supplied by banks and other companies to enable travelers to carry money without fear of loss or theft.

traveler's letter of credit—A letter of credit addressed by a bank to its correspondent banks, authorizing the person named in the letter to draw drafts on the correspondent banks to the extent of the credit specified.

trust receipt—An agreement between a bank and a borrower in which the bank releases documents, merchandise, or other property without releasing its title to the property.

value date—The date when a sum of money is transferred.

visible trade—Merchandise exports and imports.

vostro account—An old term, from Italian, used by foreign banks, meaning "your account with us" (see **Due To account**).

weight list—A list that itemizes the weights of individual parcels or bales. In the case of bulk commodities, it covers an entire cargo.

APPENDIX A

Incoterms 1990
ICC Publication No. 460
[extracts]

ICC No. 460, *Incoterms 1990*, Copyright © 1990 by ICC Publishing S.A. All rights reserved. Reprinted with permission of The International Chamber of Commerce through ICC Publishing Inc., in New York.

EX WORKS (...named place)

"Ex works" means that the seller fulfils his obligation to deliver when he has made the goods available at his premises (i.e. works, factory, warehouse, etc.) to the buyer. In particular, he is not responsible for loading the goods on the vehicle provided by the buyer or for clearing the goods for export, unless otherwise agreed. The buyer bears all costs and risks involved in taking the goods from the seller's premises to the desired destination. This term thus represents the minimum obligation for the seller. This term should not be used when the buyer cannot carry out directly or indirectly the export formalities. In such circumstances, the FCA term should be used.

FREE CARRIER (... named place)

"Free Carrier" means that the seller fulfils his obligation to deliver when he has handed over the goods, cleared for export, into the charge of the carrier named by the buyer at the named place or point. If no precise point is indicated by the buyer, the seller may choose within the place or range stipulated where the carrier shall take the goods into his charge. When, according to commercial practice, the seller's assistance is required in making the contract with the carrier (such as in rail or air transport) the seller may act at the buyer's risk and expense.

This term may be used for any mode of transport, including multimodal transport.

"Carrier" means any person who, in a contract of carriage, undertakes to perform or to procure the performance of carriage by rail, road, sea, air, inland waterway or by a combination of such modes. If the buyer instructs the seller to deliver the cargo to a person, e.g. a freight forwarder who is not a "carrier", the seller is deemed to have fulfilled his obligation to deliver the goods when they are in the custody of that person.

"Transport terminal" means a railway terminal, a freight station, a container terminal or yard, a multi-purpose cargo terminal or any similar receiving point.

"Container" includes any equipment used to unitise cargo, e.g. all types of containers and/or flats, whether ISO accepted or not, trailers, swap bodies, ro-ro equipment, igloos, and applies to all modes of transport.

FREE ALONGSIDE SHIP (... named port of shipment)

"Free Alongside Ship" means that the seller fulfils his obligation to deliver when the goods have been placed alongside the vessel on the quay or in lighters at the named port of shipment. This means that the buyer has to bear all costs and risks of loss of or damage to the goods from that moment.

The FAS term requires the buyer to clear the goods for export. It should not be used when the buyer cannot carry out directly or indirectly the export formalities.

This term can only be used for sea or inland waterway transport.

FREE ON BOARD (... named port of shipment)

"Free on Board" means that the seller fulfils his obligation to deliver when the goods have passed over the ship's rail at the named port of shipment. This means that the buyer has to bear all costs and risks of loss of or damage to the goods from that point.

The FOB term requires the seller to clear the goods for export.

This term can only be used for sea or inland waterway transport. When the ship's rail serves no practical purpose, such as in the case of roll-on/roll-off or container traffic, the FCA term is more appropriate to use.

COST AND FREIGHT (... named port of destination)

"Cost and Freight" means that the seller must pay the costs and freight necessary to bring the goods to the named port of destination but the risk of loss of or damage to the goods, as well as any additional costs due to events occurring after the time the goods have been delivered on board the vessel, is transferred from the seller to the buyer when the goods pass the ship's rail in the port of shipment.

The CFR term requires the seller to clear the goods for export.

This term can only be used for sea and inland waterway transport. When the ship's rail serves no practical purpose, such as in the case of roll-on/roll-off or container traffic, the CPT term is more appropriate to use.

COST, INSURANCE AND FREIGHT (... named port of destination)

"Cost, Insurance and Freight" means that the seller has the same obligations as under CFR but with the addition that he has to procure marine insurance against the buyer's risk of loss of or damage to the goods during the carriage. The seller contracts for insurance and pays the insurance premium.

The buyer should note that under the CIF term the seller is only required to obtain insurance on minimum coverage.

The CIF term requires the seller to clear the goods for export.

This term can only be used for sea and inland waterway transport. When the ship's rail serves no practical purposes such as in the case of roll-on/roll-off or container traffic, the CIP term is more appropriate to use.

CARRIAGE PAID TO (... named place of destination)

"Carriage paid to. . ." means that the seller pays the freight for the carriage of the goods to the named destination. The risk of loss of or damage to the goods, as well as any additional costs due to events occurring after the time the goods have been delivered to the carrier, is transferred from the seller to the buyer when the goods have been delivered into the custody of the carrier.

"Carrier" means any person who, in a contract of carriage, undertakes to perform or to procure the performance of carriage, by rail, road, sea, air, inland waterway or by a combination of such modes.

If subsequent carriers are used for the carriage to the agreed destination, the risk passes when the goods have been delivered to the first carrier.

The CPT term requires the seller to clear the goods for export.

This term may be used for any mode of transport including multimodal transport.

CARRIAGE AND INSURANCE PAID TO (... named place of destination)

"Carriage and insurance paid to. . ." means that the seller has the same obligations as under CPT but with the addition that the seller has to procure cargo insurance against the buyer's risk of loss of or damage to the goods during the carriage. The seller contracts for insurance and pays the insurance premium.

The buyer should note that under the CIP term the seller is only required to obtain insurance on minimum coverage. The CIP term requires the seller to clear the goods for export. This term may be used for any mode of transport including multimodal transport.

DELIVERED AT FRONTIER (... named place)

"Delivered at Frontier" means that the seller fulfils his obligation to deliver when the goods have been made available, cleared for export, at the named point and place at the frontier, but before the customs border of the adjoining country. The term "frontier" may be used for any frontier including that of the country of export. Therefore, it is of vital importance that the frontier in question be defined precisely by always naming the point and place in the term. The term is primarily intended to be used when goods are to be carried by rail or road, but it may be used for any mode of transport.

DELIVERED EX SHIP (... named port of destination)

"Delivered Ex Ship" means that the seller fulfils his obligation to deliver when the goods have been made available to the buyer on board the ship uncleared for import at the named port of destination. The seller has to bear all the costs and risks involved in bringing the goods to the named port of destination.

This term can only be used for sea or inland waterway transport.

DELIVERED EX QUAY (DUTY PAID) (... named port of destination)

"Delivered Ex Quay (duty paid)" means that the seller fulfils his obligation to deliver when he has made the goods available to the buyer on the quay (wharf) at the named port of destination, cleared for importation. The seller has to bear all risks and costs including duties, taxes and other charges of delivering the goods thereto.

This term should not be used if the seller is unable directly or indirectly to obtain the import licence.

If the parties wish the buyer to clear the goods for importation and pay the duty the words "duty unpaid" should be used instead of "duty paid."

If the parties wish to exclude from the seller's obligations some of the costs payable upon importation of the goods (such as value added tax (VAT)), this should be made clear by adding words to this effect: "Delivered ex quay, VAT unpaid (. . . named port of destination)."

This term can only be used for sea or inland waterway transport.

DELIVERED DUTY UNPAID (... named place of destination)

"Delivered duty unpaid" means that the seller fulfils his obligation to deliver when the goods have been made available at the named place in the country of importation. The seller has to bear the costs and risks involved in bringing the goods thereto (excluding duties, taxes and other official charges payable upon importation as well as the costs and risks of carrying out customs formalities). The buyer has to pay any additional costs and to bear any risks caused by his failure to clear the goods for import in time. If the parties wish the seller to carry out customs formalities and bear the costs and risks resulting therefrom, this has to be made clear by adding words to this effect.

If the parties wish to include in the seller's obligations some of the costs payable upon importation of the goods (such as value added tax (VAT)), this should be made clear by adding words to this effect: "Delivered duty unpaid, VAT paid, (. . . named place of destination)."

This term may be used irrespective of the mode of transport.

DELIVERED DUTY PAID (... named place of destination)

"Delivered duty paid" means that the seller fulfils his obligation to deliver when the goods have been made available at the named place in the country of importation. The seller has to bear the risks and costs, including duties, taxes and other charges of delivering the goods thereto, cleared for importation. Whilst the EXW term represents the minimum obligation for the seller, DDP represents the maximum obligation.

This term should not be used if the seller is unable directly or indirectly to obtain the import licence.

If the parties wish the buyer to clear the goods for importation and to pay the duty, the term DDU should be used.

If the parties wish to exclude from the seller's obligations some of the costs payable upon importation of the goods (such as value added tax (VAT)), this should be made clear by adding words to this effect: "Delivered duty paid, VAT unpaid (. . . named place of destination)."

This term may be used irrespective of the mode of transport.

APPENDIX B

ICC Uniform Rules for Collections
ICC Publication No. 522
Effective January 1, 1996

A. General Provisions and Definitions

Article 1

Application of URC 522

a   The Uniform Rules for Collections, 1995 Revision, ICC Publication No. 522, shall apply to all collections as defined in Article 2 where such rules are incorporated into the text of the "collection instruction" referred to in Article 4 and are binding on all parties thereto unless otherwise expressly agreed or contrary to the provisions of a national, state or local law and/or regulation which cannot be departed from.

b   Banks shall have no obligation to handle either a collection or any collection instruction or subsequent related instructions.

c   If a bank elects, for any reason, not to handle a collection or any related instructions received by it, it must advise the party from whom it received the collection or the instructions by telecommunication or, if that is not possible, by other expeditious means, without delay.

Article 2

Definition of Collection

For the purposes of these Articles:

a   "Collection" means the handling by banks of documents as defined in sub-Article 2(b), in accordance with instructions received, in order to:

     i.   obtain payment and/or acceptance,

         or

     ii.   deliver documents against payment and/or against acceptance,

         or

     iii.   deliver documents on other terms and conditions.

b   "Documents" means financial documents and/or commercial documents:

     i.   "Financial documents" means bills of exchange, promissory notes, cheques, or other similar instruments used for obtaining the payment of money;

     ii.   "Commercial documents" means invoices, transport documents, documents of title or other similar documents, or any other documents whatsoever, not being financial documents.

c   "Clean collection" means collection of financial documents not accompanied by commercial documents.

d   "Documentary collection" means collection of:

     i.   Financial documents accompanied by commercial documents;

     ii.   Commercial documents not accompanied by financial documents.

Article 3

Parties to a Collection

a   For the purposes of these Articles the "parties thereto" are:

     i.   the "principal" who is the party entrusting the handling of a collection to a bank;

     ii.   the "remitting bank" which is the bank to which the principal has entrusted the handling of a collection;

     iii.   the "collecting bank" which is any bank, other than the remitting bank, involved in processing the collection;

     iv.   the "presenting bank" which is the collecting bank making presentation to the drawee.

b   The "drawee" is the one to whom presentation is to be made in accordance with the collection instruction.

B.   Form and Structure of Collections

Article 4

Collection Instruction

a   i.   All documents sent for collection must be accompanied by a collection instruction indicating that the collection is subject to URC 522 and giving complete and precise instructions. Banks are only permitted to act upon the instructions given in such collection instruction, and in accordance with these Rules.

ii.   Banks will not examine documents in order to obtain instructions.

iii.   Unless otherwise authorized in the collection instruction, banks will disregard any instructions from any party/bank other than the party/bank from whom they received the collection.

b   A collection instruction should contain the following items of information, as appropriate.

i.   Details of the bank from which the collection was received including full name, postal and SWIFT addresses, telex, telephone, facsimile numbers and reference.

ii.   Details of the principal including full name, postal address, and if applicable telex, telephone and facsimile numbers.

iii.   Details of the drawee including full name, postal address, or the domicile at which presentation is to be made and if applicable telex, telephone and facsimile numbers.

iv.   Details of the presenting bank, if any, including full name, postal address, and if applicable telex, telephone and facsimile numbers.

v.   Amount(s) and currency(ies) to be collected.

vi.   List of documents enclosed and the numerical count of each document.

vii.   a.   Terms and conditions upon which payment and/or acceptance is to be obtained.

b.   Terms of delivery of documents against:

1)   payment and/or acceptance

2)   other terms and conditions

It is the responsibility of the party preparing the collection instruction to ensure that the terms for the delivery of documents are clearly and unambiguously stated, otherwise banks will not be responsible for any consequences arising therefrom.

viii.   Charges to be collected, indicating whether they may be waived or not.

ix.   Interest to be collected, if applicable, indicating whether it may be waived or not, including:

a.   rate of interest

b.   interest period

c.   basis of calculation (for example 360 or 365 days in a year) as applicable.

x.   Method of payment and form of payment advice.

xi.   Instructions in case of non-payment, non-acceptance and/or non-compliance with other instructions.

c   i.   Collection instructions should bear the complete address of the drawee or of the domicile at which the presentation is to be made. If the address is incomplete or incorrect, the collecting bank may, without any liability and responsibility on its part, endeavor to ascertain the proper address.

ii.   The collecting bank will not be liable or responsible for any ensuing delay as a result of an incomplete/incorrect address being provided.

C.   Form of Presentation

Article 5

Presentation

a   For the purposes of these Articles, presentation is the procedure whereby the presenting bank makes the documents available to the drawee as instructed.

b   The collection instruction should state the exact period of time within which any action is to be taken by the drawee.

Expressions such as "first", "prompt" "immediate", and the like should not be used in connection with presentation or with reference to any period of time within which documents have to be taken up or for any other action that is to be taken by the drawee. If such terms are used banks will disregard them.

c   Documents are to be presented to the drawee in the form in which they are received, except that banks are authorized to affix any necessary stamps, at the expense of the party from whom they received the collection unless otherwise instructed, and to make any necessary endorsements or place any rubber stamps or other identifying marks or symbols customary to or required for the collection operation.

d   For the purpose of giving effect to the instructions of the principal, the remitting bank will utilize the bank nominated by the principal as the collecting bank. In the absence of such nomination, the remitting bank will utilize any bank of its own, or another bank's choice in the country of payment or acceptance or in the country where other terms and conditions have to be complied with.

e   The documents and collection instruction may be sent direct by the remitting bank to the collecting bank or through another bank as intermediary.

f   If the remitting bank does not nominate a specific presenting bank, the collecting bank may utilize a presenting bank of its choice.

Article 6

Sight/Acceptance

In the case of documents payable at sight the presenting bank must make presentation for payment without delay. In the case of documents payable at a tenor other than sight the presenting bank must, where acceptance is called for, make presentation for acceptance without delay, and where payment is called for, make presentation for payment not later than the appropriate maturity date.

Article 7

Release of Commercial Documents

Documents Against Acceptance (D/A) vs.
Documents Against Payment (D/P)

a   Collections should not contain bills of exchange payable at a future date with instructions that commercial documents are to be delivered against payment.

b   If a collection contains a bill of exchange payable at a future date, the collection instruction should state whether the commercial documents are to be released to the drawee against acceptance (D/A) or against payment (D/P).

        In the absence of such statement commercial documents will be released only against payment and the collecting bank will not be responsible for any consequences arising out of any delay in the delivery of documents.

c   If a collection contains a bill of exchange payable at a future date and the collection instruction indicates that commercial documents are to be released against payment, documents will be released only against such payment and the collecting bank will not be responsible for any consequences arising out of any delay in the delivery of documents.

Article 8

Creation of Documents

Where the remitting bank instructs that either the collecting bank or the drawee is to create documents (bills of exchange, promissory notes, trust receipts, letters of undertaking or other documents) that were not included in the collection, the form and wording of such documents shall be provided by the remitting bank, otherwise the collecting bank shall not be liable or responsible for the form and wording of any such document provided by the collecting bank and/or the drawee.

D. Liabilities and Responsibilities

Article 9

Good Faith and Reasonable Care

Banks will act in good faith and exercise reasonable care.

Article 10

Documents vs. Goods/Services/Performances

a   Goods should not be despatched directly to the address of a bank or consigned to or to the order of a bank without prior agreement on the part of that bank.

Nevertheless, in the event that goods are despatched directly to the address of a bank or consigned to or to the order of a bank for release to a drawee against payment or acceptance or upon other terms and conditions without prior agreement on the part of that bank, such bank shall have no obligation to take delivery of the goods, which remain at the risk and responsibility of the party despatching the goods.

b   Banks have no obligation to take any action in respect of the goods to which a documentary collection relates, including storage and insurance of the goods even when specific instructions are given to do so. Banks will only take such action if, when, and to the extent that they agree to do so in each case, Notwithstanding the provisions of sub-Article 1(c), this rule applies even in the absence of any specific advice to this effect by the collecting bank.

c   Nevertheless, in the case that banks take action for the protection of the goods, whether instructed or not, they assume no liability or responsibility with regard to the fate and/or condition of the goods and/or for any acts and/or omissions on the part of any third parties entrusted with the custody and/or protection of the goods. However, the collecting bank must advise without delay the bank from which the collection instruction was received of any such action taken.

d   Any charges and/or expenses incurred by banks in connection with any action taken to protect the goods will be for the account of the party from whom they received the collection.

e   i.   Notwithstanding the provisions of sub-Article 10(a), where the goods are consigned to or to the order of the collecting bank and the drawee has honored the collection by payment, acceptance or other terms and conditions, and the collecting bank arranges for the release of the goods, the remitting bank shall be deemed to have authorized the collecting bank to do so.

       ii.   Where a collecting bank on the instructions of the remitting bank or in terms of sub-Article 10(e)i, arranges for the release of the goods, the remitting bank shall indemnify such collecting bank for all damages and expenses incurred.

Article 11

Disclaimer For Acts of an Instructed Party

a   Banks utilizing the services of another bank or other banks for the purpose of giving effect to the instructions of the principal, do so for the account and at the risk of such principal.

b   Banks assume no liability or responsibility should the instructions they transmit not be carried out, even if they have themselves taken the initiative in the choice of such other bank(s).

c   A party instructing another party to perform services shall be bound by and liable to indemnify the instructed party against all obligations and responsibilities imposed by foreign laws and usages.

Article 12

___

Disclaimer on Documents Received

a   Banks must determine that the documents received appear to be as listed in the collection instruction and must advise by telecommunication or, if that is not possible, by other expeditious means, without delay, the party from whom the collection instruction was received of any documents missing, or found to be other than listed.

Banks have no further obligation in this respect.

b   If the documents do not appear to be listed, the remitting bank shall be precluded from disputing the type and number of documents received by the collecting bank.

c   Subject to sub-Article 5(c) and sub-Articles 12(a) and 12(b) above, banks will present documents as received without further examination.

Article 13

___

Disclaimer on Effectiveness of Documents

Banks assume no liability or responsibility for the form, sufficiency, accuracy, genuineness, falsification or legal effect of any document(s), or for the general and/or particular conditions stipulated in the document(s) or superimposed thereon, nor do they assume any liability or responsibility for the description, quantity, weight, ability, condition, packing, delivery, value or existence of the goods represented by any document(s), or for the good faith or acts and/or omissions, solvency, performance or standing of the consignors, the carriers, the forwarders, the consignees or the insurers of the goods, or any other person whomsoever.

Article 14

___

Disclaimer on Delays, Loss in Transit and Translation

a   Banks assume no liability or responsibility for the consequences arising out of delay and/or loss in transit of any message(s), letter(s) or document(s), or for delay, mutilation or other error(s) arising in transmission of any telecommunication or for error(s) in translation and/or interpretation of technical terms.

b   Banks will not be liable or responsible for any delays resulting from the need to obtain clarification of any instructions received.

Article 15

Force Majeure

Banks assume no liability or responsibility for consequences arising out of the interruption of their business by Acts of God, riots, civil commotions, insurrections, wars, or any other causes beyond their control or by strikes or lockouts.

E.   Payment

Article 16

Payment Without Delay

a   Amounts collected (less charges and/or disbursements and/or expenses where applicable) must be made available without delay to the party from whom the collection instruction was received in accordance with the terms and conditions of the collection instruction.

b   Notwithstanding the provisions of sub-Article 1(c) and unless otherwise agreed, the collecting bank will effect payment of the amount collected in favor of the remitting bank only.

Article 17

Payment in Local Currency

In the case of documents payable in the currency of the country of payment (local currency), the presenting bank must, unless otherwise instructed in the collection instruction, release the documents to the drawee against payment in local currency only if such currency is immediately available for disposal in the manner specified in the collection instruction.

Article 18

_____

Payment In Foreign Currency

In the case of documents payable in a currency other than that of the country of payment (foreign currency), the presenting bank must, unless otherwise instructed in the collection instruction, release the documents to the drawee against payment in the designated foreign currency only if such foreign currency can immediately be remitted in accordance with the instructions given in the collection instruction.

Article 19

_____

Partial Payments

a   In respect of clean collections, partial payments may be accepted if and to the extent to which and on the conditions on which partial payments are authorized by the law in force in the place of payment. The financial document(s) will be released to the drawee only when full payment thereof has been received.

b   In respect of documentary collections, partial payments will only be accepted if specifically authorized in the collection instruction. However, unless otherwise instructed, the presenting bank will release the documents to the drawee only after full payment has been received, and the presenting bank will not be responsible for any consequences arising out of any delay in the delivery of documents.

c   In all cases partial payments will be accepted only subject to compliance with the provisions of either Article 17 or Article 18 as appropriate.

Partial payment, if accepted, will be dealt with in accordance with the provisions of Article 16.

F.   Interest, Charges and Expenses

Article 20

Interest

a If the collection instruction specifies that interest is to be collected and the drawee refuses to pay such interest, the presenting bank may deliver the document(s) against payment or acceptance or on other terms and conditions as the case may be, without collecting such interest, unless sub-Article 20(c) applies.

b Where such interest is to be collected, the collection instruction must specify the rate of interest, interest period and basis of calculation.

c Where the collection instruction expressly states that interest may not be waived and the drawee refuses to pay such interest the presenting bank will not deliver documents and will not be responsible for any consequences arising out of any delay in the delivery of document(s). When payment of interest has been refused, the presenting bank must inform by telecommunication or, if that is not possible, by other expeditious means without delay the bank from which the collection instruction was received.

Article 21

Charges and Expenses

a If the collection instruction specifies that collection charges and/or expenses are to be for account of the drawee and the drawee refuses to pay them, the presenting bank may deliver the document(s) against payment or acceptance or on other terms and conditions as the case may be, without collecting charges and/or expenses, unless sub-Article 21(b) applies.

Whenever collection charges and/or expenses are so waived they will be for the account of the party from whom the collection was received and may be deducted from the proceeds.

b Where the collection instruction expressly states that charges and/or expenses may not be waived and the drawee refuses to pay such charges and/or expenses, the presenting bank will not deliver documents and will not be responsible for any consequences arising out of any delay in the delivery of the document(s). When payment of collection charges and/or expenses has been refused the presenting bank must inform by telecommunication or, if that is not possible, by other expeditious means without delay the bank from which the collection instruction was received.

c   In all cases where in the express terms of a collection instruction or under these Rules, disbursements and/or expenses and/or collection charges are to be borne by the principal, the collecting bank(s) shall be entitled to recover promptly outlays in respect of disbursements, expenses and charges from the bank from which the collection instruction was received, and the remitting bank shall be entitled to recover promptly from the principal any amount so paid out by it, together with its own disbursements, expenses and charges, regardless of the fate of the collection.

d   Banks reserve the right to demand payment of charges and/or expenses in advance from the party from whom the collection instruction was received, to cover costs in attempting to carry out any instructions, and pending receipt of such payment also reserve the right not to carry out such instructions.

G.   Other Provisions

Article 22

Acceptance

The presenting bank is responsible for seeing that the form of the acceptance of a bill of exchange appears to be complete and correct, but is not responsible for the genuineness of any signature or for the authority of any signatory to sign the acceptance.

Article 23

Promissory Notes and Other Instruments

The presenting bank is not responsible for the genuineness of any signature or for the authority of any signatory to sign a promissory note, receipt, or other instruments.

Article 24

Protest

The collection instruction should give specific instructions regarding protest (or other legal process in lieu thereof), in the event of non-payment or non-acceptance.

In the absence of such specific instructions, the banks concerned with the collection have no obligation to have the document(s) protested (or subjected to other legal process in lieu thereof) for non-payment or nonacceptance.

Any charges and/or expenses incurred by banks in connection with such protest, or other legal process, will be for the account of the party from whom the collection instruction was received.

Article 25

Case-of-Need

If the principal nominates a representative to act as case-of-need in the event of non-payment and/or nonacceptance the collection instruction should clearly and fully indicate the powers of such case-of-need. In the absence of such indication banks will not accept any instructions from the case-of-need.

Article 26

Advices

Collecting banks are to advise fate in accordance with the following rules:

a **Form of Advice**
   All advices or information from the collecting bank to the bank from which the collection instruction was received, must bear appropriate details including, in all cases, the latter bank's reference as stated in the collection instruction.

b **Method of Advice**
   It shall be the responsibility of the remitting bank to instruct the collecting bank regarding the method by which the advices detailed in (c)i, (c)ii and (c)iii are to be given. In the absence of such instructions, the collecting bank will send the relative advices by the method of its choice at the expense of the bank from which the collection instruction was received.

c   i.   ADVICE OF PAYMENT

The collecting bank must send without delay advice of payment to the bank from which the collection instruction was received, detailing the amount or amounts collected, charges and/ or disbursements and/or expenses deducted, where appropriate, and method of disposal of the funds.

ii.   ADVICE OF ACCEPTANCE

The collecting bank must send without delay advice of acceptance to the bank from which the collection instruction was received.

iii.   ADVICE OF NON-PAYMENT AND/OR NONACCEPTANCE

The presenting bank should endeavor to ascertain the reasons for non-payment and/or non-acceptance and advise accordingly, without delay, the bank from which it received the collection instruction.

The presenting bank must send without delay advice of non-payment and/or advice of non-acceptance to the bank from which it received the collection instruction.

On receipt of such advice the remitting bank must give appropriate instructions as to the further handling of the documents. If such instructions are not received by the presenting bank within 60 days after its advice of nonpayment and/or non-acceptance, the documents may be returned to the bank from which the collection instruction was received without any further responsibility on the part of the presenting bank.

THE ICC AT A GLANCE

The ICC is a non-governmental organization serving world business. ICC members in more than 130 countries represent tens of thousands of companies and business organizations. ICC National Committees or Councils in some 60 countries coordinate activities at the national level.

The ICC

- represents the world business community at national and international levels;
- promotes world trade and investment based on free and fair competition;
- harmonises trade practices and formulates terminology and guidelines for importers and exporters;
- provides a growing range of practical services to business.

Through its subsidiary, ICC Publishing S.A., the ICC produces a wide range of publications. It also holds vocational seminars and business conferences in cities throughout the world.

SELECTED ICC PUBLICATIONS

Documentary Credits

Documentary Credits Insight
This ICC newsletter, published four times a year, gives the reader a direct connection to the ICC experts who analyze how UCP 500 is implemented in everyday situations. Contains analytical commentary and up-to-the-minute information on the UCP from the same experts who drafted UCP 500.

> Periodical/subscription 4 issues a year

Case Studies on Documentary Credits under UCP 500 By Charles del Busto
The first presentation to analyze, in detail, real-life cases involving UCP 500. Taken from queries answered by the ICC's Group of Experts, or structured from other cases, *Case Studies* links the UCP Articles with factual explanations concerning their implementation. Each of the 33 case studies in this book is referenced to a specific Article of UCP 500.
ISBN 92-842-1183.2 N^0 535

Documentary Credits UCP 500 and 400 Compared Edited by Charles del Busto
A highly effective vehicle with which to train managers, supervisors and international trade practitioners in critical areas of the new UCP 500 Rules. A vital companion guide for all concerned with Documentary Credits.
ISBN 92-842-1157-3 N^0 511

ICC Standard Documentary Credit Forms Edited by Charles del Busto
A series of forms designed for bankers, attorneys, importers/exporters and others involved in documentary credit transactions around the world.
ISBN 92-842-1160-3 N^0 516

ICC Uniform Customs and Practice for Documentary Credits (1993 Revision)
The *UCP 500* is a practical and comprehensive set of 49 Rules that address the major issues in documentary credit usage. They also reflect the major legal decisions on documentary credits by the courts in the last ten years.
ISBN 92-842-1155-7 N^0 500

HOW TO OBTAIN ICC PUBLICATIONS

These publications are available from ICC National Committees in some sixty countries, or from:

ICC Publishing S.A.
38 Cours Albert 1er
75008 Paris, France
Tel: (33.1) 49.53.29.23
Fax: (33.1) 49.53.29.02
Telex: 650 770

ICC Publishing, Inc.
156 Fifth Avenue, Suite 308
New York, N.Y. 10010 USA
Tel: (1.212) 206.1150
Fax: (1.212) 633.6025

APPENDIX C

Uniform Customs and Practice for Documentary Credits ICC Publication No. 500

A. General Provisions and Definitions

Article 1

Application of UCP

The Uniform Customs and Practice for Documentary Credits, 1993 Revision, ICC Publication N^{0}500, shall apply to all Documentary Credits (including to the extent to which they may be applicable, Standby Letter(s) of Credit) where they are incorporated into the text of the Credit. They are binding on all parties thereto, unless otherwise expressly stipulated in the Credit.

Article 2

Meaning of Credit

For the purposes of these Articles, the expressions "Documentary Credit(s)" and "Standby Letter(s) of Credit" (hereinafter referred to as "Credit(s)"), mean any arrangement, however named or described, whereby a bank (the "Issuing Bank") acting at the request and on the instructions of a customer (the "Applicant") or on its own behalf,

    i.   is to make a payment to or to the order of a third party (the "Beneficiary"), or is to accept and pay bills of exchange (Draft(s)) drawn by the Beneficiary,

    or

ii.   authorizes another bank to effect such payment, or to accept and pay such bills of exchange (Draft(s)),

or

iii.   authorizes another bank to negotiate,

against stipulated document(s),provided that the terms and conditions of the Credit are complied with.

For the purposes of these Articles, branches of a bank in different countries are considered another bank.

Article 3

Credits v. Contracts

a   Credits, by their nature, are separate transactions from the sales or other contract(s) on which they may be based and banks are in no way concerned with or bound by such contract(s), even if any reference whatsoever to such contract(s) is included in the Credit. Consequently, the undertaking of a bank to pay, accept and pay Draft(s) or negotiate and/or to fulfil any other obligation under the Credit, is not subject to claims or defenses by the Applicant resulting from his relationships with the Issuing Bank or the Beneficiary.

b   A Beneficiary can in no case avail himself of the contractual relationships existing between the banks or between the Applicant and the Issuing Bank.

Article 4

Documents v. Goods/Services/Performances

In Credit operations all parties concerned deal with documents, and not with goods, services and/or other performances to which the documents may relate.

Article 5

Instructions to Issue/Amend Credits

a   Instructions for the issuance of a Credit, the Credit itself, instructions for an amendment thereto, and the amendment itself, must be complete and precise.

In order to guard against confusion and misunderstanding, banks should discourage any attempt:

   i.   to include excessive detail in the Credit or in any amendment thereto;
   ii.   to give instructions to issue, advise or confirm a Credit by reference to a Credit previously issued (similar Credit) where such previous Credit has been subject to accepted amendment(s), and/or unaccepted amendment(s).

b   All instructions for the insurance of a Credit and the Credit itself and, where applicable, all instructions for an amendment thereto and the amendment itself, must state precisely the document(s) against which payment, acceptance or negotiation is to be made.

B. Form and Notification of Credits

Article 6

Revocable v. Irrevocable Credits

a   A Credit may be either

   i.   revocable,

      or

   ii.   irrevocable.

b   The Credit, therefore, should clearly indicate whether it is revocable or irrevocable.

c   In the absence of such indication the Credit shall be deemed to be irrevocable.

Article 7

Advising Bank's Liability

a A Credit may be advised to a Beneficiary through another bank (the "Advising Bank") without engagement on the part of the Advising Bank, but that bank, if it elects to advise the Credit, shall take reasonable care to check the apparent authenticity of the Credit which it advises. If the bank elects not to advise the Credit, it must so inform the Issuing Bank without delay.

b If the Advising Bank cannot establish such apparent authenticity it must inform, without delay, the bank from which the instructions appear to have been received that it has been unable to establish the authenticity of the Credit and if it elects nonetheless to advise the Credit it must inform the Beneficiary that it has not been able to establish the authenticity of the Credit.

Article 8

Revocation of a Credit

a A revocable Credit may be amended or cancelled by the Issuing Bank at any moment and without prior notice to the Beneficiary.

b However, the issuing Bank must:

i. reimburse another bank with which a revocable Credit has been made available for sight payment, acceptance or negotiation—for any payment, acceptance or negotiation made by such bank—prior to receipt by it of notice of amendment or cancellation, against documents which appear on their face to be in compliance with the terms and conditions of the Credit;

ii. reimburse another bank with which a revocable Credit has been made available for deferred payment, if such a bank has, prior to receipt by it of notice of amendment or cancellation, taken up documents which appear on their face to be in compliance with the terms and conditions of the Credit.

Article 9

Liability of Issuing and Confirming Banks

a   An irrevocable Credit constitutes a definite undertaking of the Issuing Bank, provided that the stipulated documents are presented to the Nominated Bank or to the Issuing Bank and that the terms and conditions of the Credit are complied with:

    i.   if the Credit provides for sight payment—to pay at sight;

    ii.   if the Credit provides for deferred payment—to pay on the maturity date(s) determinable in accordance with the stipulations of the Credit;

    iii.   if the Credit provides for acceptance:

        a.   by the Issuing Bank—to accept Draft(s) drawn by the Beneficiary on the Issuing Bank and pay them at maturity,

        or

        b.   by another drawee bank—to accept and pay at maturity Draft(s) drawn by the Beneficiary on the Issuing Bank in the event the drawee bank stipulated in the Credit does not accept Draft(s) drawn on it, or to pay Draft(s) accepted but not paid by such drawee bank at maturity;

    iv.   if the Credit provides for negotiation—to pay without recourse to drawers and/or bona fide holders, Draft(s) drawn by the Beneficiary and/or document(s) presented under the Credit. A Credit should not be issued available by Draft(s) on the Applicant. If the Credit nevertheless calls for Draft(s) on the Applicant, banks will consider such Draft(s) as an additional document(s).

b   A confirmation of an irrevocable Credit by another bank (the "Confirming Bank") upon the authorization or request of the Issuing Bank, constitutes a definite undertaking of the Confirming Bank, in addition to that of the Issuing Bank, provided that the stipulated documents are presented to the Confirming Bank or to any other Nominated Bank and that the terms and conditions of the Credit are complied with:

    i.   if the Credit provides for sight payment—to pay at sight;

    ii.   if the Credit provides for deferred payment—to pay on the maturity date(s) determinable in accordance with the stipulations of the Credit;

iii.   if the Credit provides for acceptance:

     a.   by the Confirming Bank—to accept Draft(s) drawn by the Beneficiary on the Confirming Bank and pay them at maturity,

     or

     b.   by another drawee bank—to accept and pay at maturity Draft(s) drawn by the Beneficiary on the Confirming Bank, in the event the drawee bank stipulated in the Credit does not accept Draft(s) drawn on it, or to pay Draft(s) accepted but not paid by such drawee bank at maturity;

iv.   if the Credit provides for negotiation—to negotiate without recourse to drawers and/or bona fide holders, Draft(s) drawn by the Beneficiary and/or document(s) presented under the Credit. A Credit should not be issued available by Draft(s) on the Applicant. If the Credit nevertheless calls for Draft(s) on the Applicant, banks will consider such Draft(s) as an additional document(s).

c   i.   If another bank is authorized or requested by the Issuing Bank to add its confirmation to a Credit but is not prepared to do so, it must so inform the Issuing Bank without delay.

  ii.   Unless the Issuing Bank specifies otherwise in its authorization or request to add confirmation, the Advising Bank may advise the Credit to the Beneficiary without adding its confirmation.

d   i.   Except as otherwise provided by Article 48, an irrevocable Credit can neither be amended nor cancelled without the agreement of the Issuing Bank, the Confirming Bank, if any, and the Beneficiary.

  ii.   The Issuing Bank shall be irrevocably bound by an amendment(s) issued by it from the time of the issuance of such amendment(s). A Confirming Bank may extend its confirmation to an amendment and shall be irrevocably bound as of the time of its advice of the amendment. A Confirming Bank may, however, choose to advise an amendment to the Beneficiary without extending its confirmation and if so, must inform the Issuing Bank and the Beneficiary without delay.

  iii.   The terms of the original Credit (or a Credit incorporating previously accepted amendment(s)) will remain in force for the Beneficiary until the Beneficiary communicates his acceptance of the amendment to the bank that advised such amendment. The Beneficiary should give notification of acceptance or rejection of amendment(s). If the Beneficiary fails to give such notification, the tender of documents to the Nominated Bank or Issuing Bank, that conform to the Credit and to not yet accepted amendment(s), will be deemed to be notification of acceptance by the Beneficiary of such amendment(s) and as of that moment the Credit will be amended.

iv. Partial acceptance of amendments contained in one and the same advice of amendment is not allowed and consequently will not be given any effect.

Article 10

Types of Credit

a   All Credits must clearly indicate whether they are available by sight payment, by deferred payment, by acceptance or by negotiation.

b   i.   Unless the Credit stipulates that it is available only with the Issuing Bank, all Credits must nominate the bank (the "Nominated Bank") which is authorized to pay, to incur a deferred payment undertaking, to accept Draft(s) or to negotiate. In a freely negotiable Credit, any bank is a Nominated Bank.

        Presentation of documents must be made to the Issuing Bank or the Confirming Bank, if any, or any other Nominated Bank.

    ii.   Negotiation means the giving of value for Draft(s) and/or document(s) by the bank authorized to negotiate. Mere examination of the documents without giving of value does not constitute a negotiation.

c   Unless the Nominated Bank is the Confirming Bank, nomination by the Issuing Bank does not constitute any undertaking by the Nominated Bank to pay, to incur a deferred payment undertaking, to accept Draft(s), or to negotiate. Except where expressly agreed to by the Nominated Bank and so communicated to the Beneficiary, the Nominated Bank's receipt of and/or examination and/or forwarding of the documents does not make that bank liable to pay, to incur a deferred payment undertaking, to accept Draft(s), or to negotiate.

d   By nominating another bank, or by allowing for negotiation by any bank, or by authorizing or requesting another bank to add its confirmation, the Issuing Bank authorizes such bank to pay, accept Draft(s) or negotiate as the case may be, against documents which appear on their face to be in compliance with the terms and conditions of the Credit and undertakes to reimburse such bank in accordance with the provisions of these Articles.

Article 11

Teletransmitted and Pre-Advised Credits

a   i.   When an Issuing Bank instructs an Advising Bank by an authenticated teletransmission to advise a Credit or an amendment to a Credit, the teletransmission will be deemed to be the operative Credit instrument or the operative amendment, and no mail confirmation should be sent. Should a mail confirmation nevertheless be sent, it will have no effect and the Advising Bank will have no obligation to check such mail confirmation against the operative Credit instrument or the operative amendment received by teletransmission.

       ii.   If the teletransmission states "full details to follow" (or words of similar effect) or states that the mail confirmation is to be the operative Credit instrument or the operative amendment, then the teletransmission will not be deemed to be the operative Credit instrument or the operative amendment. The Issuing Bank must forward the operative Credit instrument or the operative amendment to such Advising Bank without delay.

b   If a bank uses the services of an Advising Bank to have the Credit advised to the Beneficiary, it must also use the services of the same bank for advising an amendment(s).

c   A preliminary advice of the issuance or amendment of an irrevocable Credit (pre-advice), shall only be given by an Issuing Bank if such bank is prepared to issue the operative Credit instrument or the operative amendment thereto. Unless otherwise stated in such preliminary advice by the Issuing Bank, an Issuing Bank having given such pre-advice shall be irrevocably committed to issue or amend the Credit, in terms not inconsistent with the pre-advice, without delay.

Article 12

Incomplete or Unclear Instructions

If incomplete or unclear instructions are received to advise, confirm or amend a Credit, the bank requested to act on such instructions may give preliminary notification to the Beneficiary for information only and without responsibility. This preliminary notification should state clearly that the notification is provided for information only and without the responsibility of the Advising Bank. In any event, the Advising Bank must inform the Issuing Bank of the action taken and request it to provide the necessary information.

The Issuing Bank must provide the necessary information without delay. The Credit will be advised, confirmed or amended, only when complete and clear instructions have been received and if the Advising Bank is then prepared to act on the instructions.

C. Liabilities and Responsibilities

Article 13

Standard for Examination of Documents

a   Banks must examine all documents stipulated in the Credit with reasonable care, to ascertain whether or not they appear, on their face, to be in compliance with the terms and conditions of the Credit. Compliance of the stipulated documents on their face with the terms and conditions of the Credit, shall be determined by international standard banking practice as reflected in these Articles. Documents which appear on their face to be inconsistent with one another will be considered as not appearing on their face to be in compliance with the terms and conditions of the Credit.

Documents not stipulated in the Credit will not be examined by banks. If they receive such documents, they shall return them to the presenter or pass them on without responsibility.

b   The issuing Bank, the Confirming Bank, if any, or a Nominated Bank acting on their behalf, shall each have a reasonable time, not to exceed seven banking days following the day of receipt of the documents, to examine the documents and determine whether to take up or refuse the documents and to inform the party from which it received the documents accordingly.

c   If a Credit contains conditions without stating the document(s) to be presented in compliance therewith, banks will deem such conditions as not stated and will disregard them.

Article 14

Discrepant Documents and Notice

a   When the Issuing Bank authorizes another bank to pay, incur a deferred payment undertaking, accept Draft(s), or negotiate against documents which appear on their face to be in compliance with the terms and conditions of the Credit, the Issuing Bank and the Confirming Bank, if any, are bound:

i.   to reimburse the Nominated Bank which has paid, incurred a deferred payment undertaking, accepted Draft(s), or negotiated,

ii.   to take up the documents.

b   Upon receipt of the documents the Issuing Bank and /or Confirming Bank, if any, or a Nominated Bank acting on their behalf, must determine on the basis of the documents alone whether or not they appear on their face to be in compliance with the terms and conditions of the Credit. If the documents appear on their face not to be in compliance with the terms and conditions of the Credit, such banks may refuse to take up the documents.

c   If the Issuing Bank determines that the documents appear on their face not to be in compliance with the terms and conditions of the Credit, it may in its sole judgment approach the Applicant for a waiver of the discrepancy(ies). This does not, however, extend the period mentioned in sub-Article 13 (b).

d   i.   If the Issuing Bank and/or Confirming Bank, if any, or a Nominated Bank acting on their behalf, decides to refuse the documents, it must give notice to that effect by telecommunication or, if that is not possible, by other expeditious means, without delay but no later than the close of the seventh banking day following the day of receipt of the documents. Such notice shall be given to the bank from which it received the documents, or to the Beneficiary, if it received the documents directly from him.

     ii.   Such notice must state all discrepancies in respect of which the bank refuses the documents and must also state whether it is holding the documents at the disposal of, or is returning them to, the presenter.

     iii. The Issuing Bank and/or Confirming Bank, if any, shall then be entitled to claim from the remitting bank refund, with interest, of any reimbursement which has been made to that bank.

e   If the issuing Bank and/or Confirming Bank, if any, fails to act in accordance with the provisions of this Article and/or fails to hold the documents at the disposal of, or return them to the presenter, the Issuing Bank and/or Confirming Bank, if any, shall be precluded from claiming that the documents are not in compliance with the terms and conditions of the Credit.

f   If the remitting bank draws the attention of the Issuing Bank and/or Confirming Bank, if any, to any discrepancy(ies) in the document(s) or advises such banks that it has paid, incurred a deferred payment undertaking, accepted Draft(s) or negotiated under reserve or against an indemnity in respect of such discrepancy(ies), the Issuing Bank and/or Confirming Bank, if any, shall not be thereby relieved from any of their obligations under any provision of this Article. Such reserve or indemnity concerns only the relations between the remitting bank and the party towards whom the reserve was made, or from whom, or on whose behalf, the indemnity was obtained.

Article 15

Disclaimer on Effectiveness of Documents

Banks assume no liability or responsibility for the form, sufficiency, accuracy, genuineness, falsification or legal effect of any document(s), or for the general and/or particular conditions stipulated in the document(s) or superimposed thereon; nor do they assume any liability or responsibility for the description, quantity, weight, quality, condition, packing, delivery, value or existence of the goods represented by any document(s), or for the good faith or acts and/or omissions, solvency, performance or standing of the consignors, the carriers, the forwarders, the consignees or the insurers of the goods, or any other person whomsoever.

Article 16

Disclaimer on the Transmission of Messages

Banks assume no liability or responsibility for the consequences arising out of delay and/or loss in transit of any message(s), letter(s) or document(s), or for delay, mutilation or other error(s) arising in the transmission of any telecommunication. Banks assume no liability or responsibility for errors in translation and/or interpretation of technical terms, and reserve the right to transmit Credit terms without translating them.

Article 17

Force Majeure

Banks assume no liability or responsibility for the consequences arising out of the interruption of their business by Acts of God, riots, civil commotions, insurrections, wars or any other causes beyond their control, or by any strikes or lockouts. Unless specifically authorized, banks will not, upon resumption of their business, pay, incur a deferred payment undertaking, accept Draft(s) or negotiate under Credits which expired during such interruption of their business.

Article 18

Disclaimer for Acts of an Instructed Party

a   Banks utilizing the services of another bank or other banks for the purpose of giving effect to the instructions of the Applicant do so for the account and at the risk of such Applicant.

b   Banks assume no liability or responsibility should the instructions they transmit not be carried out, even if they have themselves taken the initiative in the choice of such other bank(s).

c   i.   A party instructing another party to perform services is liable for any charges, including commissions, fees, costs or expenses incurred by the instructed party in connection with its instructions.

ii.   Where a Credit stipulates that such charges are for the account of a party other than the instructing party, and charges cannot be collected, the instructing party remains ultimately liable for the payment thereof.

d   The Applicant shall be bound by and liable to indemnify the banks against all obligations and responsibilities imposed by foreign laws and usages.

Article 19

Bank-to-Bank Reimbursement Arrangements

a   If an issuing Bank intends that the reimbursement to which a paying, accepting or negotiating bank is entitled, shall be obtained by such bank (the "Claiming Bank"), claiming on another party (the "Reimbursing Bank"), it shall provide such Reimbursing Bank in good time with the proper instructions or authorization to honor such reimbursement claims.

b   Issuing Banks shall not require a Claiming Bank to supply a certificate of compliance with the terms and conditions of the Credit to the Reimbursing Bank.

c   An Issuing Bank shall not be relieved from any of its obligations to provide reimbursement if and when reimbursement is not received by the Claiming Bank from the Reimbursing Bank.

d   The Issuing Bank shall be responsible to the Claiming Bank for any loss of interest if reimbursement is not provided by the Reimbursing Bank on first demand, or as otherwise specified in the Credit, or mutually agreed, as the case may be.

e   The Reimbursing Bank's charges should be for the account of the Issuing Bank. However, in cases where the charges are for the account of another party, it is the responsibility of the Issuing Bank to so indicate in the original Credit and in the reimbursement authorization. In cases where the Reimbursing Bank's charges are for the account of another party they shall be collected from the Claiming Bank when the Credit is drawn under. In cases where the Credit is not drawn under, the Reimbursing Bank's charges remain the obligation of the Issuing Bank.

D.   Documents

Article 20

Ambiguity as to the Issuers of Documents

a   Terms such as "first class," "well known," "qualified," "independent," "official," "competent," "local" and the like, shall not be used to describe the issuers of any document(s) to be presented under a Credit. If such terms are incorporated in the Credit, banks will accept the relative document(s) as presented, provided that it appears on its face to be in compliance with the other terms and conditions of the Credit and not to have been issued by the Beneficiary.

b   Unless otherwise stipulated in the Credit, banks will also accept as an original document(s), a document(s) produced or appearing to have been produced:

    i.   by reprographic, automated or computerized systems;

    ii.   as carbon copies;

provided that it is marked as original and, where necessary, appears to be signed.

A document may be signed by handwriting, by facsimile signature, by perforated signature, by stamp, by symbol, or by any other mechanical or electronic method of authentication.

c   i.   Unless otherwise stipulated in the Credit, banks will accept as a copy(ies), a document(s) either labelled copy or not marked as an original—a copy(ies) need not be signed.

    ii.   Credits that require multiple document(s) such as "duplicate," "two fold," "two copies" and the like, will be satisfied by the presentation of one original and the remaining number in copies except where the document itself indicates otherwise.

Unless otherwise stipulated in the Credit, a condition under a Credit calling for a document to be authenticated, validated, legalized, visaed, certified or indicating a similar requirement, will be satisfied by any signature, mark, stamp or label on such document that on its face appears to satisfy the above condition.

Article 21

Unspecified Issuers or Contents of Documents

When documents other than transport documents, insurance documents and commercial invoices are called for, the Credit should stipulate by whom such documents are to be issued and their wording or data content. If the Credit does not so stipulate, banks will accept such documents as presented, provided that their data content is not inconsistent with any other stipulated document presented.

Article 22

Issuance Date of Documents v. Credit Date

Unless otherwise stipulated in the Credit, banks will accept a document bearing a date of issuance prior to that of the Credit, subject to such document being presented within the time limits set out in the Credit and in these Articles.

Article 23

Marine/Ocean Bill of Lading

a   If a Credit calls for a bill of lading covering a port-to-port shipment, banks will, unless otherwise stipulated in the Credit, accept a document, however named, which:

    i.   appears on its face to indicate the name of the carrier and to have been signed or otherwise authenticated by:

        — the carrier or a named agent for or on behalf of the carrier, or

        — the master or a named agent for or on behalf of the master.

        Any signature or authentication of the carrier or master must be identified as carrier or master, as the case may be. An agent signing or authenticating for the carrier or master must also indicate the name and the capacity of the party, i.e. carrier or master, on whose behalf that agent is acting, and

ii.   indicates that the goods have been loaded on board, or shipped on a named vessel.

Loading on board or shipment on a named vessel may be indicated by pre-printed wording on the bill of lading that the goods have been loaded on board a named vessel or shipped on a named vessel, in which case the date of issuance of the bill of lading will be deemed to be the date of loading on board and the date of shipment.

In all other cases loading on board a named vessel must be evidenced by a notation on the bill of lading which gives the date on which the goods have been loaded on board, in which case the date of the on board notation will be deemed to be the date of shipment.

If the bill of lading contains the indication "intended vessel," or similar qualification in relation to the vessel, loading on board a named vessel must be evidenced by an on board notation on the bill of lading which, in addition to the date on which the goods have been loaded on board, also includes the name of the vessel on which the goods have been loaded, even if they have been loaded on the vessel named as the "intended vessel."

If the bill of lading indicates a place of receipt or taking in charge different from the port of loading, the on board notation must also include the port of loading stipulated in the Credit and the name of the vessel on which the goods have been loaded, even if they have been loaded on the vessel named in the bill of lading. This provision also applies whenever loading on board the vessel is indicated by preprinted wording on the bill of lading,

and

iii.   indicates the port of loading and the port of discharge stipulated in the Credit, notwithstanding that it:

a.   indicates a place of taking in charge different from the port of loading, and/or a place of final destination different from the port of discharge,

and/or

b.   contains the indication "intended" or similar qualification in relation to the port of loading and/or port of discharge, as long as the document also states the ports of loading and/or discharge stipulated in the Credit,

and

iv. consists of a sole original bill of lading or, if issued in more than one original, the full set as so issued,

and

v. appears to contain all of the terms and conditions of carriage, or some of such terms and conditions by reference to a source or document other than the bill of lading (short form/blank back bill of lading); banks will not examine the contents of such terms and conditions,

and

vi. contains no indication that it is subject to a charter party and/or no indication that the carrying vessel is propelled by sail only,

and

vii. in all other respects meets the stipulations of the Credit.

b For the purpose of this Article, transhipment means unloading and reloading from one vessel to another vessel during the course of ocean carriage from the port of loading to the port of discharge stipulated in the Credit.

c Unless transhipment is prohibited by the terms of the Credit, banks will accept a bill of lading which indicates that the goods will be transhipped, provided that the entire ocean carriage is covered by one and the same bill of lading.

d Even if the Credit prohibits transhipment, banks will accept a bill of lading which:

i. indicates that transhipment will take place as long as the relevant cargo is shipped in Container(s), Trailer(s) and/or "LASH" barge(s) as evidenced by the bill of lading, provided that the entire ocean carriage is covered by one and the same bill of lading,

and/or

ii. incorporates clauses stating that the carrier reserves the right to tranship.

Article 24

Non-Negotiable Sea Waybill

a   If a Credit calls for a non-negotiable sea waybill covering a port-to-port shipment, banks will, unless otherwise stipulated in the Credit, accept a document, however named, which:

    i.   appears on its face to indicate the name of the carrier and to have been signed or otherwise authenticated by:

        — the carrier or a named agent for or on behalf of the carrier, or

        — the master or a named agent for or on behalf of the master,

        Any signature or authentication of the carrier or master must be identified as carrier or master, as the case may be. An agent signing or authenticating for the carrier or master must also indicate the name and the capacity of the party, i.e. carrier or master, on whose behalf that agent is acting,

        and

    ii.   indicates that the goods have been loaded on board, or shipped on a named vessel.

        Loading on board or shipment on a named vessel may be indicated by pre-printed wording on the non-negotiable sea waybill that the goods have been loaded on board a named vessel or shipped on a named vessel, in which case the date of issuance of the non-negotiable sea waybill will be deemed to be the date of loading on board and the date of shipment.

        In all other cases loading on board a named vessel must be evidenced by a notation on the non-negotiable sea waybill which gives the date on which the goods have been loaded on board, in which case the date of the on board notation will be deemed to be the date of shipment.

        If the non-negotiable sea waybill contains the indication "intended vessel," or similar qualification in relation to the vessel, loading on board a named vessel must be evidenced by an on board notation on the non-negotiable sea way bill which, in addition to the date on which the goods have been loaded on board, includes the name of the vessel on which the goods have been loaded, even if they have been loaded on the vessel named as the "intended vessel."

        If the non-negotiable sea waybill indicates a place of receipt or taking in charge different from the port of loading, the on board notation must also include the port of loading stipulated in the Credit and the name of the vessel on which the goods have been loaded, even if they have been loaded on a vessel named in the non-negotiable sea waybill. This provision also applies whenever loading on board the vessel is indicated by pre-printed wording on the non-negotiable sea waybill,

and

iii. indicates the port of loading and the port of discharge stipulated in the Credit, notwith-standing that it:

    a. indicates a place of taking in charge different from the port of loading, and/or a place of final destination different from the port of discharge,

    and/or

    b. contains the indication "intended" or similar qualification in relation to the port of loading and/or port of discharge, as long as the document also states the ports of loading and/or discharge stipulated in the Credit,

and

iv. consists of a sole original non-negotiable sea waybill, or if issued in more than one original, the full set as so issued,

and

v. appears to contain all of the terms and conditions of carriage, or some of such terms and conditions by reference to a source or document other than the non-negotiable sea waybill (short form/blank back non-negotiable sea waybill); banks will not examine the contents of such terms and conditions,

and

vi. contains no indication that it is subject to a charter party and/or no indication that the carrying vessel is propelled by sail only,

and

vii. in all other respects meets the stipulations of the Credit.

b   For the purpose of this Article, transhipment means unloading and reloading from one vessel to another vessel during the course of ocean carriage from the port of loading to the port of discharge stipulated in the Credit.

c   Unless transhipment is prohibited by the terms of the Credit, banks will accept a non-negotiable sea waybill which indicates that the goods will be transhipped, provided that the entire ocean carriage is covered by one and the same non-negotiable sea waybill.

d   Even if the Credit prohibits transhipment, banks will accept a non-negotiable sea waybill which:

   i.   indicates that transhipment will take place as long as the relevant cargo is shipped in Container(s), Trailer(s) and/or "LASH" barge(s) as evidenced by the non-negotiable sea way bill, provided that the entire ocean carriage is covered by one and the same non-negotiable sea waybill,

        and/or

   ii. incorporates clauses stating that the carrier reserves the right to tranship.

Article 25

Charter Party Bill of Lading

a   If a Credit calls for or permits a charter party bill of lading, banks will, unless otherwise stipulated in the Credit, accept a document, however named, which:

   i.   contains any indication that it is subject to a charter party,

        and

   ii. appears on its face to have been signed or otherwise authenticated by:

        — the master or a named agent for or on behalf of the master, or

        — the owner or a named agent for or on behalf of the owner.

        Any signature or authentication of the master or owner must be identified as master or owner as the case may be. An agent signing or authenticating for the master or owner must also indicate the name and the capacity of the party, i.e. master or owner, on whose behalf that agent is acting,

        and

   iii. does or does not indicate the name of the carrier,

        and

iv.   indicates that the goods have been loaded on board or shipped on a named vessel.

Loading on board or shipment on a named vessel may be indicated by pre-printed wording on the bill of lading that the goods have been loaded on board a named vessel or shipped on a named vessel, in which case the date of issuance of the bill of lading will be deemed to be the date of loading on board and the date of shipment.

In all other cases loading on board a named vessel must be evidenced by a notation on the bill of lading which gives the date on which the goods have been loaded on board, in which case the date of the on board notation will be deemed to be the date of shipment,

and

v.   indicates the port of loading and the port of discharge stipulated in the Credit,

and

vi.   consists of a sole original bill of lading or, if issued in more than one original, the full set as so issued,

and

vii.   contains no indication that the carrying vessel is propelled by sail only,

and

viii.   in all other respects meets the stipulations of the Credit.

b   Even if the Credit requires the presentation of a charter party contract in connection with a charter party bill of lading, banks will not examine such charter party contract, but will pass it on without responsibility on their part.

Article 26

_____

Multimodal Transport Document

a   If a Credit calls for a transport document covering at least two different modes of transport (multimodal transport), banks will, unless otherwise stipulated in the Credit, accept a document, however named, which:

   i.   appears on its face to indicate the name of the carrier or multimodal transport operator and to have been signed or otherwise authenticated by:

         — the carrier or multimodal transport operator or a named agent for or on behalf of the carrier or multimodal transport operator, or

         — the master or a named agent for or on behalf of the master.

         Any signature or authentication of the carrier, multimodal transport operator or master must be identified as carrier, multimodal transport operator or master, as the case may be. An agent signing or authenticating for the carrier, multimodal transport operator or master must also indicate the name and the capacity of the party, i.e. carrier, multimodal transport operator or master, on whose behalf that agent is acting,

         and

   ii.   indicates that the goods have been dispatched, taken in charge or loaded on board.

         Dispatch, taking in charge or loading on board may be indicated by wording to that effect on the multimodal transport document and the date of issuance will be deemed to be the date of dispatch, taking in charge or loading on board and the date of shipment. However, if the document indicates, by stamp or otherwise, a date of dispatch, taking in charge or loading on board, such date will be deemed to be the date of shipment,

         and

   iii. a.   indicates the place of taking in charge stipulated in the Credit which may be different from the port, airport or place of loading, and the place of final destination stipulated in the Credit which may be different from the port, airport or place of discharge,

              and/or

b.   contains the indication "intended" or similar qualification in relation to the vessel and/or port of loading and/or port of discharge,

and

iv.   consists of a sole original multimodal transport document or, if issued in more than one original, the full set as so issued,

and

v.   appears to contain all of the terms and conditions of carriage, or some of such terms and conditions by reference to a source or document other than the multimodal transport document (short form/blank back multimodal transport document); banks will not examine the contents of such terms and conditions,

and

vi.   contains no indication that it is subject to a charter party and/or no indication that the carrying vessel is propelled by sail only,

and

vii.   in all other respects meets the stipulations of the Credit.

b.   Even if the Credit prohibits transhipment, banks will accept a multimodal transport document which indicates that transhipment will or may take place, provided that the entire carriage is covered by one and the same multimodal transport document.

Article 27

Air Transport Document

a   If a Credit calls for an air transport document, banks will, unless otherwise stipulated in the Credit, accept a document, however named, which:

i.   appears on its face to indicate the name of the carrier and to have been signed or otherwise authenticated by:

— the carrier, or

— a named agent for or on behalf of the carrier.

Any signature or authentication of the carrier must be identified as carrier. An agent signing or authenticating for the carrier must also indicate the name and the capacity of the party, i.e. carrier, on whose behalf that agent is acting,

and

ii.   indicates that the goods have been accepted for carriage,

and

iii. where the Credit calls for an actual date of dispatch, indicates a specific notation of such date, the date of dispatch so indicated on the air transport document will be deemed to be the date of shipment.

For the purpose of this Article, the information appearing in the box on the air transport document (marked "For Carrier Use Only" or similar expression) relative to the flight number and date will not be considered as a specific notation of such date of dispatch.

In all other cases, the date of issuance of the air transport document will be deemed to be the date of shipment,

and

iv.   indicates the airport of departure and the airport of destination stipulated in the Credit,

and

v.   appears to be the original for consignor/shipper even if the Credit stipulates a full set of originals, or similar expressions,

and

vi.   appears to contain all of the terms and conditions of carriage, or some of such terms and conditions, by reference to a source or document other than the air transport document; banks will not examine the contents of such terms and conditions,

and

vii. in all other respects meets the stipulations of the Credit.

b   For the purpose of this Article, transhipment means unloading and reloading from one aircraft to another aircraft during the course of carriage from the airport of departure to the airport of destination stipulated in the Credit.

c   Even if the Credit prohibits transhipment, banks will accept an air transport document which indicates that transhipment will or may take place, provided that the entire carriage is covered by one and the same air transport document.

Article 28

Road, Rail or Inland Waterway Transport Documents

a   If a Credit calls for a road, rail, or inland waterway transport document, banks will, unless otherwise stipulated in the Credit, accept a document of the type called for, however named, which:

   i.   appears on its face to indicate the name of the carrier and to have been signed or otherwise authenticated by the carrier or a named agent for or on behalf of the carrier and/or to bear a reception stamp or other indication of receipt by the carrier or a named agent for or on behalf of the carrier.

   Any signature, authentication, reception stamp or other indication of receipt of the carrier, must be identified on its face as that of the carrier. An agent signing or authenticating for the carrier, must also indicate the name and the capacity of the party, i.e. carrier, on whose behalf that agent is acting,

   and

   ii.   indicates that the goods have been received for shipment, dispatch or carriage or wording to this effect. The date of issuance will be deemed to be the date of shipment unless the transport document contains a reception stamp, in which case the date of the reception stamp will be deemed to be the date of shipment,

   and

   iii.   indicates the place of shipment and the place of destination stipulated in the Credit,

   and

   iv.   in all other respects meets the stipulations of the Credit.

b   In the absence of any indication on the transport document as to the numbers issued, banks will accept the transport document(s) presented as constituting a full set. Banks will accept as original(s) the transport document(s) whether marked as original(s) or not.

c   For the purpose of this Article, transhipment means unloading and reloading from one means of conveyance to another means of conveyance, in different modes of transport, during the course of carriage from the place of shipment to the place of destination stipulated in the Credit.

d   Even if the Credit prohibits transhipment, banks will accept a road, rail, or inland waterway transport document which indicates that transhipment will or may take place, provided that the entire carriage is covered by one and the same transport document and within the same mode of transport.

Article 29

Courier and Post Receipts

a   If a Credit calls for a post receipt or certificate of posting, banks will, unless otherwise stipulated in the Credit, accept a post receipt or certificate of posting which:

    i.   appears on its face to have been stamped or otherwise authenticated and dated in the place from which the Credit stipulates the goods are to be shipped or dispatched and such date will be deemed to be the date of shipment or dispatch,

        and

    ii.   in all other respects meets the stipulations of the Credit.

b   If a Credit calls for a document issued by a courier or expedited delivery service evidencing receipt of the goods for delivery, banks will, unless otherwise stipulated in the Credit, accept a document, however named, which:

    i.   appears on its face to indicate the name of the courier/service, and to have been stamped, signed or otherwise authenticated by such named courier/service (unless the Credit specifically calls for a document issued by a named Courier/Service, banks will accept a document issued by any Courier/Service),

        and

    ii.   indicates a date of pick-up or of receipt or wording to this effect, such date being deemed to be the date of shipment or dispatch,

        and

    iii.   in all other respects meets the stipulations of the Credit.

Article 30

Transport Documents issued by Freight Forwarders

Unless otherwise authorized in the Credit, banks will only accept a transport document issued by a freight forwarder if it appears on its face to indicate:

    i.   the name of the freight forwarder as a carrier or multimodal transport operator and to have been signed or otherwise authenticated by the freight forwarder as carrier or multimodal transport operator,

        or

    ii.   the name of the carrier or multimodal transport operator and to have been signed or otherwise authenticated by the freight forwarder as a named agent for or on behalf of the carrier or multimodal transport operator.

Article 31

"On Deck," "Shipper's Load and Count," Name of Consignor

Unless otherwise stipulated in the Credit, banks will accept a transport document which:

    i.   does not indicate, in the case of carriage by sea or by more than one means of conveyance including carriage by sea, that the goods are or will be loaded on deck. Nevertheless, banks will accept a transport document which contains a provision that the goods may be carried on deck, provided that it does not specifically state that they are or will be loaded on deck,

        and/or

    ii.   bears a clause on the face thereof such as "shipper's load and count" or "said by shipper to contain" or words of similar effect,

        and/or

    iii.   indicates as the consignor of the goods a party other than the Beneficiary of the Credit.

Article 32

Clean Transport Documents

a   A clean transport document is one which bears no clause or notation which expressly declares a defective condition of the goods and/or the packaging.

b   Banks will not accept transport documents bearing such clauses or notations unless the Credit expressly stipulates the clauses or notations which may be accepted.

c   Banks will regard a requirement in a Credit for a transport document to bear the clause "clean on board" as complied with if such transport document meets the requirements of this Article and of Articles 23, 24, 25, 26, 27, 28 or 30.

Article 33

Freight Payable/Prepaid Transport Documents

a   Unless otherwise stipulated in the Credit, or inconsistent with any of the documents presented under the Credit, banks will accept transport documents stating that freight or transportation charges (hereafter referred to as "freight") have still to be paid.

b   If a credit stipulates that the transport document has to indicate that freight has been paid or prepaid, banks will accept a transport document on which words clearly indicating payment or prepayment of freight appear by stamp or otherwise, or on which payment or prepayment of freight is indicated by other means. If the Credit requires courier charges to be paid or prepaid banks will also accept a transport document issued by a courier or expedited delivery service evidencing that courier charges are for the account of a party other than the consignee.

c   The words "freight prepayable" or "freight to be prepaid" or words of similar effect, if appearing on transport documents, will not be accepted as constituting evidence of the payment of freight.

d   Banks will accept transport documents bearing reference by stamp or otherwise to costs additional to the freight, such as costs of, or disbursements incurred in connection with, loading, unloading or similar operations, unless the conditions of the Credit specifically prohibit such reference.

Article 34

Insurance Documents

a   Insurance documents must appear on their face to be issued and signed by insurance companies or underwriters or their agents.

b   If the insurance document indicates that it has been issued in more than one original, all the originals must be presented unless otherwise authorized in the Credit.

c   Cover notes issued by brokers will not be accepted, unless specifically authorized in the Credit.

d   Unless otherwise stipulated in the Credit, banks will accept an insurance certificate or a declaration under an open cover pre-signed by insurance companies or underwriters or their agents. If a Credit specifically calls for an insurance certificate or a declaration under an open cover, banks will accept, in lieu thereof, an insurance policy.

e   Unless otherwise stipulated in the Credit, or unless it appears from the insurance document that the cover is effective at the latest from the date of loading on board or dispatch or taking in charge of the goods, banks will not accept an insurance document which bears a date of issuance later than the date of loading on board or dispatch or taking in charge as indicated in such transport document.

f   i.   Unless otherwise stipulated in the Credit, the insurance document must be expressed in the same currency as the Credit.

        ii.   Unless otherwise stipulated in the Credit, the minimum amount for which the insurance document must indicate the insurance cover to have been effected is the CIF (cost, insurance and freight (... "named port of destination")) or CIP (carriage and insurance paid to (..."named place of destination")) value of the goods, as the case may be, plus 10%, but only when the CIF or CIP value can be determined from the documents on their face. Otherwise, banks will accept as such minimum amount 110% of the amount for which payment, acceptance or negotiation is requested under the Credit, or 110% of the gross amount of the invoice, whichever is the greater.

Article 35

Type of Insurance Cover

a   Credits should stipulate the type of insurance required and, if any, the additional risks which are to be covered. Imprecise terms such as "usual risks" or "customary risks" shall not be used; if they are used, banks will accept insurance documents as presented, without responsibility for any risks not being covered.

b   Failing specific stipulations in the Credit, banks will accept insurance documents as presented, without responsibility for any risks not being covered.

c   Unless otherwise stipulated in the Credit, banks will accept an insurance document which indicates that the cover is subject to a franchise or an excess (deductible).

Article 36

All Risks Insurance Cover

Where a Credit stipulates "insurance against all risks", banks will accept an insurance document which contains any "all risks" notation or clause, whether or not bearing the heading "all risks", even if the insurance document indicates that certain risks are excluded, without responsibility for any risk(s) not being covered.

Article 37

Commercial Invoices

a   Unless otherwise stipulated in the Credit, commercial invoices;

      i.   must appear on their face to be issued by the Beneficiary named in the Credit (except as provided in Article 48),

          and

      ii.   must be made out in the name of the Applicant (except as provided in sub-Article 48 (h)),

          and

      iii.   need not be signed.

b   Unless otherwise stipulated in the Credit, banks may refuse commercial invoices issued for amounts in excess of the amount permitted by the Credit. Nevertheless, if a bank authorized to pay, incur a deferred payment undertaking, accept Draft(s), or negotiate under a Credit accepts such invoices, its decision will be binding upon all parties, provided that such bank has not paid, incurred a deferred payment undertaking, accepted Draft(s) or negotiated for an amount in excess of that permitted by the Credit.

c   The description of the goods in the commercial invoice must correspond with the description in the Credit. In all other documents, the goods may be described in general terms not inconsistent with the description of the goods in the Credit.

Article 38

Other Documents

If a credit calls for an attestation or certification of weight in the case of transport other than by sea, banks will accept a weight stamp or declaration of weight which appears to have been superimposed on the transport document by the carrier or his agent unless the Credit specifically stipulates that the attestation or certification of weight must be by means of a separate document.

E. Miscellaneous Provisions

Article 39

Allowances In Credit Amount, Quantity and Unit Price

a   The words "about," "approximately," "circa" or similar expressions used in connection with the amount of the Credit or the quantity or the unit price stated in the Credit are to be construed as allowing a difference not to exceed 10% more or 10% less than the amount or the quantity or the unit price to which they refer.

b   Unless a Credit stipulates that the quantity of the goods specified must not be exceeded or reduced, a tolerance of 5% more or 5% less will be permissible, always provided that the amount of the drawings does not exceed the amount of the Credit. This tolerance does not apply when the Credit stipulates the quantity in terms of a stated number of packing units or individual items.

c   Unless a Credit which prohibits partial shipments stipulates otherwise, or unless sub-Article (b) above is applicable, a tolerance of 5% less in the amount of the drawing will be permissible, provided that if the Credit stipulates the quantity of the goods, such quantity of goods is shipped in full, and if the Credit stipulates a unit price, such price is not reduced. This provision does not apply when expressions referred to in sub-Article (a) above are used in the Credit.

Article 40

Partial Shipments/Drawings

a   Partial drawings and/or shipments are allowed, unless the Credit stipulates otherwise.

b   Transport documents which appear on their face to indicate that shipment has been made on the same means of conveyance and for the same journey, provided they indicate the same destination, will not be regarded as covering partial shipments, even if the transport documents indicate different dates of shipment and/or different ports of loading, places of taking in charge, or despatch.

c   Shipments made by post or by courier will not be regarded as partial shipments if the post receipts or certificates of posting or courier's receipts or dispatch notes appear to have been stamped, signed or otherwise authenticated in the place from which the Credit stipulates the goods are to be dispatched, and on the same date.

Article 41

Instalment Shipments/Drawings

If drawings and/or shipments by instalments within given periods are stipulated in the Credit and any instalment is not drawn and/or shipped within the period allowed for that instalment, the Credit ceases to be available for that and any subsequent instalments, unless otherwise stipulated in the Credit.

Article 42

Expiry Date and Place for Presentation of Documents

a   All Credits must stipulate an expiry date and a place for presentation of documents for payment, acceptance, or with the exception of freely negotiable Credits, a place for presentation of documents for negotiation. An expiry date stipulated for payment, acceptance or negotiation will be construed to express an expiry date for presentation of documents.

b   Except as provided in sub-Article 44(a), documents must be presented on or before such expiry date.

c   If an issuing Bank states that the Credit is to be available "for one month," "for six months," or the like, but does not specify the date from which the time is to run, the date of issuance of the Credit by the Issuing Bank will be deemed to be the first day from which such time is to run. Banks should discourage indication of the expiry date of the Credit in this manner.

Article 43

Limitation on the Expiry Date

a   In addition to stipulating an expiry date for presentation of documents, every Credit which calls for a transport document(s) should also stipulate a specified period of time after the date of shipment during which presentation must be made in compliance with the terms and conditions of the Credit. If no such period of time is stipulated, banks will not accept documents presented to them later than 21 days after the date of shipment. In any event, documents must be presented not later than the expiry date of the Credit.

b   In cases in which sub-Article 40(b) applies, the date of shipment will be considered to be the latest shipment date on any of the transport documents presented.

Article 44

Extension of Expiry Date

a   If the expiry date of the Credit and/or the last day of the period of time for presentation of documents stipulated by the Credit or applicable by virtue of Article 43 falls on a day on which the bank to which presentation has to be made is closed for reasons other than those referred to in Article 17, the stipulated expiry date and/or the last day of the period of time after the date of shipment for presentation of documents, as the case may be, shall be extended to the first following day on which such bank is open.

b   The latest date for shipment shall not be extended by reason of the extension of the expiry date and/or the period of time after the date of shipment for presentation of documents in accordance with sub-Article (a) above. If no such latest date for shipment is stipulated in the Credit or amendments thereto, banks will not accept transport documents indicating a date of shipment later than the expiry date stipulated in the Credit or amendments thereto.

c   The bank to which presentation is made on such first following business day must provide a statement that the documents were presented within the time limits extended in accordance with sub-Article 44(a) of the Uniform Customs and Practice for Documentary Credits, 1993 Revision, ICC Publication No. 500.

Article 45

Hours of Presentation

Banks are under no obligation to accept presentation of documents outside their banking hours.

Article 46

General Expressions as to Dates for Shipment

a   Unless otherwise stipulated in the Credit, the expression "shipment" used in stipulating an earliest and/or a latest date for shipment will be understood to include expressions such as, "loading on board," "dispatch," "accepted for carriage," "date of post receipt," "date of pick-up," and the like, and in the case of a Credit calling for a multimodal transport document the expression "taking in charge."

b   Expressions such as "prompt," "immediately" "as soon as possible," and the like should not be used. If they are used banks will disregard them.

c   If the expression "on or about" or similar expressions are used, banks will interpret them as a stipulation that shipment is to be made during the period from five days before to five days after the specified date, both end days included.

Article 47

Date Terminology for Periods of Shipment

a   The words "to," "until," "till," "from" and words of similar import applying to any date or period in the Credit referring to shipment will be understood to include the date mentioned.

b   The word "after" will be understood to exclude the date mentioned.

c   The terms "first half," "second half" of a month shall be construed respectively as the 1st to the 15th, and the 16th to the last day of such month, all dates inclusive.

d   The terms "beginning," "middle," or "end" of a month shall be construed respectively as the 1st to the 10th, the 11th to the 20th, and the 21st to the last day of such month, all dates inclusive.

Transferable Credit

Article 48

Transferable Credit

a   A transferable Credit is a Credit under which the Beneficiary (First Beneficiary) may request the bank authorized to pay, incur a deferred payment undertaking, accept or negotiate (the "Transferring Bank"), or in the case of a freely negotiable Credit, the bank specifically authorized in the Credit as a Transferring Bank, to make the Credit available in whole or in part to one or more other Beneficiary(ies) (Second Beneficiary(ies)).

b   A Credit can be transferred only if it is expressly designated as "transferable" by the Issuing Bank. Terms such as "divisible," "fractionable," "assignable," and "transmissible" do not render the Credit transferable. If such terms are used they shall be disregarded.

c   The Transferring Bank shall be under no obligation to effect such transfer except to the extent and in the manner expressly consented to by such bank.

d   At the time of making a request for transfer and prior to transfer of the Credit, the First Beneficiary must irrevocably instruct the Transferring Bank whether or not he retains the right to refuse to allow the Transferring Bank to advise amendments to the Second Beneficiary(ies). If the Transferring Bank consents to the transfer under these conditions, it must, at the time of transfer, advise the Second Beneficiary(ies) of the First Beneficiary's instructions regarding amendments.

e   If a Credit is transferred to more than one Second Beneficiary(ies), refusal of an amendment by one or more Second Beneficiary(ies) does not invalidate the acceptance(s) by the other Second Beneficiary(ies) with respect to whom the Credit will be amended accordingly. With respect to the Second Beneficiary(ies) who rejected the amendment, the Credit will remain unamended.

f   Transferring Bank charges in respect of transfers including commissions, fees, costs or expenses are payable by the First Beneficiary, unless otherwise agreed. If the Transferring Bank agrees to transfer the Credit it shall be under no obligation to effect the transfer until such charges are paid.

g   Unless otherwise stated in the Credit, a transferable Credit can be transferred once only. Consequently, the Credit cannot be transferred at the request of the Second Beneficiary to any subsequent Third Beneficiary. For the purpose of this Article, a retransfer to the First Beneficiary does not constitute a prohibited transfer.

Fractions of a transferable Credit (not exceeding in the aggregate the amount of the Credit) can be transferred separately, provided partial shipments/drawings are not prohibited, and the aggregate of such transfers will be considered as constituting only one transfer of the Credit.

h   The Credit can be transferred only on the terms and conditions specified in the original Credit, with the exception of:

— the amount of the Credit,

— any unit price stated therein,

— the expiry date,

— the last date for presentation of documents in accordance with Article 43,

— the period for shipment,

any or all of which may be reduced or curtailed.

The percentage for which insurance cover must be effected may be increased in such a way as to provide the amount of cover stipulated in the original Credit, or these Articles.

In addition, the name of the First Beneficiary can be substituted for that of the Applicant, but if the name of the Applicant is specifically required by the original Credit to appear in any document(s) other than the invoice, such requirement must be fulfilled.

i   The First Beneficiary has the right to substitute his own invoice(s) (and Draft(s)) for those of the Second Beneficiary(ies), for amounts not in excess of the original amount stipulated in the Credit and for the original unit prices if stipulated in the Credit, and upon such substitution of invoice(s) (and Draft(s)) the First Beneficiary can draw under the Credit for the difference, if any, between his invoice(s) and the Second Beneficiary's(ies') invoice(s).

When a Credit has been transferred and the First Beneficiary is to supply his own invoice(s) (and Draft(s)) in exchange for the Second Beneficiary's(ies') invoice(s) (and Draft(s)) but fails to do so on first demand, the Transferring Bank has the right to deliver to the Issuing Bank the documents received under the transferred Credit, including the Second Beneficiary's(ies') invoice(s) (and Draft(s)) without further responsibility to the First Beneficiary.

j   The First Beneficiary may request that payment or negotiation be effected to the Second Beneficiary(ies) at the place to which the Credit has been transferred up to and including the expiry date of the Credit, unless the original Credit expressly states that it may not be made available for payment or negotiation at a place other than that stipulated in the Credit. This is without prejudice to the First Beneficiary's right to substitute subsequently his own invoice(s) (and Draft(s)) for those of the Second Beneficiary(ies) and to claim any difference due to him.

G. Assignment of Proceeds

Article 49

Assignment of Proceeds

The fact that a Credit is not stated to be transferable shall not affect the Beneficiary's right to assign any proceeds to which he may be, or may become, entitled under such Credit, in accordance with the provisions of the applicable law. This Article relates only to the assignment of proceeds and not to the assignment of the right to perform under the Credit itself.

INDEX

domestic banking, global banking vs, 230
domestic dollars, funding global finance,
  198–199, 203
    interest rate, 186
domestic economy, 21–22
domestic letters of credit, 153
domestic trade, bankers' acceptances, 165–166
domicile, Eurodollars, 204
draft, 54, 116, 118, 140
drawback, 10
drawee, 118
drawer, 118
drawings, 323
  guide, 54
dual currency, 48
Due From accounts, 48
Due To accounts, 47–48, 50, 60
dumping, 9

E

earnings, 256–257
economic component, analyzing, 235–236
Edge Act corporations, 26, 29–30, 33
effectiveness of documents, disclaimer on, 284,
  303
eligible bankers' acceptances, 164–167
eligible for discount, 165
emerging markets, 13, 237
endorser, 118
English banking system, 1–2
ERM *see* Exchange Rate Mechanism
errors, 49
Euro, 98
  commercial paper, 208
Eurobond, 206
Eurocurrencies, 205
Eurodollars, 186, 199
  accounting features, 200–202
European Community, 8
European currency unit (ECU), 97–98
European Monetary System (EMS), 84–85
evaluate, 260
examination of documents, 137
  standard for, 301
Exchange Rate Mechanism (ERM), 85, 87,
  89–90, 95
Exchange Stabilization Fund, 96
exchange controls, 83–84, 85–86, 94–95
exchange rates, 83–84
expenses, 287–288

expiry date, 323
  extension, 324
  limitation, 324
Export–Import Bank of the United States
  (Eximbank), 215–216
export letters of credit, 144–145
export trading company (ETC), 31–32
exporter's responsibilities, 135–136
exports, 7–8, 11, 16
  payments for, 71
external financing, developing countries, 237,
  238
ex works, 273

F

factors of production, 246
farmers, 166–167
FAS *see* free alongside ship
Federal Reserve Act of 1913, 27
  bankers' acceptances, 165
Federal Reserve Regular Reciprocal Currency
  Arrangements, 96, 97
federal funds, 56
Fedwire, 57–58
field warehouses, 166
Financial Times Guide to World Currencies,
  66
financial accounts 17, 19
financial risk, credit, 179–180
financial standby letters of credit, 154
financing, 125
  types, international credit, 189–193
fixed interest rate, 186–187
fixed rate of exchange, 67
float, 67
  calculations in global payments, 56
floating policy, 114
floating rate, 67, 186–187
FOB *see* free on board
force majeure, 285, 303
foreign banks, 2
foreign banks in the U.S., 33
  setting up, 33–34
foreign branches, 27–29
foreign currency
  collections, 124
  sight drafts, 124
  trading in, 71–72
  see also currency
foreign drafts, 50, 51, 53, 55

order, 113
organization of U.S. banks, 25–37
    notes, 36–37
    problem, 36
    questions, 36
over-the-counter derivatives, 253–254
overdraft, 59
overseas branches, 28
overseas shell branches, 34

P

packing list, 116
paper currency, 40, 42
par value, 65, 67
para-statal, 182
Paris Club, 221
partial payments, 286
partial shipments, 134, 323
participants
    foreign exchange markets, 83
    objectives, 88–91
participation, bankers' acceptances, 170–171
payee, 118
payment, 39–101, 46, 285–286
    advice of, 290
    options, 108–109
    orders, 51
performance standby letters of credit, 154
personnel risk, 257–258
petrodollars, 199
place for presentation of documents, 323–324
placement, 203
policy
    domestic politics and, 11
    statements, 96
political change, country risk assessment, 240
political component, analyzing, 239–243
political evaluation, 242
political objectives, 245
por aval, 188
Porter, Michael, 6 (quoted)
portfolio investment, 13
position
    maintaining, 74–76
    taking, 82
post receipts, 110, 317
pre-advised credit, 300
precious metals, 7
premiums, 73
prepaid transport documents, 319
prepayment, 109

presentation, 280–281
    date, 136
prime rate, 186
private banking, 2, 184
private financing, 214
private placement, 207
privatization, 182, 239
proceeds, assignment of, 328
product risk, 253–255
production, trade and, 8
profit, 255
promissory notes, 288
proprietary trading, 69, 82
protectionism of trade, 9–11
protest, 121–122, 289
public warehouses, 166
purchases of funds, 203
purchasing power parity, 70

Q

quota, 9

R

rail
    bill of lading, 110
    transport document, 316–317
railroad system, global finance, 207–208
reading list, 263
reasonable care, 282
rebate, 10
received for shipment bill of lading, 113
red clause letters of credit, 148–149
Regulation K, 29–30
regulations
    foreign exchange markets, 94–96
    money market, 82
reimbursement arrangements, 152
reimbursing bank, 304–305
release of commercial documents, 281–282
remittance, 54
    air mail, 50
    orders 50
    teletransmission, 50–51
Renaissance Italy, trade financing, 112
representative offices, 30–31
rescheduling, 224
reserve assets, 17
reserves, 19, 236, 237
responsibilities, 282–285
restructuring, 224

tombstones, 192
tourism, 12, 16
trade, 2, 6–12, 64, 103
    acceptances, 122–123, 161
    balance, 19
    credit, Renaissance Italy, 112
    effect of, 11
    features of, 9
    financing, 108, 190–191
    history, 6–7
    invisible, 11–12
    protectionism, 9–11
    terms, 118–119
    visible, 7–9
traders, 69–70
    foreign exchange markets, 87–88
    objectives, 88–91
trading
    for one's own account, 82
    risks, 251–253
    separated from settlement, 252–253
transfer pricing, 184
transferable credit, 326–327
transferable letters of credit, 149
transferee, 149
transfers, 17
    individual, 12
translation
    loss (or gain), 90–91
    disclaimer, 284–285
transmission of messages, disclaimer on, 303
transport documents, 110–114
    freight forwarders-issued, 318
transportation, 11, 17
transshipment, 134
travel, 17
traveler's checks, 49, 54–55, 56
traveler's letter of credit, 153
Treaty of Rome, 84
truck bill of lading, 110
trust receipt, 124, 147

U

Ukraine, 245
unclean bill of lading, 113

unclear instructions, 300
unconfirmed letters of credit, 145
underdeveloped country, 13
Uniform Customs and Practice for
    Documentary Credits (UCP), 131, 293–328
Uniform Rules for Collections, 277–292
unsecured financing, 187–188
unsecured lending, 186
usance letter of credit, 146–147
U.S. commercial banks, 221–222
U.S. foreign exchange market, 68
U.S. market operations, 95–96
U.S. Trade Representative (USTR), 104
Uzbekistan, 245

V

value date, 56
visaed commercial invoice, 116
visible trade, 7–9
vostro accounts, 47–48

W

warehouse receipt, 166
weight list, 116
with recourse, 140
without recourse, 190
working balances, 57
World Bank group, 217–219
World Trade Organization (WTO), 221
world of global banking, 1–23
    notes, 23
    problem, 23
    questions, 23

Y

Yankee bond, 206

Z

Zaire, debt crisis, 222–223
zero-coupon bonds, 206

Thank you for using this American Bankers Association/American Institute of Banking textbook. Your responses on the following evaluation will help shape the structure and content of future editions. <u>Return your completed form to your instructor or fold in three and mail to</u>: American Institute of Banking, Attn: Manager, Product Development, 1120 Connecticut Avenue, N.W., Washington, D.C. 20036.

Name of Chapter _____

Name of Bank _____

TEXTBOOK/COURSE ATTRIBUTES

Importance Factor					Satisfaction Level			
Very Important			Not Important		Completely Satisfied			Not Satisfied
1	2	3	4	**Textbook covered all important topics**	1	2	3	4
1	2	3	4	**Content was easy to read and understand**	1	2	3	4
1	2	3	4	**The graphics and examples were helpful**	1	2	3	4
1	2	3	4	**I can use what I've learned in this course in my work**	1	2	3	4

	Excellent			Poor
What was your overall opinion of the textbook?	1	2	3	4

Did your instructor use any additional materials to teach this course?
( ) Yes   ( ) No

If Yes, please check all that apply
( ) Transparencies/Overheads   ( ) Handouts
( ) Other textbook (please specify)_____

Number of AIB courses you have taken in past three years:
( ) 0   ( ) 1-2   ( ) 3-5
( ) More than 5

AIB course taken through: (Please check all that apply)
( ) AIB Chapter/Study Group
( ) AIB Correspondence Study Program
( ) Other (please specify)_____

Currently working toward an AIB Diploma/Certificate?
( ) Yes   ( ) No

If yes, please specify:
( ) Bank Operations   ( ) Consumer Credit
( ) Commercial Lending   ( ) General Banking
( ) Mortgage Lending   ( ) Accelerated Banking
( ) Customer Service   ( ) Securities Services
( ) Supervisory

Asset size of your bank:
( ) 0-$75m   ( ) $76-$250m   ( ) $251-$500m
( ) $501-$1b   ( ) over $1b

Number of employees in your bank:
( ) 1-10   ( ) 11-20   ( ) 21-40
( ) 41-90   ( ) 91-200   ( ) 201-350
( ) 351-2,000   ( ) over 2,000

Job Title:_____

Major Job Responsibility:
( ) Lending   ( ) Marketing   ( ) Operations
( ) Compliance   ( ) Auditing   ( ) Human Resources
( ) Trust   ( ) Customer Svc.   ( ) Branch Admin.
( ) Securities Processing   ( ) Security/Risk
                                             Management
( ) Other (Please specify)_____

Years in Banking:
( ) 0-2   ( ) 3-5   ( ) 6-10
( ) Over 10

Highest Education Level:
( ) High School   ( ) Some College   ( ) BA/BS Degree
( ) Advanced Degree

Age:
( ) under 25   ( ) 25-35   ( ) 36-45
( ) over 45

Name _____
Bank _____
Address _____
City _____ State _____ Zip _____
Telephone (____) _____

( ) Please send me more information on AIB's Diploma/Certificate Program.

( ) Please send me more information on AIB's Correspondence Study Program.

Comments (please identify any specific suggestions you have that may improve the overall effectiveness of this publication):

_____
_____
_____
_____
_____
_____
_____
_____
_____
_____
_____

— — — — — — — — — — — — — — PLEASE FOLD ALONG DOTTED LINE — — — — — — — — — — — — — — —